Born
to
Win

Born
to
Win

A Lifelong Struggle to Capture the America's Cup

By John Bertrand
As Told to Patrick Robinson

SIDGWICK & JACKSON
LONDON

First published in Great Britain in 1985
by Sidgwick and Jackson Limited

Originally published in the United States of America in 1985
by Hearst Marine Books, by arrangement with Bantam Books Inc., New York

Copyright © 1985 by John Bertrand and Patrick Robinson

ISBN 0-283-99302-2

Printed in Great Britain by
The Garden City Press, Letchworth, Hertfordshire
for Sidgwick and Jackson Limited
1 Tavistock Chambers, Bloomsbury Way
London WC1A 2SG

This book is respectfully dedicated to Hughey, Mad Dog, and Beasho, Skippy, Scoop and the old Ya Bird, Chink, Splash and the Major, Will, Robbie, Scotty and young Damian, the Men from the Land Down Under who made *Australia II* go, and with whom I was privileged to sail.

—JOHN BERTRAND
Melbourne, 1985

Foreword

I heard it from an advanced soul met in one of those dimensions we sometimes reach in dreams, out by the moss-and-pine foothills of Olympus. "Heroes," she said, "are those who adventure beyond horizons, who struggle there against great odds to win great victories, and return at last to tell us what they saw." She spoke clearly and calmly, as though she knew we'd all be heroic if only we'd remember who we are.

Before I could question—Where can I apply? How can I move past a horizon? Any chance those great odds will smash me flat?—before I could ask, the dimension shifted and I woke at dawn in the safety of my bed. Heroes have always charmed me, caught my imagination, but bed is an awfully comfortable place to be. Is there a way to become a hero, I wondered, without going too far from home?

The next day, by the strangest of coincidences, came the manuscript of *Born to Win*, and there in my hand was the complete guide for every apprentice hero, printed in lightning bolts: Here's what to expect on the way to herohood; here are the steps that we must take if we would touch magic and become its friend.

That the heroes of this book are John Bertrand and his wife, Rasa, and the crew of *Australia II* sailing closehauled in pursuit of the America's Cup make it a breathtaking handbook to find, an exhilaration to read.

If you're a mystic, you could argue that John Bertrand was born to win. His own great-grandfather, Thomas Pearkes, worked year after year to build Sir Thomas Lipton's towering J-boats for the America's Cup, and never won. If you're a mystic, you'd suggest that Thomas Pearkes chose to be born once more near the sea, this time in Australia as John Bertrand, direct descendant, hungering to race again.

But many another great-grandson and granddaughter of history's sailors didn't see the prize, or saw and didn't care, or cared for a while and then quit. Reading this book, I've come to believe unmystically that

Bertrand was born to win the America's Cup as any hero is born to destiny: He found what he wanted to do and he did it. Spark together love with pure determination and you've got a laser torch guaranteed to level whatever stands in your way.

When we master the art of sail, when we master any art, we unlock the powers that lie behind all arts, powers which matter more than hardware. Bertrand shows us what he's learned and we nod agreement, always having known though we've never been to sea.

The boat that sails to victory, he says, sails not so much in the hands of a crew as in its spirit. When he changes tactics to set that spirit free, it's our own voice we hear: "Hurray! Of course!"

His is the story of the race for *mental* domination of the America's Cup, of one challenger's discovery that the prize was fastened to the New York Yacht Club not by steel and bolts but by powers of mind. Reading, we nod again. Of course! The secret that Bertrand found is the same that works for anyone: If we would prevail, we must first become the best human being we can imagine. Only then do we become eligible to win. And then we find, trophies or not, that we've already won.

This book is a delightful window on the hidden smile and secret motive of the universe. A kid from Melbourne chose a destiny to rise against all odds to win the biggest prize in the racing of sail, he practiced thirty years, and he won. Pandemonium! Yet above joy gone wild, beyond celebrations that turned midnight into rainbows, the whisper of a universe: "Take a look at what you've done. You thought you were racing sailboats . . ."

. . . and you've changed a nation. Bertrand tells us early on of what was once his country's Tall Poppy Syndrome: "Australians are afraid of big winners," he writes. "When one poppy in a field grows much taller than the rest, there is a mad compulsion by everyone to cut it back down to size." Now, destiny touched, the America's Cup lifted gracefully as a sword from the stone of history, now every Australian is a winner. What happens to a Tall Poppy Syndrome when all at once everybody's a tall poppy? Australia will never be the same!

"Take a look at what you've done," whispers the universe, above coast-to-coast explosions of champagne, "You think you've changed a nation . . ."

. . . and you remind the world of another. We love John Bertrand and his dear Rasa, Alan Bond, and all the crew of *Australia II* because they are citizens of a country to which every one of us belongs. We're born of a country called perfection, no matter how often we forget or how imperfectly we sometimes act. Australian or American, Russian, Swede or Chinese, we're citizens of a land whose frontier is excellence, whose anthem is beauty, whose flag is the sunrise.

Heroes remind us of our dreams and of our destinies. In their thousand ways, they remind us who we are. In this book, they sail *Australia II* to meet us, to take us home.

—RICHARD BACH
Author of *Jonathan Livingston Seagull* and *The Bridge Across Forever*

Contents

List of Terms

It is not necessary for the reader to understand the technical language of sailing to enjoy this book. However, as you stand alongside John Bertrand in the cockpit of *Australia II* in the heat of the 1983 America's Cup battle, it would obviously enhance your more vivid images to know that the *bow* is the front, the *stern* is the back, *port* is left, and *starboard* right.

It would also be helpful for nonsailors to understand more clearly that a yacht cannot sail directly into the wind. The yacht must sail diagonally (at about a 45° angle) to the wind. Thus, from Point A against the wind to Point B, one mile away, she could sail to the left diagonally for more than half a mile, then swing back onto the other diagonal to reach Point B in two wide sweeps. These are called *tacks*.

More usually, however, the skipper will make a series of smaller tacks, zigzagging his way to Point B. Also, he need not start going left. He may go right, as might his opponent. But they must go off diagonally to the wind. This is fundamental to all yacht racing.

There are three upwind legs on the America's Cup course, and for those who would like to savor the commands and calls of the skipper, here is a list of the terms used in the book and simple explanations of their meaning:

Bearing   Direction a yacht is going.

Birdbath   Tiny cockpit at bottom of the mast; home of the mastman.

Closehauled   Sails trimmed tight, almost in a straight line down the middle of the yacht, catching all of the wind; also known as "hard on the wind."

Coaming   Outside upper edge, which joins the deck and the hull.

Covering   Getting in front and staying directly between your opponent and the direction of the wind. (He goes left, you go left. He goes right, you go right. But he cannot sail through you.)

Dirty air   Wind that hits the sails of the leading boat first and then billows back causing turbulence when it hits opponent's sails; causes huge loss of speed, forcing opponent to tack away, searching for clear air.

Downhill run   Sailing downwind.

Downwind   Right around the big red buoy at Point B—and the wind is now directly behind instead of directly in front. Up goes the spinnaker, a big parachute, straight out in front; mainsail set out wide over the side catching every bit of the following wind.

Fetch the mark   Getting round the big red buoy at Point B.

Genoa   Large headsail that overlaps the mainsail.

Halyard   Line attached to top and bottom of mast with which sails and spinnakers are hauled up to correct height.

Header, or knock   Sudden advantageous wind change, allowing the skipper to tack immediately and aim the yacht onto a fractionally better line to Point B.

Heeling   Yacht leaning naturally away from the wind.

Jibe   When the sails come across the yacht from one side to the other with the wind behind; used at the wing mark.

Layline   The unseen line on the water that a yacht follows to the next mark without tacking.

Lee-bow position   When the opponent is trapped on your weather hip. Cannot get by because of the dirty air coming off your sail. Usually forces him to tack.

Luffing   Sails flutter as yacht is headed directly into wind.

Mainsheet   Line that controls the mainsail.

Off the wind   Sailing down any of the three legs that are to leeward on the course: the two reaches or the run.

Pointing   Aiming the bow of the yacht to the ultimate advantageous geometric angle, beyond which the sails will collapse because the boat would then be going *directly* into the wind.

Port tack   When the yacht is heading to the right with the sails and yacht leaning to the right, and the wind is coming from the left, over the port side.

Power reaches The second and third legs of the America's Cup course, with the wind abeam.

Protest flag Signal raised to opponent if you believe he has broken the rules and should be disqualified. Signifies you will make protest to race committee following the race.

Starboard tack Opposite to port tack. This sail setting traditionally has the right of way. Thus, if two yachts are on a collision course, the one on the port tack must give way.

Tacking The moment the yacht is swung through the eye of the wind to the other diagonal.

Tacking duel Caused when boat in rear starts tacking, trying to break free of "the cover," to get out to the left, or right, into clean air.

Tactician Skipper's right-hand man, his "eyes" and "ears." Plots the match racing tactics.

Tender Accompanying powerboat with syndicate officials' supplies, reserves, computer storage, supporters, etc.

Time on distance Countdown coming to starting line—i.e., 10 seconds left to cover last 20 yards.

To leeward The direction away from which the wind is coming.

To weather The direction from which the wind is coming.

To windward Sailing upwind, or into the wind.

Trim tab Small rudder attached to the keel; acts like controlling wing flaps on aircraft.

Weather helm When the yacht tends to come up into the wind with every gust.

Weather mark The big red buoy at Point B, to weather (windward) of the starting line.

Winch Machine for winding in sail lines.

Wind shadow The turbulent air the boat in the rear sails into when close to opponent.

Wing mark The buoy around which the boat swings after the first power reach, and sets off down the second. The mark is placed, literally, out on "the wing."

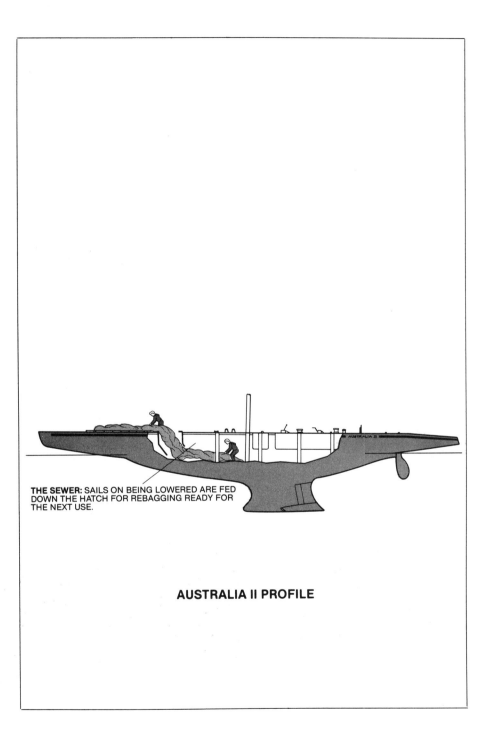

THE SEWER: SAILS ON BEING LOWERED ARE FED DOWN THE HATCH FOR REBAGGING READY FOR THE NEXT USE.

AUSTRALIA II PROFILE

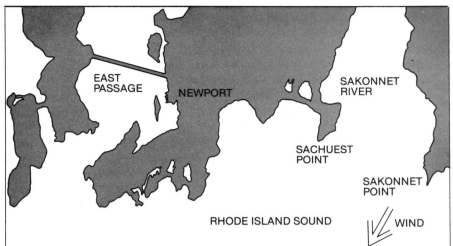

EAST
PASSAGE

NEWPORT

SAKONNET
RIVER

SACHUEST
POINT

SAKONNET
POINT

RHODE ISLAND SOUND

WIND

• BRENTON REEF LIGHT TOWER

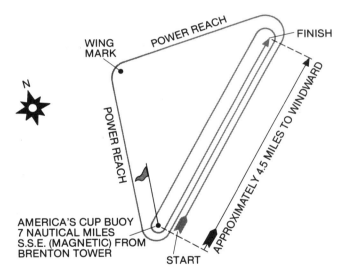

POWER REACH

WING
MARK

FINISH

N

APPROXIMATELY 4.5 MILES TO WINDWARD

POWER REACH

AMERICA'S CUP BUOY
7 NAUTICAL MILES
S.S.E. (MAGNETIC) FROM
BRENTON TOWER

START

1983 AMERICA'S CUP RACECOURSE

AUSTRALIA II CREW POSITIONS

THE CREW

1. HELMSMAN
2. TACTICIAN
3. NAVIGATOR
4. MAIN SHEET TRIMMER
5. STARBOARD TRIMMER
6. PORT TRIMMER
7. STARBOARD WINCH GRINDER
8. PORT WINCH GRINDER
9. MASTMAN
10. BOWMAN
11. SEWERMAN AND RELIEF GRINDER

The Men Who Captured the America's Cup

Alan Bond
Chairman of the *Australia II* Syndicate

John Bertrand—Helmsman

Hugh Treharne—Tactician

Grant Simmer—Navigator

Colin Beashel—Mainsheet Hand

Ken Judge—Starboard Trimmer

Skip Lissiman—Port Trimmer

Rob Brown—Trimmer

John Longley—Port Winch Grinder

Brian Richardson—Starboard Winch Grinder

Will Baillieu—Winch Grinder

Phil Smidmore—Mastman

Peter Costello—Sewerman and Grinder

Scott McAllister—Bow Man

Damian Fewster—Replacement Bow Man

Ben Lexcen—Designer of *Australia II*

Warren Jones—Syndicate Managing Director

Ken Beashel—Maintenance Supervisor

Tom Schnackenberg—Sails Coordinator

Laurie Hayden—Combat Psychologist

Sir James Hardy—Sailing Adviser

Born
to
Win

1

September 21, 11:46 A.M.

It was only one second, the blink of an eye, but it was one second with which I may have to live for the rest of my life.

It was no more than a reflex action. I took my right hand off the wheel of *Australia II* and waved good-bye to Sir James Hardy and our compatriots on *Challenge 12*. I could see his crew waving back from the pitching deck of the other Australian boat that had been with us for so long—first as a bitter and deadly rival, and then as the only sailing friends and companions we had on Rhode Island Sound that summer. "Good-bye, Jim." It had a kind of lonely ring to it. Never in the 132-year history of the America's Cup had an atmosphere been any more grim than the one that existed on *Australia II*.

We were 3–1 down in the best-of-seven series. God knows just about every foreign challenger in the 24 previous America's Cup contests had known what that felt like. But not one of them ever had a chance like we did. Not one of them had ever been quite so prepared, quite so accomplished, and quite so feared by the defenders. And it may just be that no one ever had a boat like we did.

Yet here we were, right back in the pack, along with all the others, wallowing on the point of total defeat. Just a few hours from being sent home with nothing. Grim—that was the word for it. And it was a feeling that pervaded the little Australian armada of supporters, which chugged along behind us out there, praying for the miracle that had never come in this contest since the United States schooner *America* first won the Cup from the British in 1851, before the United States Civil War.

September 21, 1983, was the date. The wind was gusting at 18 to 22 knots, the sea was lumpy, a typical day out in the Newport slop. Our foredeck was pitching up and down, in the slightly exaggerated way that we had grown accustomed to aboard *Australia II*.

I wheeled her around before the wind, glanced back at *Challenge 12*, muttering to myself once more, "Good-bye, Jim," wondering how we all would feel when we next saw the veteran Australian helmsman back on the dock at Newport. Clearly, the odds against our winning the America's Cup seemed insurmountable, too great to comprehend. I looked ahead while remembering the words I had said to the crew with such clear-cut confidence:

"This will eventually come down to pure logic. If we go out there and get beaten, they'll send us home. If, however, we win *today*, they'll let us stay and fight again tomorrow. And if we keep winning, we'll leave this country with the America's Cup. But the only thing that matters is today. We have sailed together for thousands of miles, and when you come right down to it, today is the only thing that counts, the only thing we have trained for. Gentlemen, let's just go out there, right now, and win *today*."

And now it is quiet, save for the incessant slap-slap of our bow wave as we slide downwind. The two waterproof hatches on the foredeck are battened down tight, and up before the mast Damian, our bow man who just had his 21st birthday, is already standing in green water. Grant Simmer, our young navigator, is beginning to pour out the priceless monologue of readings from his charts and instruments that will keep up for the next five hours or so. We are about 12 minutes from the 10-minute gun, which will blast off at noon, and there is already high excitement on the boat, for we are hearing scrambled messages on the navigator's radio that *Liberty* is in trouble—with, of all things, a gear failure. It is not absolutely clear what has broken, but our observers on Alan Bond's launch, *Black Swan*, seem to think their port jumper strut, high up the mast, has buckled.

According to *Black Swan*, *Liberty* buried her head in a big wave while

Dennis Conner was tuning the port setting of his sails, and the mast suddenly sagged to leeward. We are getting radio reports that the Coast Guard refused Conner's request for a helicopter to fly a spare strut out from shore. That *Rhonda,* a super-fast launch with twin 235-horsepower motors, had screamed back and has already delivered the new jumper strut. Two members of her crew apparently are lashed to the top of the mast, trying to attach the new part.

Now, nobody wants to win by default, but from our point of view, the situation is not without some pleasant irony. We had a couple of shocking gear failures in the first two races, and I thought our American opponents were a bit haughty about it. You know, "typical Australian casualness"— that type of attitude. Still, the American skipper *did* write a book entitled, *No Excuse to Lose,* so it will be interesting to see how they cope with the unforeseen adversity of structural failure now that it appears to be their turn.

I speak again to the crew. "OK, guys, now listen. The red boat appears to have a problem. But it has nothing to do with us. Remember that— nothing at all to do with us. For all we know, their boat will be perfect by the time we hit the starting line. I don't want you to think of *Liberty* as being anything less than 100 percent efficient. That way, if she can't sail properly, then we'll destroy her. But if she can, then we won't be surprised. I ask you all now to forget the red boat, and let's concentrate on preparing *Australia II* for the race of her life."

And now we are concentrating, perhaps as we have never concentrated before.

Hughey and Ya are already in conference, discussing the potential windshifts. The Major has cast me a couple of big grins, and Skippy, Beasho, and the boys are with me to a man. I reflect again that this is just about as fine a group of blokes as I have ever met.

We have not yet looked for the red boat, but she'll be there waiting for us, fighting her problems, going through all the same agonizing prerace turmoil as we, attempting to work out the wind, looking for the wind phasing and the way we might expect it to move. I bet they are desperate to win this, to get us, with our winged keel, out of the way once and for all. They might have a 3–1 lead, but they've been in a boat race, and they know it. We're not done for yet, not by a long way. We've thrashed them twice, once when we ran out of time and once for real. We've suffered two diabolical gear failures, and we've made one ridiculous mistake at the start. Or, rather, I have, and the result is that we are 3–1. But it's a narrow 3–1, if you know what I mean. No one in either boat thinks we are being thrashed by Dennis Conner and his crew.

By the way, when I talk to the crew, I don't refer to Dennis by name.

No "Dennis," no "Conner," no "Mr. Conner" or "Lord Conner," or whatever some yachtsmen believe him to be. I do not even go for the familiar "D.C. this" or "D.C. that." I don't even name his boat or any of his crew. No "Halsey," no "John," not even *Liberty*." I have tried to dehumanize the opposition completely. Whenever I mention our opponents to my crew now, I refer to them as "the red boat"—nothing more.

Suddenly, there she is—the red boat is in front of us, ahead in the mist. High above her deck and lashed to the upper part of the mast, which is swaying wildly, are Tom Rich, their foredeck boss, and Scott Vogel, their bow man. They must be getting badly bruised and knocked about up there. Grant has just called out that the wind is gusting to 22 knots. We're all in foul-weather gear, and the condition at the top of our opponent's mast must be awful and dangerous. The plight of the two Americans aloft is beyond description; I do not want anyone to think about it, or even care. I hate to sound like a schoolmaster, but to my great delight, I am now certain everyone is concentrating on the job at hand. *Win today, win today*—that's all we have to do. Two minutes before the gun, the two Americans are lowered to safety. They must be exhausted, but that has nothing to do with us. We are now oblivious to everything. Our expectations are high, extremely high. We have no interest in the thousands of spectator boats dotting the horizon. Hundreds of them, perhaps, hope we will win, but they cannot help us. No one can. It's just ourselves, our boat, our will to win. Man and machine. Nothing more. As friends, and as a close-knit crew, we are all alone. We are 12,000 miles from home, in one of the most nerve-racking sports confrontations ever staged.

Now the information is coming through faster. Hughey filters it, telling me only what I *must* know. Beasho on the mainsheet is working the great sail, robotlike. The midday gun crashes out, echoing across the water. Chink Longley's right arm jerks as if he has been shot, his thumb snapping down on our stopwatch. The countdown has begun, and I aim *Australia II* straight for the red boat. We come at them from the port end of the line, trying to hook up with them, if possible, to intimidate them, to remind them of the superior circling ability of *Australia II*. As we suspect, Conner is not interested in a close "war dance" with us before the start. He jibes away, sailing downwind away from us. "Follow 'em, John," says Hughey, and Beasho eases the mainsail as we track down after the red boat, our backs to the starting line as well as to the wall. We have gone nearly half a mile, well into the countdown, when Conner elects to go right around a Coast Guard cutter. With about six minutes to go, we see them slew around to leeward of the cutter. We are about 50 yards behind them, traveling about the same speed. I hesitate and decide to follow the red boat around the cutter. And as I do so, I know I have made a deadly mistake. I should have tacked away, rejoined them as they emerged again, and stayed right on top of them. For a split second, my time-on-distance clock fell a little behind. When we came around the cutter, we ended up on the leeward side, too far to leeward of the starting mark, and we were running out of time. Now we are starting at the port end of the line, coming up to a time-on-distance start.

By international match-racing standards, this counts as an elementary error, and I am not pleased with myself. I say quietly to Hughey, "That was bloody ridiculous," but I do not want to instill uneasiness into everyone. The tension is bad enough without that.

However, our position is now less than wonderful, and we have a very critical path to sail to the line. At 3–1 down, there can be no mistakes, but instead of being in control of the start, we are now in a scrap. The red boat is by no means in control of us, but we no longer have the luxury of being able to make even a semblance of an error without losing this life-or-death start.

Anyway, on we sail, loping up to the line. Chink is calling out the time every 10 seconds. We're inside three minutes, shaking off time, shaking off time. "Head her up, John, just a fraction more." We're burning off time, luffing the sail, burning some more. The damned watch seems to be going more slowly than it has ever gone. The red boat now looks fine, all repaired and very close to us, just to weather. It is clear that the leeward end of the line, the port end where we are, has an overwhelming advantage, being much closer to the first weather mark. The whole starting line is in fact skewed into the wind, so the left side obviously is the place to be. However, I still do not like being so close to the line with a lot of time to burn off. None of us does.

At about 90 seconds, I decide to hang there, determined to get that leeward end. The stopwatch is still going abnormally slowly, as we keep burning off time, burning it off, waiting, balancing *Australia II* in the wind, ready to pounce.

Chink is counting down fast now. Still 30 seconds to go, and we are only about a boatlength from the line. I have, of course, two fears—that we hit the mark before the gun and that we are absolutely stationary at the gun. Conner's boat is only about 15 feet away, and, predictably, she tacks off from our weather side, setting herself up for a port-tack start across the line.

We're on starboard tack and the count is in its critical stage. ". . . 20 . . . 19 . . . 18 . . . 17 . . ." We are almost stationary and there's no going back now. At "15" I order the sails to be pulled on. Beasho tightens the mainsheet, the jib hardens, everyone is poised for the action. ". . . 9 . . . 8

... 7 ... 6 ..." Christ! This is going to be close! "Head her up, John, head her up, into the wind." "No! Watch out, we'll hit the fucking America's Cup buoy." ". . . 5 . . . 4 . . ." "I'm pushing her up. I can't go another inch." ". . . 3 . . . 2 . . . 1" We're over! Crash. It's the goddamned gun and I've beaten it by one second. We have just oozed over the line as I pushed up the bow. It was only one second, the blink of an eye, but it was one second with which I may have to live for the rest of my life.

In my rage I shout at the top of my lungs, "Holy shi-i-i-i-i-i-it, John, we're early!" I grip the wheel until I think my fingers will break. Hughey says, "Easy, John; steady, John. It can happen to anyone." To anyone, all right, but not to me, please not to me. I've been trained all my life for moments like this. It's my trade, and I have spent years perfecting it. I am the man with the training and the background of two Olympic Games and three previous America's Cups. Not only had Alan Bond seen fit to vest in me the hopes and dreams of the entire nation of Australia, but I seemed to be in command of a project that had cost him enough money to very nearly wipe out the Australian national debt.

And here I stand in the cockpit of *Australia II,* having perpetrated an error of truly grotesque proportions. They say that when you are dying, your entire life passes in front of you. Well, I know what that means now. Recollections of a thousand yacht races are occurring to me—almost as if the blunder never happened, that I somehow had another chance.

The boat is deathly quiet after my first outburst. And I am still steaming with rage at myself. I have to have a safety valve, so I take advantage of the gusting sea breeze to carry away a long string of obscenities.

As I finish, still no one is speaking, and my natural reflexes are permitting me to start swinging *Australia II* to starboard as fast as I can. We are facing Newport, and the red boat probably is making about 800 knots toward the first mark. Our position is so preposterous, so completely ghastly, and the odds against us so ridiculous, that half of our supporters must be jamming the wires trying to get through to their travel agents to book immediate flights to Sydney. It is Hughey who breaks the ice. Dear, wonderful, taciturn, quiet Hughey, who never smiles in a big race. With his usual deadpan, he says, "OK, John, I'm glad we got that over with. Now let's go and beat up on the Yanks again!"

This outrageous mock display of aggression brings smiles to the faces of all the crew. Even to mine. But mine is the smile of a slightly dazed fighter who has just beaten an eight count and wishes to convey the impression he still has a lot left in him. Truthfully, at the moment, I feel that I have the cares of the world upon my shoulders. I know that to an outsider it is only a boat race, but to me it is just about my whole existence. I am witnessing what appeared to be the culmination of my life's work go clean down the tubes—for an error of one miserable second.

There seems to be so much at stake. In pure nationalistic terms, there is the matter of honor and pride. I know that in a changing world those qualities are often treated lightly, even with disdain by some. But I know I speak for all of my crew when I say that when you are locked head to head in a major international sporting confrontation, and you are sailing under the flag of your own country, well, that feeling and that responsibility cannot be measured in money or time or any of the other modern means of measuring excellence.

Honor and pride and the timeless human desire to pursue excellence for the sake of pure excellence are, believe me, the most powerful masters of all. When you are struggling against huge odds to gain supremacy on behalf of everyone in your own country, that becomes not so much a desire as an obsession. I even believe that if I had said that we could win only if five crewmen would step forward and allow their right arms to be cut off, I would have had 10 volunteers, each man prepared to be maimed in the interest of victory for *Australia II*. That is how we felt. I think it has something to do with that sense of nobility that a truly Corinthian sport like yacht racing brings out in us. We were not doing it for money, we were doing it for each other—and for a lot of other people as well. Under those circumstances, I think every sportsman will tell you there seems to be a sense of a higher calling. Something selfless, something noble. A stirring within us that is, I suppose, as old as human life itself.

But back to the action. It is about eight seconds after the gun, and I have to get this boat turned around and facing the right direction—quickly. All hands are ready. I'm still furious with myself, but I wheel her from a starboard tack to a port tack. We missed the big, red iron America's Cup buoy by about 18 inches as we jibed, the winch-grinders working like devils in the "engine room" of the boat.

It is awesome how swiftly and automatically we have slipped back on track. "OK, John, start straightening up." "Hold the mainsheet." "Trim that damned jib." "The wind is still left." All our calls are made from the perspective of upwind, even when sailing downwind. Thus, if we're going downwind and Hughey is facing me (or aft), he may say right, but from my place behind the wheel looking forward, it means left. How many times had I spoken the words to the crew—the words that I am now telling myself: "The strength of a great boat crew lies in its ability to hit right back after a setback, to rebound as if nothing had happened." The boys have rallied around after that terrible start—every one of them performing with the utmost efficiency. Finally we make it. *Australia II* heels over, sailing hard on the wind, beneath my grip. Out in front is the red boat, but she's nowhere near as far in front as I thought she would be. "Hell, John, we're in luck," says Hughey. And, sure enough, Chink Longley had correctly computed 37 seconds as the actual distance between the two boats as they crossed the starting line, but it was nothing like that much.

The truth was that the leeward end of the line was still by far the best place to be at the start. And although the Americans had 37 seconds on us officially, they were at the wrong end. We calculated that the 37-second difference as we finally slid over the starting line was in fact worth only about 20 seconds, maybe 15. "Come on, John, let's make the best of it. We're still right in this race."

Australia II feels terrific right now. I have maneuvered her so many times that sometimes she feels like an old shoe. Not only have the boys forgiven me, but so has the boat. And for the first time, the black clouds of incandescent anger—which hovered over my cockpit for the past 60 seconds (it seemed like about five months)—begin to lift, and I am now calling on all of my years of experience to fight us back into this life-or-death struggle.

We're back on course, and, with mounting optimism, every yard we travel confirms our opinion that the situation is not as bad as we had feared. But more important is that amazing strength of our team spirit. I can feel it everywhere.

"Come on, John, settle down. Watch your responsibilities. Let's sail the boat—together, the way we can." Those are the words being spoken to me by Colin Beashel. He's only 24 years old, but sometimes I feel Beasho has been on this earth for about a thousand years.

He is such a calming influence. In fact, the present calm aboard the boat exists by design, not by accident. For months I worked very closely with a sports psychologist, Laurie Hayden, who told me that there were two men in that crew who could always be counted on to sit back from an explosive situation—and rationalize it. Colin is one of those I knew I could count on. That technique took us three months to perfect. We worked hard on it, because we knew it was going to happen. Our collective search for perfection was so intense that we knew in advance that the consequences of any one of us making a mistake would almost certainly be an outburst of temper, which would be immediately counterproductive and had to be eliminated instantly. It takes a bit of preplanning to assemble a top crew, a crew who can think and act as brothers.

Anyway, the red boat is out in front to leeward of us. I'm feeling much better and we set off in pursuit of the impossible. I speak normally for the first time in a while. "OK, boys, we are going to grind them down. We are still going to win this." Privately, I am thinking, "I only hope to Christ this race does not end before we pass them. Please, please don't let us sail for 24 miles and still not get by."

We are still a fair way behind, about 3½ boatlengths, but we have good boatspeed and are climbing to windward very nicely—still on a port tack gaining marginally, but nothing to get excited about. After about four minutes, I have a feeling, a very strong one indeed. There is something wrong with *Liberty*, of that I am quite sure. Just before the start, after Rick and Vogel had come down, they had torn the luff tape on the headsail, and their jib bag went over the side. I thought they might be getting rattled by our very presence. They were terribly spooked over our boat, because they did not know what they were sailing against. Our mysterious winged keel had never even been seen by our opponents. Three minutes into Race 5, both Hughey and I sense they are in trouble. Their mast looks a bit soft high up on port tack, and my experience tells me they will be spending much time looking over their shoulders, wondering what we're up to.

Australia II sails on very, very fast through the water. My sole job right now is to sail the boat better than she has ever been sailed.

Just as Hughey and I are about to chat briefly about *Liberty*'s problems, we sense a windshift. Our bearing is starting to decrease. We are falling in to *Liberty*.

"Here comes a header, John. It's the first knock and its ours," snaps Hughey. "Five degrees knock!" calls Grant. "Tack, John, right now!" Away we go, now in the opposite direction to *Liberty*. We wait with bated breath. Will she follow and attempt to put a loose cover on us? "By Christ, she's not coming," I mutter. The red boat sails on, still on her original tack. I presume she's looking for a shift out there on the right, but in the opinion of my team, she's not going to find it. To our great joy, she just keeps going while we accelerate all on our own—out on the left side, where we had found many shifts in our races against the foreign boats.

Now here is a chance for the whole race to change. When two boats are going in opposite directions, you can get a real turnaround, and we are on a lift on this glorious starboard tack. We sail for possibly five more minutes—a long, long time under these circumstances. It is a kind of misty day, and we just about lose sight of the red boat in the haze.

Suddenly we start to knock again as the wind phases back. "Five degrees, John," says Grant. "Time to tack," says Hughey. I pull the wheel around smoothly to starboard, over comes the mainsail, and there is furious action in the well of the boat. All hands are flailing away at their appointed tasks. I head her down just off the wind, a fraction too far until she accelerates, and, as the mainsail fills, I head her up that fraction again. The great sails are now perfect, and *Australia II* heels over, as we head once again toward the red boat. The five-degree lift is excellent. We are clawing to windward now, and that lift we grabbed with such alacrity sends us all the way over toward the starboard layline.

Hughey is down the leeward side, watching *Liberty* like a hawk. He's calling out range and bearings. *Liberty* swings back to meet us, and when we converge, it is going to be damned close. We have come back from the jaws of death, and this could be bow to bow. Somehow we have caught up almost all of the official 37 seconds.

Both boats are sailing at around 8 knots now on a collision course. Suddenly Hughey calls, "Stand by for a starboard tack, John." And I can clearly see why. This is desperately close, but we have a chance to fetch up underneath them in a very safe lee-bow position.

Try to imagine *Australia II* and *Liberty* hurtling toward each other, 23 tons each, down the sides of a huge triangle. Just before the moment of impact, exactly at the apex, I am going to turn our wheel hard around to port, causing the bow of *Australia II* to swing fiercely to the left through 60 degrees. This, of course, will also cause our hull to slide broadside toward *Liberty* in a giant sideswipe/skidding motion. By this rather hair-raising method, we should end up exactly parallel with *Liberty,* we hope just a few feet apart and sailing in precisely the same direction, with *Australia II* about two-thirds of a boatlength ahead, but "underneath," or farther away from the mark toward which we are both headed.

Right now this is the maneuver Hughey and I are working on as we glide toward each other. Closer and closer: "Five boatlengths . . . four boatlengths." "Boatspeed," I call. "Seven four," snaps Grant. "Too slow," says Hughey, "get her up to seven seven." Now we're really close. "Speed," I shout, "what's the speed?" "Seven point five," says Grant. "Get her up two-tenths more," shouts Hughey above the wind. "Ready, John, stand by. Starboard tack. *Now!*"

I spin the wheel around smoothly, and the huge mainsail scrapes across our heads. I can see Damian hanging on for dear life up on the foredeck. The noise from the sails is nearly deafening as the whole boat shudders into the wind. *Liberty* seems about to cut us in half as we slew down toward her. *Australia II* locks right in alongside the red boat, the perfect lee-bow position. And now we are in brutal combat, racing neck-and-neck together as our furiously working winch-grinders, their hands gloved like those of prizefighters, struggle with throbbing muscles to move the dozens of feet of lines littering the well of the boat.

Australia II and *Liberty* are locked together, two great warring hulls in a harsh, uncompromising struggle for supremacy. The tension between *Liberty* and us is so great, so utterly consuming, that there is nothing to say. There is literally not a sound from anyone out there, almost as though to speak might be construed as a sign of weakness. In total, deadly silence, we grapple for each other's jugular.

From this close range we are trying keenly to assess the extent of the damage on *Liberty*, but it's difficult to see. The strut wire looks slack; that jumper strut certainly has broken again.

At this point in the race, we have taken 37 seconds off the Americans—not totally because of a broken strut. We outsailed them. They made a mistake. They should never have let us go off on our own. They should have followed and covered us. They should have come after us and found a way to keep us from outspeeding them, no matter what.

No doubt the strut damage did reduce their boatspeed a bit, but not as much as they thought it did. In fact, they were sailing faster than they thought they were. *Liberty* was occasionally a bit faster than we were on starboard tack, and as we sail together now, I can see that we are just about dead level, geographically and in terms of boatspeed.

I can hardly believe it, but we have the Americans rattled. They just made a judgment error. And they made it because they are intimidated by our boat. They went looking for wind when they should have been in a dogfight with us. This has to be the first time in history that a defending American crew has been intimidated by a foreign challenger. Their natural position in these races gives them a touch of arrogance resulting from always being better prepared, better trained, better financed, better equipped with local knowledge, and better equipped with the latest techniques in sail design. Now they were up against a boat and a crew that were superior in some of these areas. Like all match racers, I have a predatory instinct in these matters, so I'm obliged to say that I smelled blood and weakness on that first upwind leg of Race 5.

It is hard to explain the sensation of mounting excitement that is abroad in the Australian crew. Half an hour earlier we had been floundering, with hope almost gone. Now we are poised for what we hope is the kill. Somehow we have lured *Liberty* out to meet us on this great battleground. Now she must face us on our terms—in a tacking duel to the first mark, whether she likes it or not. And every man on our boat is uncannily aware that the American crew is at best wary, and at worst afraid, of such a tussle. One could hardly blame them for that, because *Australia II* does have one shining advantage, and that is in the mobility her keel gives her. I can spin her around like greased lightning, and I know that every time we tack we can take time and distance off our opponents.

And now the battle is on as we race together, hard on the wind, separated by a distance of less than 15 feet. Which one of us will blink first? Not us, that's for certain. And sure enough, there she goes. We have forced *Liberty* to tack away, back to the right-hand side of the course, which has served her so poorly. We immediately go with her, but the red boat tacks again, and once more, and we are facing her across the water. Again we are steaming toward each other. Right now it's feet and inches that count, not boatlengths. We must cross her bow in a very aggressive move and establish a lead. Our boatspeed again hits 7.8 knots. We have to keep this up until the last second before the tack, which will plant us squarely in front of the Americans, thus allowing us to steal their wind.

It all requires split-second timing. Grant calls out the speed nonstop, Hughey's eyes are like two gimlets on *Liberty*, I'm holding her right on the edge of the wind. It's like threading a needle. "We're going to take her now, John," says the tactician. "We have her now." One hundred yards apart . . . 90 yards . . . 80 yards . . . we're closing. This is it, whether we like it or not. "OK, John, tack *now!*" "TACKING!" I shout, and the heads dive for cover as that enormous sail sweeps around the mast. The winch-grinders' arms are a mere blur as these strong men crank away at the heavy-duty end of this deft, subtle, and cold-blooded art. *Australia II* shudders around, right across *Liberty*'s bow. And there we are, out in front in the race. We have the American boat on toast. There is nothing she can do except take on *Australia II* in the only area where we are unequivocally superior—a tight tacking duel. And she is crippled on her port side.

But as surely as I knew 10 minutes ago that we had a major psychological advantage over our opponents, I also know now, as I glance back and see them, that an angry, wounded Dennis Conner is a bloody tough opponent by anyone's standards. I am quite sure he will come back at us like a starved dog, and back he comes. Again and again he converges with us; every time, Hughey and I clobber them, as this light, sensitive white boat from Western Australia holds the great power racing machine *Liberty* on the end of our rapier.

Twelve times we have hurled ourselves at each other, like a couple of stags locking antlers. By now we all know we are in the middle of a momentous fight. Occasionally I glance over at big Dennis, watching his frustration—a real martinet if ever I saw one. You just have to admire him. What a fighter he is. Make one mistake and that son of a bitch would just roll right over you. His concentration is total. Even though we have known each other for 10 years, he doesn't give me even a glance. He just towers over that cockpit of his, master of his boat, his lips glinting from their coating of white zinc sun cream.

Now he is coming at us again. My heart goes out to the grinders. The sweat is pouring off them as we shape up for tack number 13. They must be praying for the mark, for the joyous respite of the downwind legs. But there they are—Richo, the Major, and Chink, all in superb condition, arms pounding, taking the strain. Each one of them is prepared to drive those winches to within an inch of their lives.

"TACKING!" I yell, and the whole muscle-bound circus in the well of the boat drives into action again. Still we are in front, but Dennis throws five more tacks at us before we finally come in close sight of the first weather mark.

"Let's not make any mistakes here, John," says Hughey. "We're only just fetching this mark. Will we need two tacks?" I am not sure. We are still only just in front, and I can hear that sinister sound of *Liberty*'s bow wave right behind us. I feel that we need every last second of advantage here, and slightly against my adviser's better judgment, I decide to sail the boat around the mark in one try.

Now I aim *Australia II* into the very eye of the wind. The most I can expect to miss the buoy by is about four feet, and that's really close. Any closer to the wind and we'll stall. Edging her up inch by inch, until the great mainsail is shuddering in protest, the jib shivering out above the foredeck, I hold her steady and wheel around the mark 23 seconds to the good. I may have experienced a more complete feeling of exaltation in a boat race before, but I cannot now recall one.

I look at the crew: at the grinders, whose arms must feel like spaghetti, whose hands are sore and aching; at Damian, so damned young, soaked from head to foot, now feeding out the spinnaker like a maniac; at Grant, now helping up at the mast; at Hughey, a terrific strength beside me; at Colin Beashel, who has worked furiously on that mainsheet in testing, fraught conditions with never a mistake; at Scoop and Skippy, who trimmed the jib to within half an inch; and finally at Ya, standing up to his thighs in water in the birdbath, that godawful spot on a 12-Meter where you never know if your boots are full of water or of blood.

We sailed a fabulous first leg, and we took exactly one minute off the red boat—by anyone's standards, that is extremely impressive. Doubtless the Americans would rationalize their performance by blaming the jumper strut—but they would be well advised to take one other factor into consideration. We sailed the first leg in 46 minutes flat, the fastest time recorded for any windward leg in this America's Cup series. We hit the right windshifts, on the button every time, and gained back that 37 seconds—and then we took 23 seconds off them in the tacking duel.

But now we face the two power reaches in this race. There is fierce but precision activity in setting the spinnaker. These downwind legs are not likely to show *Australia II* at her best. If *Liberty* is in any shape—and she's only just behind us—we can anticipate a real struggle. She is faster than we are on these reaches, and if we can turn into the wind an hour from now with our 23-second lead still intact, I will be a very happy, and mildly surprised, skipper.

2

22 Bristol Avenue

My grandpa, a fisherman, could tell the wind direction by instinct. He could feel the air being generated before it even got to us. He told my mum I had his gift for "smelling" the wind.

By the way, my name is John Bertrand. I live quite close to Melbourne, Australia, and during the most visible few weeks of my sailing career I was 36 years old. You may have gathered from certain parts of the preceding chapter that life for me has not always been a breeze. I seem to have spent an inordinate amount of time trying to climb mountains and scale peaks of achievement that many of those close to me considered of questionable merit.

My goals were of a lofty nature, those of the old-fashioned amateur sportsman. I was pursuing, with a kind of deranged fury, the sense of excellence, conquest, and perfection—particularly perfection—that is contained in the pure Olympic spirit. At least that is how I always perceived the matter.

Others of a more pragmatic, less charitable turn of mind were apt to regard my efforts, impatiently, as more of an egocentric pursuit of self-satisfaction, having scant regard for the financial future of myself, my wife, or my family, not to mention my descendants. I was occasionally described as a kind of globe-trotting "pot hunter," the equivalent of a ski bum or a tennis bum. Except, of course, that I appeared to have been born in a boat, preferred to live in a boat, and would very likely die in a boat—without much to show for it, either. Still, there usually are two ways of looking at things.

I suppose I ought to mention that for a very short time, when funds were not all they might have been in our household, my adorable, rock-steady, sardonic, forgiving, endlessly cheerful wife, Rasa, joined that bunch of doubters. However, driven apart as we very nearly were by a racing yacht I did not even own, we never dwell upon those moments anymore. Poor Rasa. It must have been rotten, those moments when her obdurate blind faith in my efforts momentarily gave way to the more worldly task of bringing up a young family on little money while I was trimming the jib, as it were.

I shall now take this opportunity to spend a short while in my family tree, in which I usually have been welcome, and which is, curiously, steeped in the tradition of the seas.

Like many Australians, my roots, at least on my mother's side, are English. We originally came from Southampton, that great seaport in Hampshire that was for many years the headquarters of world shipping, both passenger liners and oceangoing cargo vessels—not to mention the building of great racing boats.

It was hereabouts that one of the better-known members of my seafaring family, Thomas Pearkes, my great-grandfather, established a reputation as one of the finest ship's engineers in England.

By the age of 16, Tom had crossed the Atlantic eight times as a cabin boy. The docks and shipyards around the port were home to him, and he rose to be a master of his greatly sought-after craft. In time, the big racing yachts became his specialty, and he spent as much time working on these boats in Cowes and other Isle of Wight yards as he did in Southampton itself.'

In the early part of the twentieth century, the dominant figure in yacht racing was the legendary Sir Thomas Lipton, who spent 31 years and a huge fortune trying to win back the America's Cup for England. He was, by all accounts, a wonderful man. Born of extremely poor Irish parents in Glasgow, Scotland, he emigrated to America at 15 with scarcely a penny. Later he returned to Glasgow to found a large chain of grocery stores and a veritable empire of tea trading.

Lipton challenged the Americans for the Cup five times in his beautiful racing yachts, painted green in honor of his heritage and all named *Shamrock*—each was 130 feet long and weighed 100 tons. My great-grandfather was one of his main engineers, and he worked on these racing boats for Sir Thomas both in Southampton and on the Isle of Wight. The millionaire, with his Scottish links, usually insisted on using other top engineers and tradesmen from the great shipbuilding yards on the River Clyde in Scotland, and many of them stayed at Tom Pearkes's house, often for periods of eight or nine months, while the *Shamrock*s were being prepared for the Atlantic journey to do battle with the Americans.

Among them they did not, of course, win the America's Cup, but they sailed hard and with immense sportsmanship. The highlight of their years was probably 1920, when *Shamrock IV* soundly defeated *Resolute* in the first two races. That was the first time any foreign challenger had ever taken two races off the United States. The second was in 1934, when Tommy Sopwith's *Endeavour* beat *Rainbow* in two straight races. In 1983 I was the third helmsman to achieve this honor, if honor it be.

It was in fact my grandfather, Bill Cull, who had married the young Evelyn Pearkes, who first moved to Australia. My mother, Beryl, was only four years old when they left Southampton, and they finally settled along the Chelsea shore 19 miles south of Melbourne. My grandfather (he was always called "Bant") was a commercial fisherman, and for years he worked the waters of Port Phillip Bay in a 14-foot motorboat, making a decent living without ever getting very rich.

He was an extraordinary seaman. At the Chelsea Yacht Club, where he was vice-commodore, he was in charge of the rescue boat, a double-ended 17-foot-long power launch. He helped to build that boat, and he was one of the real stalwarts that communities on the ocean rely on. A stocky, weather-beaten man, he had a big nose and piercing blue eyes—my mum says a bit like my own. I loved Bant when I was young. He had endless patience with all children and he had the most remarkable instinct for the sea breeze. He could predict it to within five minutes. I know that sounds ridiculous, but he really could. When I wanted to go sailing, I used to run up the road from our house and get Bant and make him come down to the shore, where we would stand together facing a sea like a millpond. I would ask, "When's the sea breeze coming?" And Bant would stand gazing at the clouds and the water, assessing when the thermal convections would start the breeze. Finally, he would say something extraordinary, like, "Johnny, I think it will come at nine minutes past 12 o'clock." I was only about eight at the time, but I always thought it was hysterical. And then it would happen. The breeze would arrive *exactly* when he said it would. It was very nearly mystical. I know it was a long time ago, and memory can play tricks, but anyone around our way will tell you that Bant Cull could tell you precisely when that wind would come. And I'd say that was true about 90 percent of the time.

He just had the greatest feeling for the sea. He really could smell the wind. He could look at the type of cloud out over the water, he could tell the wind direction by pure instinct and he could feel the air being generated before it even got to us.

When I was very young, my grandfather tried to teach me about the wind and its speed across the water and its likely effect on the waves and on a small boat. He told my mum I had his gift for "smelling" the wind. But, as with most things you can luckily do without apparent effort, you tend to take them a bit for granted and don't dwell on them. But you might find a few international sailors who recall my getting a decent wind-shift in a race before they did, and if anyone ever feels like paying me a small compliment about that, I will be happy to tell them that that part of my sailor's knowledge came from a wonderful gentleman, Bant Cull, fisherman, of Bristol Avenue, Chelsea, State of Victoria, Australia.

My grandmother, Mrs. Evelyn Cull, was also a bit of a character. She and Bant lived only four houses up the road from the house where I grew up, and she was one of my great supporters. She was one of those very powerful ladies. At the age of 80, she was still a very active president of the Chelsea Yacht Club Ladies Committee. She was a remarkable strength in the community and was always talking about the power of positive thinking. She had an enormous influence on my life, regaling me for years with tales of the sea, helped in the telling by my great-grandfather, Tom Pearkes. They told me of those enormous racing boats he helped prepare for Sir Thomas Lipton, and both she and my mother told me I was the image of old Tom—same build, same eyes, same moustache. And I knew about the America's Cup as some kids know about football or baseball.

"Nan" Cull, as she was always known, did not restrict her comments to America's Cups of the past, either. She had stringent opinions about the modern-day clashes with the Americans. But in her latter years, her most forthright opinion left no room for discussion. "Australia," she would say sternly to anyone who would listen, "cannot and will not ever win the America's Cup until my Johnny is actually steering the boat." Heaven forbid!

In one of the most traumatic incidents of my life, Nan Cull died five weeks before I took the helm of *Australia II* against *Liberty*. No one deserved to know we had won more than she did, and for me personally, her death was very, very saddening—in a sense, more so after our victory.

My own mother and father lived at 22 Bristol Avenue, the last dwelling on the street, a single-story beach house with the narrow sand dunes reaching right up to the back door. My father, Alexander Bertrand, was, like me, an engineer. My mother, Beryl, was a champion swimmer and only just missed Olympic selection for Australia. She used to become very nervous before swimming, and she was violently ill before the final trials for the 1932 Los Angeles Olympics—forfeiting her place to a girl she always believed she could defeat.

The house where my brother, Lex, and I were brought up—and in which my mother still lives—could hardly have been closer to the ocean. The sound of the sea winds, the gulls wheeling over our house, and the varying sounds of the water were second nature for all of us. I cannot remember life without boats and sailing. Even when I was very young, I would go out in Grandpa's fishing boat and sail my little fleet of toy yachts behind us on a long cord. Even when he had taught Lex and me to fish with him, I still preferred to watch the angles of my yachts knifing through the water behind us.

But those were barefooted days of childhood, and I think I was about seven—Lex must have been 10—when we began our ocean-racing careers. It may not have been quite the start that great America's Cup skippers such as Mike Vanderbilt had, but it was all-encompassing for us.

We acquired a very old flat-bottomed powerboat with an engine that had long since given up the ghost as it lay rusting along the shore. We purchased a 16-foot-long pole three inches in diameter and with the aid of some homemade shrouds, we embedded it into the deck to serve as a mast. From an army surplus store we bought an old parachute, and Mum spent hours cutting and stitching it to form a square sail. Our boat was probably the most diabolical-looking craft ever to hit the historic waters of Port Phillip Bay.

I remember the day of her maiden voyage under sail. Lex and I dragged her down the beach, into the onrushing waves. We pushed and shoved and struggled as successive swells attempted to turn the boat around and send her back to dry land. Mum nearly had a heart attack as we finally timed everything correctly and rushed out through the surf into water about three feet deep. We fell sprawling over the side of the boat, grappling to get at the oars.

Lex took the port side, I the starboard, and we rowed and rowed until we were exhausted—about 150 yards offshore. This was the moment, and we hoisted the parachute sail and swung her around to leeward. The gusting wind filled our "sail" in a second, and for the first time I felt the age-old silent surge of power from the breeze, which has mesmerized sailors from the beginning of civilization. I doubt if the historic aspect of it occurred to the seven-year-old hanging on for dear life to the mainsheet and experiencing the most dramatic few minutes of his life. But in retrospect, I guess that was my first-ever square run.

We sailed the boat all summer long. In all the extremes of weather, even when the wind grew cold and whipped in from the south bringing rainsqualls, and the great length of coastline in front of our house was deserted—there was often the sight of two struggling figures pushing that old boat out into the sea and blowing back before the wind. We became extremely proficient at maneuvering our little craft, and one of the great highlights of our sailing careers occurred one blustery autumn day. We were way out beyond the surf, when suddenly we saw a capsized V.J. (Vaucluse Junior) racing yacht, her two-man crew in the water. Immediately we put into action the rescue drill that Grandpa Bant had instilled in us. We sailed around the yacht, whipping her into the wind, and hauling down the parachute sail in one lightning movement, fetching up alongside the shipwrecked yachtsmen.

I thought I would die of excitement as we made them fast to us, took the bedraggled crew on board, and, to their utter astonishment, hoisted our parachute again and towed everyone to safety. They must have been grateful, if flabbergasted, because when we got them to shore, they thanked us profusely and told us to report to the Chelsea Yacht Club the next day so they could take us sailing in a real racing yacht.

I did not sleep one wink that night. After all the years I had spent wandering around the yacht club with Lex, gazing at the boats and dreaming of the great racers we would one day own, I was actually going out in one the very next day.

I was so excited to be going out on a huge V.J.—all of 12 feet. And I will never forget the feeling I had when we set off. It was a windy day and the boat immediately accelerated. To this day I can recall the quick, efficient way everything happened, the speed and the wonderful quiet, fast ride across the sea.

From that day the yacht club, located just along the beach from our house, became the hub of our world. That was the only place we wanted to be. When we weren't out sailing, we were just hanging around looking at sailing boats. At school, and when I was supposed to be doing my homework, I did almost nothing except draw and paint boats, fantasizing about the great races I thought I would one day win.

I was still only seven when Lex and I took delivery of our first real sailboat—a little eight-foot snub-bowed Sabot. And now, as local yacht owners, it was clear that we had to be admitted to the club—which had an age limit of 18, since they were wary of the place becoming a kindergarten. After all kinds of stormy meetings, the club officials finally agreed to lower the age limit to 10. Lex Bertrand was admitted as the first-ever club cadet, and, since we clearly could not be separated, they let me in as a half-cadet, a privileged status that I still enjoy at the Chelsea Yacht Club.

Then the trouble began. As yacht owners and club members, we established a chain of command. As the elder brother, Lex was skipper and helmsman. I was bow man and mainsheet hand. He sat in the stern, steering and being important, and I sat in the bow of the boat, hanging on to the mainsheet. For two months this was fine, but then, as I suppose I have felt all of my life, I wanted to steer, to have my turn at the helm. This caused major trouble, since Lex was clearly not happy about relinquishing his position as skipper.

It required a full family meeting to reach agreement that I was entitled to my go at the tiller, and a half-hourly rotation system was established. A very large alarm clock was placed on the beach, and it went off every 30 minutes—signifying an immediate switching of roles. If either of us went five minutes too long, there was hell to pay. We fought and argued. Once I tried to dislodge Lex with a boathook.

Mum stepped in and said she would be the final arbiter with a white tablecloth—if anyone overstayed his half hour at the tiller and ignored the alarm clock, she would come down and wave the tablecloth, and her decision was final. That cloth meant the man at the helm gave up his position no matter what delicate stage of the proceedings we were in.

Still we fought and argued. Sometimes there would be such a row on the boat, such shouting and yelling, that Mum would be running along the beach with the tablecloth—to the absolute amazement of passersby. The very sight of the cloth was supposed to end all discussions, but still the arguments were unbelievable.

Finally, one day on the beach, my dad was standing next to the boat in a black fury, with a huge ax poised like the sword of Damocles. "THAT'S THE END!" he bawled. "NO MORE! I'm going to chop this bloody thing in two." I remember Mum pleading with him not to annihilate the boat. "Darling," she begged, "why don't we just get another little boat for the boys."

It took her about two hours to get him to listen, but the ax did not fall, and shortly afterward we got another Sabot. I kept the old one, which was called *Flying J*, and the new boat, of course, was called *Flying L*. Oh, it was all wonderful. There was a big *J* with wings on my boat and a similar winged *L* on the other. Each was about four feet high. It was lovely old-fashioned stuff, and I will always remember those days with the utmost fondness.

Quite soon Lex and I became very good at sailing the Sabots. We looked after them with incredible care, keeping them in our little white beach hut—number 940 in a long row of such bathing huts stretching down to the club. We used to lift the boats down the steps and then rig them on blankets that we took off our beds—which again nearly drove Mum mad. Also, we used to move aside furniture in the house and take the little boats right into the living room to paint and varnish them away from flying sand. We cared for those boats as though they were Grand Prix racers. The Bertrand family reward finally came when Lex won the State of Victoria Junior Championship. At the age of 13 I won it as well, and I cannot ever explain how proud Mum and Dad were.

Shortly after those great triumphs, Dad agreed that we had to progress to a real racing boat, and we began to look for a V.J.—the fantastically fast Vaucluse Junior, 12 feet long, with twin "hiking boards," a speed machine that can travel as fast as the Flying Dutchman. This is a high-performance training boat, and its power-to-weight ratio is nothing short of phenomenal. The crew slide out on these hiking boards with only their feet touching the side of the boat. The boats have fully battened mainsails, and in a 20- to 25-knot sea breeze, they can do 15 knots. One way or another, they are hair-raising little boats, and you need the nerves of a World War I pilot to sail them.

However, Father, Uncle Bill, and Lex decided we should move up to that very yacht. And there is one thing about my father for which I will always be grateful. If Lex and I wanted to do something badly—by that I mean *desperately*—he would do everything in his power to see that we had the best equipment. We did not have much money in those days, but he still wanted to give us a proper chance for success in whatever we attempted.

Most V.J.s then cost about £120, which seemed like a fortune to all of us. We looked around at many of them and eventually wrote to the secretary of the V.J. Association in Sydney, where huge fleets of these stream-lined racers formed the biggest class in Australia. We received a most helpful letter from the secretary, Arthur Wardle, and we made the decision that for £230 we would buy a brand-new Fairbrother hull, to be built by Australia's finest boatbuilder, Don Fairbrother in Sydney.

Months went by, and Lex and I were in a frenzy of anticipation. Finally the day dawned. There was a letter from Fairbrothers informing us that our new V.J. was ready.

This was a dream come true, and in high excitement we all piled into the family car, a Ford Zephyr Six, and Mum and Dad and Lex and I drove the 600 miles to Sydney to collect the boat. We took a blanket from my bed to wrap it in, and when we got there, and I first laid eyes on that boat—well, I just couldn't believe it. I could hardly stop shaking as we stitched the blanket around the hull and hoisted it up onto the roof rack alongside the beautifully cut Gary Foggs sails (of pure Egyptian cotton) and the highly polished mast. She was more magnificent than anything I had ever seen, far ahead of anything anyone had ever seen in Victoria. She was made of cedar plywood, weighing just 90 pounds in total minimum class rules. It was the most beautiful piece of workmanship—12 feet long with the bowsprit.

Dad had saved for ages to buy that boat, and she was everything I had ever dreamed she could be. We named her *Be Be* (for Bertrand boys), and we had a six-foot *B* stitched onto the sails. I would also like to record that I have never been so frightened of a boat since then. That hull could plane to windward and reach fantastic speeds. Lex, who was 15, was skipper, and I, 12, was terrified. I was on the jib and supposed to work on the forward swing board. While the boat was going at fantastic speeds, I was supposed to stand with my feet spread apart on that highly polished, richly curved piece of carpentry, about six inches above the water, and hang on to the jibsheet. I must have fallen off a dozen times in the first week. I was so frightened that when we entered a race, I was too scared to put up the spinnaker. Lex kept yelling at me to get it up, but I couldn't. I was too afraid to move, and there was no way I was going to let go and stand up and haul up the spinnaker. I suppose the lasting tribute to that lightning-fast machine was that we still won the race—it was *that* fast.

We cherished that boat for two years. She carried us to the V.J. championship of Victoria, which to us was equivalent to the World Championship. We had to compete against all the living legends from around our coastline, including the reigning state champion, Brett McEwan. In the very first race, sailed off the Sandringham Yacht Club on our home waters of Port Phillip Bay, we beat him by a good distance, and he never turned up to race us again. We never even saw him again for several years. And imagine the look in our dad's eyes when Lex and I were presented the Cup for the best young V.J. sailors in Victoria. He was so proud he could have died.

By this time Lex was a very good skipper, exceptional under pressure. However, I, as usual, was a lousy crew. I *can* complement people, but I get so frustrated because I want to do it myself. I always feel it could be done better. I was able to contain myself with *Be Be*, and it was not until we traded her for a brand-new Fairbrother V.J. hull, named *Ballerina*, that the old troubles started again. We had terrible fights on the boat, and shortly after we finished third in the National Junior Championships, sailed off our home club at Chelsea in 1960, well, we split up.

Lex went off and sailed for Peter Hoskings, a top racing yachtsman and a dear friend of our family. I took over as skipper of *Ballerina*, and for the first time I was solely in charge. The first thing I did was to confide in Mum that this boat would not win me the championship of Australia, which was my burning ambition. I was not quite 15, but I knew that I needed a racing hull by Laurie Chivvers of Western Australia. Mum agreed, and somehow we sold *Ballerina* for a good price and took delivery of the new boat without paying out much money.

Never was I so disappointed in a new boat. The finish, by my standards, was awful. As usual, I completely dismantled our living room, laying out the sheets and moving in the pots of varnish and brushes. And I completely sanded her down in the house, stripping her back to bare wood and slowly bringing her up to the standard lately enjoyed by *Be Be*. Once more my boat looked like a piece of antique furniture. My crew was Geoff Augustine, age 14, and when he trimmed that mainsail, I knew we had a flying machine on our hands. Fast? She was like lightning, and I named her *Triad* for the union of three elements—in this case, sun, wind, and water. She was also named after the boat of another dear family friend, Bill Osborne, the 14-time National Australian Champion in the 14-foot class.

No two teenagers ever worked harder sailing a boat than Geoff and I. We practiced for hundreds of hours out there on the bay. Eventually, there was nothing we could not do with that boat, under any conditions. She was fantastically fast, and we could sail her on the razor's edge of every limit known to man. She would hurtle across those waters hitting record speeds, and I knew that one day we could win the National Championships.

It was 1961, just before my 15th birthday, when we finally decided to make the long cross-country journey to Western Australia, to the Swan River in Perth, where the championships were being held that year. Lex would have his driving license, and we would take the car, by road to Adelaide and then on the train to the West.

That year, however, provided another trauma in my young life. My dad died and I was devastated. He was such a wonderful friend, and Lex and I owed him everything. It was he who had seen our potential so early and he who had sacrificed so much to give us both a real shot at championship-class sailing. Now he was gone, and the gap he left in my life was as big as Port Phillip Bay. It took me years to get over it, if indeed I ever have. And I have never once won a major event without thinking of him.

But life somehow goes on, and greatly encouraged by Mum and my grandparents, I worked away at getting to Perth. Lex got his license at 18, and within a few days we began the long journey to Perth to the National Championships.

Lex, by the way, was not acting as an unpaid chauffeur for Geoff and me. He was crewing for Peter Hoskings in the Lightweight Sharpie Class, and the entire thing was a huge adventure. We set off from Bristol Avenue at first light, with the boat lashed to the roof rack of the old Zephyr. It was 400 miles to Adelaide and about halfway there, the engine blew up. We found our way to a garage and waited while a new Ford engine was fitted. With our budget for the trip thus obliterated, we continued driving all through the night to catch the train from Adelaide.

By some miracle we made it, and, down nearly to our last pennies, we pressed on across the Nullarbor Desert, 1,000 miles on the train, with sandwiches, bottles of lemonade, car, boat, sails, and everything. We arrived in Perth broke.

It's funny what you remember about a journey like that. I remember Geoff and me soaking our hands and bottoms three times a day with methylated spirits to protect us from what we called "gunwale bum," a burning sore condition caused by hiking out on those swing boards. We thus developed extremely tough backsides to take the battering necessary to get out on those boards quickly, at high speeds, skipper and crew leaning five feet out over the side.

For that time, the very early 1960s, that was a rather professional attitude. Most racers tended to be less driven then, and none of our competitors had practiced anything like the amount we had. We practiced because we loved it. The pursuit of excellence has always driven me. We did not do it for domination but to achieve sailing perfection. In this sense, we were ahead of our time, and we were in that position because I had always been fascinated with the refinement of the sport, a mental attitude that took me a long way without requiring me to become vicious about it.

Now, in this Junior National Championship we were obliged to line up for five races on the Swan River against the best young V.J. sailors in Australia. Geoff and I did not just beat them, we killed them. I remember that I took a monumental risk in Race 1, and we capsized at top speed. But we did what we always did—got right back in and still won by more than six minutes.

We outsailed everyone, winning all five races by huge margins. In every race we sailed right into the middle of the senior fleet, which had set off 10 minutes before us. It was hitherto the most important moment of my life. I had only turned 16, and I remember feeling close to tears because my dad couldn't see me.

As I stood there with the trophy, the thoughts flooded over me again. This man who had given me everything never even saw me win it. It did not seem right then, and it doesn't now. It still makes me sad to think that he never knew. However, in my heart I think he knew, just as I think Nan Cull knows that *Australia II* finally won the America's Cup, with her "Johnny" steering the boat, just as she had always predicted.

Naturally the word of our victory in Perth was sent from coast to coast by the newspapers—with particular emphasis on the manner in which we had won. Of course I was assailed by my usual self-doubts about my ability, whether or not *anyone else* could have won in the lightning-fast *Triad*. But I sold her soon after that, and she never won another series. I suppose that says something.

Another important aspect of Perth 1962 was the arrival of the reigning World Champion in the Flying Dutchman Class, Rolly Tasker. This Olympic silver medalist came down especially to see me race, and apparently he did not forget what I had done. He contacted Jim Hardy and told him I was a potential crew member for the America's Cup. So in a sense my destiny was already beginning as we performed our daredevil antics on the Swan River that summer.

Looking back at my new status as Junior V.J. Champion of Australia in 1962, I think it must have given me a sudden maturity, because not only did I feel an overpowering urge to helm a much bigger boat, but I also began to be diligent at school. In the ensuing 24 months, I became head prefect of the school and received the Dux Scholar Award. I also won a place at Melbourne's Monash University, where I would study hard for four years and earn a degree in mechanical engineering.

I was 22 by the time I graduated from Monash, and by then I had won three Junior National Championships, one Senior, two runners-up, and one third. I had been State Junior Champion at 13, and, quite frankly, I had been unbeatable in an old motorboat powered by a secondhand parachute. In my more excitable moments I sometimes wondered whether Great-Grandfather Pearkes and Sir Thomas Lipton might not have found a place for me on one of those mighty *Shamrocks*.

Oh yes—one more minor point. My thesis for my engineering degree was a long treatise on the aerodynamics of the sails of 12-Meters—a subject that would more or less consume me until the 26th day of September in 1983.

3

Harsh Encounters

Then the spinnaker got badly snagged and our foredeck man, Paul Salmon, was washed overboard; the mainsheet man was half drowned; and the New York Yacht Club flung out our protest with autocratic disdain.

As a free-spirited soul who answers the call of the oceans and the beckoning of great sailboats, I should perhaps record that one of the most important moments of my youth occurred not upon some broad seascape with the wind in my hair, the slash of salt spray on my face, and victory in my nostrils. It occurred in a rather dark discotheque in the back streets of Melbourne, with some awful jazz music in my ears, a few beers beneath my belt, and lust in my eyes.

I was just 18 years old, and it was the first night I was ever allowed to drive the family car on my own. With two high-school mates I was trying to pick up a couple of girls at a local jazz dance, and I first spotted her across the room in a corner. Emboldened by the thought of the six powerful cylinders that waited outside as a kind of sensual ally, I ventured forth as a proper grown-up hunter of the opposite sex and introduced myself. She was very pretty, and she drove my imagination wild when she coolly announced that she was a nurse. "A nurse!" The very embodiment of every schoolboy's fantasies. I thought, "This is fantastic. They know everything." I nudged my companions, winking furiously. Suddenly I was besieged by doubts. Biologically I was not all that sophisticated, and I wondered if I could handle this.

Well, as it turned out, the pretty little nurse whose favors I sought was exactly 17 years old. She was two weeks into her training, fresh out of a Catholic convent. She was about as much a nurse as I was.

In fact, I nearly lost her the first night, and my troubles began as soon as she told me her name. Now I have a dreadful memory for names at best, and when she came forward with Miss Rasa Padgurskis, well, that just about finished me. I used to have trouble with Anne. I ended up taking her home, which was a dwelling in the back of beyond, the suburb of Rosanna. I think I asked her how long she had lived in Darwin. And at 4 A.M. she got out of the car and I set sail for home, where my brother was combing the streets for me, about 10 minutes from alerting the local police, Coast Guard and presumably Interpol.

The following day I awoke with cheerful anticipation of seeing the delectable Miss Whatsername again as soon as possible. And then it hit me. I had forgotten to write down her address or phone number. Worse, I did not remember her name, but one of her friends had called her "Mary."

"That's it," I thought, "I'll phone the hospital and ask for Mary."

"Hallo, is that St. Vincent's Hospital?"

"Speaking. Would you like emergency, surgery, or the wards?" [a busy male voice]

"Well, er, actually I wondered if I could speak to Mary."

"Mary who?" [slightly irritated]

"Er, Mary, the nurse."

"This is a Catholic hospital, sonny. There are about a thousand of them. What's her last name?" [VERY irritated]

"Well, there's *no way* I can tell you that."

"Get more information, son." Click. I was terminated. I would never find her again.

But once more the sea proved to be the key to my life. I suddenly remembered Dobsons, the finest builders of wooden masts in Australia. I dimly remembered driving past their yard just before I dropped "Mary" at her home. Thank God for Dobsons. The following day I was playing football for the South Melbourne Club under-19 team and I had to drive past the mastmakers to get to the game. I found the house and rang the bell.

Lo and behold it was answered by Miss Rasa Padgurskis, whom I was privileged to marry in 1969. She is today the mother of our three children, she has seen me through two Olympic Games, four America's Cup matches, heaven-knows-how-many setbacks, and God knows what I would ever have done without her these past 15 years.

Rasa's unusual name came from her Lithuanian parents, who had fled from their Russian-occupied country. Her father had escaped in an army vehicle and made his way to Germany, where he had traveled from farm to farm to find work and to eat. The family finally got together again in Australia, but Rasa's mother was tragically killed in a road accident when Rasa was just four. Her father, Leonas, with great courage worked as a builder and raised the family.

To this day he is ruled by the traditional Slavic work ethic, and for years he could not comprehend why I was always sailing boats, not being in possession of what he considers to be "a proper job." Old Leonas has never mastered the English language, so I have never quite been able to explain to him why I am often at home at strange hours of the day—or am occasionally missing for weeks on end. In the middle of one America's Cup campaign, I became so determined that he should not consider me a total waster that I told him I was a milkman and worked very early in the morning. This delighted him no end. "Ah, John. That's good. Proper regular work. Very good. You will make my Rasa fine husband." We never discussed my career again, but the business of racing big boats, or even manufacturing sails for them, continues to confuse him. He regards all of that as some kind of irresponsible vacation. But as long as I am able to hold down my job as a milkman, well, "That's good. Regular work, John. That's what counts."

In the very beginning I am not sure that I represented a great improvement in the standard of living from the days when Leonas was trudging around German farms. When Rasa and I first married, I had no money, I had not yet begun a serious job, and my obsession with fast sailing boats would condemn us to a terribly restless, almost nomadic existence.

Back in the summer of 1968, more than a year before our wedding, I had been approached by Jim Hardy about sailing under his command on Sir Frank Packer's new America's Cup challenger, *Gretel II*. At this time I was well into my aerodynamics thesis for my degree at Monash, but the prospect of joining the Australian crew bound for Newport in 1970 was a pretty heady thought for a third-year undergraduate—particularly for one such as myself, for whom the America's Cup held such an overpowering mystique. It was a call that touched my every instinct. I had thoughts as usual of Great-Grandpa Tom Pearkes (who had, after all, died at

Grandma's house in Chelsea only four years previously, at the age of 94), of the great *Shamrocks*, and of the rich family tradition of the sea that I had been so lucky to inherit.

They flew me to Sydney and I stepped aboard *Gretel II*, the first keeled boat on which I had ever set foot. I thought it was awe-inspiring, and I felt very sure I had something to offer, especially in the area of highly sensitive sail-trimming, which is second nature to the small-boat racing yachtsman. Jim took me sailing on *Gretel II* and I was most impressed. He wanted me involved very early on, and my reaction to this siren song, under pressure, was not really that of the cool, methodical marine engineer and skipper I fervently hoped to become one day. I resolved forthwith to leave university immediately, shelve my aerodynamics theory for two years, and run away to sea in a headlong rush for glory.

About this time I experienced the feeling that a runaway thoroughbred colt must receive from a master horseman. With my reins being held in a grip of iron, I felt myself being hauled to a standstill. "Now you listen to me, John," said my mother, the redoubtable Beryl. "I am not going to let you do anything crazy. That boat and that crew will wait for you until you have graduated. I have much more faith in you than you have in yourself, and in my opinion you cannot be replaced on that boat no matter how hard they try. When you start sailing on *Gretel II*, I would prefer you to be there as a graduate of Monash with a first-class engineering degree, which will serve you for the rest of your life. I do not want you to leave university until that is done."

Well, it was instantly clear to me that Mrs. Bertrand was not at all sure to whom she was speaking. Nor indeed had she considered that I was 21 years old, and I was old enough to vote, fight for my country, and die for my country. I was also Lightweight Sharpie champion of my country, which everybody knows wants a bit of doing. I told her in no uncertain terms that the opportunity to sail on *Gretel II* was a once-in-a-lifetime chance, a fantastic break too great to turn down. The whole project contained hitherto unfathomable opportunity. There was a lot she failed to understand.

Anyway, I went straight back to the university and finished my degree. Not for the first time in my life, I have had many years to contemplate the hard common sense of my mum. Thank God for Beryl.

But the call of *Gretel II* did not go away. I finished my thesis, got my degree, married Rasa, and accepted a position as port trimmer on Sir Frank Packer's boat. My new young wife and I moved to Sydney, to a small apartment, and I was offered a job with Warwick Hood, the naval architect who designed *Dame Pattie*, the second of the modern Australian challengers for the America's Cup. *Dame Pattie* was, of course, the luckless

12-Meter that ran headlong into the U.S. superboat *Intrepid* in 1967 and was demolished 4–0 without further ceremony.

It was October of 1969, and it was, I suppose, the beginning of my 14-year quest to wrest the America's Cup from the New York Yacht Club. Unlike many of my shipmates, I was there only to win. The only reason I *ever* sailed on a 12-Meter off Newport, Rhode Island, was to *win* the America's Cup. I always believed it could be done.

And so my adventure began that October on *Gretel II*. We sailed only on weekends in those days and spent much of the time during the week modifying the boat. Sir Frank, a big, tough, lovely guy who made a fortune in publishing, used to pop in on weekends to see how everything was going. Every aspect of our preparation was behind schedule. We were miles behind with the designs, blocks were still being built for the boat at a time when they should have been in place, the mast and its rigging were a shambles. We used to get down to the yacht at the appointed sailing time of 8 A.M., and we would not get the boat out until one o'clock in the afternoon, because they were still working on the hull. Our designer and manager, the brilliant Alan Payne, was completely overworked, yet in the middle of his many critical problems, he once found time to telephone me at work and solemnly ask me what size sneakers I wore.

Even in those early days, I could not help reflecting on the incredible mismatch of people running an America's Cup campaign with all of its utterly critical timing areas. Our management displayed a total bewilderment at using time effectively, and this was reflected throughout the campaign. Our leadership proved incapable of getting the project on track—simply because no one knew enough about it.

There was a great rivalry between Jim Hardy and Martin Visser for the right to skipper *Gretel II*. A concerted effort, geared to produce a tight-knit fighting combination to go to Newport and represent Australia, didn't exist—we were, quite frankly, without hope. In terms of the America's Cup, this was Amateur Night in Australia. That 1970 outfit would have had a hard time beating most of the *challengers* in the 1983 Cup races.

But to Newport we went, with Jim Hardy, heir to one of the oldest wine-producing families in Australia, at the helm. The first obstacle loomed in the shape of the immensely proud and impeccably dressed Frenchman, Baron Bich. The ballpoint-pen king was challenging on behalf of his homeland with a very beautiful 12-Meter named *France*.

He arrived with a fleet of 12-Meters, old ones he had purchased as trial horses. Accompanying him were about 60 sailors, two chefs, and more wine than Jim Hardy's family had produced in the twentieth century. Happily for us, this all created real chaos—as only a group of very excitable Frenchmen can. Amid all kinds of gesticulating and yelling, Bich fired skippers, reinstated them, changed the crew, and lost the first three races to us in rapid succession. He made us look organized.

For the fourth race, things were bound to be different. The Baron, resplendent in white gloves, took the helm of *France,* but he became lost in the fog and finally accepted a tow home, his $4 million challenge, as they say, down the old tubes.

This left us looking not too bad, although the two big U.S. Twelves, *Intrepid* and *Valiant,* dueling for the right to face us, seemed pretty formidable. Olin Stephens's new boat, *Valiant,* was skippered by Rear-Commodore Robert McCullough, while *Intrepid* was helmed by the tall, baldheaded Californian architect Bill Ficker. These two men went at it in the hardest match racing I had ever seen. Their boats were big and heavy, but their crew organization was terrific—at least a decade ahead of us. Their sails were far superior to ours, even though the sails on *Gretel II* were considered very good in those days. And their greater match-racing experience afforded them the knowledge of when to use their sails and which ones to select.

Yet there was a suspicion that *Intrepid* was not as fast in 1970 as she had been when she demolished *Dame Pattie. Gretel II* was a fast boat, and there were people who thought we had a chance, despite our lack of experience.

We did acquire one rather unlikely supporter in the form of Ted Turner, the boisterous American who would skipper *Courageous* to victory in 1977. In 1970 he was a real renegade, blackballed as an upstart by the New York Yacht Club, and, as a Southerner, prone to fly a Confederate flag on the transom of his boat, *American Eagle.* Ted had his whole crew decked out in T-shirts with Confederate colors, and he made his men available to help us. I doubt anything like this had ever before occurred in the history of this great race, but it was fun for us to have him as an ally. He helped us tune our boat and he raced with us in some highly competitive trials. He was never what you would describe as quiet or refined, but he loved the sport and he was very colorful. Turner is a terrific guy in many ways, the kind of man we Aussies admire: a hard, aggressive yachtsman. It was a privilege to have sailed in his company.

Turner was the first top American sailor I had ever come to know, but I had seen from close quarters the professional structure set up by the men from the United States. And long before we faced *Intrepid* on the starting line, I had decided that I wanted to stay on in the United States. I felt that to be an international racing yachtsman you had to race and sail in America. I wanted to find out all about it. I wanted to learn their techniques, their training methods, their tactics, and, above all, I wanted to meet the men who would be sailing their 12-Meters in the coming years. It occurred to me that if one day I was to take the helm of an America's Cup boat from Australia, I would be better placed to deal with an enemy that I knew, rather than one that was totally unknown to me, as the men on *Intrepid* were now.

I felt that the key to my remaining in this new and exciting country was as a student, so I wrote to Professor Jerome Milgram at the Massachusetts Institute of Technology, the most advanced scientific, technological, and engineering university in the world, and requested a scholarship to study for my master's degree in marine engineering. To my delight, I was granted a teaching assistantship, which would begin immediately after the America's Cup races.

Meanwhile, before the races against *Intrepid,* I realized that the Americans were not the superhuman sailors many people would have us believe. They are merely products of a system that combined constant match racing in hot competition, the very best equipment, and unlimited financial resources. But the vision of the mighty Bill Ficker and his immortal crew . . . no, I did not accept that—any more than I would one day accept the invincibility of Dennis Conner and his crew. They are all just good sailors, like us, with those three key differences.

Mind you, we did endeavor to make the Americans look pretty spectacular in the first race of 1970. All the way out to the start, we were still screwing pulleys and blocks onto the boat—a fact that, in retrospect, was nothing short of amazing. Then our hierarchy, including myself, elected to hoist a genoa we had never used before. This is roughly akin to a race car driver starting a race with a new engine that's never been tuned.

The Americans came at us like a wolf pack, aggressive to a degree that struck terror into the heart of poor Jim Hardy. His response was to hoist our protest flag. Then the spinnaker became badly snagged. When our foredeck man, Paul Salmon, was washed overboard, it took us six minutes to pick him up. Then the mainsheet hand, David Forbes, fell overboard and was pulled in, half drowned, clinging to a rope. Bill Ficker won by six minutes, and the New York Yacht Club flung out our protest with autocratic disdain.

Race 2 very nearly put the whole lot of us in the New York Supreme Court—which was what Sir Frank Packer had threatened when the New York Yacht Club disqualified us *after* we had won the race. He raged that protesting to the NYYC was like complaining to your mother-in-law about your wife. But he might as well have saved his wrath. We never had a prayer with the protest—first because we were not in the right, and second because we were not familiar enough with the rules.

That second race in 1970 is to this day the subject of angry discussion.

The problem started when Jim Hardy, still reeling from the intimidation he had received at the hands of Bill Ficker in Race 1, decided to hand over the start to Martin Visser, an emotional fellow who was keyed up almost to the point of hysteria as the two boats approached each other. I was port sail-trimmer, and I remember *Intrepid* being to weather as we were coming in on the starboard layline at the weather end of the starting line. We were coming up to the committee boat, and *Intrepid* had nowhere to go—except around our stern (which meant we would have won the start easily) or between us and the committee boat (which was a fast-closing gap).

They elected to dive for the gap, but it was an incredible gamble. If you have no room there, you have no room there—and you are *out*. They missed the committee boat by a couple of feet. Martin Visser realized that we had asked for the sails to come on too late, and we were not going to be able to close the gap in time.

Martin was so involved emotionally that he literally had blood in his eyes. He struggled desperately to block *Intrepid*'s way, but he went too far and luffed the sails to beyond closehauled. This meant he was no longer in control or even sailing on a proper course. He was just hoping to drift into his opponent and ram her like a renegade from the Spanish Main— which is against the rules. You must stay closehauled and keep sailing a course. Anyway, we hit *Intrepid* with an almighty thump and smashed our bow. The artificial coaming, the whole front section, just fell off—as Salmon and Forbes had done the day before. There were protest flags all over the place, and then, amazingly, we went on to win the race.

The American protest was upheld, and *Gretel II* was disqualified. The Australian press went berserk. There were headlines screaming outrage: "We Was Robbed" and "Home-Town Decision Robs Australia." But I remember what it was like. I was holding the genoa, and I was the one who had to let it go because we were going above closehauled and it was back-winding. Then, when we crossed the finish line, Bill Fesq, the navigator, got out the rule book and read the relevant passage. Among the crew there was a thunderous, stunned silence as the full significance became apparent. Our afterguard did not know the rules any better than we had known them in Race 1.

There was little question about it in my mind, but everyone started to rally 'round and try to formulate evidence to suggest we were not in the wrong. Of course, in such a situation you have to do everything you can to succeed, and in the end we had convinced ourselves that we were right. And when the New York Yacht Club announced their findings, it was Bob Bavier, president of the North American Yacht Racing Union, who put the matter into perspective. Privately he said, "The Australians deserved to win on the race course. However, they simply do not know the rules."

That made us 2–0 down, and then Ficker won the third race. But in our fourth start, in a 12-knot breeze, we finally got *Gretel II* moving, and she walked away from *Intrepid*, winning by more than a minute. After a long tacking duel in Race 5, we finally went down 4–1. But we had pursued them closely in what proved to be a potentially faster boat. I resolved then that when I returned one day at the helm of an Australian challenger, I would have a topnotch organization and a match-fit crew with hundreds of hours of racing experience, and I would have a rules expert in my camp, preferably on my boat, to make sure that I only *lost* races and never *gave* them away.

I think we were all in a reflective mood after that drubbing, but Jim Hardy seemed to read my thoughts on that final evening before we broke camp. We had developed a very good relationship, and that night he suddenly said to me, "John, you will one day end up steering a 12-Meter yourself, as the skipper of an Australian challenge."

In any event, in 1970 I left Newport for MIT in Cambridge with mixed feelings. I knew that a rather slow American boat had just whipped a pretty fast challenger by pure efficiency—and in a way that offended many of my natural instincts. I had quite enjoyed the adventure, but I was frustrated in some ways about the conduct of our campaign. It seemed to me that everything could have been done very much better.

Also, I had a young and pretty new wife for whom Newport also held very mixed emotions. For a start, she and I had been separated summarily as soon as we arrived. Wives and crew do not mix in Australian sporting circles. In fact, the women were treated shabbily. For years this presented a major problem with the America's Cup. It all stemmed from the Australian macho image. Management refused to consider where women could fit into the scheme of things. It was as though the problem was too big and too embarrassing to tackle. You can't make people suddenly function independently; otherwise you are talking about people who are divorced. You have to find a way to bring the women into the whole thing. The failure of the Australians to tackle this problem has always been, for me, a major disenchantment.

In 1970 we were very separate, and Rasa was concerned about this, particularly since our crew had a bit of a reputation among the ladies of the town. The trouble was that the commitment did not exist in those days. It was more fun to play than to be in quarters by 11 o'clock. They were all heroes in Newport. Being Australians, they were always the center of attention among the girls. They were fit, suntanned young men full of good humor, and they were having a wonderful time. If you had asked them what their real purpose was in Newport, an alarmingly small number probably would have said they were there to win the America's Cup. Incidentally, this has always worked in the Americans' favor, because they were not subject to the same temptations. An American in Newport in an America's Cup summer is just one of the mob. It's the lads from Down Under who are the prize catches, and this always irritated Sir Frank Packer.

I remember one night when he was at the crew house, trying to enforce his 11 o'clock curfew. He was sitting inside the hall on a chair, wearing his enormous spectacles with lenses about three-eighths inch thick, checking off the boys, one by one, as they came in. Finally, he instructed us all to line up in the billiards room, where he made a speech in his deep, gruff, raspy, ex-middleweight fighter's voice. "OK, lads," he said. "We're here for one reason, and that's to win yacht races. We're not here to stay out half the night fucking women. We're here to win yacht races. Do you all agree?" We all lowered our heads, and he said, "OK. Anyone who comes in after 11 o'clock from now on will be sent straight home to Australia. Good night." And that was that. From then on, everyone came in on time. No one wanted to go home, and no one doubted that he would have carried out his threat.

Rasa was a lot busier than most crewmen's wives, because she was going back and forth to Massachusetts to fix up our little furnished apartment in Medford for the fall semester at MIT. She was also arranging work for herself at two hospitals. One involved taking care of drug-addicted babies born to heroin addicts. And in another private hospital, where doctors used to induce births on Fridays because they were playing golf on Saturdays, Rasa worked as a midwife. Those jobs were very heavy and contrasting experiences for young Rasa, and she made a major mark in the latter position, because she was one of a group of midwives who reintroduced breast feeding, which had been frowned upon for many years by the wealthy clientele.

Finally we moved into the apartment and I reported to that great learning institution in Cambridge. We had almost no friends, no money, and there was a constant struggle to pay the $45-a-week rent for the apartment. My scholarship paid for my tuition, but our room and board had to come out of Rasa's nursing salary, which was the only money we had. It was a bit of a struggle. We were always broke, but Rasa kept me going, doubtless wondering where it was all taking us—except to yet another racing boat. For my part, I attacked my studies with a fierce will and managed to complete the course in 20 months instead of 24. Professor Milgram approved of this with a warm smile of admiration—which was clouded only when I had to borrow $45 from him to pay the rent.

Naturally, throughout those long, hard months I gravitated to the water. My closest friend was Robbie Doyle, who would go on to be sail-trimmer for the new American boat, *Courageous,* in 1974. He introduced me to the highly competitive Finn racing class, and I sailed on the Charles River in Boston. Surprisingly, I very quickly mastered this little boat, which races in one of the most viciously combative events in the Olympic Games, with yachtsmen shouting and screaming at each other, capsizing, colliding, and God-knows-what. This is the stock-car derby of Olympic watersports, and, quite frankly, it was right up my street. I got so good at it that I entered the U.S. National Finn Championships, held at Marion, Massachusetts. We were, I believe, the only gypsy entrants at those Championships in 1971; after a good regatta, I managed to finish seventh, which pleased me no end. We were on the first leg of a 9,000-mile cross-country summer vacation which took us to Los Angeles and back, all through the old South on a secondhand motorcycle. We met many wonderful people and it was the start of a great love affair with America and the American people, which Rasa and I still treasure to this day.

I had a few months to go at MIT, so I next decided to go to Toronto for the Finn Gold Cup, which is the World Championship. In Canada I had a very fierce competitive regatta and finished fifth against the best Finn racing sailors. This was the highest any Australian had ever placed in World Championship Finn racing, so I decided to return home for the Australian National Championships and get myself selected for the 1972 Olympics in Munich.

However, I faced two fairly major problems. I had scarcely enough money for a bus ride over to the Charles River, never mind two air fares home to Melbourne. Also, I did not have a Finn Class boat. So, speaking as a hotshot America's Cup sailor, I decided to fire off a few letters to Melbourne businessmen to see whether I could raise some sponsorship.

To my great delight, a Melbourne car dealer, whom I had never met, decided that I must have a lot of brass neck, if not talent, and he forwarded $2,000. Much later I found out that the Olympic manager, David Linacre, had a great deal to do with this heaven-sent sponsorship.

When we returned to Australia, I went into strict training on behalf of myself, my young wife, my mum, and the saintly car dealer. For five weeks I prepared to take on the might of the Australian Finn fleet, many of whom had been racing in highly competitive European events for four months as preparation for the National Championships. And every one of them turned up at the Sandringham Yacht Club. Did I need to win this? Bloody Oath I did.

It was a wicked close struggle, at the end of which I narrowly brought my borrowed boat over the line in first place. Rasa and Mum and my brother, Lex, were delirious with happiness. In a sense I had named the boat for Rasa, painting on the side "Eik Gretia," which is Lithuanian for "go fast."

Now I was really under way, and if Rasa thought we had hitherto been acting like a couple of oceangoing bedouins wandering around the world, she had seen nothing yet. I was now qualified to receive $20 a day from the Australian Yachting Federation to conduct a 3½-month sailing campaign in Europe, culminating with the 1972 Olympic Games in Munich, in which I was my country's number-one hope in the Finn Class. And once more we boarded a plane heading north, bound for the open seas and competition against the best in the world.

We set off for Kiel Regatta week in northern Germany, the site of the Olympic watersports later that summer. I was nowhere near ready, and when the German event started, I was still screwing fittings onto the boat in a grotesque parody of the experience with *Gretel II*. I finished 35th, probably the worst performance of my entire career.

Rasa and I packed up our few belongings and, with our list of hostels and cheap hotels, we set off for Medemblick, a little resort on the Zuider Zee, that great Dutch near-landlocked ocean (like Port Phillip Bay) due north of Amsterdam. I finished seventh in the European Finn Championships there; by now I had the boat properly tuned. Next, we turned south to Italy, crossing the Alps and driving down the coast to the port of Anzio, where the Finn World Championships were to be held. I sailed like a demon and finished second, beaten only by the great Jorge Bruder of Brazil, who, at his best, could be just about unbeatable in Finn Class sailing. He beat me decisively, but I was a very solid second.

Rasa and I were beginning to enjoy this adventure. We did not have much money, but everyone was very kind to us, and we were often invited to stay overnight and have meals with other sailing people. Remember, being a yacht racer is not like being a tennis player—where you wind up being wealthy by the time you attain my level of accomplishment. This is sailing. Your principal reward is the overpowering sense of achievement, a boost to your psyche, after defeating the opposition and doing it with style.

I felt very good as we headed north again for the National Championships of Finland. We took a long and picturesque car journey that was magical for Rasa and me. We arrived at the Little Island course and at last I was the master of my little boat. I won the championship, wondering whether my dad could see me as I stood beneath the snowcapped mountains on the edge of those northern waters, so many thousands of miles from home. Lonely Finland, with all of its beauty, looked like heaven to me. I felt that Dad and Bant, who taught me about the wind so long ago, must not have been very far away.

We turned our rented Peugeot south for the Olympics.

No sooner had we arrived at the Olympic Village in Kiel after our long drive than Rasa was asked to leave. There was a major upheaval, once again involving Australian officials who were as usual trying to ban competitors' wives. Rasa had been with me all summer. She was my on-land coach and my supporter, mentor, and friend. Without her, there would have been a terrible gap in my life, and here were these guys trying to split us up. It was absolutely ridiculous: Rasa and I had shared everything. We were a partnership: I could not have done my best without her. I made a stand and caused a great fuss, and David Linacre once more stepped in to help me. He put his reputation on the line and insisted that Rasa and I be allowed to stay together. Eventually we got her into the Village, and I will always be grateful for his support. It was very important that Rasa stayed with me, because I was under a lot of pressure and made a lot of mistakes. I could not have coped without her.

Before the Games, we took some time off and drove to the border of East Germany. Standing together on a hillside, we looked at the armed guards protecting the border, at the grayness and the somber quality of life beyond them. I just looked across and felt thankful for having been born an Australian, but for Rasa it was a much more emotional experience. Somewhere out there, out beyond the Soviet border, lived her beloved grandmother in Lithuania, a long way behind the Iron Curtain. Rasa's entire heritage somehow remained beyond the guards. After standing there for about 20 minutes, she just took my hand and we walked away without saying a word.

In the Games I finished fourth, earning for myself the leather medal, an experience I wish never to have again. It is a very funny thing, but in most trades or professions, if you are the fourth-best practitioner in the world, you have at least fame and probably fortune. In our game it's different. There are first, second, and third: gold, silver, and bronze. Everyone else is last. Nothing is as tough as the Olympics. I packed up our Peugeot somewhat ruefully, a rookie Olympian who had just undergone what seemed like a fiery baptism in my first Games. At the closing ceremony in the great stadium, Jorge Bruder, who had beaten me in the World Championships in Anzio, came up and put his arm around me. He was a charming man, that Brazilian, but he just could never come out on top in the Olympics. He always froze up with nervousness. But he was very nice and always very generous to me. He had switched from the Finn Class to the Star Class, and he, too, had finished fourth. "John," he said, "now we have both done it. We've both won the leather medal."

By the time I was ready to leave the Olympic Village that summer, I had already been approached by the Sydney boat designer Ben Lexcen. He asked if I would assist in the preparation of a new assault on the America's Cup in 1974. The challenge apparently was being funded by a highly ambitious real-estate developer from Perth. I accepted with some alacrity. I did not know where this new path would take me, but as usual, the prospect of a very fast boat was like an aphrodisiac to me, and I could not resist. The man who headed up the new syndicate was named Alan Bond.

4

The Green Hills of Yanchep

To my astonishment, he left the wheel, right out there in the Indian Ocean. He hurtled below, swinging through the ropes like a gorilla, fighting to get at the gigantic Rob Stirling.

I might as well come straight out with it. In the previous chapter I was so busy telling about my efforts to become the greatest sailor since Captain Cook that I quite forgot to mention that Rasa was pregnant during the 1972 Olympics. Lapses of memory on a personal level are a bit of a failing of mine. I tend to be weak in remembering birthdays, anniversaries, and other significant occasions. However, it has recently occurred to me that I may have been something of a nightmare as a young married man—yes, unforgivably thoughtless—thanks to my obsession with yacht racing and my consuming dream of a triumph in Newport.

Just consider, for a moment, Rasa's life with me thus far. Without a penny to our name, and no proper home, we had made the following three-year journey together: Melbourne, Sydney, Newport, Boston, Melbourne, France, Germany, Holland, Italy, Finland, Germany. And now here we were on our way to Mum's house again along the shore near Melbourne. And we were still without a home of our own, with Rasa on the verge of producing our first son, Lucas. When you are young, you think you can cope with anything. But Rasa was really being tested, for I was about to begin work on *Southern Cross,* and we were again obliged to move back to Sydney and rent a small apartment.

Just before I joined Alan Bond's first challenge, an interesting boat became available for the Australian National Soling Championships being held on the Swan River in Perth. Called *Alexia,* she had once belonged to King Constantine of Greece. Benny Lexcen had sailed her in the 1972 Olympics, but he had recently fallen down the hatch of a 45-foot Admiral's Cup boat he had designed—*Gingko* by name—and broken his ribs. (This maneuver is not untypical of Benny. He's always blundering about and getting wounded somehow or other.)

Anyway, Ken Berkeley, the owner of *Alexia,* asked me to skipper her in the National Championships on the other coast of Australia, 2,000 miles away. Despite two major problems—experience with these lovely three-man racing boats, and money (I had none of either)—I did accept, in return for a couple of tickets from Sydney to Perth for Rasa and me. However, things were not very smooth thereafter. Rasa was eight months pregnant, the owners of the boat suddenly could not make the trip, and I could not afford to stay overnight in a pub. So there we were in Perth with no crew, no funds, and no hope. Well, as luck would have it, I ran into Peter Anderson, a wonderful guy who has become a lifelong friend. Peter was also competing, and he took in Rasa and me as his houseguests. After using my gigantic Rasa as ballast for a couple of days while I tuned *Alexia* into some sort of racing order, I managed to round up a couple of guys to sail with me. Neither one was world championship class material, but at least I managed to take part in the races.

I thought that showed quite a lot for my organizational abilities under pressure. Also, it enabled me to meet a legendary sailing champion, the favorite for the Soling title that year, Kenny Beashel. I also heard·about Warren Jones, Peter Anderson's partner in his machine-tool renting business. When the company was eventually sold out to the Bond Corporation, Warren would go with it, and he and I and Kenny would meet again.

Oh, yes, the regatta—the 1973 Australian Soling Championships. I did win it. As a matter of fact, I won the first six races straight and did not have to sail the seventh because I was so far in front. *Alexia* was a lovely boat. I don't think anyone has ever before or since won six straight in this championship.

Three days after Lucas was born, I left on a six-week world tour on behalf of Alan Bond's syndicate, my task being to examine the subtleties of sailcloth. I was briefed to keep a weather eye open for any new developments, but also to ensure that we stayed within the terms of the Deed of Gift, which governs all challenges for the America's Cup.

I have to admit that I was more concerned with my new assignment than with the other infinitely more important gift with which my wife had just presented me. My departure, as well it might have, put a dreadful strain on our marriage. Rasa hated being alone in the tiny apartment in Sydney, and she returned to her father's house with Lucas for three weeks. Finally I returned, and we put things back together, but I must say that I am in no way proud of my behavior during those early days back in Australia. If I could live them over, I would not repeat my mistakes.

Since I got back to business pretty quickly then, I suppose, having unburdened my conscience, I might as well return to it now. I checked out sailcloth and weaving all over the world, and then I began to work with some of the weavers to develop our own material for *Southern Cross*. Eventually the boat was built in Sydney, with the rig on which I had worked so diligently, and was shipped to Western Australia. Therein begins a tale that for months and months hovered dubiously between the hysterical and the amazing, the ridiculous and a lunatic-peak of naked ambition.

Alan Bond was his name. When I first met him for an interview in Sydney, a few days before my world tour, he was 35 years old. He looked like a fighter, walked like a fighter, and spoke like a fighter. He was only about five feet six inches tall and he had a neck like Muhammad Ali. He spoke like a machine gun, taking note all in one breath that I had a top degree in engineering, that I had done a splendid thesis on the aerodynamics of 12-Meter sails, that I had a master's degree in marine engineering from MIT, that I was a national sailing champion of Australia, that I had taken part in the Olympic Games, that this job on *Southern Cross* was a great way to continue with naval architecture, that I looked like the kind of fellow he would get along with, that we would give the Yanks a bloody good hiding, that he hoped my wife would like his new city in Western Australia . . . and when could I start?

At one point I very nearly spoke, but not quite. Someone came into the office with a long and rather drawn-out argument about some project or other. Alan Bond cut it to smithereens. He obliterated it, scooped up the pieces, and flung them all out the window. At the end, the guy seemed to be devastated. But back came Bondy (everyone calls him that) with a big smile and the innate, terrifying charm of the true salesman. Within a few minutes the visitor walked out with a huge smile on *his* face, to tackle his problem anew, perhaps in a slightly different way, just as he and the boss had agreed. It was a mesmerizing performance, and I was reeling. This chap, a former sign painter with little education, had just staged the most brilliant piece of analytical argument I had ever seen. Life with Bond would probably not be dull, and by the time he had given me another couple of pep talks, I figured that the Americans might just as well airmail the America's Cup direct to his office in Perth, since they clearly had no chance whatsoever of defending it. Unfortunately, however, I had not yet given serious thought to the forthcoming glories of his new little home in the West, "Yanchep, Sun City—Home of the Twelves," site of the 1974 Australian preparation for the America's Cup. And, he anticipated, the site of the 1988 Olympic Games.

Once more Rasa and I, now with Lucas, set off. We packed up and left our tiny apartment and flew more than 2,000 miles to the great city of Perth, capital of Western Australia, the former British Swan River Colony. Home of Alan Bond.

I had last visited Perth 10 years earlier, when Geoff Augustine and I had arrived on the train broke and left with the Junior Championship of Australia. It was here that Rolly Tasker had first spotted me, here that I had taken my first steps toward the America's Cup. And here I was again, this time arriving on a transcontinental jet as one of the leading lights in a new and extremely exciting Australian challenge for the "Auld Mug." Last time we had made our way to the Swan River in the old family Ford with a reconditioned engine. This time Alan Bond was right there to meet us with his new, air-conditioned Rolls-Royce Corniche. There we sat, in the lap of luxury, being taken on a deluxe guided tour of Perth. Bondy was behind the wheel, all the while extolling the virtues of his city, showing us multimillion-dollar land bargains, explaining how Perth would very soon be the capital of the universe, the true city of opportunity in the land of plenty. Rasa and I, of course, could hardly afford an ice cream, but I must say one thing for Bondy: He'll sell to anyone.

The Corniche turned north. The air-conditioner throbbed relentlessly against the heat outside, which was about 110 degrees. The loudest noise in the Rolls was not in fact the ticking of the clock. It was Alan Bond, still pitching, still selling all the pluses and plausibilities of Western Australia. Smoothly we sped along the West Coast Highway. The Indian Ocean was off to our left, its waves rolling in unchecked from Calcutta or Bombay or somewhere. We glided on up to a tiny fishing inlet called Two Rocks. The final four miles did not produce much variation in the way of scenery, but the sandhills were of a very good quality. There were thousands of them—all white and dusty and rolling all the way to the horizon. There was no vegetation save for scrub bushes. As far as I could see, survival was impossible. I half expected to see a burnoosed Arab come trotting into view on a camel. The place was completely white, and I had just exclaimed, "You have to be joking. You can't sell this land for development. It's just sandhills. The whole place is a desert." But right about then, half the landscape turned bright green. I thought I'd gone mad or was seeing a mirage. Perhaps the air-conditioner had given up and I was having a hot flash. But the sandhills were suddenly a rich green. "Christ!" I said. "The grass is growing. Have you put in irrigation?" "No," said Bondy. "I've painted the sandhills to make the brochures look better." By this time I could not remove my gaze from the green hills of Yanchep, and I could not take my eyes off this progressive marketing wizard who was driving me through his new domain. I found my head switching rhythmically from the sandhills to Bondy and back, as if I were following a tennis match. I found it hard to believe what I had most certainly just been told. But Bondy confirmed it all with an offhand wave of his palm. "Just helping the grass along a little."

The temperature was well into the hundreds and there was a dry, dusty, southwesterly gusting in from the ocean. This was it. For my salary of $85 a week, plus room and board, Rasa and I and Lucas would make our home here for 10 months, after which we would fly to Newport to challenge the United States for the America's Cup.

Rasa and I, by some miracle, were still married at the end of the afternoon, and we settled, as best we could, into our tiny house. Soon the boats arrived: *Southern Cross,* the new aluminum racing shell from Sydney; *Gretel II,* the fast, lightweight loser of the 1970 contest. Yanchep's little harbor now looked a bit more like the home of the Twelves. But this was real frontier stuff. It was like the Wild West. The heat and the flies were nearly unbearable. One day I came home and found Rasa sitting in the middle of the floor of the living room and crying hysterically.

"What's the matter?" I asked.

"I can't take it. I can't take it another minute," she sobbed. "The flies are driving me crazy."

And there they were, dozens of huge dead flies lined up along the windows. I had jammed the fireplaces with paper, I had jammed every crack in every door and window, and still they got in.

And where, you might ask, was Bondy during this boiling hard-labor preparation? Well, he was exactly where you would think he would be. In his Corniche, with the air-conditioner turned up high—selling, selling, selling.

I remember getting a bit of a jolt when the crew was first being assembled. Our helmsman, John Cuneo, an optician from Brisbane, was lecturing one morning in the big boatshed, and as I arrived, I could see that everyone was watching him with riveted attention. My crewmates were being shown how to tie knots and coil ropes. I thought, "Holy shit! Am I going to race with this lot?" It was a bit like seeing a bunch of Grand Prix drivers turn up for a big race without a driver's license among them.

Out on the water, conditions were as hard as on land. The wind used to get up in the afternoon to about 30 knots, and racing was difficult. Even out there, the heat never abated.

Cuneo and I clearly were never destined to become close friends. He is one of those persons who would have made a very fair schoolmaster. He was completely autocratic and had a big office where he sat right at the end, about five long paces away from the door. We all had to knock and walk in and sit down in front of his desk before he seemed able to focus his attention on any one of us. Even though I was his tactician and number-two man, I had to go through this ritual. He would sit and gaze like a headmaster at a wayward pupil. We were supposed to be a team, but John Cuneo found it difficult to master the subtle art of making people want to work for him.

In the end I resigned as tactician, and I went in to see Alan Bond.

In one hour, Bondy converted me from a disgruntled second-in-command to a supremely happy mainsheet hand. I had taken a major demotion, yet Alan Bond had made me feel good about it. What a salesman.

We had other troubles at Yanchep. For example, it turned out that another adversary was the seaweed at the mouth of one of the harbor entrances. Bondy had gone ahead and built the harbor without much study of the ecology and he had somehow managed to alienate the local fishermen, because they anticipated the commercialism of the new marina. Anyway, nature came down fairly heavily on the side of the "fishos," as we call them. All the extra iodine in the atmosphere caused chronic stress corrosion in our fancy steel rigging, and that came down fairly heavily on us—almost literally. The mast just crashed down at the end of one race. Alan, who was on the boat, nearly died of shock. It could have killed someone. But when the reason for its demise became known, the fishos loved it. The marina that they hated had created the seaweed problem, which caused the iodine increase, which caused the mast to topple. As far as those Western Australian fishos were concerned, that collapse was undoubtedly the highlight of the entire campaign.

Alan Bond, wealthy though he undoubtedly was, experienced a great deal of pressure that summer. And as he struggled his way through a myriad of commercial pitfalls in land development, we did want to do well for him. Naturally, everyone wanted the new boat, *Southern Cross,* to be fast, really fast. A lot faster than the defeated *Gretel II.* And I think that subconsciously we were prepared to do almost anything to make this a reality, whether it was true or not. For instance, we always put the best

sails on *Southern Cross* and the bad ones on *Gretel*. We never even gave
ourselves a chance to find out whether or not we were truly faster than
the lovely old wooden boat that had occasionally laid up very tight with
Intrepid, hitherto the fastest Twelve ever built. No one wanted to have to
break the news to Bondy, the newest of the America's Cup entrepreneurs,
that the boat on which he had just spent a million dollars was possibly
slower than Sir Frank Packer's old wooden hull, built four years earlier.
We just kept doing everything in our power to make certain *Southern Cross*
appeared faster—and that was that. Unfortunately, we knew no better.

We also had a difficult time with fittings. We were supposed to fit out
this boat ourselves, and many of the crew had not worked much with
metal before then. It took us about six months to stop the bits and pieces
from falling off her.

But, in hindsight, my main memory of that 10 months in Yanchep was
of the awkwardness I felt with my skipper. It is impossible to describe the
difference between a contented, close-knit crew and a group of men who
are not united by good leadership. It was a lesson I never forgot. And
nine years later, I would make 100 percent certain it never happened on
Australia II.

Mutiny was in the air in Yanchep. John Cuneo was a superb sailor.
Two years earlier he had won an Olympic gold medal in the Dragon
Class, and no one could question his technical ability. The hitch was his
attitude toward his teammates. He seemed to be a person apart, with no
real empathy for the problems of his men. And "Cunes" could fly into a
rage that was very nearly boundless. On one sweltering hot day off
Yanchep, for example, Cunes was not in the best of moods. He was, if
you know what I mean, white-knuckling it, squeezing the wheel with
frustration. In those days, most of the winch-grinding was done below
deck, and those poor bastards never saw the light of day. It was like being
in a Roman galley. Sometimes, for a joke, we'd toss them a bunch of ba-
nanas.

Well, something went wrong on this particular day, and Cunes glanced
at the sails and of course knew immediately which one of our boys was not
doing his job. The culprit was big Rob Stirling, who weighed in at about
240 pounds of pure muscle. *"Blast Stirling!"* he yelled. "What's that?" I
asked. *"Blast him, blast him,"* confirmed Cunes, who was by now five feet six
inches of trembling fury. To my astonishment, he left the wheel, right out
there in the Indian Ocean hard off Yanchep, Sun City, "Home of the
Twelves," and leaped from his cockpit and hurtled down into the below-
deck area of the boat. The whole place was covered with ropes and wires
and God-knows-what, and Cunes went swinging through them like a gorilla, fighting to get at the gigantic Rob Stirling, whose nickname was

"Rat." He probably would have liked to whack poor old Rat in the mouth, but he could not reach that high, and he was about to whack him in the chest when Rat picked him up. He pinned Cunes with his huge, hamlike hands, holding the gallant little helmsman's arms to his sides, and lifted him right off his feet. It was purely a defensive measure by Rat, but he had put our skipper in a position where he could not swing his fists. When I last looked, the legs of John Cuneo were still flailing away and Rat was desperately trying to look serious. It was most important to Cuneo that big, powerful men like Rat should feel they would work themselves to death for him, but, as I have mentioned before, crew relations were not the long suit of that particular America's Cup skipper.

Cuneo was a Napoleon-like figure. Everyone was scared to death of him as he tried to rule the *Southern Cross* camp with a rod of iron. It was never going to work. Benny had designed a big boat, slightly longer than the normal 12-Meter, and, looking back, I think I always knew that she was not as fast as *Gretel*. But I would not have dared to say so. Not back in 1974, when I was still relatively inexperienced and when I was still reluctant to utter what no one especially wanted to hear.

This motley group finally set off in search of the Holy Grail. We all boarded the plane for the United States, and *Southern Cross* and *Gretel* were shipped to Newport, Rhode Island. By now I feared we were in the wrong boat, and Cunes was having a hard time of it. There was no fighting unity about us. This was lambs to the slaughter, and it could not have been anything else. We only had hope on our side, and as we began our trials in Rhode Island Sound, it became shatteringly clear to me precisely what we were up against.

Out there on the American waters, one of the most bitterly contested dogfights in the history of America's Cup racing was taking place. The new American boat, *Courageous,* was locked in combat with the old wooden-hulled Queen of the America's Cup, *Intrepid,* and going into the final race, the scorecard read 4–4. Gerry Driscoll was steering *Intrepid* and the old girl was putting up a terrific fight. On the very last day that a defender could be named, *Courageous* finally won narrowly, and *Intrepid* was excused. *Courageous,* with probably the most battle-hardened crew ever assembled in big-boat racing, had gone through the most intensive match-racing trials of any other American defender, before or since. She had bid farewell to *Valiant,* and *Mariner* helmed by Ted Turner, and now *Intrepid.* She was tried and tested in real combat. We, on the other hand, were tried and tested in nothing.

On top of everything else, Bondy was having a fight with the Royal Perth Yacht Club, under whose dignified banner our challenge was mounted and who naturally trusted that the splendid little insignia of the club would be displayed proudly on our transom as we set sail. What they did not know was that Bondy wanted the proud little insignia of Yanchep, Sun City, "Home of the Twelves," to be also placed on the transom, and there was a diabolical quarrel being conducted across the telegraphic wires of the world.

Then Bondy fired Cuneo, calling in Jim Hardy to take the helm of *Southern Cross,* with Hughey Treharne as his tactician.

Whatever personal problems we all had, there was still the serious business of the actual racing. And once more the imposing figure of Baron Bich stood between us and the races against the Americans. And once more the Baron stepped forward to make us look terrific. He was in total disarray, and we gave him a wicked beating and then proceeded to prepare for the most formidable task any challenger had in the history of the America's Cup.

We were up against not only a match-hard crew in *Courageous,* but also a real thoroughbred of a 12-Meter, the best one ever built at that time. Also, a subtle change appeared to have come over the entire American camp. Suddenly, it seemed, there was a ruthlessness that no one had seen before. The New York Yacht Club stunned the yacht-racing world when they fired Robert Bavier, the urbane and brilliant helmsman who had steered *Constellation* to momentous victory over the British in 1964. Virtually on the eve of the race, he was relieved of command in favor of Ted Hood, the hard, taciturn professional sailmaker from Marblehead, Massachusetts.

Simultaneously we were also seeing the meteoric rise of a new match-racing specialist from San Diego, California, the 28-year-old near-obsessive Dennis Conner. His rise to prominence had been very, very quick, causing an enormous amount of comment and whispers throughout the summer. He had come from nowhere in a very tough league, starting off as tactician for Ted Turner on *Mariner,* later being promoted to helm that boat, and finally being invited into the cockpit of *Courageous.* The New York Yacht Club wanted this burly Californian, who would turn out to be the first of the modern match-racing skippers, to start *Courageous* against *Southern Cross.* And Conner's burgeoning reputation for total aggression at the start was well earned.

And in 1974 there was this new atmosphere of unheard-of severity among the Twelves. In 1970 the America's Cup races were still very much like an amateur regatta. But now there was a hard, relentless streak—almost as though these millionaire syndicate bosses were trying to squeeze out the very last degree of perfection from their boats. But it was nevertheless a significant change, and when sports competitions take such a turn toward cold professionalism, they never return to what they were. And people become the victims, the debris all along the path to glory.

Back now, if you will, to the plight of *Southern Cross*, aboard which we were heading to the starting line of Race 1. Jim Hardy had us in good position and Conner had *Courageous* to leeward of us. We glided over the line and for one shining moment I thought we had it made. Then it happened. Conner came right out from underneath us. It seemed that in the blink of an eye he had cold-bloodedly lee-bowed us—sailing right alongside, to leeward but just nicely in front, backwinding us. I remember thinking, "This is going to be a short summer!" Then Hughey spoke quietly, "The American points higher and is moving through the water faster." That is known as sudden death, and you cannot fight it. Hughey's words are the precise words that no helmsman ever wants to hear about an opponent. But so it was. And *Courageous*—which had a much shorter waterline than we did, but more sail area and a much better power-to-weight ratio—eased away smoothly. Downwind she was just as competitive. The Americans knew their own spinnakers so much better than we did. They always set more efficient-looking spinnakers, generally smaller than ours and more stable, and *Courageous* slid away on the reaches and the runs and won the first race by 4 minutes 54 seconds.

She won again the next day as well, by 1 minute 11 seconds. At this point Bondy pretty well lost control. This tough little man, the king of Yanchep, Sun City, "Home of the Twelves," was already running hard to save his face and his image, and he reacted as many a self-made man before him had done under circumstances that proved out of his reach. Bondy lashed out. He fired the navigator. In the same burst of energy, he also fired Hughey, the tactician. Then he made a decision that I have always regarded as the most eccentric move I have ever seen in international racing. He rehired John Cuneo, this time as tactician. This in turn presented another difficulty. As I have explained, Cunes is not a very big fellow, and we had had the area behind the wheel built up quite high in the original design to accommodate him as helmsman. Hughey and I, both very tall, were the tacticians—me before I resigned, Hughey before he was fired—and we would stand lower than the helmsman. John Cuneo, recalled from dockside for tactician duty, could not step up high enough, so we made racing history by having the only tactician who could hardly see over the deck. Cunes had trouble seeing the water and we were beaten in the next race by the colossal margin of 5 minutes 27 seconds. Alan Bond's new lineup did not improve much on the old one in the last race, either. *Courageous* thrashed us by 7 minutes 21 seconds. We had run into a veritable juggernaut in *Courageous* and Hood and Conner.

We had gone from moderate to bloody awful, and I felt I had wasted two years of my life. I'd put up with heat and flies, dust and Yanchep. For a year I had felt as though I were living on the edge of the world in that baking, disagreeable, and political environment. It was like being in a vacuum, but it was a vacuum of endless backbiting and selfish personal ambition.

Never have I wanted to leave a place as badly as I wanted to leave Newport, Rhode Island, at the end of that summer. Rasa was my support until the end, but neither of us could wait to pack up and leave. I didn't care if I never saw the place again. I thought it was the pits, and I could not imagine ever trying again for an America's Cup. I was left with the overwhelming thought that I had been for too long totally lacking in the control of my own destiny. And I felt I would never get enough control in this most unusual contest. There were just too many outside forces, too many people influencing the course of events—so many of them hopelessly unaware of what would be required to win the Cup, not just to come and be beaten. Anyone can do that.

I'll never forget the acrimonious atmosphere, even after we had packed up. Half of us never even said good-bye.

The next stop for Rasa and me was to be the American Midwest, because once more we had decided to stay in the United States. We had made that decision even before *Courageous* gave us such a beating. With great eagerness I had accepted a position with Lowell North, the famous American sailmaker, who was himself an Olympic gold medalist and one of the nicest and most knowledgeable men in the world of international yacht racing. Lowell had phoned me and suggested that I spend a couple of years in the States, working at one of his lofts, with a view to opening a franchise of North Sails in Melbourne. I was very excited about this all summer, and it provided a ray of light and hope in what I look back upon as our darkest days. We flew from Boston to the Midwest, two wasted war veterans bound for the peace and serenity of Pewaukee, Wisconsin, which would be our home, and in a sense our salvation, for two wonderfully happy years—the first years we had ever spent in a house of our own, albeit only a rented one.

First, however, we stayed at the home of Buddy Melges, one of the finest helmsmen in America, an Olympic gold medalist in the 1972 Soling Class in Munich and a man who would become one of the great friends and influences upon my life. It has always been a privilege to know Buddy for his kindness, his selfless gift of knowledge and tactics, his friendship, and his wit—for all of which I will always be full of admiration and gratitude. When we arrived at Lake Zenda, Wisconsin, it was dark. As we got to his house, Buddy announced, "This is the City of Zenda and I am the largest employer in Zenda." He waited until morning to tell me that

Zenda had slightly under 500 people in it and that he was in fact the *only* employer in Zenda. Melges Boatworks and Sails.

We stayed with Buddy beside his lake for two weeks, until Newport seemed like a faraway dream and no longer a nightmare. Then we went on to Pewaukee and moved into our rented house on the cool, verdant shores of Pewaukee Lake. It was so beautiful and so utterly serene that to us it seemed like paradise, a paradise far removed from the dog-eat-dog atmosphere of Newport, to which I never wished to return.

And yet I thought, as I sat endlessly daydreaming in our garden, watching the ripples on the water, could I at the age of 28 really abandon the dreams I had dreamed as a child, as I listened to old Tom Pearkes and looked at the pictures of the great *Shamrock*s with Bant and Nan, as I stood on the shore with my grandpa and gazed out over Port Phillip Bay? Could I, before I was even 30 years old, walk out on my golden ambition? The answer to that was supplied by Rasa, who once said suddenly that the call of Rhode Island Sound and the big 12-Meter racing boats would never leave me. It was a ghost that would never be still in my mind, until I had forced the committee of the New York Yacht Club to unbolt that big silver trophy and hand it over to me and a racing crew from Australia. "That's when you'll forget about Newport," she added. "And I doubt if you will ever get it out of your system until that day. God knows what will become of us as long as that thing stays in New York. It's in your blood."

At that point, nothing would induce me even to consider the 1977 challenge, which Alan Bond already was threatening. Now I had time to reflect, a luxury that I had never before experienced. I had time to sit and think in peace about the lessons of the 1974 challenge. I had made indelible mental notes of those critical aspects of the path to success that cannot be ignored—team spirit; sensible, experienced, well-liked, and respected leadership; brutal testing of the boats; a methodical technical program; and a feeling of solid camaraderie among the crew. If your team happens to be weak in any one of these areas, there is no point in going to Newport, Rhode Island.

Meanwhile, I had to have a major sailing goal—I always had one of those—and after the *Southern Cross* debacle, I chose the Olympics again. I would go to Montreal in two years and win the Olympic gold medal for the Finn Class. That seemed to be a suitable ambition. I would sail in Pewaukee, train on the lake, race throughout North America, and return to Australia for the Olympic selection trials. Life stretched out before me in a contented, comfortable journey, with just enough bite attached to that Olympic ambition to make it interesting.

At North Sails I had a marvelous time. I helped in the design of the Vanguard Finn Class yacht, built in Pewaukee and now the premier boat in this 16-foot class. I love the Finns—one sail, one man, the roughest class in all the Olympic sailing events—and at North I was also able to develop a sail that is still the most popular in the world for that class. I designed and tested it, and that sail has won the World Finn Championships for the past five years. It is as totally dominant in its class as a certain parachute was among old motor launches on Port Phillip Bay 20 years earlier.

Designing sails and sailboats on the picturesque northern waters in the spring of 1975 confirmed my general view that Pewaukee was indeed paradise. I was in the heart of a fine group of American sailors and enjoying every moment. My big break came about halfway through the summer, when another friend, Peter Barrett (who had won the Olympic gold medal in the 1968 Star Class with Lowell North in Mexico City), was obliged to withdraw from the Canada's Cup Match-Racing Event, which is sailed on Lake Huron off Detroit.

Peter had been struggling manfully as tactician in a yacht called *Golden Dazy*, designed by Ron Holland. As I recall, there were six U.S. boats— two-tonners, 40 feet long—involved in what was effectively a mini-America's Cup contest. The competition among these fast boats, with their crews of eight, was run exactly as the New York Yacht Club runs the Cup trials off Newport. It is pure match racing, and it was like a dream come true when I was asked to replace Peter as the tactician on *Golden Dazy*. The bad news was that *Golden Dazy* was firmly placed last at the time. She had lost race after race, and the crew was in the depths of despair, the boat being known unflatteringly as "Golden Duck." The competition was intense, the races were about 12 miles long, and altogether I think I raced 50 times. This was precisely like America's Cup racing, and here I was, right in the middle of the American camp, racing all the time against their best men. In the end, we even managed to win the Canada's Cup.

In the process I had taught myself match racing with the best of them. If any newspaper had taken a picture of me out there on the lake, they would have had a nice photograph of an Aussie with a wrench, ready to loosen the bolts of the America's Cup down there at the New York Yacht Club. When the summer of 1975 had started, I had had a pretty good idea that the Americans could be beaten, and now I *knew* they could. I had just helped to do it, and among those I defeated were some major America's Cup sailors—men such as Robbie Doyle, Andy Rose, and Dennis Durgan, people who are myths in their own right. Now I knew that I could match race with them.

Shortly after the Canada's Cup win, Rasa and Lucas and I drove to New Orleans for the U.S. Finn Class Championship and took delivery of my brand-new Vanguard Finn. I summarily set sail and clobbered the 40 best Finn Class sailors in North America to win the national title.

I was now prepared to go home to Australia for *their* national championship, in which I would attempt to gain Olympic selection. On the way home I went to Malmö, Sweden, for the Finn World Championships, a Gold Cup event. I hate "if onlys," but I would have won that, if only. . . . Unfortunately, I was disqualified for being two pounds overweight in the clothing I wore in one of the races, which I won. That cost me the championship, but no one could take away from me the fact that I had finished first—never mind the two pounds—and we returned to Melbourne feeling on top of the world. I next went off to Brisbane and sailed in the Australian Olympic trials, and I won that as well. So I was on my way to Montreal. After spending Christmas at home with Mum, Rasa and I and Lucas flew back to Pewaukee to complete my preparation for the Montreal summer Olympics.

After intense preparation throughout the spring of 1976, we left our charming lakeside home in Pewaukee and headed for the Olympic regatta site at Kingston, where I carried the Australian flag in the opening parade. I sailed better than I had ever sailed before, of that I am certain. There are seven races in Olympic classes, and you eliminate your worst result. This means that six of your placings count, and if you were second in all of them, or even third, you could win a gold medal. What you cannot do is come in first in five races and 22nd and 27th in two others, because one of those results must be counted, and it will kill you. Those, of course, are the rules by which we yachtsmen live. I was having a terrific time—until the 11th hour, when something happened that I will never forget and that was to have a profound and lasting effect.

Five races had been sailed. It came down to a straight fight among Australia (me), East Germany (represented by Jochen Schumann), Russia (represented by Andre Balashov), and Brazil (represented by Claudio Biecek). Conditions were perfect, with a 15-knot wind as we broke for the first windward leg. David Howlett from Great Britain was in the lead, but he had had two bad ones, and two victories would not get him a fourth overall. I was second, with not one bad race, tracked hard by the East German. He was almost on my transom as we headed down to the wing mark of the first triangle. Approaching the bottom mark I was planing at between 10 and 12 knots, and I kept glancing back at this impassive blond German about three feet behind, nearly touching my boat. Until the day I die, I will remember the feeling that rushed over me. Suddenly, from out of the blue, I thought, "Am I good enough?" It was my first moment of self-doubt in the entire competition. Defeatism is like a forest fire in a big international event. Quickly I thought, "Can I hold him off? Am I being pushed beyond my normal limitations?" These were my first negative thoughts in the Olympics. And, seized by a need to make a positive move, I decided to take a chance that I would never have dreamed of taking in a normal race. I would not even have done this in practice. But I took the opportunity of transferring the mainsheet from the boom through the ratchet block in the floor of the boat. I was under total stress at the time, and I knew this particular maneuver would save one step, would save me precious time and inches, would stop the East German from gaining an inside overlap at that mark and from giving him the opportunity to pass me. I could not even bear to think about that possibility.

Then I lost control of the mainsheet, and the main boom shot out to leeward, beyond the position for stability control of the sail. The boat immediately flipped out of control and capsized to weather. The boat was upside down and I was underneath. "Holy God! What have I done?" was my last thought as I hurtled into the water. I had gone from very nearly being in a control position to being totally out of control. If only I had had the presence of mind to do what I had been trained to do. If only I had made the methodical moves I knew were right, under that intense pressure, I would still be sailing along, still in front with miles to go in which to get him, even if he did get an overlap. Instead of that, I tried to drown myself. I had fallen into the trap that nearly every Olympic competitor falls into. I had taken a stupid risk, losing the significance of the race and my position in it. I had done the opposite of everything I had been trained for. And now I was upside down.

Puffing and gasping, I righted the boat, climbed back in, and finished seventh—which left me in an almost impossible position with regard to a gold medal. The East German finished second, very steady, very controlled. I have no idea why I suddenly was bothered by him. I had never even heard of him—it was not exactly like being locked in combat with Paul Elvstrom at his peak.

And so to the seventh race. I was in an equivocal position. If I match raced the Brazilian and beat him, I would be assured of a bronze medal. If I went for broke and sailed to win that final race, I could still win the gold as long as the East German was beaten for second place. However, in going for broke in this class, you have to take chances, and the prospect of capsizing again was personally unappealing. The dread of a second leather medal haunted me. Australia had finished fourth in this class in three of the last four Olympics, and I did not want to make it four. I decided to play it safe and to match race the Brazilian. After leading the entire field for some of the way, I finally found myself on the wrong end of a windshift on the opposite side of the course from the East German and the Russian. They went on to take the gold and silver medals. I stuck hard by the Brazilian and beat him easily for the bronze. (I might add, as a footnote to those Olympics, that on the very same day the U.S. placed third in the Tempest Class. The helmsman who won the bronze medal was Dennis Conner.)

I had achieved some of my ambition by winning a medal in the Olympic Games, and it was a very proud moment for me—very satisfying yet very thought-provoking. My main regret was that I took that one chance—but for that, I could so easily have won.

I suppose most beaten competitors have at least one regret—but I took that one negative moment deadly seriously. I reflected on it many times after the regatta because it had happened at a critical time, and it spurred me on to become a keen student of sports psychology, of the psychology of winning. I still felt I had what it takes, but it did give me some new insights into myself. It amazed me how cool, or at least apparently cool, that East German had been, even though he had never before won a European championship or any major regatta. He just kept doing what he had been trained to do, reproducing his training under extreme pressure. That East German just seemed to be enjoying the atmosphere and the competition, and that was what I should have been doing, achieving that same degree of self-control. I should have been able to step back and analyze the opposition, without allowing my performance to deteriorate. I wanted to find out more about myself and why I had reacted as I had in the heat of the moment. Was I afraid? If so, of what? Why should defeat hold such devils for me? How could I develop the perfect poise in these situations and summon the correct response for these moments? These were the questions I asked myself, and these were the questions I would have to cope with in the coming years. Winning America's Cup skippers cannot, after all, afford the kind of weakness that I had displayed so spectacularly on that Canadian lake.

Life is full of lessons, and the key is to use them as building blocks. That is *a* definition—*my* definition—of experience. And, like time, you cannot buy it. You just have to use it, to serve your apprenticeship. When I was very young, Mum would tell me that everything always happens for the best. I remember thinking that this could not possibly be so—setbacks, in my mind, being setbacks forever. Only in later years, especially after my reflective months beyond the 1976 Olympics, did I fully realize what a very positive attitude this is, to turn life's disasters into positive knowledge.

The trouble is that you need so many disasters in order to make yourself into the complete athlete, fighter, yachtsman, or whatever. You need years and years of trying, of serving your time. You just cannot say we will win because we will win because we will win. That will not do it. You have to catch every blow an opponent aims at you and store it up to develop an innate sense of wisdom. Yacht racing, like any big sport, has precedents, and you need total recall for these lessons learned in the past. Like statesmen and generals, an international sports competitor who does not understand the past will not be much of an authority on the present.

It is always the lessons that count. There is no question in my mind that without my defeat at the careful and emotionless hands of Herr Jochen Schumann, of the German Democratic Republic, on July 27, 1976, *Australia II* categorically would not have won the 1983 America's Cup.

5

The Olympics
That Never
Were

*Thousands of futile miles of practice beneath her keel. This gallant little boat
which had gone so far, behind the Iron Curtain, all for nothing.*

When I returned to Australia after the 1976 Olympic
Games, I was 29 years old. Shortly thereafter, I de-
clined an invitation to join Alan Bond's 1977 challenge for the America's
Cup because I had developed a burning ambition to live until I was 30.

"Death by frustration" would seem to be an unfitting coroner's verdict
for an Olympic medalist. The 1977 campaign, and all that it stood for,
sent shivers through me. I seemed to have traveled a thousand light years
since those ghastly final days in Newport in 1974. And I felt that the new
campaign, and those who were in charge, had progressed very little.
There had been, of course, a few major changes, the primary one being
that Alan Bond had sold Yanchep, Sun City, "Home of the Twelves", to
the Japanese, and practice was proceeding in a rather more civilized en-

vironment some 60 miles to the south on the Swan River—a stretch of water that holds deep and affectionate memories for me.

There was also a new boat, *Australia,* designed jointly by Ben Lexcen and Johan Valentijn (who later designed *Liberty*). But in my soul I knew that the lessons had not been learned, that Bondy still did not have the organization, or the team spirit, or the correct psychological buildup, or indeed the top Olympic-level crewmen he would need to cope with the Americans. I had just been there, and I knew what they were up against. I would have been staggered if *Australia* had won a race from the Americans, regardless of whether the defender was Ted Turner's *Courageous* or Lowell North's *Enterprise.* And all of my suspicions seemed justified when I received from out of the blue a phone call from the best sailor on *Australia,* David Forbes, the mainsheet hand/tactician. I thought he sounded a bit hesitant, even stammering a bit, rather unlike him. And then he blurted it out. "John," he said, "this is a bloody nightmare. Would you consider taking my place and going to Newport with *Australia*?"

"Are you mad?" I roared. "No, really, John," he said. "I can't just walk out, and I think you'd enjoy it." Well, after I stopped laughing, I told him, with all the good humor of a slightly smug bystander, "Back off, Forbesey, old mate. I'm afraid it's your problem this time—which is only fair, since I had it last time."

I realize that it sounds rather cavalier to be turning down blithely a chance to race in the most dramatic sailboat contest in the world. And I do not mean to sound blasé or ungrateful at being asked, or even self-important. These are the very last qualities I would wish to convey, even in retrospect, to Alan Bond. However, my fears for his challenge were genuine, and my certainty about his inadequate organization were feelings I could not hide. I was not interested in a valiant and bold challenge in front of the whole world. I was only interested in going to America and *winning* the America's Cup. And until I was quite certain we had a real shot at victory, I did not want to go at all. It was not as though Alan Bond had been asking me to straighten out everything and have a major influence on how his challenge was conducted—he already had a full team of helpers doing that. He just wanted me to join the system he had created and become a part of what I considered a lost cause.

At this time, I was in the process of setting up my franchise of North Sails in Melbourne. I had serious business on my mind, as well as a wife and a family. I was trying to raise money, rent property, buy a house, and establish ourselves in our home town as a proper family for the first time. And while the lure of a professional attack on the America's Cup would have drawn me like the call of the sirens to those Greek deckhands who sailed under the command of Ulysses, I did not have one hour to spare to prepare for a losers' challenge in Newport, Rhode Island.

At the time Forbesey called, I was trying to borrow $20,000 for my new business, and I was under some pressure, since the only collateral I had was my Olympic bronze medal. However, luck favors the bold, and when I said this in some desperation to a seemingly friendly manager at the Australia and New Zealand Bank, I was delighted to learn that he had also taken part in an Olympic Games, as an oarsman in 1956 in Melbourne. "If you sailed under the Australian flag and won a bronze medal, you must be OK," he said, and he loaned me the money forthwith.

With my loan capital I rented 3,000 square feet of factory in Beach Street, Mordialloc, and got started. I hired Chet Proctor from the U.S. and a small group of sail cutters, and the business flourished immediately. It continued to prosper in a very labor-intensive market through all the years I owned North Sails (Melbourne). The business provided us with a sound foundation upon which we could all live comfortably, and I could, now with some security, continue to further my ambition to prove I could be the best in the world.

Australia and her crew went off to Newport without me to face Ted Turner's *Courageous,* in what turned out to be a massacre. Turner and his tactician, Gary Jobson, were too good. *Courageous* was much faster, and they thrashed the Aussies 4–0. Bondy's new boat was never in front at any stage of any race—not even at one mark—and if that did not teach them something, then nothing ever would. Ted Turner, our old pal from 1970, apparently was just marvelous. With his big cigar clamped between his teeth, he swaggered about Newport, shouting and laughing, still irreverent about the New York Yacht Club. He had clobbered both of the new American boats, *Independence* and *Enterprise,* in the trials, and he disposed of the Australians in short order with a loud rebel yell as they flew over the line. He also set a regal cap on his famous victory, in the true style of the outrageous character we all know him to be. In the middle of the postmatch press conference, he collapsed, heroically drunk, with an empty bottle of rum still gripped in his fist.

It was a display of gloriously drunken joy. And, of course, it was frowned upon by the committee of the New York Yacht Club, which included five former defenders or contenders—Bob Bavier, Briggs Cunningham, George Hinman, Bob McCullough, and Bus Mosbacher. Rather than frowning, they should have installed a brass commemorative plaque in the place where Turner fell, for this was without doubt the last gesture of carefree amateur recklessness that would ever be seen in the America's Cup.

For even as the bold Turner hurtled blissfully to the floor, out beyond the plains of Arizona, hard by the Mexican border, a new and mighty force was gathering. It was a force that would once and for all turn the America's Cup into a business for pure professionals, and it was a force that would forever guard the competition from the ambitions of casual amateur sportsmen like Ted Turner. The name of that force was Dennis Conner. And ever since I first saw him lee-bow us with such brutality in the first race between *Southern Cross* and *Courageous* in 1974, our paths seemed destined to travel in unison.

Both Conner and I won bronze medals at the Olympics in Montreal, and there we got to know each other a little better. Although we did not meet in the 1977 America's Cup, the following year I went to Miami for the Southern Ocean Racing Circuit, and Dennis invited me to sail with him on the 46-foot offshore racing yacht *Williwaw*, with its highly trained crew of 12. My exploits in *Golden Dazy* might not have cut much ice in Australia, but American ocean racers do not miss much. Dennis misses nothing, and he wanted me to go along and add my expertise in sail-trimming, plus a little bit of steering as an alternate helmsman to him. As usual, Dennis had the best boat, the best campaign, the best preparation in sail selection, and more preparation in fitting out *Williwaw* than any other competitor in the regatta. And also as usual, the dice were loaded in his favor, for that is the way Dennis likes it, and his victory in those 1978 SORC races was almost a foregone conclusion. The fact is, Dennis only sails to his full potential when he is much better prepared than everyone else. He has to feel, mentally, that he has the advantage. That's what sets him up for the kill. All through his book, *No Excuse to Lose,* that philosophy is reinforced. He feels that he must work harder in the technical area than anyone else, and he takes it to a point where he has such a major advantage going into a race that he cannot lose. Well, that's one way of doing it, although it would not sit well with men like Ted Turner.

As for myself, well, I think I am more like Dennis than Ted. I have that methodical streak that goes with being a marine engineer. I like to be well prepared and to have a boat that will compete on equal terms. But I want no more than that. Give me a fair chance and I will race anyone right down to the wire, man to man, one on one.

Back in 1978 I accepted that offer to sail with Dennis with great enthusiasm. We raced together four times, and I learned an awful lot from him. He is a man of many facets and one of the most interesting features is his attitude toward his crew. He has a marvelous ability to involve everyone in every aspect of the race. He will suddenly shout questions to inappropriate people—he will ask the bow man, for example, what he thinks of the shape of the mainsail. He will ask the port trimmer whether we are going fast enough. He will ask the main winch-grinder whether the last tack was a good idea, or whether the wind looks better down to the right than the left. This technique has the effect of making people feel important. A guy who has a routine task suddenly finds himself involved with the master about overall cockpit strategy. It makes everyone feel great, and Dennis was the first boat skipper to show me how effective his method is in producing tight team spirit.

What surprised me, however, was the apparent change in the skipper's attitude after we docked. When we reached Nassau, *Williwaw*'s owner greeted us and told Dennis about our hotel accommodations. Then Dennis just jumped off the boat, went up to the bar, and ordered a drink for himself and his patron. He seemed to want nothing more to do with his own crew. He spent hours holding court with other skippers, discussing how he had beaten them all. It seemed to be so ego-oriented. But the rest of the crew just laughed it off. "That's Dennis. The race is over, so now he has to hold court. That's what he does." I had watched him involve his crew superbly in the race, but now it seemed like such a hollow involvement. He seemed not even to want to have a drink with them, after they had sailed so far together.

Someone, somewhere, wrote that in another life Dennis might very well have emerged as Alexander the Great, so ruthless is he about yacht racing. I would not dispute that, and I can confirm that he has a streak of cold determination that is impressive to behold. His capacity to start a boat race is something to be seen. It is fascinating just to watch him assessing the situation, ice cool, totally methodical, in a very tight environment. I remember one start with him in particular. We were to leeward of three or four boats, all reaching down to the line on an off-the-wind start. Dennis was at the wheel, talking quietly and calmly, assessing the speed of *Williwaw* compared to the competition. Checking the watch, judging his time-on-distance ratios, computing all the variables, and finally making his move. Two fast tacks, the sails suddenly full, *Williwaw* heeling over into the line—a start almost breathtaking in its perfection. It was a privilege to have watched him at such close quarters, for his performance was nothing short of fabulous.

As we hit the line, I glanced at his face. He had a strange, faraway look in his eyes and just a little smile on his face—a private smile, introspective, aimed only at himself. He had just done it again. I realized at that moment that Dennis is a man who has to prove himself to himself all of the time, and he has to have his ego fed, although only he can really feed it. This is all part of his incredible drive. I think Dennis Conner wants to go on sailing 12-Meters for the rest of his life, to prove to himself that he is the best there is and the best there ever will be.

I believe that we finished our SORC races together with a great deal of mutual respect. I somehow felt an inevitability about our futures, sensing that we would become implacable enemies on the only mutual battleground available to us, the waters of Rhode Island Sound, each sailing a

12-Meter for the America's Cup. Dennis knew it too. He knew of my ambitions, and since he was quite certain of his overall dominance as the greatest helmsman in the U.S., he knew that one day he would have to stop me from taking away that Cup. He is not a man to elaborate much, or indeed to waste much time stating the obvious. One afternoon, very casually, almost too casually, he said to me, "John, I don't think the Australians are ever going to be competitive in the America's Cup until you are steering the boat." He said no more, but it was one of those moments. He knew what I knew. One day it would be the U.S.A. (D. Conner) vs. Australia (J. Bertrand), and may the best man win.

It was hard to know what Dennis really thought, whether he looked forward to such a match. But I knew I wanted to race him, principally because I thought I probably could beat him. No, cancel that. I thought he was beatable. I had watched him very carefully, and, by God, he was good. But he was human, and I remember thinking that if he represented the very best there was in 12-Meter racing, that would not be good enough to keep me at bay forever. My overall assessment of Dennis at that stage was that he did make the occasional error, and when he did, he was not always absolutely certain what to do. I never thought he had quite my instinct for it. I always had the feeling I could "smell" the wind a bit better, and I knew my engineering background made me superior as an analyst. I also knew that if you made one major blunder in a race against Dennis Conner, he would wipe you off the face of the earth, almost as though you had never been there. But the inevitability of our eventual man-to-man combat was there for both of us. When I eventually saw the press clippings of those SORC races and the summer interviews he occasionally gave, I noticed that he invariably mentioned my name. So I guess I was not all that far from his thoughts six long years before we finally met eyeball to eyeball.

We said a very friendly good-bye, and our paths did not appear destined to cross again for some time. Dennis was masterminding the two-boat West Coast–backed defense of the America's Cup in 1980, and I was hoping to go to the Moscow Olympics that year.

A gold medal in Moscow was my goal, and this time I would sail a Soling, the sleek and lovely three-man keelboat in which my old mentor Buddy Melges from Wisconsin had demolished 25 opponents in the 1972 Olympics with one of the most devastating racing performances ever seen. He steered his boat to three victories—interspersed with a second, a third, and a fourth—to win his gold medal by miles. No one had seen anything like that in living memory. Greatly inspired by many winter fireside chats with Buddy back in Pewaukee and Zenda, I was wildly excited by the prospect of sailing this very fast boat in Russia. Then, slightly to my surprise, no less a figure than Alan Bond stepped forward with $25,000 of sponsorship money to speed me on my way. I must say that Bondy has always done right by me, and I trust that in some distant year, when that buzzing little dynamo from Perth has time to reflect on his rambunctious life, he will consider with a smile that I did right by him.

I was not entirely certain that I could win the highly competitive Australian Olympic trials for the Soling Class. Only one boat would represent Australia in Moscow, so it was very much a win-or-bust situation. To win, I had to face Mark Bethwaite, a formidable old rival whose ambition for the Moscow gold was exactly the same as mine. He was just as determined, just as accomplished in a sailboat, twice as experienced in a Soling, and just as uncompromising a competitor. Mark was the reigning Australian champion. We were deadly rivals, about the same age, and we first met back in 1968, when I won the National Sharpie Championship off Chelsea. He finished third or fourth, and we seemed to have been sailing against each other ever since. He's a mining executive by profession, very disciplined and a lot of fun. When we get into different boats in competition, however, it seems to produce a savage rivalry. Mark is unbelievably competitive, even going in for that psychological body language. You know—when he shakes hands, he does it very strongly, in a domineering way, coming at you with his hand over the top, his knuckles facing the sky, immediately placing you on the defensive.

Before the Olympic trials, there were four selection races sailed over two days. These determined the competitors who would be eligible to compete in the trials. Mark and his boys won all four of those races. That, I suggest, would make anyone nervous. The night before the first race, I decided to go for a drive by myself. I set off up the highway and I could not get out of my mind the fact that Mark had been sailing these boats for three years, while I had been at the helm of mine for only one. He had announced his ambition to go to Moscow a full two years before we had, and his experience had been evident in pre-trial events.

As I drove along, all by myself, I suddenly noticed a drive-in theater and decided to stop and see the movie, regardless of what was playing, just to get my mind off the forthcoming competition. The film being shown was *Rocky*. I really loved it, and it provided the perfect stimulus for what I needed. It showed that graphic story of the fighter who overcame everything. It showed the power of the mind, how it can turn you into an all-conquering athlete. As I drove out of the theater, I thought I *was* Rocky. From the strength of that character in the film, from watching him struggle and work, driving himself on, I drew strength and aggression. At that point, I couldn't wait to get at Mark Bethwaite, and the following morning I beat him in the race as I had never beaten him before. If our race had been in Philadelphia, I'd have taken those steps at the Art Museum eight at a time, just like Sly Stallone himself.

We went on to win the trials, with Mark and his boys in second place. We also won the National Soling Championships within that group of races. Thus, to the tune of "Rocky," I was on my way to Moscow. Mark, hiding his profound disappointment, came up to shake hands afterward, putting me once again into the defensive mode, of course. And then, with what I consider to be immense sportsmanship, he volunteered to go to Moscow as a reserve boat to us, and to act as our training partner. It was an incredibly generous offer, and in my mind it sealed a friendship that I hope will last always.

Meanwhile, Alan Bond's 1980 challenge for the America's Cup was proceeding in Sydney without a new boat. Ben Lexcen had made some alterations in *Australia* and claimed she would probably go about a knot faster—at least that's what he told me. Well, 12-Meter racing yachts do not suddenly get a knot faster. They might get about one-tenth of a knot faster, but no more, and the awful specter of Newport 1974 again reared its head. All this false hope, all these illusions and fantasies, everyone saying we will win. Why? Because we will win, because we will win. Simultaneously, on the other side of the world, armed with the biggest budget in the history of the America's Cup, Dennis Conner had a brand-new fast boat in *Freedom* and had been methodically racing against a very expensive, revamped *Enterprise*. At a meeting in the Melbourne Hilton, unsurprisingly and with as much prudence as I could muster, I declined the opportunity to skipper *Australia* in the forthcoming races against Dennis Conner's chosen boat. I was very, very happy sailing my Soling, and I was certain that victory in Moscow would give me all of the proper authority I needed for the Ultimate Challenge in Newport.

Throughout the long Australian summer of 1979–80, I was totally preoccupied with matters like boatspeed and sail trim. So preoccupied was I that on December 28, 1979, I scarcely noticed the main item in the Melbourne *Herald*—that on the previous day the Red Army of Leonid Brezhnev had marched south into Afghanistan and appeared to have no intention of returning to Russia in the foreseeable future. Within a few weeks, the gigantic political machinations that enveloped the free world had spread to all potential Olympians. It was a terribly emotional time for all of us. My entire future seemed to me to be hanging in the balance, solvable only in the great halls of the Kremlin or the White House. Finally, we knew. In the Melbourne *Herald* it was coolly announced that the Australian Yachting Federation, along with the United States and more than 50 other countries, would boycott the 1980 Olympic Games to protest the invasion of Afghanistan. We were not going to the Olympics, and that was that. We were not even going to have a shot at the gold medal.

Now I fully understand the basic moral judgment behind this decision. How can we permit the Russian Bear to commit a diabolical act of international piracy, against all accepted forms of behavior in the modern world, and then go off and play games with Ivan in his own backyard? Like most questions that are worth answering, the complexities of that one were enormous. I fully appreciated the views of the politicians, but from the point of view of an athlete, it was a shattering blow. I had spent a total of $50,000—sponsorship money as well as my own funds—in perfecting the boat and going to Europe for pre-trial races. We had practiced for hundreds of hours in pursuit of Olympic glory. Our boat had already been shipped to Russia, but we were not going to be able to join her. It really was awful.

I remember the day, several months later, when our boat came back. The bundle came off the ship and I helped unwrap it. There she was, just as we had prepared her for the Olympics that, for us, never were. Dusty and unused, with thousands of miles of futile practice beneath her keel. This gallant little boat that had gone so far, behind the Iron Curtain, all for nothing. It was sad, that moment.

I decided to pick up my sailing career somehow or other and to spend a few weeks thinking about alternative plans. But I never had time for that. A thunderbolt named Alan Bond called in June from Newport. "Olympics? Forget them, John. That's water over the dam. We really need you here. You've got to come. We can't win without you. You have so much to contribute. . . ."

"Stop, stop! I can't. It's too late. You must know that," I said, declining the America's Cup yet again. But Bondy was in full cry, cajoling, persuading, inspiring. "Come as tactician," he blurted. "Number-two man on the boat. Jim Hardy's right-hand man. It'll be terrific. We can win this."

"But, Alan, it's so late. . . ." Three weeks later, Rasa and I and our three children, Lucas (8), Andre (4), and Sunshine (2), touched down at Kennedy Airport and were driven to Newport, Rhode Island. Bondy, the old sorcerer, had done it again. Here I was back at the place I had vowed to avoid until I could be in command. But still, I was going to be number-two man—a step in the right direction. At least I *thought* I was to be second—until it became transparently clear that Alan Bond had more of a chance of routing the Red Army from Afghanistan than he had of dislodging Ben Lexcen from the tactician's job on *Australia*. Ben was firmly ensconced and had been there for months and months of practice. He was Alan's chief boat designer, the crew had faith in him, and he was doing a very good job.

This lovely great bear of a man had also crashed his fist through a flimsy hotel wall and broken his wrist in fury when he read in the paper that I was arriving to take over his job. Of course I knew nothing of all this, and the first time I saw him, I said "Hiya, Benny. What have you done to your wrist?" No wonder he looked as though he were developing apoplexy. Bondy, of course was avoiding me, ducking and diving all over the place, unable to spare me 30 seconds of his time. People kept coming up to me and saying, "Hi, John. What are you doing here?" I kept saying I was supposed to be tactician on *Australia,* but this quickly became a very obvious piece of fiction. Finally, I nailed down Alan in his office and asked him to explain to me exactly what he thought I was doing in Newport. Alan, without even a touch of remorse, said he could not possibly fire Benny, since the crew really believed in him.

I knew what was on Alan's mind. He wanted me there for my technical advice, which was all very well, but he had told me he wanted me as tactician. "John," he said in his most sincere manner, "everyone wants you to be involved. We want you to sail on the boat. All of us. Australia wants you to sail on the boat. You can have any title you want. You can be crew coach. You have so much to contribute." By this time I was nearly knee-deep in bullshit, and then Alan finally brought himself to utter the words he suspected would send me to a travel agent. "We would like you to sail," he said, "as our port trimmer." This, of course, was the position I had occupied back in 1970, 10 years earlier, on Sir Frank Packer's *Gretel II.*

We sat gazing at each other for several seconds. Finally, I spoke. "Alan," I said, "try to see this from my point of view. I have just won the National Soling Championship of Australia. I was my country's chosen representative to skipper a boat in the Olympic Games. There were many people who believed we would win the gold medal in Moscow. Even the Americans thought we were major contenders. The very last thing I want to do is to hang around a 12-Meter as port trimmer, when my personal expectations are so much higher than that. It is unfair of you to have brought me here under the guise of becoming tactician. I could have made a contribution in that role. I did, after all, win a major championship for the U.S.A. as a match-racing tactician. But port trimmer? My heart is not in it. I've been there and done that before."

Now, there was another aspect to consider. I was, in fact, having this discussion with my biggest Olympic sponsor, one who saw his $25,000 go down the drain. In fairness to Alan, I must say that he never mentioned the subject. But he said everything he could think of to get me to stay, including making one or two minuscule allusions to the fact that 1980 was a mere $1.5 million holding pattern for him. That he was just keeping his finger in the pie. That 1983 was the year of the major Bond attack. That we would fight together another time, and win together—of that he was sure.

With my head reeling, I left Bondy's office and set off for the tiny apartment in which Rasa and the children were ensconced. Poor little Sunshine had developed pneumonia, and the place was in some chaos. The children were crying, Rasa was coping gallantly, and I was in a total quandary. All of my instincts told me to tell Alan to bag it, before Rasa bagged me. I could not imagine how she could stand two more months of this in these cramped quarters. But, as usual, I could count on my shrewd and long-suffering wife for the cold, dispassionate advice I needed. I had asked Alan for 24 hours to make my decision, but Rasa made it for both of us in about one minute flat. I can hear her now. "John," she said, "I know your pride is hurt, and I know this is a blow to your ego, but you have not been diminished in my eyes. I think that we should stay and you should sail on the boat, just for the experience. We have come all this way, and you will learn a lot out there. Let's face it—you will be able to take part in an America's Cup campaign without having gone through all that rubbish for the last two years. Let's stay, and you get out there and do your best."

One way or another this was a most impressive little speech because Rasa's experience in racing high-performance boats is minimal, and her record probably would not cause Paul Elvstrom to cut his throat. A famous day in 1969 springs to mind. It was shortly before we were married and she skippered my lightweight Sharpie *Triad* in the Ladies Day event at Chelsea. I took my place as for'ard hand, with Peter Evans making up the crew. Well, we were winning nicely, out in front of the pack when I called for a tack. Rasa, not concentrating much, did it about twice as fast as she should have, and flung the boat over, capsizing us completely. I hit the water first, backward, with the sails crashing down on top of me, but I remember the last sight I had before I plunged beneath the surface. Rasa was pinning her hair.

But now, eleven years later in Newport, Rasa had put her finger on exactly the right decision here, and that was it. I went down to Bondy's office first thing the next morning and told him he had a new port trimmer. Bondy's face lit up as he bounded around his desk. He reached up, flung his arm around my shoulders, and shouted, "Those are the words of a true champion. Thank you, John. Thank you very much."

As soon as I was officially a member of the Australian crew, I went out in a powerboat to take a look at *Freedom* and to greet big Dennis. It was fun to see him again, and we had a long chat. He told me all about the boat and his crew and carefully avoided the subject of my not steering *Australia*. But he left me certain of one plain, unvarnished fact. There was no doubt in his mind that he would win. Defeat was nothing more than a preposterous and rather silly concept. Besides, Dennis had no respect for Benny and Jim, the two decisionmakers aboard *Australia*. He felt that he had the ability to beat them in any one-on-one contest. He loved to go through the analogy of comparing every aspect, every man, one boat against the other, and he believed *Freedom* was out in front in every case. His confidence and his arrogance were total. And I knew, as I spoke to him, that you *have* to feel like that in order to win a big international event. That talk with Dennis was extremely revealing, and it demonstrated to me once and for all the critical aspect of crew psychology. I vowed to become a master at it before I ever set foot in Newport at the helm of an Australian challenger.

Before we continue with my adventure as port trimmer on Alan Bond's challenger, I ought to point out that I have no wish to paint Bondy as a kind of eccentric Barnum-and-Bailey figure with no thought for anyone but himself. He is not that, and that is not how I perceive him. In fact, I always regard him with great affection and tend to see his more extravagant side with the utmost humor. This, of course, has the result of making him sound like some kind of wild man who paints sandhills and recruits tacticians under false pretenses.

Alan Bond is a very serious, very formidable, and very, very successful businessman. He has succeeded to a remarkable degree by dint of ferocious hard work, high intelligence, and a bulldog approach to business matters. He is shrewd, innovative, multitalented, a fantastic salesman, and the most intuitive observer of a situation that I have ever met. He is also a complex soul—not so much a loner as a lonely person with few real friends—and he unashamedly seeks power through money, and money through huge business deals with a network of powerful acquaintances generated by his fame, high profile, and well-publicized commercial skills. He is reported to be worth some $200 million—which is not bad for a former sign painter who started with absolutely nothing and was a millionaire at 25. For a start, Alan Bond is the owner of Swan Lager, the big Australian brewing concern. He also owns all kinds of real estate and is heavily involved in the gas and oil business all over the world. He is a tycoon in the old-fashioned sense, with an eye for a good deal. He often walks around totally preoccupied with the cares of his business empire. He is also as tight as a mackerel's bum. He hates spending money when he does not need to do so.

Bondy very rarely takes any of his crew out to dinner, I think mainly because he is too busy, too preoccupied. His mind never stops thinking about business. I remember one night in a restaurant when I could see him becoming progressively more bored. Suddenly he started to recite to his guests a list of everything he owned. It was outrageous. "I own this. . . . I own that. . . . I will soon own. . . ." At first I thought he was just massaging his own ego, trying to show how powerful he is. But, on reflection, I think he was snapping himself out of his lethargy and conducting a fast little meeting of his auditors, all on his own. I don't think he cared whether anyone was listening or not. He just likes to keep things moving.

But his intuition in any situation is remarkable. He can be away from the 12-Meter camp for a month or so, but when he arrives, he starts firing questions and making comments by the dozen. Some things he says are not relevant, but then many things *are*. Unnervingly relevant. No one can separate the wheat from the chaff like Alan Bond can do. He also has a lovely ability to take a person aside, have a little chat, and make that individual feel good. After such an encounter, you come away thinking that he is some kind of god, or at least a fairly senior saint. It takes a bit longer to realize that what he did was to realign you totally with his every thought and desire.

His occasional talks to the team were not consistently good. They were always a little off base, nowhere near as effective as when Alan talks to an individual. He also has a rather kind streak. Any one of the boys could go to Alan with a problem and he would take the time to listen very carefully. If Alan was busy and you wanted to buy a new spinnaker, he wouldn't give you the time of day, but if your wife was ill, he would drop everything. It's a funny sort of dichotomy.

He could be a good sailor. In fact, I have often thought Bondy could be a world-class helmsman if he spent a lot of time at it. But he doesn't, so he's terrible. I know that he knows how to do it. I have seen him start in a race and have occasionally noticed a glimmer of expertise. But Bondy at the helm is much like me playing golf. I don't do it enough, so I'm terrible. If you leave him at the helm long enough, he will mess things up, because he only wants to get in there and have a bit of a go. He is bored after about 30 seconds of steering. His mind is everywhere. He is talking, chatting, plotting and scheming, laughing, procrastinating, and thinking about a thousand things that have nothing to do with the present task. The boat could go in a full circle and he wouldn't notice.

At the other end of his personality is this wickedly determined, stubborn, hard man, with an incredible desire never to give in. Never. He is like a fighting bulldog under pressure, and it has shown up repeatedly in his business, when he has hung in against all kinds of odds. And, suddenly, things have broken right for him. He may have the grim determination of the British bulldog—he was born in a London suburb and did not move to Australia until he was eight years old—but when attacked with a protest in a major race, Bondy comes out with both fists flying, shooting from both hips, shouting his mouth off—never mind the facts. Select your metaphor. An enraged Bondy will make it instantly applicable.

Luckily, Bondy also has the good sense to provide himself with a keeper, a chap who keeps him under control when the heat is on. This person is Warren Jones, the syndicate manager who, happily, has become more and more skilled at his appointed task over the years. One of his main duties is to tame Bondy, to keep the boss on a tight leash until he has fed him all the facts. At least then Alan knows the arguments that will be flying back at him. Warren has become a master at this, and as we left the 1970s and moved into a new decade, Bondy never came out swinging at the New York Yacht Club until he had a meticulously prepared case, beautifully put together by the very, very meticulous Warren Jones.

Warren knows the boss as well as anyone. I remember commenting about Alan's amazing skill in running a difficult meeting I had just attended. Warren told me something that is almost certainly accurate—that Alan's biggest strength is his ability to manipulate a board meeting. He will listen endlessly, abstract the important information, and make a decision instantly. He is terrific at untangling problems. And his strategy when he is attempting to get his own way is truly mesmerizing. Of that I can provide more firsthand evidence than I prefer to admit.

Essentially Alan Bond is a very rough diamond growing smoother by the years. Back in 1977 there was an incident to illustrate this fact. I found it astonishing and illuminating. Another of the tough Australian tycoons, Syd Fisher, a former middleweight fighter from the Depression era, detests Alan Bond, and the feeling is mutual. One day during the Admiral's Cup trials in Melbourne, old Syd Fisher went aboard Bondy's *Apollo IV* just to have a look around. Bond had him thrown off the boat by one of his deckhands. Syd was furious, and he had Bondy's boat cradle dismantled and flung in pieces out onto the highway. A little later that evening, I had occasion to have conversations with both of them—separately, of course. It turned out that they both loved the fracas. They both were laughing and joking and felt terrific. With a huge smile, Syd called Bondy everything. Bondy, grinning from ear to ear, made the same observations about Syd. But there were no hard feelings. They both thought it was wonderful. A couple of very hard men, those two, right out of the same mold.

Anyway, in Newport in 1980, Bondy was ecstatic by the time we eliminated the Swedish, British, and French 12-Meters and became the official challenger. Meanwhile, *Freedom* had crushed all opposition among the American boats, reaching the final with a record of 40 wins and three losses (against the old *Courageous, Enterprise,* and *Clipper*). It had been an exhibition of relentless power sailing by Dennis Conner and the crewmen who follow him everywhere—"my guys," as he laconically refers to them.

Now we had to face them—a crew and a skipper with three times as much sailing together as we had, and three times as much match racing. We placed our hope in our new bendy mast. We knew we could not win in the area of skippering or crewing or tactics, but we might give it a shot with a cunning piece of new equipment. The British boat, *Lionheart,* had gone from being noncompetitive to very competitive with the aid of a new bendy spar that gave her extra sail area. Bondy and Benny had observed this, so our engineers clandestinely rushed to build us a similar spar for use against the Americans in the final. We knew our new mast would be particularly important in light air, when that extra sail area would give us an edge. So we decided to go for broke and haul up that new mast the moment we could. Nevertheless, I do not think any one of the *Australia* crew felt they had a chance of beating Conner and "his guys."

6

Demolition in Newport, 1980

"We are coming back in 1983 with a major challenge—and we are going to win." The guys cheered and clapped. "My skipper and my helmsman," he added, "will be John Bertrand."

Ben Lexcen is essentially a bear of a man. He is a great big, wisecracking king of one-liners, blinking with disarming mischief behind his spectacles. He is gloriously extroverted, full of fun and irreverence, adored by the press for his wicked barbs. He is also a genius of boat design, a gifted sailor, a close personal friend of mine and Rasa's, and the greatly loved unofficial godfather of our oldest son, Lucas. When something is bothering Ben, no one knows it better than I, and I have seen him under great pressure react in a variety of ways—some dogged, some a bit eccentric.

I will admit that I was surprised at the depth of aggression he showed in combat in the 1980 America's Cup against the British, the Swedes, and the French—which is why it was such a poignant and unexpected moment for everyone when Benny, the great iconoclast, was finally silenced and became a puppy instead of a fighter. A big, blue 12-Meter called *Freedom* was the culprit; at first sight, it knocked all the bounce and aggression out of our bear. Benny very nearly saluted Dennis Conner as the American slid down to the start of Race 1 in the 1980 America's Cup. Benny's personality had undergone a total transformation—from the killer in the cockpit who took apart Baron Bich's lovely *France III* to a pensive little foreign sailor, nervous about his opponent, quiet, without jokes, laughter, or shouting. He was suddenly a man whose fire had gone, who no longer believed that he had a chance. In place of aggression, Ben now displayed respect. From my forward position, up among the ropes, I wanted nothing more than to run back for a few seconds and shake him, to shout, "Come on, Benny! These bastards are just human like us. They're fallible and they can be beaten—but you *must* believe you can win."

Benny, however, did not believe that. And there he stood, right behind me, a victim of the American aura, yet another member of a challenging afterguard whose faith in himself and in his men had wilted suddenly and then vanished. I had seen it many times before. Men reduced to jelly before the mighty American system, with all of its power, its arrogance, its money, and its efficiency. It was just more pronounced in a great, noisy, wonderful character like Ben. And I vowed it would never happen to me or to any of my boys when eventually I became skipper of an Australian boat.

The series was a catastrophe. Predictably, we lost it, 4–1. At the end, I made some very critical notes about our performance. They read as follows:

Race 1. Not sailing our boat well enough to contain *Freedom*. She seemed faster, but events proved that in these conditions she should not have been. We failed to get maximum out of our boat. 1–0.

Race 2. Conditions light. Perfect for us, could have won more comfortably. Put up wrong spinnaker. Select wrong side of course. Get overtaken. Scrape home by four lengths. 1–1.

Race 3. Conditions potentially good for us. Should have been equal with them. *Freedom* has hopeless problems, losing time with first torn spinnaker, then torn jib. Then over two minutes with pole in the water. And we *still* lost. 2–1.

Race 4. Sail selection again wrong. Mainsail too small. Misjudged weather. Lost by 3 minutes 45 seconds. We have not had enough practice with our sails. We *cannot* possibly win with this lack of preparation. 3–1.

Race 5. *Australia* is not competitive when the wind is more than 14 knots. *Freedom* just sails clean away from us. Total disaster. 4–1. Go home as usual

At the end of the race, the usual pandemonium had broken out. *Freedom* and her crew were being mobbed by hundreds of small craft and spectators. Dennis Conner was being escorted home like some conquering Roman gladiator. Then the speedboat from *Black Swan* came out, bearing Bondy, Warren Jones, Rasa, and other wives. Lines were flung out to us from *Black Swan* as we made fast for the tow home. Bondy came bouncing over the side, full of vim and smiles. "Don't worry, boys," he yelled. "That was great, we gave it our best shot." He did not seem to give a damn whether we had won or not. But Bondy is nothing if not very, very astute, and my mind flashed back to that conversation when he hinted that 1980 was just a low-budget holding action, and that 1983 was what would count. As we approached Newport Harbor, Bondy assembled the crew and confirmed what I had suspected. "I have decided," he said, "that we are coming back in 1983 with a major challenge. We'll have the budget and the boat. And we are going to win the America's Cup. Right?"

The guys cheered and clapped. "Ben Lexcen will design the boat and my skipper and helmsman will be John Bertrand."

There may have been a sense of relief on the boat. My very presence there in such paradoxical circumstances had been so offputting for the people in the afterguard, such a peculiar aspect of the campaign, that it was as if Bondy had finally put everything into its proper perspective. He had, after all, recruited an Olympic medalist and multiple national champion as his tactician and then turned him into a deckhand. Now I felt deeply honored and very proud. Rasa looked pretty surprised, but hardly more so than I. Bondy had never consulted me about skippering his major challenge for the Cup. I just stood there, smiling happily at the honor he had bestowed upon me, but I didn't say a word. I never thanked him and I never accepted. And I had no intention of doing so until he made his precise plans very clear to me and I knew exactly what he was now getting me into.

Over the next few weeks, Alan Bond and I talked often, both in Newport and in Australia. I am obliged to say he sounded as determined as only Alan Bond can. When he is a bit determined, Bondy sounds obsessive; when he's really determined, he sounds like Genghis Khan. During these talks, it became obvious that he had always known he needed the time after the defeat of *Australia* in 1977 to get things precisely right. He never held out any hopes for the 1980 races, and he was plotting and planning for 1983. He was so determined that 1983 was to be *his* year, there is no doubt that he intended it to be his fourth and final challenge. He had always helped me in my career, and I think he had always nursed the idea of appointing me as his skipper—typical of a well-organized businessman who always keeps one eye on the future.

As usual, I did not even know what the devious little wizard was up to until it was too late. I kept telling myself, "Don't be fooled by him, take your time, you don't have to make a decision right now." Of course, he had already made my decision without my realizing it. There was no way I was going to turn down my ultimate lifetime goal of skippering an America's Cup boat, and with all of Alan Bond's assurances, it seemed that things would be run precisely as I had always wanted them to be.

Bondy was also keenly aware of the activities of Dennis Conner and that big two-boat *Freedom/Enterprise* campaign. He knew beyond doubt that in order to win he would have to match that campaign with money and boats. After sailing against *Freedom,* Alan Bond had a close look at the trial horse for whatever new boat the U.S. would come up with for 1983. Very early on, he told me that I would have a two-boat campaign just like Dennis Conner. He said I would have principal say in all crew matters, selection, tactics, technical refining, sail refining, crew psychology, and boat tuning. He told me I had his total support. There would be no budget restrictions. He believed that I was his man, and that together we would win the America's Cup and make history.

I used to just look at him standing there—grim, pugnacious, and as determined as any human being on the face of the earth. I knew right from the start that he would back me 100 percent, that he was going into this with me through thick and thin. I never doubted that we would quarrel, but Bondy and I were going through to the end of September 1983 in Rhode Island as a team, and I knew he would be as good as his word. "My skipper and my helmsman will be John Bertrand," he had announced. I was his man and that was that.

I did make my position utterly clear to him. I told him that I would take no gambles whatsoever. I told him that if Benny could give me a boat equal to the Americans'—nothing drastic, nothing different—I thought we could win. I felt now that I had the experience as well as the mental backup in terms of my knowledge of major sailing regattas and match racing. My one fear was a gamble in design—I did not want any offbeat boats constructed to be different just in case it gave us an edge. I told Bondy that *Southern Cross,* with its long waterline, was a wild card. *Australia* had been a gamble in 1980 with its bendy mast. These boats were typical of what I perceived as the philosophy of Alan and Benny. They had been pressed beyond their limits and were searching for something to pull them out of the fire—hence their decision to go with an unorthodox waterline length and an unorthodox mast.

My formula for winning was imbedded in my mind. Give me a boat that will make us equal, and then let me harmonize the crew. Let me motivate them. Let me bring everyone together, thoughtfully, with respect for each other. Just let me form the great democracy that a big racing-boat crew should be. Let me instill in them that feeling of self-reliance and reliance on each other. Let me use all of my sports-psychology lessons. Just give me the chance to make them pursue excellence as I myself pursue it. My team will be totally involved in my own entire reason for living—to be respected and admired by your peers. I want them to be assailed by the feeling that the only thing in the world you can never do is to let each other down.

That is how I perceived the America's Cup being won—by a fantastically tight team. Men who would go to the wall for each other, inspiring, covering, supporting, helping out everywhere, each backing up the others, watching each other through the difficult areas, each ready to jump in and help, to slave away at whatever was necessary. I wanted a team of winch-grinders who would pound those steel handles until their arms felt they would collapse. And then they would go back and do it again. And again. Not because they had to but because they wanted to. Because the prospect of letting down their mates was so utterly, so humiliatingly unthinkable.

The three America's Cups in which I had sailed had been rich and vast exercises in experience. Without them, I would not have known what to do or say as I stood on the verge of accepting Alan Bond's offer. I would be devoting more than two years of my life to our obsession with becoming the first challenger to remove that big silver ewer from the New York Yacht Club after what would be 132 years, the longest winning streak in sports history. By anyone's standards, that is not so much history as immortality. I'm not sure who wanted it most, Bondy or me. Maybe the press would always call me, "John Bertrand, the quiet, humble skipper of *Australia II*." That is what they may think, but deep inside I know I am as tough, hard, and determined as Bondy, with all the arrogance that an international racing helmsman must have if he wants to live with the best in the world.

So Bondy and I reached an agreement. It took six months before I finally agreed formally. "I would be honored to accept your invitation to helm your new boat for a 1983 challenge in Newport for the America's Cup." I stood there for a few moments, dreaming of glory, of the Mount Olympus we would climb together. For a few seconds, I was almost overwhelmed by the sheer nobility of it all. "Talk to my solicitor," said Bondy, as he strutted out the door to tie up a land deal.

We had already decided to build a new racing yacht and try to get selected for the Admiral's Cup races in Cowes on the Isle of Wight, off the southern coast of England. This is a major championship series of races, and Australia usually sends three boats. We planned to use the new boat as a testing ground for our future America's Cup crew. It would be a fast boat, a 43-footer, and Bondy asked me to coordinate our entire onslaught on the Admiral's Cup, with few budget restrictions. The boat was to be called *Apollo V,* and I was charged with the responsibility of researching the design, figuring out who should do it and who should build it, and, most important, who should sail on it. I decided that the design should be done by Doug Peterson, one of the more conservative members of his profession. I thought we had better tackle the area we knew best, because the last thing we needed was a trick boat to try out, under high-pressure circumstances, the men who ultimately would graduate from *Apollo V* to the new America's Cup boat.

We intended to take a crew of 11 to Cowes, and one of the first I chose was a young engineer from Sydney, Grant Simmer, who had followed me as National Lightweight Sharpie Champion of Australia. He was inexperienced, but I was impressed with him, and I felt he could be a serious contender for the America's Cup crew. I also recruited the vastly experienced John ("Chink") Longley, the former schoolteacher from Perth, and I immediately struck up a great relationship with this big, burly veteran of the previous three America's Cups. While sailing on *Australia* against *Freedom,* I had also liked the look of the 28-year-old bow man, Scotty McAllister, so I asked him to join us on *Apollo.*

In the Admiral's Cup races we did fairly well. Australia as a nation finished fifth in the overall scoring, but *Apollo* was third point-scorer in all the inshore races. It was a lot of fun, and I enjoyed skippering her. Alan Bond was on board, making some attempt to give the matter at hand his very close personal attention but succeeding only marginally. He was very calm and quiet, but he did a lot of procrastinating and a lot of discussing. He was as usual a man who had an enormous amount on his mind—not the least of which was the fact that he was about to authorize the expenditure of nearly $5 million in order to get us all to Newport in first-class shape two years hence.

It is a strange thing, but all major sports have a kind of bush telegraph among interested parties that treats nearly everything everyone is doing as public information. It did not take Bondy and me long to find out that some 7,500 miles away, Dennis Conner was developing the most unbelievably extensive campaign for the 25th defense of the America's Cup, which he presumed would be against us. Apparently he had already affirmed in a long interview that they were regarding our challenge very seriously. He was quoted as saying, "I have the utmost respect for

Bertrand." And anyone who knew Dennis would realize what a remarkable thing that was for him to say. He believes, as I have pointed out, that he is the best there ever will be at sailing Twelves, and that kind of ego normally does not spend much time having the utmost respect for anyone. No one could recall his having said anything like that before. Actually, it made me feel a bit nervous. I am more at home being perceived as an underdog and then pouncing. Generally speaking, I prefer to conduct my own psychological warfare, but if Dennis wants to let his crew know that I might be a bit of a handful, well, I suppose that's OK with me.

As we stood around on *Apollo V* that summer discussing the 1983 campaign, we were more interested in boats than in sailors. It appeared that Dennis had already taken the unprecedented step of commissioning *two* brand-new 12-Meter yachts to trial against the victorious *Freedom*, winner in 1980 of 47 of her 52 races. The rumor was that the two new Twelves would be tried in the spring of 1982 off Newport and then shipped for extensive winter trials to California, before returning to Newport in the early summer of 1983 to make ready for us. In addition, it seemed that the other American syndicate, the *Defender/Courageous* group, would also have a full-blooded two-boat campaign, with their top helmsman being the great silver-maned match racer Tom Blackaller, among whose most noteworthy characteristics was a thorough and total dislike of Dennis Conner.

In the mind of big Tom, Dennis probably was going mad. He poured scorn on the man from San Diego, demanding to know what in the name of God he thought he was doing by spending a year producing boats and preparing equipment, and then a year and a half practicing sailing—all in order to win a sailboat race. Why, Blackaller wanted to know, did Conner not get a job in the Pentagon and start plotting the downfall of the Red Army or Navy or something? He observed that Dennis took himself very, very seriously, that he took the America's Cup very, very seriously. What had become of sportsmanship?

Meanwhile, Blackaller apparently was planning something very nearly as high pressured. He would trial *Defender* against old *Courageous*, and they would also go to California for the winter. One way or another, it appeared to me that the Americans had finally decided that the America's Cup races were to be treated something like the aftermath of Pearl Harbor. All this media stuff from the United States seemed to make Bondy a bit jumpy—but then he was always a bit jumpy.

I thought it was all pretty dramatic, because when you slice through all the rubbish, you still are going to end up with two 12-Meter boats on the starting line, each with a boatspeed of perhaps a touch more than *Freedom* had and a touch more than *Australia* had in light wind in 1980. Each would have a crew of 11, with all the most advanced sail techniques. Each would have all of the most advanced equipment. And each would be thoroughly prepared.

In the end, either Dennis or Tom was going to have to sail his boat against me and the boys from the land Down Under. And I was going to have to sail our boat against either old D.C. and "his guys" or Tommy and his team. Whatever the buildup, one shining fact had emerged and was not going to go away: The long-awaited showdown between Dennis Conner and myself could happen in 1983. Twenty-four months is not a long time to prepare a top-class 12-Meter campaign, and Dennis was already being quoted as saying this was going to be the race of a lifetime. I did not dispute that, and I did have a powerful sense of history in the making, as the parallel paths that Dennis and I had trodden for so long were now on a nearly irrevocable collision course.

My discussions with Bondy were shaping our strategy, and one in particular that took place on *Apollo* was to have a major effect on our design thinking. It was conducted after a 250-mile race to France. I was at the helm for that race, and the boat we would have to face was Peter de Savary's *Victory,* which he was using as a tryout boat for potential America's Cup crew members. The British would certainly be one of our main opponents in Newport in the elimination races, and Bondy was very anxious to beat them.

There were a lot of other boats in the race, and as we nosed our way out into the tossing waters of the English Channel on a cool, blustery day, I was not at all sure we would ever find them, never mind race them. After a few miles, however, *Victory* and *Apollo* were clear of the field, neck and neck out there on those cold, gray waters. We sailed tight-hauled into the wind. Both of us were on starboard tack as the wind whipped up the Channel from the southwest, its coolness belying the fact that it had come from someplace warm like the Azores. For mile after mile we raced together, very close, sometimes converging to within 100 yards, locked in that intimate, stern combat that epitomizes top ocean racing. It was glorious racing. We beat not just the British boat but everyone else as well. Bondy, who was dying to top de Savary, was ecstatic. I think we achieved some kind of dominance over the crew of *Victory* on that day. The British were very good and very competitive, but I think they developed a respect that was a little overdone, and they would carry it with them to Newport. For us, that was a major psychological breakthrough. I felt I would have enough trouble going up against the Americans, never mind further complications from a nation that had done nothing worthwhile in the America's Cup for the better part of half a century.

Alan Bond was in high good humor as we pulled into the little harbor at Dinard. We had a long, relaxed chat, and I had a couple of beers, when suddenly he said, "Come here, John, there's something I want you to see. Something Benny sent me."

The name *Benny* suddenly reminded me. Where the devil was Benny? I hadn't seen him for ages. Mind you, he has a propensity to disappear— once he took off for months without telling anyone. He just left Australia and went to live on the Isle of Wight and no one knew what had happened to him. But of course he turned up again. He is the most wonderful, kind, and lovely guy, like a little boy in so many ways.

I haven't explained very much thus far about Ben and his career, and since Bondy at this point was about to produce something startling, a little more about Benny is in order. He was born Bob Miller and was brought up mainly by his grandfather. He never had a real mother, like most kids, and he always has said that he started school at 11 and left when he was 13, so he is not all that long on formal education.

He came from a little town called Boggrabi in western New South Wales, about 200 miles from the sea. His father was a soldier who abandoned young Bob. After Bob's grandmother died when he was nine, he says, "The sea became my parents." His grandfather gave him a pretty free rein but did insist that he go to school when he was 11. At this point, old Ben (I think I'll stick to calling him Ben) could not read or write, but within six months he was at the top of his class. In those days, he used to borrow or steal little boats to learn to sail. He was never far from the water, and eventually, after being apprenticed as a boilermaker with the state railways, he joined a Brisbane sailmaker, Norman Wright, one of the legendary skippers of the 18-foot skiffs in which Ben himself would very soon star as a brilliant sailor. Since he did little but daydream about boats and draw boats, it was not long before Ben joined up with Craig Whitworth in Sydney, and they developed a flourishing sailmaking and yacht-designing business. However, after a terrible row, Ben found himself on his own. He also found that, because of legal entanglements, he could not take his name with him. So he changed it. He called himself Ben after his dog, and Lexcen after a family name of his wife's. And there you have Benny, a man with a gossamer mind, like quicksilver, who named himself after a bloody woofer and never really grew up.

I think Benny's lack of formal education has been an advantage in many ways because, as a designer of fast yachts, he feels no constraints, so he has always been a free spirit at the drawing board. He will suddenly feel an inspiration and proceed to sit down and sketch his idea. The formally educated naval architect might very well spot something that seemed impossible and not even bother to start.

Benny's wonderfully adventurous mind has led him down many paths of discovery and hitherto-unattained excellence. He has been designing racing boats for a long time. In 1981 he was 45 years old, and more than 20 years earlier he had designed a fantastically fast 18-footer that caused a revolution in the future structure of these very popular, extremely fast boats. It did not take him long to progress to ocean racers, and the first big boat of his design that went to a major international regatta was *Mercedes III*, the high-scoring yacht in the 1967 Admiral's Cup. Then he designed a spectacularly fast, revolutionary boat called *Volante* for a man in New Zealand. Pretty soon after that, Alan Bond spotted Benny's extraordinary talent and had him design the beautiful, long-keeled *Apollo*, the first of an entire fleet he would design for the millionaire from Perth.

Shortly thereafter, Alan Bond established a permanent designer/sponsor relationship with Benny and gave him a retainer. I am not exactly certain how this works, but Bondy commissions Ben to design all of his America's Cup boats, for a fairly hefty sum of money, which takes all financial pressure off Benny and allows him to run riot with his thoughts.

Bondy knows he is dealing with pure genius, so he allows Benny's mind to roam at will, exploring all kinds of unlikely avenues in the search for success. Benny is by nature a completely lateral thinker, and he is not afraid to tackle things that many designers would shy away from. He has the most glorious flights of fantasy, always talking about the depths of the oceans, about dolphins and other great fishes. My children love him, because in a sense he is very like them, full of wonderment at a world he believes is probably undiscovered. Despite Bondy's total indulgence of our resident genius—even Ben likens his relationship with his mentor to that of a court painter with a Medici prince—the master of Swan Lager knows all about his designer's foibles and weaknesses. For Ben is not by nature a precision engineer, and we all have lived for years with what we call "Bennyurisms"—which, broadly speaking, refers to things that keep falling off the boat.

Benny's general attitude in his search of pure boatspeed has always been that if it doesn't break, it must be too heavy. Light, fast boats are his idea of heaven. And whenever anything goes wrong, which is fairly often, Benny goes into a complete flap. He will blame anyone—welders, carpenters, engineers, sailmakers, riggers—anyone. I have *never once* heard him admit that there may have been some intrinsic fault in his design. I do not think artists like Benny can face that type of failure. They just have to ignore it, pretend it had nothing to do with them, and move on.

A few years back, when Ben was in his sailmaking loft, he used to get so furious that he would let out an enormous scream of rage and then stand up and hurl a huge pair of scissors across the factory floor. The first time he did it, all the sewing machinists working away in that strange rhythm of a sail loft (THUMP-da-da THUMP-da-da THUMP-da-da) dived for cover, flinging themselves every which way in case he threw more of those dangerous missiles. However, it quickly became a habit with Benny, until the evasive action became not so much predictable as regimented. In the end, the girls got it down to a fine art. Benny would spring to his feet, quivering with fury, his scissors poised. "Aaaahhhh!!" he would bellow, and every machinist, without looking up, would dive under the table, all of them hitting the floor as one, conversation unbroken, as the scissors flew harmlessly over their heads. It was like the foxhole system in Korea.

As a designer, Benny has also had his failures. The long-hulled *Southern Cross* was one of them. *Australia* was not a lot better in 1977, although she improved in 1980. Benny has admitted, reflectively, that in 1980, when he was tactician, we should have done better than 4–1. But he is inclined to blame the sailing, for that. With typically disarming candor, he told me that we lost because everyone went "bloody soft," and that he, Benny, was "the dopiest of all, being nervous of *Freedom* just because she had walloped all the American boats." He is the most wonderful puzzle, never afraid to tell a story against himself. Never afraid to laugh at himself, he once told me that when a new boat of his was being launched in Sydney, he was so afraid it might sink he went to the top of a nearby hill and watched the launching with a pair of powerful binoculars.

Benny is no stranger to failure and no stranger to success.

But back to Dinard in 1981. Alan Bond was rummaging in a locker, saying, "Wait till you see this. Wait till you see what Benny's come up with." I stood there, full of curiosity, but not very excited, because Benny is so prolific that he is always coming up with something. Even as Bondy rummaged, Ben was in Holland, working at the Netherlands ship model testing facility, which employs 600 people and is the best in the world. He had spent $350,000 on test models in his search for the perfect 12-Meter for 1983. These models, made of wood and measuring 27 feet long, cost $60,000 each to produce and tank-test. Benny had been working and dreaming diligently in Holland for three or four months. He had already perfected a conventional design with, he claimed, a 1-percent-improvement test, and that boat would ultimately become *Challenge 12*.

Bondy finally showed me his precious new plans. He unrolled them and spread them out, and my eyes were riveted to these grotesque images of a new concept in keel design. I nearly flipped. After all that I had told him—no gambles, no risks, no trick boats, just put me in there on equal terms—Benny turns up with something that looks like a bloody rocket underneath my cockpit.

I thought to myself, "Here we go again. We're back to 1974, trying to tackle the world with a strange-looking boat. If it's different, it must be better. The only way to win is to be different." That old, tired philosophy, born of men who do not believe in all the other areas of their endeavor, the areas of practice, practice, practice. Top men on the boat. Sails cut perfectly. "Oh no, this won't do it. You have to be different." I thought, "My God, I just don't want to be involved with a lemon. Not again."

Bondy saw my dismay before I even had time to speak. He must have known I would be appalled, because he quickly said something I will never forget. He said, "John, do you really believe that in 20 years airplanes are going to look as they do today?" He had hit me right in my engineer's weak spot. He knew how conscious I was of the speed of modern development, and his words had the effect of wrecking the argument I had not yet had time to voice.

So there I stood, speechless, in Bondy's hotel room in France, gazing with horror at what Ben had wrought. Staring at the extraordinary shape of a revolutionary new keel. Mentally pouring scorn, derision, and cynicism on the design for the 12-Meter racing yacht that would one day become *Australia II*.

7

The Keel
in Bondy's
Suitcase

But what would happen when the heaving waters of Rhode Island Sound got underneath the new keel? Could she really win by 20 minutes, or were we drifting along on yet another pipe dream?

The little French seaport of Dinard, nestled at the southern end of the picturesque Gulf of Saint-Malo, beyond the Channel Islands, is a glorious haven for tired long-distance yacht racers. In lateral terms, it is situated slightly farther south than Paris, and its warm summer evenings, idyllic views, mellow wines, and beautifully prepared fish and salads often seem created especially by a higher power to cast care from the shoulders of the most world-weary helmsman.

That particular balmy evening, we were an enigmatic little group, with Bondy full of excitement about Benny's possible breakthrough and Rasa highly conscious of my own doubts and fears. I did not wish to voice my personal skepticism about the proposed new keel, since my syndicate chief and, in so many ways, my friend and longtime supporter, had just spent more money in a few weeks in the Dutch testing tank than I had earned in all of my life. Bondy was certain Benny was onto something. But throughout that leisurely victory dinner, I was plagued by two stultifying thoughts—first, that both Bondy and Warren Jones would be far more amenable to a radical new design than to a traditional boat; and second, that Benny might have misjudged the speed of a 12-Meter yacht yet again, as he had in 1974 and 1977.

On a lovely, unhurried cruise the following day, I could not rid my mind of the apparition of that mad keel and the drawings thereof, which lurked in Bondy's suitcase. I was still in this unsettled mood when we arrived back at the Isle of Wight. But when Bondy hits the dock after being at sea for a few hours, things tend to happen in short order. "OK, John," he said, "we are going to Holland." "When?" I asked, taking my time over securing *Apollo V* for the night. "Now!" he yelled. As on so many previous occasions with Bondy, the ensuing hours were a blur. Weather forecasts were checked, helicopters booked, then canceled, cars hired, chauffeurs primed, ferry schedules checked, and before I knew what had happened, Bondy, Jones, John Longley, and I were heading for a 10-seat private jet in great secrecy, personal escorts accompanying us to a deserted part of a terminal at Heathrow Airport. Destination: a military airfield, "somewhere in Holland."

It was all I could do to stop myself from calling Bondy "James." But he loved it all, as he does anything that seems to be clandestine and clever, which all of this most certainly was. We took off immediately, racing above the north Kent coastline and hitting 30,000 feet, above those turbulent waters where the English Channel becomes the North Sea. Somewhere over the Dutch countryside, we descended to a military airport. There we were met and driven immediately to the Netherlands Ship Model Basin, where Benny had been living and working for nearly four months. During this time, he had gone through all of the concepts, and, with the aid of extensive computer work, a three-dimensional flow package had been developed that charted pretty accurately the lift-drag characteristics of the keel. These three-dimensional flow studies apparently had suggested that Benny's new winged keel was a sensational improvement. And they had gone ahead and built a model on the basis of the computer readout.

Well, I might have done a double take when I saw the plans back in Dinard, but when I saw the actual model, I just about died. Under stress, I usually have two principal expressions of alarm. When I saw that winged keel, and everything seemed suddenly to have roared into life, if not Technicolor, I just stood there and used them both. "Jesus Christ!" I said.

"Holy shit!" Had I not told them so many times? Give me a similar boat and we'll go out there and sail it better.

But before I could make any kind of observation, Benny was telling Alan that the computer statistics had a precise one-to-one correlation with the tank-testing results. The two programs were not linked, but both of them ultimately dealt with the effect of water on the airfoil—in this case, the keel, which is just like the wing of a plane. The size and shape and flow of water were put into the computer in three dimensions that take into consideration the vortex, which is the three-dimensional curvature of the water off the tip of the wing (or keel). It then predicted the lift and drag characteristics of that keel. The model, which of course had the same geometry, was then towed up and down the 700-meter testing tank with about 10 people, who logged every possible statistic. Four weeks and $60,000 later, out came those results. Benny apparently had tried all manner of shapes and wing sizes before he finally settled on his main model, but the results were amazing. They were not just good, they were fabulous, and both computer and model had reached almost exactly the same conclusions.

I was worried that the tests did not take into account variations in rough water and the Newport slop, but I had to agree that the results of these tests were so overwhelming that we would be crazy not to build this boat. Benny was beside himself with excitement. His tests proved that this new boat would be 5 percent better than any conventional boat going to windward. "We're not just going to win the America's Cup," he exclaimed. "We're going to win it by miles. We're going to win some of these races by 20 minutes!" You see, Benny never believed we could do it on a one-on-one basis, and neither did Alan. They had been broken too many times by the American system of world-class preparation. Neither of them could contain their joy, and while my skepticism had evaporated only marginally, I did feel that we *had* to build this new boat with its winged keel. The tank tests, after all, had said that in 20 knots of breeze we *must* win by 20 minutes.

Alan Bond ordered the boat to be built. We all agreed that we should have a crash program to get it done as soon as possible. At that moment, as we all stood together next to that huge testing tank, I think Benny hit the high point of his life that far. He was like a little boy let loose in a toy shop. I am sure that in those moments he saw himself on the verge of immortality. The designer who made the biggest breakthrough in years in the construction of a winning 12-Meter yacht—this was the boat that finally would put Benny on the map for good. There they stood—Benny, Bondy, and Jones. Rarely have I seen three such infectiously luminous smiles as those worn by these three men on the verge of their destiny. It was an exhilarating moment, and the start of more than two years of riotous optimism about the boatspeed of the yacht with the winged keel.

Speaking as the driver, however, I found myself preoccupied with the memories of the old Newport slop, those short, choppy waves that throw off balance any boat that is not perfectly ballasted. The bow will start chopping up and down, or the stern will ride back and forth, making a poorly balanced yacht nearly impossible to steer. There before me were the calm, still waters of the testing tank upon which Benny had based his research. Still speaking as the mere driver, I found myself wondering precisely what would happen when the heaving waters of Rhode Island Sound got under the new keel and she heeled away from the wind. Could she really win by 20 minutes, or were we drifting along on yet another pipe dream?

Alan Bond, who has always had a rather uncanny ability to read my innermost thoughts, was keenly aware of my misgivings, and I think he understood them as we prepared to end our four-hour stay with Benny. But Alan can wear two hats—one as the enthusiastic entrepreneur in sight of a winning deal, the other as a shrewd businessman with no self-delusions whatsoever. And as we headed back to the airport, he said to me, "John, you know as well as I do that our boat and the American boat will be about the same speed in the end. When you get through all the rubbish, they always are. Maybe we'll be a bit faster, maybe a bit slower. But in general terms, there won't be much in it." I remember being very surprised at this cold streak of realism from Bondy, but, like me, he'd been there and done it before. So, however enthusiastic he was now, he never lost sight of what could still happen and what had happened before.

We flew back to England, leaving Benny behind to refine the plans and get them passed by Lloyds of London, which must approve all specifications and the structural integrity of every boat which seeks Lloyds insurance. Our aim was to show Lloyds the plans with a conventional keel, for although they gave us their assurance that everything was treated in strictest confidence, there was no way we were going to place our trust in that.

The plans we did show them were very similar to what we would build, stressing the same point of the center of gravity, but I don't think Benny ever let them see the final plans of *Australia II*. The die was cast. I was destined to take a revolutionary boat to Newport, despite the fact that we had done this before and had never been within a bull's roar of being competitive, never mind winning. But Bondy's words remained with me for months: "In the end, John, we'll be about the same as the Americans."

Work began almost immediately at the boatyard of Steven Ward in Perth. The boat was constructed in the utmost secrecy behind locked doors. The keel pattern was made at workshops in Sydney and shipped to

Perth, where it was cast in one piece by the government foundry, in a massive container that had to be broken open by small dynamite charges. Benny made it bigger by about one-eighth inch, so it was planed down by hand, laboriously, until it was perfectly correct. Without this precision finishing, the keel apparently could not work.

By January 1982, it was time for me to begin the long and difficult task of crew selection, but, like everyone else in the Australian camp, I became preoccupied with the progress on the new boat. Twice I flew to Perth to see the graceful 64-foot-long hull, and we also put together a technical committee to oversee the campaign. This consisted of Benny, myself, Warren Jones, Chink Longley, and Tom Schnackenberg, whose place in this campaign ranks, in my opinion, with the very highest echelon of our team. Tom's area is sails—the engine of the boat—and we recruited him under the most awkward circumstances. Tom happens to be a New Zealander rather than an Australian, which disqualifies him from taking part in an Aussie challenge for the America's Cup. Not that a minor detail like that would stop us. We wanted Schnackenberg, or, more specifically, I wanted Schnackenberg, and if that was what was required, Bondy would see that "Schnacks" became an Australian. As such, he quickly became a resident with a house in—guess where? That's it: Yanchep, Sun City, "Home of the Twelves."

Tom Schnackenberg, at the age of 37, grinning widely behind his big, bushy moustache, became an Aussie like the rest of us and took his place on the team that would go to Newport. And what a fantastic asset he was, this wonderful fellow from the North Sails loft in Auckland, whose grasp of the most complex and overpowering computer problems and readouts had men like Bondy and Warren Jones blinking in bewilderment. Bondy, being ever the pragmatic executive, could not understand what "Schnacks" was talking about half of the time, did not know how to deal with him, and immediately evacuated the territory, leaving that type of problem to me.

Tom Schnackenberg, who has a lovely wife called Annie and two little boys, immediately became a huge favorite with the crew. When he came on board at the beginning of the campaign in 1981–82, he immediately began to contribute. I already knew his worth. Back before the 1980 races against *Freedom,* he had told me that when he was a perfectly legal sails consultant on the American yacht *Enterprise* during 1977, they could get their sails recut overnight whenever necessary, whereas the Australians had to wait more than two days for altered sails. In 1980, I had been instrumental in arranging for Schnackenberg to be listened to, because when I got to Newport, Tom's credibility as a sail adviser was very low, mainly because the hierarchy could not understand him. I recruited John

Marshall from North Sails, and together we arranged a meeting and did a real P.R. job on Bondy, selling the massive talent of Tom Schnackenberg to the millionaire from Perth. Finally Bondy agreed, and Tom's credibility was established once and for all. I was very impressed with him in 1980, and it was a prerequisite that if I accepted the helm for the 1983 campaign, Tom Schnackenberg would be my chief sails coordinator from the start of the campaign to the bitter end.

By trade Tom is a nuclear physicist (he nearly finished a Ph.D. at Vancouver University in Canada), and, like many intellectuals of his type, he is quite often not listened to, even when it is painfully obvious that his thoughts are brilliant. I insisted that for the 1983 campaign he be given total control of the sailmaking program, which, unlike previous America's Cup efforts, finally gave us a proper direction. In the old days we used to rely on Ben and various sailmakers, none of whom had Tom's talent with this difficult and time-consuming subject. Now Tom would coordinate the whole package from start to finish, using to the utmost his gifts for extraordinary diligence, total methodical planning, copious notekeeping, a stringent filing system, and, above all, his remarkable brain, working like a computer at solving the most intricate technical problems in a way that I have never seen matched.

His contribution was probably the overriding reason why our sail development program went from strength to strength—all the way to the starting line of Race 7 against *Liberty* in Newport. I was such an enthusiastic supporter of his that I take pride in the fact that my backup, with my assessment of actual boatspeed and some analytic input, to Tom's data base gave us a nearly unbeatable advantage. Add to all this the strong technical input of my tactician, Hughey Treharne, the other major sailmaker on the boat, and the contribution of navigator Grant Simmer, and you can see why, given any major decision, there was a very high probability that we would arrive at the right answer. No America's Cup campaign had ever been as efficient as that, including the American ones.

Tom had already worked for a year helping the British syndicate's *Victory '83,* and by the time he reported for duty to us as a full-fledged Aussie, he was, in my opinion, the number-one employee of the entire North Sails worldwide organization. He was probably the world's leading authority on 12-Meter sails. He can speak on a variety of subjects and is a rather whimsical type of person, by nature fantastically noncompetitive—otherwise, he would be in the computer industry's fast lane now, earning about four times more money than he does.

Tom was always a great part of the team, and he would often run with us in the morning, even when he had been up half the night, if not all of it, recutting sails or redirecting our entire computer-analysis programs.

His arsenal was huge. He estimated very early on that we would be taking to Newport 40 genoas, 10 mainsails, and 50 spinnakers, with probably 20 sails on the boat for any one race. Each sail's shape, configuration, and driving power were Tom's responsibility. And he attended to every single detail throughout the campaign. He was not interested in extravagance, only in scientific conclusions. For instance, in the American camp, if a sail is not doing its job, Dennis Conner will just whistle up a half-dozen new sails. In earlier campaigns, we had a tendency to do the same thing. Tom detested this approach. He thought it was crazy because he did not think sail manufacturing was sufficiently accurate. He thought recutting was more progressive, correctly working to a scientific conclusion. Once we had a sail that was good, we just kept recutting it, sometimes to a fraction of an inch, keeping it good, dealing with the stretch instead of starting again with a new one. In that way he was extremely conservative, but he was at the same time extremely potent, because he made sure we always had our fingers on every pulse with great accuracy.

Amusingly, after all this heavy concentration on his job, Tom's hobby is sailboarding. He is, I suppose, totally consumed with the effect of the wind in the intricate science of driving a boat, of whatever weight, forward. Money does not do it for him—nor, apparently, does recognition, for in his own country he is just about unknown, despite his international reputation. Tom's raison d'être is, I suppose, the pursuit of excellence for the sake of pure excellence. That is an ennobling way of living your life and one of which I very much approve.

Meanwhile, in Steve Ward's boatyard in Perth, they were pursuing excellence, more accurately, *Lexcellence,* with the cool nonchalance of the truly skilled boatbuilder. Every six weeks, sometimes every four weeks, the technical committee would gather. Benny would discuss the latest expectations from our radical hydrofoil; Schnacks and I would plot the rig and the aerodynamics of the sails; Chink Longley, who knows as much about the interior workings of a 12-Meter as any man alive, would help with overall workability problems; Warren Jones would coordinate the effort down to the minutest detail, as only he can.

At this juncture, because of a lingering suspicion that I may have been thus far less than charitable to this immensely talented, if rather difficult man, I ought to stress that his contribution to our team was nothing short of colossal. In any effort so diverse and technically complicated, some details are certain to fall into the cracks. In other campaigns, that is. Not in ours, because we had Warren Jones. His eye and his concentration on detail, no matter what the area or the time of day, are quite phenomenal. It is almost a fetish with him, and it used to make the crew laugh—but it never made me laugh. I used to be astounded by the overall grasp of the man who acted as our executive director, our legal expert, and our America's Cup rules expert, and the man who would know if the deputy cook's assistant had purchased three eggs too few for breakfast.

On the subject of breakfast, there was always a light interlude before Warren stood up to make the daily announcements just before we left for the dock. He would stand up and say, "Gentlemen, it is now twenty-seven-and-a-half minutes to eight," banging officiously on his orange-juice glass with his knife. Ding! ding! ding! ding! ding! ding! This would be greeted with a howl of derision from the crew.

"Hold it, Warren, just a minute. I believe it is twenty-eight minutes to eight."

"No, no! Surely it's twenty-six minutes to eight!"

"Warren, this is bloody ridiculous. I'm certain it is twenty-six-and-a-half minutes to eight."

"Christ, Warren, can't you get anything right? It is at least twenty-five-and-three-fourths minutes to eight."

And on and on. Right out of elementary school. All naughty boys together, becoming more mischievous by the minute, with our executive director gazing stonily ahead, amused, but unsmiling. The only worthwhile observation about these episodes is that if Warren Jones said it was eight minutes and 43.7 seconds to eight, and the great world time clock at the Greenwich Observatory in London suggested that this was wrong by 6.2 seconds, I'd stake my life savings on Warren, and I would be completely secure in the knowledge that the Poms would have to put their bloody clock right.

That is not an exaggeration. Warren Jones, with whom I have not always seen eye to eye, was, in my opinion, utterly, irrevocably irreplaceable to the campaign of *Australia II*.

Anyway, that was the team entrusted by Alan Bond to ensure that his new baby, the embryonic *Australia II,* hit the warm waters off the Fremantle Sailing Club as nothing short of the fastest 12-Meter ever to leave a boatyard. And, with the exception of the boatbuilders, and of course Bondy, they were the only people allowed to see the boat with the amazing keel. For, as the project developed, the security became tighter and tighter. The huge door that guarded the hull was kept battened down at all times. No one was permitted inside. Tarpaulin was wrapped around the boat from the time that keel was cast. In the final stages, painters worked inside the tarpaulin. When she was launched in June 1982, she emerged in all her splendor under wraps. Still no one saw her deadly secret. She was lowered at last into the water for the traditional champagne-breaking launching, but no one knew precisely what was going on beneath her skirt.

The following 48 hours saw her full rig completed. We checked her over and over—the committee, the boatbuilders, and Alan Bond—until we were all satisfied that *Australia II* at this early stage was everything she should be, from bow to stern, from keel to masthead.

She measured 64 feet overall, 18 inches longer than *Gretel II,* 18 inches shorter than her ruby-red opponent, *Liberty.* At the waterline she measured 46 feet, drawing nearly 10 feet. She weighed more than 23 tons, but she was nearly 1½ tons lighter than *Liberty* would be. Her hull was painted pure white, and along the side was her battle livery of green and yellow stripes (Australia's national colors), two of each, stark and straight, a few inches below the gunwales—with a tiny, demonic kangaroo poised symbolically just before the point of her bow.

Australia II had a rather sharp bow and a very restricted foredeck area, with a slight hook to it, like an upside-down eagle's beak. This deck was painted in a washed-out green to reduce reflection. It was scientifically blended to create a restful area for tired eyes—eyes aching from the strain of staring out at bright sunlit water, eyes sore from the ordeal of peering across the glare of those reflective waves for hours on end, in search of ripples, in search of wind, sometimes in search of the enemy in the distant haze. Farther back, away from the point of the bow, behind the carefully angled spray deflectors and spinnaker brace, are two waterproof hatches leading to the "sewer," where the sails are kept. The hatch covers here, which are so often under water, were built to the standards of a nuclear submarine—total overkill, totally waterproof—not only to provide maximum assistance for the man who fills the murderous role of the sewerman, but in rueful remembrance of the fact that we had to pump *Australia* all the way around the race course in 1980 in a big sea. In the months to come, I would thank God for those hatches, particularly in one race where we never even had to pump, and the Italian challenger had to abandon the race because she was sinking.

Immediately behind the hatches rises the mast, 96 feet high and nestled in a cluster of major winches that work the screaming halyards of the spinnakers and the driving genoa, the topping lift winch that raises the spinnaker pole and the genoa tacking-line winch. In the middle of this lot are the diabolically cramped quarters of the mastman. Measuring four feet by 30 inches, about two feet deep, it is known as the birdbath or the pit. It always fills with water, and the ropes are hurled into this hole as they come whipping off the winches. It's like a madhouse in there when the pressure is on.

Behind this is the main working deck of the boat, to the rear of which is the cockpit of the afterguard. This is all about two feet lower than the level of the foredeck. Mere inches from the front of this main area is the big, crescent-shaped boom-vang track, which holds down the huge boom and controls the aerodynamic twist of the mainsail. This amounts to a hydraulic railway train to reduce twist. Dominating the forward end of this area are the two huge coffee-grinders (primary winches). There are positions here for four winch-grinders, and it is the main powerhouse of the boat, where all retrimming of the genoas takes place.

Farther aft are the tailers' cockpits, each about four feet deep, where two men will work, clearing the genoa sheets when tacking to windward, which is often. Behind this, in the center of the deck, is the center pedestal, home of the mainsheet trimmer, who controls the bank of multifunctional hydraulic controls, the boom vang, the mainsail outhaul for boom tension, the backstay control, and the hydraulic jumper struts for side bend control.

The navigation area, just in front of the steering wheel, has an onboard computer and various equipment, giving us the true wind speed and direction and the apparent wind speed and direction. There, too, are the little speedometer, accurate to within .01 knot, and the instruments that will tell us how far to go to the layline. Everything developed after months and months of testing. My own area is essentially shared with my tactician. *Australia II* has two wheels so that I can have the best possible view on either tack. The wheels are four feet in diameter, with brown leather nonslip grips to keep your hands from freezing in the wet. I like a wheel to be on the small side, but I had both of these raised two inches to give a tall person like myself maximum comfort over the long summer of racing. If they were too high, the huge mainsail boom would hit them.

Behind the helmsman's position is the mainsail traveler, a large aluminum track, right above my head, on which the boom sheet slams back and forth. On the transom are painted the words, "*Australia II*," and, in smaller letters, "Royal Perth Yacht Club." I have no idea why, but I always felt slightly humble when I looked at those words. A couple of radio aerials and the final destination of the backstay completed our equipment, right above the waterline. One way or another she was quite a weapon, an instrument of war.

The day of her maiden voyage was a major occasion. It seemed as though half the world, including dogs, wives, and children, had turned up at the Fremantle Sailing Club. The place was packed, and Benny was floating somewhere between the dock and seventh heaven. It was a heartwarming sight. Here was this huge, good-natured, slightly chaotic man, who can swear like a drunken bushwhacker, walking around as if on air, with his arms often spread wide before his new creation, as if conducting a Vivaldi concerto, a subject in which he is also very well versed. Benny radiated warmth. In his considered view, *Australia II* made all other boats seem ugly. And now she was ready to show her paces. Well, almost. In fact, the moment she hit the water, it was clear she was floating incorrectly. Her bow was way too high in the air, and we had to add 1,000 pounds of ballast before she settled properly on her lines. In the general spirit of joy and good fellowship, this was written off as a minor oversight. In fact, it was a bit of a screwup—a classic "Bennyurism."

Before we go for our first sail in *Australia II,* consider for a moment the sheer guts of her designer. By coming up with this winged keel, he was putting his entire reputation on the line. He has no inhibitions whatsoever, so this would not bother him, but no American designer would have dared to take such a radical step so late in the campaign. Benny had known multiple failures with winged keels, with dorsal fins, and God-knows-what, back in the mid-1970s. They rarely worked adequately, never mind speedily. Benny has designed some awful boats, and for Alan Bond he once designed a truly tragic boat, *Apollo III,* a big 50-footer that may well have been the greatest dog of all time. And it was not so much that she would not go. She wanted to lie down and die. But Alan never held it against Benny. He just kept giving him his head, knowing, or at least believing, that one day the quixotic Sydney artist would come up with something wonderful.

As we all waited for *Australia II* to be prepared for her maiden voyage, Benny believed he at last had the answer. It seemed completely logical to him, that winged keel, and he was prepared to pile Alan Bond's money behind his, Benny's, brain. As usual, he had constructed the boat very lightly, adhering to his famous maxim, "If it doesn't break, it has been too heavily constructed." This, of course, is not great for a bloke who is not long on dollars, but for an America's Cup campaign, with virtually unlimited money and time, you spend months beefing up components that Benny had approved in his original design.

And now she was in the water, and the large crowd turned it into an emotional moment. There she floated, the hope of all Australia, and there was a huge amount of "oohing" and "ahing." "Doesn't she look fantastic?" "Doesn't she look fast?" I refrained from mentioning the fact that they all look fast at this stage, in their new paint, varnish, and rigging. Ten years earlier, *Southern Cross* had also looked pretty fast at this stage. But how fast would the new boat look as the short waves of Rhode Island Sound shoved her bow skyward, and the green water crashed over the deck, and sweating aching grinders, hands gloved, fought the lethally stretched halyards and sheets? How would she look in a 25-knot breeze, hard on the wind, perhaps in pursuit of the Americans, with every inch of her construction stretched to the point of screaming? How would she shape up in one of those tight, vicious America's Cup tacking duels, perhaps three dozen at a stretch, with the boom cracking across, wrenching her from one tack to another, with the winches howling above the shouts of the afterguard, and the monstrous shuddering of the giant mainsail? How would she look then?

I remember every part of the boat on that idyllic afternoon, how she looked and what she meant to me. The foredeck looked small for an area that often accommodated three men, but the big steel hawser that secured the forestay looked tough, shiny, and new—something secure for a soaked, tired bow man. Then there were the winches, gleaming new in the sunlight with their little computer screens in the center recording infinitesimal details of the boat. They looked beautiful, and their state-of-the-art appearance drew much admiration. I knew, however, that those diabolical machines were not much better than medieval instruments of torture for the poor bastards who had to drive them. I peeked down the hatch at the beautifully fitted sewer, where we keep the sails. Its aluminum and wood were finished to a standard better than most cruisers. Given a few cushions and bunks, you could live down there on a lovely afternoon like this. Out on Rhode Island Sound, that sewer is nothing less than a hell hole. It's like a swamp down there, with enormous spinnakers being pulled down by one man, soaking wet with arms grabbing and pounding, from underneath, left right, left right, left right, like a speeded-up movie. A four-hour stint down there—soaked and exhausted, hands and arms aching and sometimes bruised—has caused powerful men to collapse on the sails at the end of a race, too tired to drag themselves on deck, too tired to care.

I looked also at all the computer systems on which we would rely so much. I looked at the towering mast—heaven forbid the bloody thing should break, as *Southern Cross*'s had done. And finally I looked at my cockpit, from where I would now have the opportunity to prove whether all of my dreams of triumph could be realized or whether they were just another Australian pipe dream. And amid all of the exclamations of admiration, I tried to keep myself entirely separate. I could not afford to let myself become in any way involved in the emotion of the moment. I had to be prepared to take that wheel for the first time and, coldbloodedly, like the engineer I was, assess the potential speed of the hull and be absolutely prepared if necessary to blow the whistle if I thought for one split second that we were going down the wrong road. I *had* to be in a position where I could say, "This is not going to work. Let's scrap this boat right now. Melt her down and start again. Let's not get trapped by *Australia II* and run out of time. Let's start again, fast."

Little did I know it, but on the other side of the world, such phrases already were about to be used by Dennis Conner on his new boats. Right now, all I knew was I was only there to win the America's Cup, not to fool around trying to hoodwink myself into steering a slow boat that would be defeated savagely by Conner.

We towed her out into the deep water, and Benny and I stood together. He wanted to take the wheel for the first few hundred yards, and I will always remember him turning around and saying, "I'm really worried about the stern weight, John. Do you think it's too big? I think it should be a bit different at the back." I nearly fell overboard. "Oh, shit, Benny," I groaned. "You have to be kidding me. Don't say things like that." "No, I'm serious," he added blithely. "I knew I should have tested another model."

Now any skipper who knew Benny less well than I might have been forgiven for giving up, right there and then, resigning his commission and going home. But one thing is important to understand about Ben. In his ephemeral mind, he just cannot cope with the fact that we are on *this* boat, with *this* crew, trying to sort out *these* problems, and improve *this* performance, right at *this* moment. He is not interested in that. He has mentally left town, gone off on some distant keeled boat way in the future. At that moment, Benny was designing *Australia III*, for the 26th America's Cup challenge, wherever that might take place. That's how he is. The hard, day-to-day problems of refining what he had created had nothing to do with him—in the same way that he would ignore everything if the boat turned out to be a dog.

Well, now I found him standing next to me muttering about rebuilding the hull. As we nosed our way out of Success Harbor, hard by the trawler port, Benny aimed *Australia II* out into the Indian Ocean and formally handed over the wheel to me. It might not have meant much to everyone else who was watching, but it was a pretty important moment for me. Twenty years had passed since I first sailed these waters with my pal Geoff Augustine and we had won the Junior Championship of Australia in our lightning-fast V.J., *Triad*. And now I stood at the helm of *Australia II*, in command of my first 12-Meter, and we were going to try to win the Cup my great-grandfather and Sir Thomas Lipton had sought so often more than half a century ago. It was quiet now as we ran lightly downwind, and I wondered then what old Tom Pearkes would have thought if he could have seen me. I was about 18 when he died. I remembered his funeral. Bant Cull, my grandpa, was also gone by now, but Nan was still alive well into her eighties. Mum and Lex of course knew where I was. But I would have given anything, truly anything, for my dad to have been able to see me at that moment. Just for a few seconds. I nearly cried again, thinking about him, just as I had done here in Perth when they gave me the trophy back in 1962.

But that sadness I always feel when I experience a successful or heady moment in racing yachts is only fleeting, and now I warmed up to the task of taking *Australia II* a couple of miles under sail to see how she felt. Well, she felt good, not great, but certainly like a nice boat. The trouble with the America's Cup is that you never get much chance to compare until the actual races against the Americans. You simply do not know how fast you are until you are alongside your opponent. Neither, of course, does he. But it still places everyone in a vacuum, the challenger's usually a lot bigger than the defender's, because at least *they* have the advantage of being able to race against the boat that won the previous time. We are always tuning up against a loser.

Well, after a mile and a half, I decided to turn her around and sail to windward. And at that moment, I knew something was afoot. *Australia II* did not merely turn, or even turn fast. She whipped around faster than any big boat I've ever sailed. It felt almost like a turn on a hairpin bend. She spun tight and fast, her winged keel holding her magically almost on a dime—rather, I imagine, like an ice skater on an inside edge. This was a definite breakthrough, because tight turns in match racing are critical, especially before the start. This was not, in fact, the main thrust of Benny's enthusiasm for the boat. That was based on pure speed, winning by 20 minutes and everything. But as spinoffs go, the turning speed of *Australia II* might prove priceless. I guessed at the time that this might also have something to do with the lack of drag Benny had forecast. The keel, essentially a lifting device, reduces the sideways slipping of a boat through the water. And Benny had designed this one to be narrow at the top, where it joins the hull, and wide at the bottom, where the wings extend out to the sides. This slim section of the keel near the waterline reduced the amount of water near the hull, cut down the drag, and reduced the wake very significantly. The wings, being heavy and made of lead, also lowered the center of gravity more than a normal keel would do, and, in my opinion, all of these factors had caused Benny to hit upon a perfect formula for outstanding mobility. "If we can just go forward fast enough and ride through that Newport slop," I thought, "we are going to win the America's Cup."

That maiden voyage was very exciting and very successful. Benny, of course, was ecstatic. For although he is not a world-class sailor under pressure, he is extremely gifted and very knowledgeable. And he realized almost as well as I did how swiftly his new boat had turned. We both figured we would be able to out-tack whatever boat the Americans threw against us. Privately, I also thought the boat would turn out to be very fragile, with more than its share of Bennyurisms, and ahead of us we would have many weeks of sailing devoted solely to discovering them. I did not care what bust in the Indian Ocean, as long as we held together in Newport.

Aside from the endless hours of practice required to refine the crew's sailing technique in a 12-Meter, our main task over the next three or four months would be to get *Australia II* into top shape. It would be a long time before we met our real opponent, and that was the missing practice ingredient that had brought down almost every challenger that had ever gone to Newport.

The boat that would ultimately provide the first racing test against *Australia II* was *Challenge 12*. She was designed by Ben Lexcen, refined in the Dutch testing tank, and based conventionally on the old *Australia*. At first Alan Bond had intended to finance the boat himself, but when he was approached by a new syndicate from the Royal Yacht Club of Victoria, who wanted to buy Ben's plans and *Challenge* to make a run for the Cup themselves, Bond accepted with alacrity. Here was a heaven-sent opportunity. Somebody else's money was going to buy the crack trial horse we needed, and the two syndicates agreed to cooperate. The Victorians appointed the former world Etchells 22 Class champion, John Savage, as skipper, but the syndicate ran into serious financial trouble shortly before *Challenge 12* was to be launched in October 1982. We could not possibly permit their effort to die, since that would have left us without a training partner, so Bondy stepped in, paid about $150,000 of their expenses, and promptly leased the boat from them, thus giving us the option to take to Newport whichever boat we liked best. This was a comforting but *unhealthy* condition for us. In a subtle way it was just as dangerous as in those days back in 1974 when we put the best sails on *Southern Cross* in order not to be disappointed in our trial races with *Gretel II*.

But for the moment, immediately after the launch in June, we were without a racing companion, and while we prepared to flounder about in the inevitable vacuum that situation creates, I was concentrating first on the Bennyurisms, and second on selecting the Australian raiding party, the twelve crewmen who would accompany me aboard *Australia II* on the mission to Newport the following year.

Hugh Treharne—tactician. As we headed out to the race course, he would lie on a genoa belowdeck, staring silently at the ceiling for two hours, his mind churning over and over, relentlessly plotting the downfall of *Liberty*. (All individual crew photography by Grace Trofa of Rhode Island)

Grant Simmer—navigator. Known as "Mad Dog Simmer." "He and John are very much the same in defeat," says Rasa Bertrand. "Just two plain, ordinary, everyday, highly unpleasant, nasty people."

Colin Beashel—mainsheet hand. I hated to ask anyone to go up for Scotty, who had now blacked out, trapped at the top of the mast by his broken arm. Conditions were terrible. The mast swayed uncontrollably and Colin Beashel, with immense heroism, stepped forward immediately and said, "Hitch me up. I'll get him down."

Ken ("Scoop") Judge—starboard trimmer. Not for the first time I thanked God for Scoop—suave, brilliantly confident, sure of himself, of me, and his crew mates. He just sat there, buttering his toast, eating his eggs and bacon, laughing, chatting away as if nothing was happening.

John ("Chink") Longley—
port winch grinder. Chink
stood up in a lava of sweat
and anger, and he turned
toward *Liberty*, screaming
out at them like a wild-
man, his teeth gleaming.
"Come and get us—come
and get us, you bastards!"

Skippy Lissiman—port
trimmer. He is doing the
most fantastic job now balancing the boat, and I
mutter to him, "Keep it
up, Skippy; for Christ's
sake let me keep hearing
your voice, keep telling
me." It was almost as if
my lifeblood, my very oxygen were coming from
Skippy's words.

Damian Fewster—replacement bowman. I immediately took a liking to him because he was not in awe of the Americans. In fact, he did not care a damn for them. He was a very fit and tough kid, afraid of nothing. He'd go up the mast, go under the boat if you like; he'd go anywhere.

Brian ("Splash") Richardson—starboard winch grinder. Splash Richardson moves into the breach holding *both* winches down by himself. He just loves the pressure, glories in the drama of it. He has dreamed of this, the heat of battle in the America's Cup, and by Christ, he's in it right now.

AUSTRALIA II

Robbie Brown—trimmer. Sounded like Salt Bush Bill, King of the Overland, when he hit the airwaves on his walkie talkie. "Jabberoo, jabberoo, jabberoo to snake bite. From where I'm camped, she blows steady out to right at 335°."

Will Bailleu—grinder. This 6'5" Olympic oarsman was our first choice for the position of port winch grinder, principally because his terrific contribution to team spirit and crew morale gave him an important edge. A fluke injury and infection, however, put him in the hospital two days before the final races against the United States and big Will never sailed against *Liberty*.

Kenny Beashel—chief of maintenance for *Australia II*. Transpacific sailor, champion yachtsman, shipwright, and boatbuilder, has no peer when it comes to the professional functioning of big racing yachts and the stress factors thereon. And I had ignored him. And now he was devastated. And it was my bloody fault.

Warren Jones—head of administration. Became more and more skilled as Bondy's "keeper" as the years went by—and he kept the boss on a tight leash until he had at least fed him the facts. When Bondy came out swinging, he always had a meticulously prepared case, presented to him by the very, very meticulous Warren Jones.

Major Peter Costello—main winch grinder and number two for'ward hand. In daily charge of our sails, one of the strongest men I have ever met. Under pressure he could do the work of three people. He had no respect for the opposition, because he hated it, pure and simple. He had fire in his eyes throughout the campaign, and he was a total inspiration to everyone.

Phil ("Ya") Smidmore—mastman. The three seconds longer it takes Ya to answer, three seconds longer than any human being I know, seems like eternity. Then he calls it. "The breeze is stronger to the left, John. Stay where you are." The Americans and the Australians have agreed to differ.

Ben Lexcen—designer of *Australia II*. He is a fascinating man with the most glorious flights of fancy, always talking about the depths of the oceans, of dolphins and other great fishes. My children love him, because in a sense he is very like them, full of wonderment at a world he believes is probably undiscovered.

Scotty McAllister—bowman. The noise was still deafening in the plastic Kevlar sails as I held *Australia II* into the wind, and no one heard that bloody crane up there at the top of the mast suddenly slam down on Scotty's arm, smashing it in two between the elbow and wrist, trapping him completely. Scotty's scream was shipped away by the wind.

Sir James Hardy—helmsman of our warm-up partner, *Challenge 12*. The turnaround was dramatic, a bit too dramatic—and it flashes through my mind that Jim is going easy on us, skillfully instilling some extra confidence in us before the battle. No one on earth wanted us to beat *Liberty* more than Sir James Hardy.

Tom ("Schnacks") Schnackenberg—sail coordinator. Schnacks was a wonderful boffin from Auckland whose grasp of the most complex and overpowering computer problems and readouts had men like Bondy and Warren Jones blinking in bewilderment.

Australia II rounds the fifth and final mark 21 seconds ahead in the deciding seventh race of the 1983 America's Cup—"and I risk a glance behind, to see what I hope is the red boat in her death throes." (Richard Benjamin, *Journal-Bulletin*)

Finn class champion of North America, 1975. With Lucas after victory in New Orleans.

Number 22 Bristol Avenue, Chelsea, the little house on the beach where Mum still lives, and where Lex and I grew up. (Greg Noakes)

The moment of truth: *Australia II* and *Liberty* locked together two minutes before the start in this monstrous struggle for supremacy. The final race for the America's Cup, September 26, 1983. (Richard Benjamin, *Journal-Bulletin*)

On the fateful fifth leg, race seven. *Australia II* has sailed across the bow of the American boat and leads by one and a half lengths. "Dennis keeps jibing. In my view, he's panicked. I'm in a cold sweat myself." (Richard Benjamin, *Journal-Bulletin*)

8

Twelve Good
Men and True

Above the shuddering sails, you could still hear the Major down in the sewer, arms pumping, yelling at the top of his lungs, "AAARR! AAARR! AAARR!" as he hauled in the sails.

You can kill yourself on a 12-Meter yacht. That is, unless you know precisely what you are doing. The stress loads on some of those halyards, sheets, and shrouds is fantastic—in a 20-knot breeze, they are stretched steel-tight. With enough rosin on his bow, a decent violinist could probably play "Flight of the Bumblebee" on them.

A 12-Meter can be an incredibly dangerous place because violent breakages are not all that uncommon. Dennis Conner sometimes wears a crash helmet at the wheel. I don't, and one day while testing *Australia II* in a high wind, a block sheared off the side of the boat with enormous force, missed my head by nine inches, and embedded itself in the mast 75 feet up.

Injuries are fairly regular; strains, gashes, and pulled muscles are commonplace. Bruises and bad backs and pinched fingers, sprains from lifting huge loads and flailing away at the winches—all are everyday occurrences. Broken limbs are more regular than anyone would like. Bravery, strength—brute strength—are as crucial to a 12-Meter as the mainsail itself. Yet you cannot just recruit 10 gorillas and a helmsman, because you also need brains. Specialist brains, seamanship, and instinct. Ten college-educated gorillas with marine training will not do it, either. Not on my boat, because I need something you cannot buy, cannot learn, and cannot train for. I need men who, in addition to all of the above, have the God-given killer instinct to win, who naturally perceive themselves as winners, who believe unquestioningly in our own invincibility.

The selection of the men who would sail *Australia II* in Newport would be, in the final reckoning, my decision. I would be helped greatly by the collaboration of Bondy, Benny, and Warren Jones, each of whom had much to contribute. Warren was manager in the previous two campaigns, and Benny was a man with a great natural capacity to see characteristics and natural instincts of people. Our big problem would be the same one that has hindered every Australian syndicate. We do not have enough big-boat racing to generate enough people with the expertise required to get a 12-Meter moving at its maximum speed. It's one thing to have top-class dinghy sailors on your crew, but it is quite another thing to get them up to world-class standard on a 64-foot-long, 23-ton racing yacht in the America's Cup.

My policy was to look at every aspect of every person who applied to join us, and if that did not produce the right men, then to go out and recruit them. My plan was always to form a final crew and then to keep on trying to improve it. This, I understood, would produce much disappointment among those who would not make it, and for that I often felt very sorry. But I know of no other way to build a crew when you are always going to feel shorthanded. Although our boat would essentially be a great democracy on the water, there was no room for the weak. We sought, throughout the entire country, only the strong, the healthy, the secure, and the ambitious.

Starting from the bow of the boat, I shall take each position in order and describe in as much detail as possible the men who were chosen as the final crew and who went to Newport in 1983 as our number-one choices. Although the story thus far is hovering around the July-through-October period of 1982, these profiles span the time from 1981 to March 1983, when the position of tactician was finally settled.

1. BOW MAN. This position requires a man of great agility with a tremendous amount of big-boat experience. His strength and power-to-

weight ratio must be excellent, because he is required to shimmy up the mast and out on the foreguy to the end of the pole. He needs fantastic balance, because there are no lifelines on this boat, and he must work in a very small area. Crunching through waves at more than 7 knots can be very, very formidable. The bow man is often in green water up to his eyeballs, horizontally hanging on to the forestay for dear life, as the waves try to sweep him over the side. The one thing he cannot do is to leave the ship under any circumstances, because that will cost us the race. This is no spot for the fainthearted or the inexperienced.

When Paul Salmon went over the side in 1970 in the first race against *Intrepid,* it was purely because we were doing things we had not practiced, and he took a chance he should not have taken. The cry, "Man Overboard!" is instant death in an America's Cup race.

The basic job of the bow man is to feed the genoa up or down, but this can take place with the bow dipping two or three feet below the surface. He must bound around the foredeck, hanging on where he can, attending at the same time to all the mechanical work forward, remembering that no matter what happens, he must not fall over the side. He wears a wet suit, boots that always fill up with water, and big leather gloves to keep the ropes from burning his hands to pieces.

And the man we chose to fill this arduous position was Scotty McAllister, age 33, from Perth. He was, in a sense, an old mate of mine. He had sailed in the 1980 campaign and as our bow man on *Apollo V.* He also sailed with me in England in the Royal Lymington Cup. He was a really neat guy. However, I had it in my mind that I was disappointed with him in that English regatta. He had not applied himself to the degree that I expected, he made too many mistakes, and I was worried that he was no longer as keen as he once had been. He had also sailed in the America's Cup in 1977, which I missed, and I was not sure that he still had the same desire, or that he was capable of forgetting the old defeats and becoming part of a winning combination.

He came over to join us in December 1982, when the boats were in Melbourne. And on the third day that he sailed, having watched him very carefully, I decided to take him aside and see what he was made of. "Scotty," I said, "you have got to decide whether you really want to become the best bow man in the world. If you want to be that, then you should continue trying out with us on this boat. If you feel you are only capable of a mediocre performance, I would like you to leave now. I believe we can win the America's Cup, and the only way I know how to do that is with people who are going to be committed totally to this project." I told him I was disappointed in his performance thus far, and I added, "Scotty, if that is the level at which you are going to be able to contribute to this campaign, then it is not going to be good enough. I want you to decide right now whether you want to be the very best, and I am afraid that is a decision only you can make."

I do not enjoy making that sort of speech, but I did not know any other way to deal with it. Shock treatment, I figured. Scotty said nothing for a while. Then he grinned and said. "OK, John, I accept that. And I hear you. . . ." And as he walked away, he turned around very slowly and said, "And I bloody well do want to be the best."

From that moment, Scotty set about proving his point. He persevered and tried his level best all of the time. And he made it clear that he wanted to be a part of the team. That was his ambition. By nature he is not a team leader, he is more of a follower, but he got involved. We had a setup in Melbourne that was like a mini–America's Cup. The boys from out of state (they had come from all over) lived at the old customs house at Williamstown on Hobson's Bay. It was Scotty who organized the boys to clean it and kind of took charge, showing real leadership quality. He got his mind and his act together, and his eventual selection was automatic. I was delighted that everything had gone right for him, and the end of Scotty's career on *Australia II* in 1983 was nothing short of tragic.

2. NUMBER-TWO FOR'ARD HAND, or SEWERMAN. This is one of the toughest jobs on the boat. You work up on the foredeck, sprinting around and helping with the sails. You also have to get down the hatch and get the sails out of the bilge, seven genoas weighing 80 to 120 pounds each, plus 10 spinnakers. They all have to be packed inside the boat and marked clearly. Sometimes we change them going to windward in a sea or coming downwind. We might do anything, and when we do, it's like a jungle down in the sewer through that hole. It is literally full of sails and is nothing less than a quagmire, sails oozing seawater everywhere, all different colors. The sewerman has to pack them up while the boat is pitching up and down. He ends up a perfect study in sweat and grime. When the bow man is pulling down the sail and shoving it down the hole at the same time at high speed, it's a nightmare down below. The sewerman's arms are going like pistons, hauling them down on top of him, pouring water everywhere, grabbing them anywhere he can, like fighting a huge, colored monster.

The man we selected for this job was Major Peter Costello of the Australian Army, an intelligence officer from Brisbane and one of the toughest men I have ever met. I first met the Major on board *Australia* when I arrived in Newport in 1980, and during this time he was undergoing some kind of a transformation. He had arrived for that challenge with short-back-and-sides hair and the quiet dignity of a military officer, polite and unassuming. Within a few weeks, he turned into some kind of a wild man, with a thick mane of blond hair and a huge moustache, bigger than mine and Groucho Marx's put together. He was a winch man in 1980, and even then it was clear that he tackled everything with a vengeance. They gave him the responsibility of handling all the sails, which is a very laborious job. With a couple of guys to help, he had to get all the sails down at the end of the day, get them unwrapped properly and dried out, and get them back on the boat each morning. It required a lot of work and was very, very monotonous, particularly for a chap like the Major, with little sailing background. It also required a man with a lot of substance to take on all that responsibility and not once mess it up. The Major did it perfectly, and he switched from a rather insignificant army officer to a macho man, six feet three inches tall, over 220 pounds of power and muscle. The key was that he was involved in something that fascinated him. I used to observe him from my position as port trimmer. He had no respect for Dennis Conner, largely because he did not know any better. All he wanted to do was to get out there and tear the bastards apart, crush them with sheer power. He would have led a boarding party. He hated the opposition, and he wanted to destroy them. Of course, he was naïve in even thinking we could win, but he did think that, and he never believed it was over until the final gun sounded.

Well, come 1982, I telephoned the Major as soon as I took command and invited him over. We flew him to Fremantle, and after he sailed on the boat just one day, I knew that we *had* to have him. I was not sure in what capacity we would use him, but his attitude was so positive that I did not even care if he sold ice cream on the foredeck, just as long as he was there. He was about 38 years old, married to a Rhode Islander named Sheila. When I formally invited him that night to join the crew of *Australia II,* he never even blinked. He just stuck out his hand without smiling and said, "Thanks, John. I won't let you down."

Work? That man would work like a maniac. I can remember days in a big sea when there was water all over the place, Scotty shoving the sails down the hole, the sail shuddering deafeningly as we rounded a mark. You could hear the Major down in the sewer, arms pumping, yelling at the top of his lungs, "AAARR! AAARR! AAARR!" as he hauled in the sails, fighting with them, just willing the bow man to get them in faster. I swear there were times when he could do the work of three men. No one could get those sails in faster. But everyone remembers about him most of all that he wanted to *win,* and he believed he *would* win. With his rather secretive intelligence-officer background, it did not take the crew long to nickname him the "trained killer." He was a former champion long-distance runner, and he worked hard at the weights. He never denied his nickname, and he never gave anyone cause to question how appropriate it was.

3. MASTMAN. The main task of the mastman is mechanical. He has to coordinate all the halyards around the mast. When the spinnaker goes up or down, he pulls it or releases it and also tails it off the winch. The severity of these tasks depends on who is hauling back the rope. In our case it was the Major, hauling away like a maniac—"AAAARR! AAAARR! AAAAARRR!"—driving the mastman crazy with the speed the rope was flying back, a literal blurr of flying Kevlar fiber, as though 10 men were grabbing rather than just the Major.

The man we chose to be our mastman was Phil Smidmore, a 30-year-old sailor with a civil engineering degree that he has never used, because he has spent a lifetime messing about in boats, finally working as a painter at a yacht club on lovely Pittwater, north of Sydney. All his life Phil has loved boats and has been involved in winning 5.5-meter world championships twice. He also crewed on an Etchells 22 in the 1982 World Championships and finished third. He was in the 1980 crew on *Australia*. He answers to the nickname "Ya," because in the middle of a race, no matter what the circumstances—I can be yelling instructions at him, Hughey can be shouting something to him—he just keeps replying, "Ya," "Ya," "Ya," to everything. He never speeds up, no matter how great the pressure. He just keeps working away at the same speed, but he has lots of natural ability and lots of experience, and he will not let you down. Even when the Major is positively hurling lines at him, old Ya just keeps rolling along, getting it done, tidily, efficiently, always at the same pace, never messing it up. He has almost no competitive instincts, and the word *faster* is to him a completely foreign expression. He has one speed, and that's it. Also, he is not a great physical presence, being built more or less on the lines of a full-grown turnip, with powerful tree-trunk legs, huge wide feet, and a slim muscular back. At the time, he had a devastatingly pretty girl friend, Valerie, to whom he is now married.

Alan Bond never had the slightest idea why Ya was in the crew at all. He was always saying, "He's not big enough, not tough enough, not sharp enough." What he did not say was that Ya was one of the very few world-class yachtsmen we had available. As I have mentioned, you can't have 10 gorillas, and in Ya we had a man who was a specialist in sensing the wind, like my grandpa, Bant Cull. He was a very canny tactical observer, and on occasions where the solids hit the fan, Ya could be invaluable. As we raced the boat, he kept making key observations, very steadily, very coldly. No panic. No hurry. Just cold, sure facts. Ya, for instance, would *never* have been rattled and capsized as I did six years before in Montreal. In a critical situation, he could see the wind on the water, the ripples and what they meant. That gift is God-given, and not many people have it. Most crew members can give a helmsman good feedback when the pressure is off, but when it is on, there are very few people who can step back from the action and demonstrate a sense of what is important, updating the tactician all of the time. Ya, under stress, could just stand there watching, steadily calling out a windshift and what it was doing, which way it was veering 100 yards ahead, or 200 yards, or half a mile up the track. These were the careful, skilled observations of the lifelong racing sailor, projecting thoughtfully the angles of the yachts way out in front, watching them as if they were weathercocks, preparing for the changes. "New breeze coming, Hughey," he would call, while the rest of the boat was bordering on frenzy. "But it still looks a little stronger to the left. We're doing the right thing. Stay right where you are. It might fade a little in a few moments. This is just a gust. We're right, Hughey. Stay as we are."

There are so few men who can see the wind on the water, with all its subtleties and patterns. Ya had that gift, and it was a gift that would be brought into devastating focus the following year in Newport in a certain fifth-leg battle in which the fate of the America's Cup was hanging in the balance.

4. PORT WINCH MAN. This is one of the real power positions on the boat. Very broadly, it requires massive strength, brilliant coordination of limbs and muscle, and the stamina of a bull elephant. How do you pick such men? The traditional way is to find the biggest tree in the jungle and get a couple of bulldozers to shake it until the gorillas start to topple out of the top branches. The last two down would be my boys for *Australia II*. That is an exaggeration, but strength is what you need down there in the engine room. Our starboard winch man was John Longley, who was also our shore-based manager and a former schoolteacher from Perth, veteran of the previous three America's Cups. He is a big (six feet four inches), powerful man of 220 pounds—not as big as his brother, who is six feet eight inches. In 1983, John was second in command to Warren Jones, working in the administration for two years. He knows a great deal about the mechanics of a 12-Meter. He also can be a bit overbearing and tends to be rather zealous about organizing people. However, with 10 years of America's Cup racing behind him, John was invaluable, indeed irreplaceable.

At first he found it very difficult to concentrate on his two jobs, one as shore-based manager and the other as a grinder on the boat. He has enormous experience, having sailed in four Admiral's Cups and two Congressional Cups in the U.S. But it is almost impossible to do two jobs, one on land and one at sea, however much experience you have. Once he got used to the idea of making the boat his absolute priority, he did a very, very consistent job. He has a tendency to rush about and try to do too many things, rather than just stick to his own area. And while I thought at times that he should not be quite so busy, there were times when I thanked God for him, this huge bull of a man who seemed so often to dominate the lower deck of *Australia II*. In an unexpected crisis, they don't come much better than John—or "Chink," as he was known because of his narrow eyes. If something awful happened very suddenly, something that took everyone by surprise, I would still be shouting, "What's going on down there?" when Chink was already at the point of the trouble, snapping out instructions, pointing his finger, telling people precisely what to do—the most experienced 12-Meter man in Australia, sorting things out with immense authority. There was nothing, not one inch of a 12-Meter, that Chink Longley did not know intimately. He used to be a sewerman, but he had a couple of shaky knees, so he had to give that up. But he was still as strong as the Major, and he was just as much of a tower of strength. His very involvement in the winch-grinding was an inspiration, because he showed us exactly how it should be done, what precise timing was required, and how perfect winch-grinding can unload the problems of everyone else. He made winch-grinding an art form, and he also stifled potential problems because he kept his eyes and ears open all of the time. To have this experience in the center of the boat was invaluable.

Chink went from strength to strength, eventually taking over the middle of the boat with such a rod of iron that we all ended up calling him "The Führer"—in the most affectionate possible way, of course.

5/6. STARBOARD WINCH GRINDER. We had two very powerful men vying for this position through 50 races in Newport. One was Will Ballieu, an Olympic rower in 1972, who was not short of money and had not, to my knowledge, spent much time as a member of the Australian work force. He was six feet five inches tall and was a great team-spirit man. His rival was 36-year-old Brian Richardson, who had the incredible record of 14 King's Cups for rowing in Australia, and in fact stroked the Aussie eight in the Moscow Olympic Games (the rowers did not join the boycott). He is probably the best rowing coach in Australia, another huge man and very fit, with a big moustache. The selection was pretty much determined by the flip of a coin—they were both very good and worked so hard for so long. But we chose Will because of his terrific involvement with team spirit. Brian Richardson was devastated when we selected Will for the final seven races. But fate swung around for him. Poor Will had an infected knee in Newport two days before the America's Cup, and he was rushed to the hospital, where it took two liters of penicillin to save his life. It was just one of those freak things, but the doctors said 10 years earlier, he would have died. It was all caused by a scratch on his kneecap and the entry into the wound of some tiny germ or virus from his foul-weather gear. Will, of course, could not recover in such a short time, and we recalled Brian Richardson (who answered to the name "Splash" because he once fell overboard). Splash, by the way, was about six feet wide as well as tall, and he thought he could outgrind any man in the world. But he couldn't outgrind Longley, and he would not have outground the Major, either. Just to be included in a league with those two is nothing but an honor, and it was fun to sail with Splash, this former Melbourne grammar school math teacher. When the going got tough, this massive athlete enjoyed perhaps his finest hours, and he did Australia proud all the way.

7. STARBOARD TRIMMER. This is a job that requires a man to stand in a deep hole, or pit, and trim or adjust the headsail. He needs very fast arm action to tail the ropes off the winches, because if he does not keep up with the mess of line, it gets wound around the genoa drum and causes what we call "a bunch of grapes on the drum." You have to be very fast in this position. The man we selected for this job was Kenny Judge, from Perth. He is a lawyer and a senior executive with the Bond Corporation. Greatly respected by Bondy, he is a man with an extremely high I.Q. He tends to be a little abrasive with the crew, probably because of some impatience, which so often goes with high intelligence in a young person. Kenny was 27 and answers to the nickname "Scoop," because he was so well advanced in local knowledge, particularly that of a slightly scandalous nature. He had been in two previous America's Cups, in 1974 and 1977, but was not an expert technical sailor, although he also sailed in two Congressional Cups. He started off competing for this position against the Sydney 18-footer champion Robbie Brown, but in the end Scoop won it overwhelmingly. Robbie was very good when everything was going well, but in a crisis, Scoop was the man. He is very fast in everything he does, and especially fast on his feet. He thinks on his feet, the commodity I value most in a tailer. When something went wrong down there with those sail sheets, Scoop would always come through with clear, cool, and calculated observations, while others would be dithering, shaking on the grinder handles, kneecaps knocking. He would say suddenly, very clearly, "We shouldn't change now. That would be making a mistake. In my opinion, we should hold on to it." He is like a block of ice when the going gets tough, and the tougher it got, the better Scoop was. And he knew it and loved it. He loved the atmosphere, and the rush of adrenaline in the heat of battle made him grow.

Scoop's nickname was not the only thing that gave him a close affinity with the press. He always found his way into the forefront of photographs. No matter who was being pictured—Bondy, Warren, Ben, Hughey, or me—you would usually find Scoop right in the middle. He used to love to get behind the wheel of *Australia II,* and he did so some days when we were being towed out to the racecourse behind *Black Swan.* The rest of us, who had been up since all hours, would dive below and snatch some sleep on the sails. Scoop would be up there at the helm, his blond hair flying, holding *Australia II* hard on a course behind the motorboat, his thoughts perhaps far away on some distant America's Cup when he may yet be in charge. His bright eyes were darting around at spectator boats—the boys always said he was watching for photographers from *Life* magazine or *Newsweek* to bring into sharp public focus, once and for all, his dream of glory.

Please do not misunderstand me. All of these observations are based on the kind of interplay you get in a boat crew. Scoop was a top-class member of our crew, and he was also one of our very few avowed winners. He honestly believed he was the world's best at what he did, and I would not dispute that. He also believed implicitly that we as a group had the capacity to destroy the Americans, and, for that alone, young Scoop was irreplaceable.

8. PORT TRIMMER. This is a position in which you have to behave yourself, because in this case the skipper knows a bit about it. We selected Skip Lissiman, a 26-year-old sails adviser from Perth who was also on the 1980 America's Cup challenge and now works full time for Alan Bond. Skip is the professional type of sailor, not unlike Ya in his approach. He is not an Olympic-class sailor, and he cannot see the wind like Ya, but he is good and solid in a crisis, always knowing what to do. Skip is not as quick to jump into the breach as his opposite number, the fleet-footed Scoop, but then neither is anyone else. Skippy has vast ocean-racing experience— twice sailing in the Admiral's Cup plus a Whitbread round-the-world series—but his competitive fires are medium at best. He never lets you down, but he just goes along cheerfully, a totally accomplished happy-go-lucky professional amid a lot of talent and a lot of emotion. He has a perfect physical build for tailing the lines—long arms, short trunk, and big shoulders, the classic 12-Meter physique. You do not want to be standing too high in the boat when you're tailing, and you need very fast arm action.

Skippy was almost obscure, because he never missed a beat, and I do not once recall his getting into trouble with overruns. When things get out of hand in this area, it causes an instant and awful mess, with the overrun rope everywhere and totally out of control and a bunch of grapes whirling around on the genoa drum and people shouting and screaming with anger and frustration. Skip Lissiman *never* let that happen, and I will remember him as one of the quiet heroes of that Australian crew—always positive, solid, and reliable. He was a brilliant example of the person who is taken for granted, the type of chap you would never miss until he was gone and there were lines all over the place and chaos on the winches. He is a very unassuming guy—with the kind of confidence you might expect from a man who sailed round the world in the biggest international race of this type—he was a mainstay in that crew; and they won it.

9. SAIL-TRIMMER: Robbie Brown, 28-year-old Sydney electrical design engineer, one of the three sail trimmers we would take. Will ultimately go against Scoop for a place in the final crew to face the Americans. But I will use all three as we progress through the Trials. Robbie is an 18-foot skiff skipper and has competed in the Admiral's Cup. He sailed on board *Australia I* in the 1980 America's Cup and has a special talent in assessing what the wind is doing right now, and what it is going to do in the forseeable future. I am always slightly concerned that he is not quite powerful enough in his upper torso and that his arms may not accelerate fast enough. But I like Robbie enormously and he has a tremendous feeling for team spirit. Should he not make the final crew he will be a vital and integral part of this team. He is a tireless worker and excellent for morale, cheerful and determined. There are other places where an uncanny ability to spot the wind, like Robbie's, can be put to use. But right at this moment I am not at liberty to discuss them.

10. MAINSHEET HAND. Every 12-Meter skipper has found it a major problem to fill this position in a challenge for the America's Cup. It is absolutely critical, and the man who does it perfectly is very rare indeed, because he has to be a super world-class sailor, blessed not only with the physical strength to work his very powerful winch, but also with great sensitivity for boatspeed and trimming of sails. He also has to be extremely smart, for he will spend much of his time staring at the computer, talking to me directly, trying to correlate what he can see in the sail shape to coincide with what I can feel beneath the wheel as the boat drives forward. He must control the setting of the mainsail, the major driving force of the boat, and he must also help coordinate the overall trim of the boat. Not surprisingly, he occupies the center position aboard the yacht, supervising the tuning, trying to maximize boatspeed, working on the twist of the sail, judging how hard the sail is being pulled in, assessing the curvature of the main, sometimes changing it, molding up new shapes according to change in wind velocity and tactical positioning of the boat.

Our choice for this job was only 24, a shipwright by trade, born to the sea, and his name was Colin Beashel. He had been national Laser champion in 1980 and the world's 5.5-meter champion in 1981. Beasho grew into one of the shining stars of the entire America's Cup—at the end of which I believe he was the best mainsheet hand Australia had ever had. He and I could work almost with telepathy. If the boat slipped out of balance, it was Beasho who would have to change the shape of the mainsail. I'd call out to him, "Flatten the mainsail!" or, "Let's deepen it up!" But by the time I uttered the words, Beasho was almost always in action, already making the adjustments, because he could feel us faltering at precisely the same time I could. Our thought waves were locked together in that desperate, intense struggle for supremacy out there on Rhode Island Sound. His instinct for the boat was nearly uncanny. Sometimes I would just feel a suggestion of speed loss, a tiny fraction of a knot, and I'd glance up and Beasho would be subtly changing the gears, as we say, perhaps letting the main out a half inch, his eyes riveted on his controls, a truly formidable study in concentration.

Beasho's father is Kenny Beashel, our chief maintenance man, and a sailor so experienced that he was of folkloric proportions in Australia. Colin works for his father on their marina along the beautiful shores of Elvina Bay in the yachting area of Pittwater, north of Sydney. Kenny himself is one of the great skippers of winning 16-foot skiffs. Because of Kenny's major job and his son's seniority, there were times when *Australia II* seemed to be engulfed by cries of "Beasho! Have you got a minute?" They both had the same nickname, and they were both so busy at the dock that sometimes it was very nearly chaos—Beasho this and Beasho that for hours on end. On one occasion, an American reporter walked up to the Major and asked, with great seriousness, "What exactly is a Beasho?" Well, this was too much for Peter. Trying to look thoughtful, he explained, "Well, it is just a very strange little animal that breeds back in Elvina Bay in Pittwater." "Wow," the reporter replied in his American drawl. "No kidding?" "Yes," Peter added ponderously, "we occasionally get one on the boat. They are strange little creatures, buglike in appearance. And you have to watch it, because they can be a bit bad-tempered." Eventually the reporter wandered off, probably still imagining a major Beasho hunt taking place below decks on *Australia II,* the crew armed with brooms and spray cans. We could hardly wait for the headline "Beasho Plague Hits Aussie Wonderboat—Crew Alert."

In all seriousness, we would have been in a spot of trouble without those Beashos from Elvina Bay—Kenny to keep us from falling apart, Colin to keep us going at top speed. It is difficult to find words to express my personal gratitude to them both.

11. NAVIGATOR. This is the most technical position on the boat, because modern navigation is pure computer analysis. We don't use the stars much anymore. We have that intricate, space-age guide for sailors known as Loran—which calculates perfectly where you are, as long as you have programmed it correctly. This is precision to a degree followed by Air Force jet fighter pilots and astronaut module commanders. Split seconds and small distances. The navigator has to interpret that computer with enormous skill. He must be able to tell us exactly where we are, how far it is to the layline, how far to the marker, which we often cannot see in the mist ahead. He has to tell us the compass bearing to the layline, and how long it should take to get there. He has to keep us updated at all times. He also has to produce computations of what sails we should be using. And all this has to be refined from thousands and thousands of hours of testing that he has done before we actually arrive on the starting line against the Americans. He has to be an information cipher system capable of handling the most sophisticated computer systems and plotting us around marks and telling us the quickest way to get to them. He also must be our electronics fix-it man.

Our man in that critical spot on *Australia II* was 27-year-old Grant Simmer, an engineer from Sydney, the dual Australian Lightweight Sharpie Champion. Grant was known variously as "Mad Dog," "Mumbles," or "Mullet," depending on whether he was bursting with fury, talking to himself under fierce concentration, or still moaning about the "bastards" who left a dead mullet in his sailboat and practically caused him to have the beach fumigated. A bit of a character is Mad Dog Simmer.

He first became involved with us when Alan Bond and I took him to England to sail as trimmer on *Apollo V* in the 1981 Admiral's Cup. I was very impressed with him right away, for his extensive experience and his natural feel for racing a sailboat. Long before that regatta was over, I was pretty sure that we would take Grant to Newport as a trimmer on the future *Australia II*. However, Bondy and I were already tackling the problem of who would take the navigator's spot. Neither of us really believed that we knew anyone who would be good enough. Bondy had already talked about approaching Qantas Airlines to see if they had a pilot or airline navigator we might be able to lease for a couple of years. I think Bondy said something a bit less subtle. Something like, "D'you think if we bought one of those 747s from Qantas it would come with a decent navigator we could use?"

Anyway, I must admit that at this time the navigational problem seemed of only mild concern then, and not yet a screaming priority. However, Bondy evidently was a bit more concerned about it than I thought, because he was creeping up on the subject in a rather stealthy manner. He spent a lot of time talking to Grant, and one day he came up to me and said, "John, I think I've found our navigator. Grant Simmer. If you ask me, he's a wizard with that computer. He wants to have a go, and I think we should let him try." So that Admiral's Cup was not a bad trip to Europe for Bondy. Not only did he get himself a boat that looked like a rocketship, which he loved, but he also, with a stroke of pure genius, got himself a very, very clever young man to point it in the right direction.

12. TACTICIAN. The moment the gun goes, this man is my eyes and my ears, leaving me free to concentrate on urging the maximum speed out of the boat without having to look all over the place to see what else is going on and which way we should go. For the long hours of an America's Cup race, he must be continually sizing up the tactical situation, the permutations and the combinations of the two boats, and assessing what we should do. He must keep me apprised of everything, filtering for me the information being fed back to us from the crew. The tactician is the last link in the chain of command. It is to him that I will ultimately listen, and it is also his job to see that I am not swamped with information. His job as a filter is extremely important. The tactician stands right next to me throughout the entire race. Tacticians are hard to come by, and world-class ones are nearly impossible to find in a community as small as Australia. The best man in the country was not going to be available, so instead I had been attempting to train Peter Gilmore for the job. Bondy was adamant that Peter would not make it because of his lack of experience, and, in the end, Peter decided to go for an Olympic place in the Soling Class. When he left our campaign, a potential gap turned into a very large one. So without much hope, we decided to approach the outstanding tactician in Australia, the tall, unsmiling head of Sobstad Sails in Sydney, a man with five Admiral's Cup campaigns to his credit, the crack ocean-racing veteran Hughey Treharne. Hughey was the tactician who nearly nine years earlier had been fired by Bondy from *Southern Cross* and had been replaced by the former skipper, John Cuneo, in the middle of the America's Cup challenge against *Courageous*. Well, that was a long time ago, and Hughey, who was now married with two children, said he would give a lot of thought to our new offer. He took a long time to make up his mind, but finally he agreed to join us, more or less at the 11th hour, just before we left for the U.S. I believe he had turned down an offer to join the *Challenge 12* syndicate, and I was delighted that he had. Hughey is a

very cool customer, a man of few words and deep thoughts. He has raced in Congressional Cups and various world championships. He also knows a great deal about match racing. Technically he is excellent, one of the very best sailors in the country. He and I have often been in competition, both as sailmakers and as rivals in yacht races. I had known for years that he is very, very good, and he proved to be a major asset.

It took us a while to get our relationship exactly right, but this is not surprising, because the helmsman/tactician partnership is a very subtle balance in communication. We worked very hard, and together we decided that I should take charge of the prestarting, with the luxury of the best tactician in the country right beside me for a second opinion. Generally speaking, I would take Hughey's advice in any tense situation that required a lot of action on my part. Only if our performance was deteriorating would I check out the situation for myself. Hughey understood everything perfectly, and our relationship became superb. We didn't quarrel once. I regarded this first-class international yachtsman as a vital member of the team, and I will always remember his contribution with the greatest appreciation. Hughey, I think, appreciated sailing with a skipper who appeared to understand the rudiments of the job we were supposed to be doing.

In the middle of the America's Cup trials, Hughey was under contract for a few days to go to England to sail in the Admiral's Cup. Apparently he had become so used to sailing next to me that he found the guy in the Isle of Wight less than first class, and he started yelling and screaming with frustration. He was practically asked to leave, since he apparently could no longer cope with that level of incompetence. He might be a bit on the quiet side, but Hughey is not one to suffer fools gladly. If he had a fault, it was only that Hughey was slightly inclined to get upset and absorbed in the anger of the moment. He sometimes had difficulty stepping back and staying as cool as he normally is. But he and I developed a first-class comprehension. Hughey, who joined the team merely as an acquaintance of mine, is now, I hope, a lifelong friend. It was a privilege to have sailed with him.

So there you have them. Twelve good men and true, the men from the land Down Under, bound for Newport. Man for man, we would not ultimately measure up to the crew of *Liberty* in pure credentials. They had about six world champions on their boat, while we were essentially a bunch of Aussies trying to give it a go, mate. I thought we had a very good close feeling right from the start. The only trouble was that on the day we left for the United States, I felt that only four of them believed deep in their souls that we could and would beat the Americans.

However, there was a fifth man among the optimists whose belief in our efforts, and in particular in mine, was about 1,000 percent. According to his wife, Barbara, he has been saying since before 1980, "They will *never* win the America's Cup until they get young Johnny Bertrand to steer the boat." I know this chapter is supposed to be restricted to the men who sailed *Australia II*, but I cannot judge it complete without paying a personal tribute and offering some insight into a man who did not sail with us but was in a sense always there. His name is Kenny Beashel—my chief of maintenance, my friend, my mentor, and Colin's father.

Kenny is a legend in Australian sailing. He is a champion, his father was a champion, and his son, Colin, is a champion. He was an "old salt" before he was 30, a true son of the sea. Stories about him abound along the Australian coast. The best one occurred when he was taking part in a world championship for 18-foot skiffs in New Zealand and a thoughtless press ferry zoomed past him and swamped him in the wash. Kenny sailed up to the boat, clambered on board, whacked the skipper in the mouth, jumped back into his own boat, and continued racing. He is generally considered to be one of the best boat builders in the world. He can fix anything, any part of any boat. Also, he can make you a model of any hull you can name. He carved a model of *Australia II* for my son Lucas in his spare time. He once worked for a big boatyard in America, and when he returned to Australia, he sailed the Pacific with his family, including young Colin, in a big sailing ketch called *Salty Goose*. There is another famous story that Kenny was called into a local court to testify that a friend of his was driving a car while drunk. When asked about the specifics, Kenny replied blandly, "Well, I could not really say anything about that. I was hanging onto the roof rack at the time, and I was drunker than he was!"

Kenny is about five feet 10 inches tall, hard and wiry, and lives in a lovely waterside home on a peninsula that can be approached only by water. He always calls me "Johnny" and always believed, to the bottom of his gigantic heart, that we would beat the Americans.

If I had to name the one man I could have sailing next to me if I ever ran into serious trouble in any boat on any sea in the world, I would say without hesitation, "Give me Kenny Beashel." One day I will send my sons to spend a year working with him at his marina on the Upper Pittwater, just so that they too may learn about the important things in life—about the sun, the winds, the oceans, and the tides; about the moon and the stars and navigation; how to use a knife, a hammer, a screwdriver, and a saw; and perhaps how to race sailing boats, how to catch a fish and cook it, how to fix an engine and climb a mast; how to tie a bowline and a reef and a clove hitch. After that, they may disperse to become poets if they wish, or historians or salesmen or bankers. But one year with Kenny Beashel will give them something available to so few in a modern computerized world. And it is in that high regard that I hold the man we chose to prevent *Australia II* from falling apart when battle commenced.

9

Psychological Warfare

Stress conditions beyond normal limits—in the "Red Zone," with grinders operating in the 180- to 200-heartbeat region—must be experienced, and tolerated. The aim is to achieve inner confidence under all race conditions.

"Gentlemen," I said, "you are now part of the *Australia II* team to go to the 1983 America's Cup. When you arrive in Newport you will feel the powerful, all-encompassing presence of the very confident Americans, which may tempt each one of you to feel inferior. I would just like to say that, as sailors and Australians, we will be superior to the Americans in all positions, on a strict man-on-man basis."

I do not recall the precise date when I first made this point, which is just as well, for it was probably the biggest single lie I have ever told. It did, I suppose, possess the saving grace of being a delicate, political white lie, uttered in the public interest. But it was nothing short of a full-scale, southern-fried whopper. And I shall be proud of it for the rest of my life.

Because at that moment, this bunch of Aussies—some of them uncertain, some of them apprehensive—began their mental buildup for Newport. I supposed it reached some kind of a peak immediately after we walloped *Victory '83* in the elimination final. Members of my crew—inspired, I suspect, by Major Peter Costello of the Australian Army—had our boat towed surreptitiously around to the *Liberty* dock, where her entire crew was working away on board. Stopping *Australia II* about six feet away, they turned up our battle hymn, "Down Under," to full volume and stood on our foredeck, chanting loudly, fingers pointing, feet stamping, eyes gleaming: "YOU'RE NEXT! YOU'RE NEXT! YOU'RE NEXT!"

That is known as confidence, massive confidence, and neither I nor any Australian, nor certainly any American, had *ever* seen anything like that from a foreign invader. But then, of course, we were not your regular challenger. We were the best there had ever been, and by then every one of my boys knew it. Arrogance, thy name is *Australia II*.

It had, however, been a long road and one not founded on hollow promises. It took months and months of training, hard mental training, to prepare each man psychologically for the onslaught on his psyche that he would experience in the U.S.A. I did not feel terribly old, but with this crew I was a seasoned, battle-hardened veteran. Yet, I did not have a single Olympic yachtsman with me. And we were off to face the inevitable boatload of them in America. In the absence of stars, there was but one commodity we could develop, and that was team spirit. In every walk of life, a tightly grouped, determined, well-trained team will so often overcome pure genius. All they need is an explicit belief that they can fight and win, that they can overcome opposing cleverness with unshakable determination, tireless work, and the desire to back each other, to cover each other's mistakes, and ultimately to triumph through sheer sense of communal purpose.

I decided to start with the word *democracy*. *Australia II* would be a completely democratic environment. Every member of the crew mattered, and I must say I stole from Dennis Conner the idea that had been implanted in my mind ever since I sailed with him in the southern waters beyond Florida in 1978. I refer to his very clever method of involving everyone, of suddenly asking the port winch grinder what he thought of the shape of the jib, of shouting to the starboard trimmer about the windshifts, of asking key questions of people who were not reasonably qualified to know the answer and who were operating in an entirely separate area. The answers were irrelevant, but it made people *feel* great. Above all, it made them think and it made them keep thinking all of the time. And 10 people who are racking their brains together are likely to be a lot more useful than three.

I had worked out in a massive graph that 80 percent of my mistakes occurred in the middle 90 minutes of a major regatta. My pattern seemed to be that my concentration went soft during that period. I started with a bang and finished like a tiger, but in those midrace mental doldrums I was going to need all the help I could get. The biggest shock a helmsman can receive is to be yelled at suddenly by a crew member who is not supposed to be yelling. "Come on, Bertrand. Wake up and sail this fucking boat!" It provides a wicked shock to the system, particularly to one's pride. But it jerks you wide awake, to refocus with your senses racing. A lot of people don't like it. For instance, Benny was not mad about my sitting up forward and snapping back my thoughts to them in the 1980 America's Cup. But I did it to him and I *wanted* people to do it to me. I suppose I do not feel threatened by this kind of input. I also believe it has fantastic value. I made the crew practice it. Sometimes I would take them out and we would have a competition—the first one who spoke, said anything at all, would have to buy beer all around when we got home. This was merely disciplinary, first to exemplify to the crew that only a few words are required to communicate, and second to stamp out superfluous remarks. Thereafter I tried to train everyone to pay attention to every detail, and I organized a chain reaction of feedback. I told them they *must say what's on their minds.* The men near the foredeck would speak through the vastly experienced Ya, the rest through Hughey, both filtering the vital information to me. Silence means tension, and that's no good. I must have told the crew a thousand times: "When we come off the starting line, I want this boat as loose as a goose. I want feedback, opinions, everyone tuned in, making observations, helping in every way—everyone totally involved, contributing. Everyone is crucial to this effort."

I told them about 1974, when people froze with emotion on the starting line, when we started the race with trim that was way off, when the crew took a third of the race just to loosen up and get a feel for boatspeed. I told them about all the myths about Dennis Conner and all this garbage about the Americans being unbeatable. I told them about 1980, when I had watched an Australian crew fold up like puppy dogs. I told them I *would not* let that happen. I told them I would not allow our boat to go quiet, frightened by our opponents, scared into insignificance.

In the very early days, I used to yell questions for the first half hour, demanding that they tell me their thoughts. In time, it would become second nature to be aware, not to be nervous, to communicate to Hughey and me anything that seemed significant. This type of communication therapy has major advantages. It gives us the combined strength of 11 brains rather than one and it also breeds a powerful camaraderie, somehow making each person feel that it was up to him, that to fail would be to let everyone else down. I've seen skippers try to force out this feeling by bullying, but you cannot do it that way. Team spirit is a one-way street. It evolves only when people *want* to fight for each other.

Very soon after the initial crew selection, I ran into a problem that in my view is uniquely Australian, and it is a problem that may never have existed in America. It is known, colloquially, in Aussie sports circles as "the Australian knocker image." It is a national, ingrained state of mind that tells us that we are a remote nation, far from the rest of the world, far from sophisticated big cities, and that we are not able to play in the big league. It is a state of mind which we have generated over many years and one which we specialize in perpetuating among ourselves. Sometimes it is called the "Tall Poppy Syndrome"—meaning that when one poppy in a field grows much taller than the rest there is a mad compulsion by everyone to cut it back down to size. Australians are afraid of big winners, and we attack them with humor at first, dry humor, almost as if proving that we don't respect the person anymore just because he has earned some distinction. "Basically, mate, you're just the same as me, same as you always were. . . ." I think much of this problem stems from our English ancestors, and it is damaging to a major sportsman. People who make it financially in Australia are sometimes considered to be villains or crooks, or at least on the verge of being so. In contrast, people who make it big in America usually are widely admired and considered to be role models.

The Australian knocker image causes us, both as a nation and as individuals, to underestimate our own self-worth. It is almost anti-Australian to perceive yourself as a winner, and much of the fault for this lies in our schooling system, where they seem to find it impossible to inject wholesome self-pride into the kids. They emerge lacking confidence, the absolute opposite of American children, who are told almost from birth that they are winners, almost a master race. In some ways this makes Americans a bit too brash for some people, but it gives them a major advantage in international sport, which is why they habitually run faster, jump higher, throw further, punch harder, play tennis better, play golf better, and generally get down to winning titles, which is what they are good at.

As I took over the psychological training of a bunch of Aussies, I could not tolerate this situation. I could not turn up in Newport with a bunch of shrinking violets. Yet I could not overnight cause them all to decide they believed in themselves, so I pursued a course of psychological training that would bring them, through a series of winning concepts, to the obdurate truth that they were as good as, if not better than, their American opponents. They needed to learn arrogance, to strut their stuff before the world—not necessarily in a bombastic way, but with the pure inner confidence of men who knew they would win.

My basic message was: "We are going to attain a standard that will put us 20 years ahead of our time. We all know that standards will change and athletic endeavors will improve during the coming years, but we are going to cut down those years and sail like that *now*. We are going to sail *Australia II* as no 12-Meter has ever been sailed. We are going to get better and better, we are going to open up new horizons and new levels of finesse, until even the Americans are going to have a hard time being competitive with us. We are going to turn this thing around. We are going to make them intimidated by us."

A neighbor of mine, at home in Melbourne, is Herb Elliott, who is considered by many experts to be the greatest miler and 1500-meter runner the world has ever seen. He once told me that in his buildup to the Olympic Games he was looking at a world 1500-meter record in 1958 of around three minutes 37 seconds. Herb decided he would run 1500 meters in a time of three minutes 30 seconds, seven seconds less than the existing record, thus obliterating any semblance of the old standards of running the distance. In fact, Herb used to train by running for exactly three minutes and 30 seconds, pulling up at this point on the stopwatch some 50 or 100 yards short of the finishing line. Of course, he never quite got there, but he got nearer and nearer, and his stupendous efforts brought smiles of joy to the face of his coach, Percy Cerruty, who was also a man at least a decade ahead of his time. Together they ignored everything that had ever been done in running the mile or the metric mile. They set standards of their own that were hitherto undreamed of. Even today, the miling records get chipped away by tenths of seconds, rarely more.

Well, back in 1958 Herb Elliott set off to achieve what I wanted for *Australia II* in 1983. To take the mile time first, the world record stood at three minutes 57.2 seconds by Derek Ibbotson of Yorkshire, England, set in 1957. The following year, Herb Elliott ran it in three minutes 54.5 seconds, bringing a new dimension to world miling.

In the Olympic Games, Herb came to the final of the 1500-meter event in 1960 with his own world record standing at three minutes 36 seconds—nearly five seconds faster than it had been four years previously. In Rome, everything changed—Herb Elliott won it in the new world record time of three minutes 35.6 seconds. And it should be remembered that this time was over three seconds faster than John Walker achieved winning his Gold Medal in Montreal 16 years later; and nearly three seconds faster than Sebastian Coe clocked winning his Gold Medal in Moscow 20 years later. Herb Elliott, who won 44 consecutive mile or 1500-meter races between 1954 and 1960, nevertheless retired disappointed. "I never got the full seven seconds knocked off the time, did I," he says wryly. And that philosophy is precisely the same as that which I wanted to instill into the Australian crew—let us seek the level of perfection they will have in the year 2000. Let us forget what will be good enough now, let's go for it, big. Let us generate a driving force to go better and better, as no Australian crew ever has.

We also talked about the most accomplished yacht racer of all time, the great Dane, Paul Elvstrom, who has inspired me since I was a little boy. Paul won four consecutive Olympic Gold Medals in the Fire Fly and Finn Classes—London in 1948, Helsinki in 1952, Melbourne in 1956, Rome in 1960. Four bullets, as we say. Dominant? He was a sensation. In Helsinki he won three of the first four races and in this seven-race series he was so far in front he never even had to go out and race on the last day. But he sailed anyway, and won again, to take the gold by nearly 3,000 points. Like Herb, he was about 20 years ahead of his time. When everyone was sitting on the side of their boats, Paul was out in his hiking straps, full hiking all on his own. When everyone else caught up and they were all in the full hiking position, Paul was horizontal-hiking. He was a step ahead of everyone because he did not have the normal mental limitations and the normal boundaries of what was perceived to be common practice. When he was campaigning he had no artificial horizons to limit himself. He was almost a replica of my other major psychological assistant—Jonathan Livingston Seagull, a very fast bird who learned to dispel imaginary horizons.

I told the crew of *Australia II* about Jonathan Livingston Seagull, impressing upon them the lesson Jonathan has for us all—that there are no limits if we will only seek our perfection, achieving like the seagull various progressive levels of excellence. I remembered having read the book a few years before, how Jonathan had crashed badly coming out of a vertical dive at 70 m.p.h., then again, into the seas at 90 m.p.h. But he kept going, turning away from the voices which told him what seagulls are supposed to do, and what they are not supposed to do—the voice that said inside him, "I am a seagull. I am limited by my nature. I must forget this foolishness. I must fly home to the flock and be content as I am, as a poor limited seagull."

I never forgot the day Jonathan breached new barriers—the first full night dive ever attempted by his day-flying species, the moment when he eased out of his dive at 140 m.p.h. and shot above the waves, "a gray cannonball under the moon." And then there was the day Jonathan hit 214 m.p.h. on a vertical dive from 5,000 feet with his wings tucked in like those of a falcon—how he progressed from one plateau of excellence to another until finally he became so darned good he was able to fly in his mind. It is a lovely little book, very simply and very beautifully written. It is also very inspiring to those of us with the will and the receptiveness to listen and absorb the lessons, particularly that touching moment about halfway through the book when he met a new group of gulls. "Here were gulls who thought as he thought. For each of them, the most important thing in living was to reach out and touch perfection in that which they most loved to do, and that was to fly. They were magnificent birds, all of them, and they spent hour after hour every day practicing flight, testing advanced aeronautics." That was the attitude that was going to win us the America's Cup, the relentless search for our own perfection—but first I had to make the boys believe in it.

As we proceeded with our training, I told them of people who inspired me, of people with attitudes and philosophies that *worked*. Finally, these seeds began to fall on fertile ground. The approach was working.

I believe very firmly that in the power of the mind lies the key to winning, as opposed to performing well and losing. As I have explained, after the Montreal Olympics, I became a keen and serious student of sports psychology, so as soon as I was appointed skipper of *Australia II*, I began to look for the right man to deal with the mental attitudes of my crew. In the latter part of 1980, I contacted a prominent Australian industrial psychologist named Joe Braysich. He sent me tapes that dealt with visualization, self-esteem, and various motivation ploys. This was very helpful. At about the same time, I looked around Melbourne for sports psychologists, because I was determined to deal properly and professionally with this most important and wildly underestimated area. Had I not just witnessed a total mental collapse of our afterguard at the very sight of the *Freedom* crew with Dennis Conner at the helm?

Eventually I met Laurie Hayden, a sports psychologist and lecturer at Melbourne State College and adviser to the Carlton Football Club. He started to introduce me to some thoughts that were further extensions of my own ideas. The basic problems we faced were: (1) in the beginning, motivation without a tangible opponent, and (2) in the later stages, stress control. In Fremantle we were entirely on our own for three or four months immediately after the launch. We would see little of Benny, who tends to grow bored when not much is going on. About every two weeks he would fly in for a couple of days just to check up on everything. If we crew members were not at that time showing great signs of winning every race by at least 20 minutes, he would fly out again, because he did not want to know about that. Since the designer whose boat we were tuning was bored, and we were involved in thousands of miles of practice sailing on our own, we needed a great deal of hard motivation. Laurie Hayden was a great help in this area. He pointed out that we needed something to hang our hats on while Newport seemed so far away, he felt that my ideas about training were 20 years ahead, and he stressed the idea of bringing the Americans down to size in our own minds. I kept telling the crew about Newport and what to expect, the overpowering image of the Americans, their boats and their professionalism. I tried to give each one of them his own vision of Newport, and each day as we went out, I would lecture them, quietly, on deck. I tried to instill in them the aggression I wanted from them, trying to make them familiar with the enemy, to give each man his own private vision of the great battleground on which he must fight. Benny, Bondy, and Warren Jones never heard these group discussions. These were private, intimate talks with the crew.

I never stopped trying to break down those myths about the Americans and their invincibility. I tried to downgrade the Americans in the eyes of the younger crew members. I said I did not care which boat they dished up against us. "They still have to get the right spinnaker up, and it may take them 12 seconds. It often does. But we are going to hoist ours in eight seconds, faster than anyone has ever hoisted a spinnaker in history. We are simply going to do everything better and faster. I can assure you all that I am personally going to beat Dennis Conner, or whomever, in Newport, and each individual in this boat is going to beat his opposite number on the American boat. You are going to be better than they are." It remained the biggest lie I have ever told, but it made these guys believe in themselves as no Australian crew had ever done before.

I remember saying to Scoop, "When we get there, I want you to look across at the starboard trimmer on the U.S. boat and I want you to *know* that you are better." This was exactly what Scoop wanted to hear. Then there was the day I said something like that to Major Peter Costello. I told him he was the best ever at what he did. That was like showing a red cape to a bull—it nearly drove him mad with pride and determination. He'd have punched a hole in the aluminum hull of the American boat with his bare fist if required.

Although this mental preparation seemed like a very logical area for us to tackle, it was not treated with quite the same urgency, or even seriousness, by our senior management. On the subject of Laurie Hayden, Alan Bond varied between lukewarm and freezing. Warren Jones had just about the same attitude, and at the time I hoped that he was not saying merely what his boss wanted to hear. What he did say was something like, "Who needs a sports psychologist? We know all that needs to be known. I've played plenty of sport. Sure, we need a physical-fitness person for the crew, but why should we have anyone screwing around with our minds? We are all tough enough ourselves. We can handle it." Of course, neither Warren nor Bondy had any idea what he was talking about in this area. Bondy once said to me, "What's this bloody character Hayden doing?"

Although Alan's smooth image was still being developed, inside he was still about as delicate as a train crash. "This guy's just excess baggage," he added.

I was quite sure that both of them were wrong. On September 28, 1982, I wrote Warren a letter pointing out that Laurie's team, the Carlton Football Club, had just won the V.F.L. Grand Final—in the inexplicable absence of the immortals of Collingwood—and I explained how they had been prepared mentally by Laurie. "Just before the Carlton players ran out," I wrote, "some of them were seen embracing each other. In other words, they were going to *war* together . . . a matter of life and death."

I also pointed out that when it comes down to the wire what really counts is the ability to perform beyond normal expectations within a high-pressure environment. "This is what Carlton achieved last week, and it is the only area that has never been properly and professionally addressed by our 12-Meter campaigns in the past." I told him that I was having a hard time selling this idea to Alan and himself, but that I considered it vital, that Laurie Hayden was interested only in doing a job, that his commitment was unbelievable, that both he (Warren) and Bondy should respect my judgment on this. "I am still concerned that you once asked me how a person like this could help me and my crew."

I tried to explain that the environment on the eve of the America's Cup final—I actually wrote, "after *Australia II* has won three races. . . ."—would be quite different from anything any of the crew had ever experienced. The tension would be extreme. I told Warren that I felt very strongly about the subject and that I wanted to start talking with Hayden on a multitude of issues concerned with operating and competing under stress.

The subject still made both Warren and Bondy nervous, so on October 12, I wrote another long memorandum to the senior management. Below are some excerpts, which I think are quite interesting in the light of what ultimately happened.

> WINNING sportsmen are *aggressive in competition*. Losers are not. Under stress, *enhanced* aggression promotes superior winch-grinding, more initiative, more eager windshift searching, more creativity in tactics, tuning, sailing the yacht. On the other hand, lack of aggression leads to poor starts, lack of fine tuning coming off the starting line, and a general "lay down and die" attitude. Ever wondered why *Courageous* in 1974 did not seem to get much farther in front of *Southern Cross* after 10 minutes of sailing? Lack of sincere inner aggression was one reason. We can cultivate this positive aggressive side in

some individuals using Hayden's help, and it is not just a "rah-rah" exercise. A lot depends on the individual and his "personality profile"—used all the time in the Olympic Games and by East Germany in particular.

STRESS INOCULATION. To set up stress conditions beyond normal limits, i.e., to operate in the "Red Zone," with grinders operating in the 180- to 200-heartbeat region. Helmsman and tactician undergoing extremely rapid decisionmaking process, which can be simulated by Hayden. Once the "Red Zone" is experienced and tolerated, when the going gets really tough and we are stretched to the limit, each member will become confident in his ability to compete successfully. The aim is to achieve inner confidence under *all* race conditions.

PROFILE MANAGEMENT. Each crew member has a personality style. It is the psychologist's aim to help each member become totally predictable when the crunch comes (the 10-minute gun), and as such, they don't do anything they are not supposed to do. We should know how all members are doing at any point in time leading up to the competition, so that recommendations can be made both to the individuals and to myself. Having someone in a position to monitor each crew member is important, and, to be frank, this has not been adequately covered in the past.

The key to motivation is that it comes from *within* the group. Extremely important that this is recognized and worked on. Assuming all our other bases are covered—yacht design, tuning, sails, boatspeed potential, physical toughness—then the final mental toughness and approach through the 45-odd races will mean the difference between winning and losing. Although every *winning* elite athlete is an amateur sports psychologist himself, to get professional outside help will be a major asset and, to be quite frank, far superior than any of us within the management can achieve. This has already been proven in other sports. We are not reinventing the wheel.

It should be stressed that Hayden plays a nonthreatening role. He is there to *help* each of the squad members and therefore increase their effectiveness for the team.

My basic aim is to put together a team of *winners*—to develop a winning team for 1983. I will be candid and say we have not been close in the past, and that's after experiencing the race atmosphere in three America's Cups. We have been too comfortable in losing. Just as we use the latest in developments and technology to design the boat, develop our sails, and sail our boat, we must use the best support in training the mind.

Gentlemen, I am deadly serious about winning the America's Cup. Nothing less will do.

JOHN BERTRAND

Although it took time and effort, I am happy to say that I was permitted my own way, but it was not without a lot of soul-searching by both Warren and Bondy. Warren even decided to conduct a little poll among the crew, which was a terrific idea. None of them knew anything about the subject—not one of them could draw on the experience of being out with the leaders in an Olympic final, neck and neck with an East German, coping with the stress, and cracking up because of a total lack of mental preparation when compared with the man from behind the Iron Curtain.

Bondy and Warren in turn developed another attitude that I could sense very clearly—Maybe we have chosen the wrong person in John Bertrand. Maybe if he needs a head shrink there's something wrong with him. Perhaps he's just not tough enough.

I understood that this very modern and slightly subversive subject might not receive a great welcome from everyone, since it is widely, and accurately, believed that the real roots of sports psychology lie in the netherworld of brainwashing. This, in turn, is a more keenly refined art, and much more eagerly practiced, in countries where the citizens traditionally are locked in to prevent them from going to live elsewhere.

For years, sports officials behind the Iron Curtain have worked very successfully on the minds of their athletes, breaking them down and then building them up to face the opposition with that cool, confident implacability we have so often seen in Soviet and East German rowing crews and track and field teams. We have also seen it in gymnastic teams from the Soviet bloc, with mere children coming out under the most unbearable Olympic pressure, before a mammoth world audience, and banging out their greatest ever performances, on demand . . . at an age when they have not yet given up sleeping with teddy bears.

These performances are not evolved from mere practice. This is something deeper, much, much deeper. These athletes have gone through a process that expels self-doubt, fear of losing, fear of going beyond your own limitations in the heat of the moment.

This is sports psychology, and this is what you are seeing when Soviet-bloc athletes arrive to compete in the company of four, five, or even six "coaches." It does not take that many people to get muscles into order. The others are there to deal with the mind. And it is these psychologists who form the bedrock of so many of those extraordinary victories achieved by the athletes of the Warsaw Pact countries in the sports arenas of the world.

During the 1970s, some Western countries did attempt to employ these "brainwashing" methods, but no one in the free world knew much about it then. And some mistakes were made that brought the process into disrepute, particularly in the United States. However, a small group of professional men persisted in the field, and it is to this rather rarefied group that Laurie Hayden belongs.

Laurie came on board at my insistence, and he did his part. His opening project was to introduce all of us to an examination perfected at the California School of Professional Psychology called the Test of Attentional and Interpersonal Style (known in the business as the TAIS Test). This is believed to be the best of its type because it increases our understanding of athlete behavior and our ability to predict performance outcome, and it provides information leading to, in the psychologist's jargon, "greater control over performance-relevant processes" (e.g., concentration and brain arousal).

In layman's terms, this 144-question test would tell us a great deal of the inner workings of the brains and self-regard of the men who would sail *Australia II*. It would determine whether men are natural leaders or followers, winners or losers. Whether they will be able to cope easily with a brand-new environment, how they will react under pressure, how much they can take, mentally and physically, without "losing it." The test examines a man's attention span and his interpersonal style, his ability to concentrate and, perhaps above all, his ability to make decisions under stress and to accept an extra workload should the occasion arise.

The test provides an insight into the moments when men might, as we say, "choke" under pressure, for psychologists are certain that this tightening up results from increasing brain arousal and an almost mysterious interaction between attentional processes and physiological arousal that prevents the athlete from regaining control.

There are a myriad of subscales in the TAIS Test which cover such critical ground as measuring a man's ability to "react to multi-environmental cues" (which broadly means keeping your bloody wits about you when things don't look all that great). The test measures a man's tendency to become distracted, overloaded, too analytical in his thinking, unable to take a sudden change of environment into consideration (i.e., getting overtaken). It measures a man's tendency to act impulsively, his energy levels, his feeling of self-confidence, his need for privacy, for expression, his need to challenge others, to express negative feelings, and in my view the most vital of all—his willingness to express support and positive feelings.

There is, of course, an ethical side to all this. You cannot go delving into a person's mind without explaining to him precisely what is happening. And naturally, some of the boys were a bit wary—particularly those who were not absolutely sure of themselves and felt that the test might be used as a final selectional tool. They feared that Laurie was somehow a hatchet man employed to search out weaknesses and get rid of them. But this was not so, nor did I ever use the test as such. It was to disclose as much as possible about each member of the crew in order that we could improve and develop our strengths, and in turn deal with our weaknesses. By the time Laurie started to work, the final squad for Newport was selected. The final two winch-grinders and the two trimmers would be selected just before the final in Newport.

The reactions of the crew themselves, at being presented with the questions, was revealing. Hughey Treharne had not yet joined us, so I will start at the back of the boat and go down the list.

Grant Simmer. He was reserved, but very keen and inquisitive, his own analytical brain being teased by this thoughtful new process. He did not ever feel threatened, so he was eager to get what he could from the test. He was one of the few who kept going back to Laurie to examine his own mind further, to try to improve all the time.

Colin Beashel. Very reserved. Colin has a naturally conservative mind. He is extremely self-confident, but this type of thing registered with him as a bit farfetched. He answered everything and listened carefully, cooperating fully, but I doubt whether any of it expanded his thinking.

Kenny Judge. Loved it. Here was an opportunity for him to find out some even more impressive things about himself. He did not *take* the TAIS Test, he dived headlong into it, wringing it dry for information, going back to Laurie, exercising that supple intelligence of his, striving to get every ounce of information that could help him get even better. He did not give a damn for his weaknesses, and he loved to hone his brain. He wanted to help, to build up his strengths, and the test showed graphically that he enjoyed a large number of tasks. Basically, Scoop would take on anything. He was *never* threatened, and he filled out his test paper in about 20 minutes flat.

Skip Lissiman. He was semireserved. First of all he had never heard of such a thing as this test, and he had never given anything of this nature a moment's consideration. He was certainly not bothered about it, and just filled it out when he had time, and to the best of my knowledge, he never gave it another thought.

Phil Smidmore. The old "Ya bird" did not know what to make of all this. He took a very, very long time to fill out the paper. About a month, as I remember. He had to work up to it, give it a lot of thought, and then fill it out slowly—he was very deliberate, very accurate, and very thoughtful.

Without breaking any confidences, I think I may say that the test revealed that Ya does not like to be given a multiple number of tasks, but he takes enormous pride in his reliability, steadfastness, and completeness.

John Longley. Chink was apprehensive, a bit defensive, because he did not want anyone discovering too much about him. In fact, Chink did not want to know about the TAIS Test, one of the main reasons being that his close colleague, Warren Jones, had been pooh-poohing the whole thing.

Brian Richardson. My mighty main winch-grinder was the most interested man in the entire crew, mainly because he was used to it. Brian had been to the Moscow Olympic Games, where he had reached the final and faced the men with steel arms and steel minds in the heat of competition. On that day he had gone head to head with the oarsmen of East Germany, the USSR, Czeckoslovakia, Bulgaria, and Hungary. He and the seven men behind him had hauled their way almost into oblivion along that desperate 2,000 meters, finishing fifth, beaten by seven seconds by the East Germans. But he knew all about the TAIS Test and its value, and he knew what it was to know and rely on your colleagues.

Major Peter Costello. Totally cooperative, though noncommittal about how much value he placed upon the test. He said very little, but I have always been sure he knew much more about this subject than he ever divulged to anyone.

I have not mentioned Robbie Brown or Will Ballieu or Scotty McAllister, because I was never aware of their reactions to the test.

Naturally, I took the test, too, and I suppose I was the most avid student. I understood that the test is not based on what someone else thinks of you—it is based on what you think of yourself, what your own personal answers reveal about you. This is of course the most reliable gauge to any person, because you always know if you are good at something. On the other hand, you know with equal certainty when you are not good at something; and then you become progressively worse because you tend to avoid it.

These tests were confidential, and I must use discretion, but not about myself. The tests indicated that I had probably the highest self-regard in the crew, and, while that may not be altogether attractive, at least it was appropriate. No one wants a doubting skipper.

It also revealed that I was often too deliberate, too cautious, too much of a perfectionist in my decisionmaking. It showed that I sometimes take too long to get the right answer. It revealed my inner worry over this, because I was so anxious to get things right, and I knew I would have to be quicker than came naturally to me. Things that should have been almost reflexive I tended to turn into a board meeting. I have always known my weakness here, and to have it spelled out for me was a tremendous help. I worked on this long and often—and, I think, successfully.

Also, I did not tend to compliment people enough on their achievements. Laurie told me what the test revealed and then added that whatever I said was keenly listened to by the crew, all of whom perceived me as highly credible and totally sincere. So he advised me to be a bit more free with my praise, and he evolved this from everyone's test, including mine. This, of course, came back to peer recognition, which is the most powerful possible psychological motivator of a team.

Laurie would tell me over and over, "Remember, John, these guys are all you have. There are no others. The only thing you can do is to make sure you get the maximum out of each one. There are problems everywhere, I know that, but you must keep reinforcing the men." All through the ensuing months, I would come in from practice, usually in some ill temper and frustrated about the performances of various members of the crew. Laurie would always say, "That figures. That's what we know we are going to get from this man. But he is all you have, so you must work within it." I will give some examples of Laurie's advice:

"John, just do not bother yourself to rush Ya, or to bombard him with three or four things to do at once. You're wasting your time and his value to you."

"You can give Scoop as many as six things at once to take care of, because he loves it."

"Be very careful with Grant, and do not be careless with words when you talk to him. He is very, very sensitive and he will dwell upon what you say to him. He respects you terribly, so make a point of talking to him, carefully. Because if you don't, you could lose him, and you would never even know it."

"The Major has a fantastically high level of aggression and willing responsiveness. Be careful not to excite him too much because he will literally do *anything* you ask for, for the cause. Do not ask him to do what he *cannot* do because he may become disillusioned. He is just super-responsive and that must not be abused. You have the power to wind him up and send him into battle. You can kill a man like that because he'll keep trying till he drops dead. Utilize him wisely."

"When you have technical problems, the Major, Skippy, and Damian have to have solutions presented to them which are simple and clear. They must have a light at the end of their respective tunnels to retain their personal levels of optimism. Never let any of these men believe that the hierarchy is in any way baffled."

"There is no need to pamper Brian Richardson in any way whatsoever: He understands the task totally, and he understands all about the mental pressure. He will not crack, and he will walk to the end of the earth for you."

I should point out that 95 percent of Laurie's working time was spent with me. He was my personal sounding board to the crew; he was the link between their state of mind and the skipper.

Another aspect of the test that emerged was my own propensity for blowing my stack from time to time, and it was Laurie Hayden who went a long way toward solving this—not the actual stack-blowing, but a method by which we could all minimize the effects. There were two people in the crew who would *never* blow their own stacks but would become icy-cool under the most formidable pressure—Beasho and Scoop. Laurie knew that I respected them both immensely—Scoop for his excellent brain and powers of instant assessment, Beasho for his God-given seamanship and calmness. These two were appointed the "Bertrand-watchers," and their responsibilities were to keep an eye on the skipper and try to spot the telltale signs of ragged nerves and irritability. They were to be ready, if possible, with the soothing remark. "Come on, John, we're going great. Keep sailing the boat. Forget about that foulup." That kind of thing.

Young Robbie Brown came up with an inspired idea also, quite early in the campaign. In one of the early trial races, I went berserk when Splash and Will were grinding the genoa instead of the spinnaker.

I let out such a string of invectives and was so furious that no one spoke at all. Scoop was doubled up with laughter and Beasho was busy keeping his head down. Anyway, that night I was a bit contrite. Actually I was very contrite, and just as we all finished dinner, Robbie came over with a circular red cardboard medal on a string. On one side was a smiling face and on the other the words "Have a Nice Day." He informed me that it was an award to be presented in perpetuity throughout the campaign to the person judged by the remainder of the crew to have been most throughly obnoxious during that day's sail. In the months, weeks, and days leading up to September 26, 1983, the medal would be awarded often to me, but on a couple of spectacular occasions to the Major for bellowing at Chink. And once to Sir James Hardy, for passing a loud and impolite message across the waters of Rhode Island Sound to the Committee of the New York Yacht Club. Generally speaking, we took great pains to conquer the symptoms of psychological breakdown and loss of control.

Laurie Hayden employed one of the most modern of all sport psychology techniques—mental visualization. The basis of this is that athletes quite often move into an advanced zone or environment, in which they have never been before. Because of the accent on youth and strength, the Olympics is filled with top competitors who have never been there before.

Likewise a challenging boat for the America's Cup. For most of my men the experience of an America's Cup challenge, and being out in front, was going to be brand new.

It's quieter in the lead. Back in second place, where we nearly always are, the environment is quite different. The noise from the fleet seems to drown out the noise from the American boat, the sounds of the water are different, the words that we hear are often depressing, the atmosphere down.

Out in front it would be different. We would hear the rare sound of a foreign bow wave right behind us, the cries and commands of the American afterguard, the new urgency in their voices that *no crew* had ever heard before. The tension on our own boat would be high, but the feeling that we had all been there before would have to be part of our psychological makeup. Laurie knew all about this, and produced a plan for the mental visualization of victory in Newport. Remember, you cannot go anywhere, if you have not first imagined yourself there. People achieve that which they have imagined themselves achieving over and over in their own minds. That which you have never even dreamed of is that which you will never attain.

Brian Richardson was the most enormous help here. He lectured us on how he and his rowing eight had prepared for the 1980 Summer Games. He told me how he was shut in a dark observation room with electrodes on his pulse, strapped to his chest and temples, his every reaction, every brain impulse being monitored, as he rowed the Olympic course against the foreign countries in his own mind. Brian would sit there alone, the Aussie stroke, poised for the start. His concentration was total as he envisioned the moment he would drop his oar into the water and heave. Down the course he would go in his mind, hauling every stroke. At around the 500-meter mark he would be gazing through his own psyche at the East Germans, breaking out in a sweat, his breath starting to come in short bursts. As he hauled away toward the line, hearing with crystal clarity the sharp cries of his own cox—"NOW . . . TWO . . . THREE . . . FOUR . . . FIVE . . ."—his chest would throb and he would feel mentally exhausted as he ripped across the winning line in his green and yellow Aussie vest, always within two seconds of their standard time. It was all in his mind, but the symptoms were real, and by the time they lined up in Moscow, Brian and his boys had been there.

This was the psychological barrier we had to tackle. And no one knew more certainly than I how critical it was. Because my boys were going to a place they had never been—to victory in the America's Cup.

Laurie and I discussed the fact that I, with no experience as skipper in Newport, must go into some really positive and powerful visualization.

And we imagined the cries of the Americans, which we expected to hear. That all too familiar "YESSIR!" "OK, you guys, stand by to take their stern." The familiar cry of the men from the U.S.A. rolling downwind from behind: "M-A-A-ST LAHN!" "OK, Aussies, we're coming to get you." All that stuff we would hear once we got into the lead. And it was all designed to expand our comfort zone to an area where none of us felt unfamiliar. Laurie taught us to go into a trance, eyes shut tightly, each imagining his own little world in the battle-worn hell of a 12-Meter in a big sea, neck and neck with the enemy.

We tackled the problem of the history of the America's Cup and its psychological effect on the crew. Let's face it, no one had been able to win it in 132 years. If we allowed ourselves, even subconsciously, to start wondering why we should win it, then we could find ourselves beaten by history before we even started. The antidote to history is logic. Laurie and I worked on this thought pattern. The past has no bearing on this series of races, not in a tangible way. None of the other challengers will be with us in Newport. Our chances of success are not in any way affected by their antics in the previous 24 challenges. We are here. It is us against them, and the only significant aspect of the history of the America's Cup is that we are about to change it in a very major sense. I told the crew, "Forget the past. Let the best team win, right now, only let's make sure it is us."

I talked to the crew about the psychological ability to back off a little and not force a decision under pressure. Because public pressure, out there in front of the world's television and press, produces a curious compulsion to make a decision, any decision, even when you may not be exactly sure what to do. It induces an outright fear of just standing there doing nothing, and, with the adrenaline pumping so hard, you might do anything, and that might be rash and foolish. If you can step back for a split second, the decision will still come very quickly, but it will not be forced and off balance. You must give your natural reflex a chance to come through, and you must be aware when you have it. If you train long enough and hard enough in a winning frame of mind, your reflex will always save you, as long as you are not too hasty.

All these winning philosophies for which we strived were designed to give the men of *Australia II* the highest possible image of themselves. In the end, we became almost arrogant. In the end, we could smell, taste, and touch that feeling of total self-control, never just giving it a shot and hoping for the best. No America's Cup crew has ever been more deadly serious than we were. Our compatibility was excellent as the months went by, and everyone enjoyed working with, and working for, that team. Sure we had our problems, like any crew, but we were far more compatible and far more tight together than any other crew in Newport in recent years.

Every night before I went to sleep, I shut myself away and lived in my own mind the feeling of being out in front, in the quiet, in the midst of the tension. And as I dreamed my separate dreams, it became easier. The power of the mind is enormous, and together we sensed ourselves making it happen. Sometimes I would finish my 15-minute-long session with my heart pounding and my pulse racing, and the others said the same thing. And Laurie always said, "Your mind can take you there, John. You may not understand what this is doing until you and the boys are finally asked the question, 'Can you beat the Americans, on this day, and win the America's Cup?'"

I was anxious to create a particular sense of pride among our crew every time we stepped aboard *Australia II*. It was important for them to feel a rising tide of pure emotional pride in themselves every time we left the dock at Newport. To help with this, we needed a special flag, and the old Aussie kangaroo, which had been rather boringly and intermittently used before, was not going to be good enough. Now Warren Jones was the instigator, and he sought professional advice from advertising men who knew about the effects of a first-class symbol. Eventually he came up with our now-legendary standard, which fluttered on high from our forestay whenever possible—the big, bouncing yellow Australian kangaroo ready for action with scarlet boxing gloves. Sometimes he fluttered just below the flag of Australia, the Blue Ensign with an embroidered pattern of white stars. He was a southpaw beneath the Southern Cross.

That flag played a significant and emotional role in our preparation. With our boxing kangaroo raised high, we looked like an outfit that was going to war, and it made us feel as if this was indeed the case. All flags have military beginnings. In the sixteenth and seventeenth centuries, they were carried in European wars as a rallying point for scattered regiments in national armies. They represented a point where tired commanders could regroup and new tactics could be deployed, and they marked the place the enemy should avoid if they knew what was good for them. I am averse to none of those sentiments, and we held our standard in much the same regard.

We also had a battle hymn, and while you would not have confused our particular musicians with the massed bands of the Grenadier Guards, you would have to admit that the Australian rock group Men at Work were capable of a bloody good noise. We adopted their song "Down Under" from their rock album *Business as Usual* as our signature tune. It sounded utterly Australian and in time it would become a sound that literally terrorized our opponents. Long before we left, we placed an order high on Warren's checklist for the two biggest amplifiers and loudspeakers on the east coast of America to be fitted onto the upper deck of our tender, *Black Swan*. When we left the dock in Newport, everyone was going to know it was the Australians going to war. Our sound was magnificently distinctive. You simply could not miss us. And it was just another psychological advantage we developed. We did not sound like a crew that was going to be beaten by anyone.

As we began to pull our act together in Fremantle with crew selection and psychological preparation, we had in our midst one final instrument of pure intimidation—our winged keel, set menacingly beneath the white hull of *Australia II*. Actually, it was set more awkwardly than menacingly, and before we had been sailing for very long, Benny decided it was in the wrong place, so we had to haul the boat to reset the keel forward eight inches. It was in a sense a super-Bennyurism. But that is also just part of the fine-tuning of a big racing boat.

But it is important to concentrate on the psychological impact that this unseen rocketship was going to have on our forthcoming opponents. If you want to make someone very, very nervous, the first thing you want to convey is mystery, secrecy. There is nothing quite as worrisome as not knowing what you are trying to defeat. Alan Bond loved this part—shrouding the keel every time *Australia II* came out of the water, talking guardedly about the keel *no one* was allowed to see. In that late summer of 1982, word got back very quickly to the Americans that the Australians were working with a radical new keel design that could turn their boat into a flying machine. In my own view, the Americans probably placed the new keel firmly in the category of the long-hulled *Southern Cross* and the bendy-masted *Australia,* writing it off as just another gimmick. Not until we started winning a lot of races did they become concerned, and then they rapidly developed paranoia about *Australia II*. I am sure that if we had never bothered to hide what we had, they would have been far less nervous, although they might have made a halfhearted attempt to copy us. However, we knew long before we ever left Fremantle that if we were first rate in Newport, and no one knew how our boat was constructed, there would be panic in the American camp. But I don't think we ever realized, even in our most exuberant moments, just how rattled our "invincible" opponents were going to become.

The final psychological lesson I would take with me was delivered one week before I left for Newport. The headmaster of Haileybury College, near our home in Brighton, told me an interesting little story that I am sure he hoped would give me extra strength. And he was right. He told me of perhaps the last visit Sir Winston Churchill made to Harrow, his old school, when he was very elderly. The great man rose to his feet and said to the boys that he had but nine words of advice for them all: "Never give in. Never give in. Never give in." And I took those nine words on a very long journey. Not as far as Sir Winston's, but nevertheless a long way.

10

Bloodbath on Port Phillip Bay

We were being forged in a frenzy of competitiveness, and in my heart I was glad when we got our arses kicked. It made us fight, and it made us tough together.

Match racing 12-Meter yachts is a totally specialized form of warfare. It has little to do with big regattas, where dozens of boats set off together, all going as fast as they can, every man for himself. Match racing is more subtle and more brutal, and it has the nerve-racking characteristic of throwing two helmsmen against each other, one on one, for all the world to see. In a way it's like a prizefight, but it is also like a diabolical game of chess with only two lethal pieces, each one as much a master of defense as offense. In the final reckoning, history will judge very simply and probably very clearly what happened in the struggle between Dennis Conner and John Bertrand. And by that I do not mean the instant predigested journalistic views of Superboat vs. Super Helmsman, with all of the customary childish oversimplifications. I mean real historical judgments, which tend to take several years to evolve, which take into consideration the myriad points of view of the principals, and which require the time to absorb the complexities these grueling races generate.

Match-racing excellence was what would decide the fate of the 1983 America's Cup, and since Dennis was widely regarded as the best in the world, I knew months—even years—beforehand that I must practice wherever I could and I must walk the awesome line that divides my own search for perfection and Alan Bond's search for corporate sponsorship dollars. This particular cash flow could start to dry up fast if I got hit with a few defeats in the public eye. But, in the spring of 1982, Alan and I agreed that I would have to go off and put my reputation on the line in the world's major match-racing events—an exercise not many America's Cup helmsmen are prepared to do because of the sponsorship problem. But I badly needed the practice. I had not been in charge of a boat in such competition for about seven years, and I knew I must be rusty and lacking in the latest techniques. Alan Bond made the cold business decision: Bertrand getting beaten all over the world would be awful, but not as awful as losing in Newport. He told me to get on with it.

My first stop was Los Angeles, California, for the Congressional Cup, a competition acknowledged as the world championship of match racing. I fervently hoped Dennis would give it a shot, but, unsurprisingly, he declined to put his reputation on the line. He had been there the previous year, and I think he finished sixth. I then drew the same boat and finished eighth. Nevertheless, it was very good practice for me. Incidentally, the American press gave me a hard time, and articles came out saying the America's Cup was clearly safe, since the Aussie helmsman was not up to much. The American defender would murder me in Newport. That was all I needed. My competitive fires were blazing, and I could hardly wait for the next skirmish.

This took place the following month, April, in Auckland, New Zealand. It was a very big event called the Citizens Watch Match Racing Championship. They invited a glittering lineup of helmsmen from all over the world. A local hotshot named Chris Dixon, a former world youth champion, won it, and we were a close third. It was a dramatic improvement, and I was delighted, returning in high spirits to Australia to await the launching of *Australia II*.

Meanwhile, I had another interesting invitation. Peter de Savary, the head of the English syndicate for the 1983 America's Cup, was already in Newport practicing with his vast crew and staff, and he wanted me to go there and helm *Australia*, upon which he considered me to be an expert. I thought it would be extremely helpful for me to see what was going on over there, and I arrived to take the helm of the boat on which I had been port trimmer in 1980, but, unknown to the British, had steered for only about five minutes in my life. The British were in high gear, and I was impressed with how much effort they were putting into it. My 2½-week visit got me all fired up, recharged about the Cup. I skippered *Australia* throughout, mainly against Phil Crebbin at the helm of *Victory*. It was very educational, ulterior motive battering against ulterior motive. The British were pretending I was giving their boys a good spell of hard race practice, when they obviously were interested in seeing how good I was. Alternately, I was pretending to enjoy sailing the old Australian boat, when I was sizing them up with every sense I had, for I knew that before we met the Americans, we were going to have to put away this lot first. De Savary's outfit was huge, about 100 people, and they had what I thought was a very fast boat, particularly in flat water, and downwind.

The aspect of this that shook me, however, was the sheer size of the British effort. They did not know exactly what they were about, so they were trying to solve their problems with a gigantic shotgun approach, spending millions of dollars, using consultants from the Royal Air Force and research men from the Royal Navy and the Army. Their computer analysis program was huge, and they were spreadeagled in every direction, buying every which way, counting on blanket coverage to make up for their lack of expertise and their inability to get their effort onto a tight, critical path. They had sails everywhere—some they needed, a lot they did not. Tom Schnackenberg could have changed their lives. But we had him, and the longer I spent in Newport, the more I realized he was worth his weight in uranium.

I saw signs that they already were hemorrhaging internally, with quarrels breaking out. A lot of the staff had been involved too long and had worked too hard expending too much effort. People just cannot work that hard for that long without going nuts. They have to have time on and time off.

At the end of my time there, I flew back to Australia in July. We were all alone with no one to race against, but after seeing so much action and urgency in the U.S.A., I found renewed zeal for the task we were trying so hard to accomplish. We underwent intensive training programs for nine days at a time. Nine days on and five days off. We used to fly to Perth and stay in the local motel and practice out there for eight hours at a stretch. The time seemed endless as we waited for the launching of *Challenge 12*. I would drill the crew day after day, practicing, practicing in my search for perfection. One day I made them hoist the spinnaker 20 times in a row until it flew in eight seconds flat. That was how quick it would have to go up in Newport, so we might as well get used to it. That afternoon nearly killed my foredeck crew.

There is only so much you can do in this kind of vacuum, and the pressure was beginning to build in me. We had no opponent and we greatly needed *Challenge 12* to get into the water, but suddenly there were rumblings from the other syndicate in Victoria that they were running out of money. If that boat did not start to race us soon, we would be in nothing less than a crisis situation. Bondy and Warren knew it as well as I, and Alan immediately stepped in and announced that he would pay the bills, lease *Challenge 12,* and get our racing program under way. Meanwhile, we kept on sailing alone, trying to pump up the adrenaline, which comes so easily against another opponent but is so hard to raise when you are racing just against yourselves and a seagull. In the end it is like dancing with your grandmother, totally noncombative. As we drifted into October, I was beginning to get very worried.

I felt as though I had the cares of the world on my shoulders. Back home in Melbourne, poor Rasa was having nightmares about the America's Cup. She was totally reticent about the whole thing and hated Newport. She never recovered from 1980, when Sunshine had pneumonia and everything was so dreadful. There was no question that she did not want to go for a fourth series of races against the Americans, and we started to grow apart because the campaign was taking up all of my time and energy. I thought she was going to leave me and take the children with her, and I felt absolutely torn. Sometimes as we struggled on in Perth, dealing each day with the absence of *Challenge 12* and our own sailing problems, I used to feel that I just could not stay there with my home life approaching a ruinous situation. On the other hand, I could not leave the crew. Plus there was a major match race coming up for the Australia Cup in Perth and I could not avoid that either. I was being pulled in every direction, and some days I wondered whether I would be able to hang on to my sense of reason. The pressure was getting to me terribly. I was totally strung out, and when I did get home between the Intensive Training Programs all of my frayed edges were showing. Right about this time I was at such a peak mentally that I really thought, "If Rasa is going, she is going right about now." But whatever the problems, Rasa and I have a deep and abiding relationship, and just when I was beginning to think that everything was going to fall apart, her love for me came through, exactly when I needed it the most. She knew the pressure I was under—she used to call it the Big P and rib me about it when I lost my cool, which was often. And I think her heart really went out to me. At the very end of October, I wrote in my diary, "Rasa is gathering strength about this. She is showing more interest each day. It has all been a terrible strain on her, but she is starting to warm to the idea of my involvement at last."

With just a few days left before the Australia Cup, the next in the match-racing series, I started to explore some mental relaxation techniques with Laurie Hayden. I had Grant Simmer, Colin Beashel, and Phil Smidmore in my crew, and I was jumping between the Viking 30 we would race against the heavy lineup of world-class yachtsmen in Perth and *Australia II*. *Challenge 12* was due to go in the water just about the time of the Australia Cup. I entered a rather plaintive cry in my diary, "We *really* need this boat to be launched. We are running out of steam without her. We need an opponent desperately. We can only think about the seagull for so long."

Meanwhile, the tension over the match racing was becoming unbelievable. Bondy, Ben, and Warren seemed to be poised on the fence like three vultures—watching, waiting to see if their boy would deliver the goods. I was determined to win, but I kept finding myself wondering what would happen if I should be beaten. Bloody oath, I needed this victory. Laurie Hayden kept telling me to diversify my thoughts, not to concentrate on just one issue. But I could not sleep, and I spent hours awake each night going over the races in my mind, trying to cast aside the possibility of losing. One of the added pressures was that in addition to facing the reigning world champion, Scott Perry, I would also face John Savage, the helmsman of the Victoria syndicate who would take over *Challenge 12,* and Iain Murray, who would helm the third Australian boat, *Advance.* Even Jim Hardy, the three-time Cup skipper whom I had always felt was not as good as I was, was going to race. For about three hundred different reasons, I would have died rather than lose.

The home-town buildup was amazing. Everything seemed to focus on me. Would Alan Bond's designated skipper come through? Among my own crew it was important, too. They had to believe in their own skipper, and if I were beaten by Savage or Murray, it would be almost unbearable. I kept telling myself that all I had to do was to control my emotions, tear them apart at the start, and I would be bound to win. But at times it seemed a very lonely position—whom could I count on as a trusted friend? I believed in Alan and I did trust him, but what was he thinking? What would Benny say if I lost? Was I still the right man to be entrusted with the boat that he believed was the culmination of his life's work? Anyway, the competition arrived and it was a blistering contest among the Viking 30s. There were protests all over the place, claims of foul, with me right in the thick of it, sailing literally for my life. Right down to the last races, it looked like a fight among the three Australian helmsmen, Savage, Murray, and me. Savage was rumored to have a slight edge in boatspeed, and there was nothing I could do about that. But I was dying to get at him in the last critical race. We won the start, but Savage, in that slightly faster boat, passed us on the first beat to windward. It was a desperate struggle.

He hung in there all the way, but on the square run, we nailed him. We turned the last mark just in the lead and had a harsh tacking duel to the finish line, but, we got there first. Bondy was so relieved he nearly fell straight into the Swan River. So did I. As victories go, that was one of the sweetest, and I don't suppose I shall ever forget it.

There was little time to savor this triumph, however. We all had to get back immediately to *Australia II*, upon which we were still treading water, still without an opponent. There was yet another delay for about three weeks, and the politics were heating up between the Victoria syndicate and our Perth syndicate. Finally, on November 17, 1982, Bondy signed the contract to charter *Challenge 12*. We still had to get her in order, and we still had to sail alone, and the days were long and tedious. Rasa and the kids came to visit, which was great for family unity. It showed Lucas what Dad was wasting his time on, 3,000 miles from home, and it did seem to help Rasa become more at peace with her husband's ambition in this crazy venture.

About a week after the launch of *Challenge 12*, we had her almost in shape. I took her out for a sail and liked her very much. She was going to be a very worthy opponent for *Australia II*—perhaps even a bit *too* worthy. Before we even had a chance to race the two boats together, we received a stunning report from our tender crew, John Fitzhardinge.

Fitzy came back to the dock one day and blithely announced that *Challenge 12* towed more easily than *Australia II*. With both yachts being pulled behind him, he had an excellent vantage point for observing the hulls moving through the water, and he was very definite. There is less drag on *Challenge 12*, he confirmed. She travels more smoothly through the water. Well, that was all I needed. Fitzy's news spooked everyone involved with the actual sailing of the boat. It would, in fact, be another week before the two boats were raced together, and these interminable delays were putting us further and further behind.

In the midst of all this, I decided to go back to Melbourne for a few days. Back home I found Rasa being very brave by herself and looking after everything. But the whole thing was taking an awful toll on her, and I was afraid to think too much about the effect it was having on the children with their father being away so much. I remember it as a peaceful visit, however, because Rasa was going to do everything she could to make my long quest for the America's Cup as smooth as possible for me. We were having a lovely time together, when one evening the telephone rang. It was Chink, calling from Perth after they had tried the two boats together for the first time.

"John, we could be in big trouble."

"Whaddaya mean?"

"We tried *Australia II* and *Challenge* today. *Challenge* was higher and faster in 15 knots of breeze. I think all our sails are up the shoot."

That was a personal blow to me as the skipper and a sailmaker. I'd been looking at them for the last four months, tuning the boat and using the most sophisticated computer data and design packages in the world. The sails were our main area of expertise, and we were developing the hardware and software components of our computers. Our analysis systems were close to perfection, and here was Chink telling me this was all rubbish.

He was also telling me that John Savage and "Frizzle" Freeman had just pulled their sails on, having never tuned the new boat before, and had blown *Australia II* out of the water. Chink had helmed the boat, with Grant Simmer tuning. Then Benny had gone aboard and said the mast rake was all wrong and the whole thing was just up the shoot. They had been hammered, and did I have any ideas?

I had ideas, all right, and most of them had to do with murder. So I got on the next plane to Perth, arriving in the morning with a lot on my mind. They met me at the airport and drove me to the testing grounds in Alan Bond's speedboat. About four miles offshore, I boarded *Australia II*. Conditions on the previous day had been 15 knots with a chop—our very worst conditions—and today things were not as bad. I took her for about four miles, eking out a two-lengths lead from *Challenge 12* in flattish water and about 8 knots of breeze. Overnight they had raised the boom and put on a hard, new D-ring. We tested all day and I tried everything I knew, but we could not split them. With a four-month start, we seemed to be identical to *Challenge,* and they were ecstatic. "Give us four months," they reasoned, "and we'll wallop these buggers and their bloody keel." The *Challenge 12* skipper, John Savage, already thought the keel was "bullshit" and said so, and would say so again in Newport a year later.

I was worried. *Australia II* was fractionally faster, but only just, and it is hard to get in front and stay there. I felt the rig needed to be moved forward about nine inches—but we were not slow to windward, nor were we slow downwind. For the moment, John Savage and his boys could have their boat. Because of the ill feeling that had developed between the two camps, we had a natural desire on our part to crush them in races as soon as possible. But it was Tom Schnackenberg who took me aside one day and put the situation into better perspective. "John," he said, "we must help *Challenge 12,* as much as we are helping ourselves. As long as we are racing and training against each other here, we have to make the competition as tough as possible. If we don't have world-class competition, we are wasting our time. It's just like going back to 1974. Unless we make our only competitor competitive, and give them the tools to beat us and turn it into a real contest, then we are doing no good to ourselves or them."

Of course he was right, and he added one other rather puckish little warning. "If you can't beat *Challenge 12,* I don't suppose you want to go to Newport, do you? If you can't beat them, you sure as hell can't beat Conner, and you wouldn't like that, would you?" He ended that little discussion by saying something else that helped me a lot. "Listen, John, no matter what we do to *Challenge 12,* she will not in the end beat you. If you take the helm of *Challenge 12,* then *Australia II* will not win the trials. The boat you drive will win. It's that simple." In my soul I believed that as well, but I felt immensely gratified that Tom had said it.

So we set about helping John Savage in every way we could. We took him out often in *Australia II* and showed him how to sail a 12-Meter. We even let his tactician, Frizzle Freeman, come out and see it all, look at the sails, even photograph them. Often I took my boys over to *Challenge 12* and we did all we could to fine-tune her.

Shortly after Christmas we arrived in Melbourne to begin the final stages of our preparation on my home waters of Port Phillip Bay. One afternoon I drove to Mum's house for a cup of tea, and since I was a bit early, I stood down on the beach outside the old boathouse. I think it was the first time I had been truly amazed by the terrifying swiftness of time. Thirty years had passed since we first lashed our parachute sail to the mast, 30 years since I had stood here with my grandpa and listened to him pinpoint the time of the freshening breeze, watched his bright blue eyes staring out of that weatherbeaten fisherman's face, focused hard on the water for ripples. Nearly 20 years had passed since my dad had joyfully helped Lex and me aim the gleamingly varnished *Be Be* into the waves. I stood there in the hot sun on the deserted beach, this little patch of sand and tide that had given my grandfather his living and shaped my entire destiny.

"John!" Beryl's voice had never changed down the years. She was standing outside the house now, looking at me, and I don't know how long she had been there. She just said, "Come in for a cup of tea when you're ready. Don't hurry. I know what you're thinking." Beryl has always known what I've been thinking, or at least she has known for an uncomfortable lot of the time—and now she knew I was thinking about the past. She too was probably involved in the strangely powerful nostalgia I felt outside the boathouse—and while I was wondering, as I often did, whether Bant and Dad would be able to see me racing *Australia II* on Port Phillip Bay, Mum was probably speculating on her constantly voiced opinion about the America's Cup . . . "Australia will only win it when my John is skipper." Beryl knew as well as anyone as she looked past me beyond the horizon of the bay that I'd be out there next week fighting *Challenge 12* on the waters I'd raced over so many times before, the waters upon which I had learned.

I walked to the house, where I sat with Mum in that sunny-light room on the water for about half an hour and then drove home in an agreeable mood. Rasa was welcoming and the children were all over the place, happy faces everywhere. All of our lives changed for the better now that I was home again, and as I sat there later having a drink with Rasa, I reflected that I appeared to live in two entirely different worlds—one was this peaceful family environment so close to where I had grown up; the other was a kind of nuthouse along the beach at Melbourne, where the sense of acrimony between the two 12-Meter crews was at times overpowering.

I ought to mention here that Warren and Chink had devised a master plan to simulate living conditions in Newport. We borrowed from the state government the old Melbourne Customs House, next to the Royal Yacht Club of Victoria, home of *Challenge 12,* and moved everyone in, under precisely the same conditions we would encounter in the United States. The plan was designed to give the boys a psychological insight into being together for months at a time. It was an exercise in compatibility, under what was turning out to be identical stress as we struggled to attain mastery over the other boat.

This was very important for us, because when we ultimately set off for the United States, we *did* know each other, and not merely superficially. Most important was the fact that the hierarchy knew beyond a doubt that the final squad was compatible, and we did not need to look forward to those disruptive arguments and petty jealousies and misunderstandings that so often plague sports teams far from home. Living out of a suitcase halfway around the world has some very special problems, and now we had dealt with them. With all of that, Laurie Hayden was a great help. He is a quiet, calm man, and I was using him as my personal sounding board to help me better understand each member of the crew, and I would continue to do this throughout our stay in Newport. He pointed out to me all of those silent, unseen, critical emotional areas that have such an overwhelming effect on the morale of the crew—a man's temperament, his emotional control, his reaction to criticism, his sensitivity, his trustworthiness, his ability to cope with responsibility, his interpersonal style, his ability to process information, and, above all, his powers of concentration. Not just for 15 minutes, but for stretches of up to 4½ hours, the average length of an America's Cup race.

It was during the soul-searching first week at the old Customs House that Bondy finally blew his stack. "Bullshit aside, John," he snapped. "I've had enough of *Challenge 12.* The bastards are getting too good. Tell them nothing more. No more cooperation, or they are going to end up beating us. Tell Schnackenberg that if he sees that their sails are up the creek, leave 'em there. And get them out of the Customs House. I don't care if they sleep on the beach. I don't want 'em listening to us."

The paranoia about defeat by the *Challenge 12* mob was getting to the Perth tycoon. "Bugs!" he yelled. "There are probably bugs all over the place. The minute those guys from *Challenge* are out, I want the place searched for bugs and electronic listening devices and anything else they might use to spy on us."

From my point of view, it was wonderful—remembering 1970, 1974, and 1980. The old calm, noncompetitive atmosphere had been like a slow-motion film. And suddenly here we were in the middle of World War III. This was for real, and it would inspire people to work themselves to a peak of motivation, to push beyond any normal levels of expectation at this stage of our training.

It was in an explosive atmosphere that our races started. *Australia II* vs. *Challenge 12* —I doubt whether there has ever been anything like it in Australia. It was daggers drawn all the way. We used to race together for miles and miles, sometimes separated by just a few feet, and sometimes, at the end of a 10-mile struggle with John Savage, there would be about 10 feet between us. We *never* could establish mastery over them, and we *never* could get away from them. When those two boats were rigged with equal sails, there was just about nothing in it. I remember arranging for them to sail in a dead straight line with us for 10 miles in a 10-to-14-knot wind, and at the end there was less than 10 feet between winner and loser. Most times we won, but sometimes they won, and if we did not sail our best, they kicked our arses—hard. *Australia II* was feeling good to me, but we were in trouble downwind. We always got caught by *Challenge 12* on the square runs, however fast we hauled up our spinnakers. We kept racing and learning, working on our sails, crew techniques, strengths, and fitness. I still had major reservations about our performance in any kind of a chop, but I continued to be pleased with our boatspeed overall. Nevertheless, an entry in my diary reads, "I am trying, all the time, to reassure myself that *Australia II* is really good."

The trials proceeded, and hostilities were beginning to break out on the water—shouting and yelling like you could not believe. We made Conner and Blackaller in Newport sound like Girl Guides. The things we bawled at each other were really wicked and it involved everyone. Chink and I and Grant Simmer were really terrible. Luckily, spectators could not really hear us because our obscenities were whipped away on the wind. But it was commonplace to suddenly hear someone yelling, "YOU F. . . . . CRAZY B. . . . . .S PISS OFF . . . . YOU DON'T KNOW THE F. . . . . RULES AND YOU NEVER WILL!!!!!" I doubt that any bunch of 11 sail-ors has ever been referred to so often and with such venom as a bunch of "arseholes" as the men of *Challenge 12* were, by us, for so long, over a mere yacht race and vice versa. You would have thought lives depended on it. Once I had to consider lashing Grant to the mast, because he wanted to get close enough to board *Challenge 12* and beat someone's brains out. It was just terrible, and very unsporting. Not like it was in Sir Thomas Lipton's day. And God knows what old Tom Pearkes would have said if he'd seen me out there shouting and swearing and hurling obscenities at my opponents. I'm not sure what my mum would have said, never mind Tom Pearkes. It was war. And every day it was made worse by the newspapers. Whenever *Challenge 12* won a race, the local Melbourne headlines were amazing. "CHALLENGE 12 COMING ON STRONG"; "AUSTRALIA II DESTROYED"; "VICTORY FOR THE MEN FROM MELBOURNE." Every time I read one of them, a knife turned in my gut. No matter how much I knew it didn't matter, it still got to me, and I despised myself for being so gullible.

Of course on the day of those sort of headlines the atmosphere was worse than ever. We were scarcely speaking to each other, and I'm surprised you can't still see the blood on the water. There was a day when Grant and Chink were both insane with anger and we had literally to grab our navigator back from leaping onto their boat. He was going to punch their tactician right in the mouth and was saying so loudly. I saw Chink get a hold of him and he shouted back to me, "We'd better hold him down, he's trying to board *Challenge*!" Pirates board ships. So do members of the Coast Guard. But in the sport of yacht racing this is rare, and I record it really to provide some idea of the shocking tension and desperate will to win that existed out there between us.

The thing is, Melbourne is a typically parochial city—and everyone in the place was cheering for *Challenge 12*—partly because they felt that the very popular Dick Pratt had been screwed financially by Bondy with some fairly steep interest payments, and partly because the home-town boys were very much underdogs. The Melbourne papers did their damage with the aid of a very well-organized and very biased *Challenge 12* publicity machine. Anytime the *Challenge* crew did well, the machine would slip into gear, telling the residents of Melbourne that *Challenge 12* was going to steamroll *Australia II* and win the America's Cup, in that order. Much of this was geared for the sponsorship effort being run by the syndicate—which was, of course fair, since they had to raise money from the public. But we found ourselves painted as outsiders from Western Australia, and here in my own home town, I was being pictured as some kind of a villain. The propaganda for *Challenge 12* was so good that people would stop Rasa in a shop and say, "Sad for poor John. I hear *Challenge 12* is going to win the America's Cup." That sort of thing made me furious and drove me into a frenzy of combativeness. The entire population of the city was fervently hoping that *Challenge 12* would come through—as perhaps she might, but over my dead body.

My diary entries at that time do reflect some anxiety on my part. One reads, "With the dust settling on the performance of our winged keel—well, there's not much advantage but we can win. The boat is a very good match racer."

Another read, just after Hughey Treharne came on board as tactician: "Just finished one of our final I.T.P.'s in Melbourne. Hughey has joined us. We are good after the start, but we are getting hammered in the pre-start maneuvers. I am still not using my own initiative enough. Hughey was calling the starts all the time and I was doing as I was told. But it's not working. The helmsman *has* to start the boat—there is so much split-second decisionmaking going on. The initiative has to be made by the person in charge of the boat. *Challenge 12* is very competitive right now and will come on strong in the U.S.A. It's always a worry. We lost yesterday in flat water, in a 7-to-10-knot breeze, by 15 seconds. It was a losing start for us, but we went very well upwind. Still bloody doubtful downwind."

After a 15-second loss in one of the practice races, the press went wild. "CHALLENGE 12 DOMINATES." And the boys on Dick Pratt's boat started to believe all this. They started pumping themselves up and hired a sports psychologist, and they were strutting around saying they were better than we. These upstarts, whom we had invented. Alan Bond's syndicate was the father of *Challenge 12*. We designed it, built it, saved it from bankruptcy, and then taught them to sail it. Now they were trying to reverse the roles from the obvious. We were the teachers and they were the pupils, and that is how we thought the situation should remain. After all, we made it happen for them. And that lopsided publicity machine of theirs was driving us all mad, especially the Major, the Führer, Mad Dog, and me. We were stirred up, we wanted to crush them, to humiliate them, but we could not do it. *Australia II* was not fast enough, and I could not get away from them. We did win the majority of races, but if you had read the local press, you would never have known that.

Of course all this was nothing short of perfect. In fact, to use an old Australian cliché, it was bloody fantastic. In this supercharged atmosphere, we sharpened our teeth and honed our skills. Without those blistering battles on Port Phillip Bay, we would never have had a prayer in Newport. We were being forged in a frenzy of competitiveness, and in my heart I was glad when we got our arses kicked. It made us fight, and it made us tough together, and it forced us to develop our technical ability to the fullest. The difference between our vacuum in Fremantle and this dogfight in Melbourne was never more graphically apparent.

Sometimes there would be quite a large spectator fleet watching. Sometimes Mum was out in a boat watching from afar. She never told me when she was coming but I usually knew when she was there. And sometimes I thought of her, standing outside the old boathouse straining for a glimpse of *Australia II* on the horizon, beyond which I was probably bellowing vulgarities at John Savage. Although the mood was nothing short of poisonous at sea, life at home was much better, but still had many complications. From time to time I gave up writing in my diary, because I was not emotionally able to cope with it, and sometimes Rasa made little entries in this big book. I noticed this one, about the time we were locked in combat with *Challenge 12*. "My aim to become more at peace with myself," she wrote, "is slowly coming to fruition. Have felt very loved and cared for by all my friends and family. Lucas still very up and down but I have been a much tighter disciplinarian and not screaming at them nearly as much. Andre is working well and can now read. Sunshine becoming even more of her own person." At this point I have drifted away from being the focal point of her life. She has drifted into talking about the children and how her friends are giving her her main strength. Although Rasa was trying valiantly to give me the support she knew in her heart I desperately needed, it was now, in the midst of these grim struggles on Port Phillip Bay, that we very nearly parted. That was the terrible toll that the America's Cup took on my life. It took all of my energy and it nearly destroyed my family. But in the end, luckily, it was worth it, and Rasa and I did not let it finish us.

Meanwhile, at this stage big Dennis was struggling halfway around the world just like us, slogging away at his opponents, one on one trying to get it right, drawing ever closer to the race he had predicted four years before. "Sooner or later, John, I guess it's going to be you and me."

On Port Phillip Bay the struggle continued. The last times we would race would be in the Advance Australia Cup, sailed off Melbourne in March all the way along the bay—Rasa could just about see the yachts from her front door. Before we started, I talked to the crew for a long time. I laid it right on the line. "The only way for us to beat the Americans is to be in this kind of a scrap against our fellow Aussies first. That is how the Americans have done it for years. The biggest races they must win are their own trials. Beating the foreigners is a piece of cake after what they have to go through in their own preliminaries. Our destiny on *Australia II* is to go and face the U.S.A., the Champions of the World. And, dammit," I shouted, "if we cannot beat *Challenge 12*, let's not go at all. Let's just stay at home where we belong. Let me clear this up for you. If we do not beat *Challenge 12* because they are too good for us, I'm not going to Newport, and that's that." My words struck home, no doubt about that. What I did not tell them was that I *knew* we could beat *Challenge 12*. And I knew we *would* beat them.

Alan Bond arrived. Benny followed him in. We were in a war for sponsorship dollars, and Alan made it very clear that victory was essential. This was no longer just training. There was big money at stake here. Corporate bucks. Defeat was out of the question. Before the Advance Australia Cup started, Bondy took me aside and told me quietly, "If we can't beat these bastards, it's going to be very expensive." The general ballyhoo was amazing.

In the final, we were down to 3–3, and everything was riding on the last race. Bondy was as nervous as a cat, because the whole city was involved, and the spectator fleet that sailed out of the harbor to watch was the biggest armada of powerboats ever seen in Melbourne. You would have thought that if anyone would lose his nerve it would be me, but I swear Alan Bond came as close as I have ever seen him come to spitting the dummy, as we say. He called me from Brisbane and said, "Now hold on, John, bullshit apart, this is getting serious. I estimate that this last race is worth a million dollars to me, one way or the other, in corporate sponsorship." I think he may have been trying to frighten the life out of me.

The day of the race was like an America's Cup final, with hundreds of boats jockeying for position to see us fight it out. The press went insane with excitement. In the middle of this, I went off and tried to find a boat for the crew members' families and girl friends. In the end, I got the commodore of the yacht club to arrange a boat for them, and finally, before the start, everyone was out there, including Rasa and all the kids.

On Port Phillip Bay we hooked up together just before the 10-minute gun, and throughout the countdown I could feel the new and terrific resolve that was present among the crew. Their determination and aggression were obvious. Our adrenaline was high, but as we came together toward the starting line, neither boat held the advantage. We forced them to tack away, giving us a slight edge, but just after the race began, they went ahead. The breeze was light and the flat water was a godsend. Hughey was calling the shots clear and cool. We were concentrating hard, the crew was locked in. Soon a knock developed. Grant called it very quickly, "Five degrees, John," and Hughey murmured, "We should tack now!" *Australia II* came around to port tack. *Challenge* came back at us on starboard, and in total silence we tacked underneath and took the lead. Essentially the race was over. My concentration and that of this crew was total, and there was no way in the world we were going to lose that race. *Australia II* drew farther and farther away. It was the first time we had ever been able to clobber them, and it was particularly gratifying to do it on this downwind leg, where we had been so weak for so long.

Our thoroughness was now paying off, and we could not be stopped. We seemed finally to have conquered, our Achilles heel and we "wobbled" away from them. (I say "wobbled" because *Australia II* was not a very smooth rider of the waves. That low, heavy, lead keel took our center of gravity quite deep into the water, so we were terribly sensitive below, shuddering often because of the big weight swinging about at the bottom of the keel instead of being concentrated at the top.) But now we felt as if we were flying, and as most sportsmen do when the pressure is on, our opponents began to get a bit rattled. The men on *Challenge 12* suddenly looked ragged, and their sails were deteriorating. The breeze freshened still more, until there was no contest. We absolutely wiped them out by three minutes, and that was the last time we raced each other in Australia. It made all of us feel marvelous, and I was mildly surprised the following day to note that the Melbourne papers did in fact carry the result.

For most of the *Australia II* camp, that was the end of it until we would meet in Newport two months hence. The boats were being packed up and our sail inventory was being given a final check as we made preparations for the move to the United States. For me, however, and for some of my key men, there was more to do. I needed still more practice. Hughey Treharne and I flew to England to take part in yet another of those wickedly competitive match-racing competitions, the Royal Lymington Cup, and we won this prestigious championship on behalf of Australia.

Next we flew to New Zealand for my second attempt at the Citizens Watch Match Racing Championship. We were a bit unlucky not to win that, finishing a very close second to Rod Davis, the crack U.S. helmsman and 12-Meter sailor, and a future Olympic champion.

And that, ladies and gentlemen, was the last race I sailed before we arrived in Newport, on June 1, 1983, to prepare for what I now believed was my ultimate destiny—to beat Dennis Conner in the final race of the America's Cup.

11

A Bunch of Bloody Aussies Arrive

Her skirt was lowered to shield Benny's keel from prying eyes, and, cloaked in mystery, Australia II *was put away for the night, under guard, in the little seaport where her name would be forever remembered.*

We were a disparate little group on that blustery Wednesday morning as we flew, half asleep, toward the historic American city of Boston. There were 10 of us, the final contingent of our group, and we had been traveling for more than 24 hours from deep in the Southern Hemisphere. We wore no formal uniforms, just our blazers, and we were, I suppose, unrecognizable as any kind of a sports team, save perhaps for the deep-water tan and the sun-bleached hair, which often distinguish the racing yachtsman. But to our fellow passengers we were doubtless just another bunch of Aussies, a bit more quiet and reserved than your average happy tourists, but nevertheless a group of guys going to Boston. No big deal. . . .

Somewhere out to the left I could just see the Charles River where I had first learned to sail the Finns 13 years before. My old university, MIT, was down there, too, and it seemed a long time since Rasa and I first lived there. Down below, as we dropped under the cloud ceiling, we could see the long swells of Massachusetts Bay rolling up the harbor. Those of us seated next to the windows gazed down, assessing the wind speed instinctively, watching the waves. They look a bit short, a bit lumpy. The sea looked gray and unfriendly, which is more or less what you might expect from a stretch of the home waters of America's sprawling East Coast yacht-racing network. As we banked into our final approach I wondered again about the white boat from Perth and how she would feel tomorrow when we headed her out into Rhode Island Sound. Could I and my casual-looking raiders from Down Under really get our hands on that monstrous piece of silver in New York's West 44th Street, the one which drives grown men insane every three years?

June 1, 1983, was our arrival date at Boston's Logan International Airport, and we immediately drove south 60 miles to the little seaport of Newport, which would be our home and battle headquarters for the next four nerve-racking months. These would be times that would try the mettle of Attila the Hun—never mind this cheerful group that looked as if they were just out for a few laughs in the bars of Newport's rollicking Bannister's Wharf. That, I assure you, is living proof that appearances can be deceptive. The one thing we were not after was laughs, and in the ensuing weeks, we would set an all-time America's Cup record for nonappearances at parties, balls, and other social functions. We never had a nighttime curfew, because we never needed one. Not one of the crew would ever stay out late, no one smoked, and no one was interested in anything stronger than two or three beers after work.

We drove into town in our shirtsleeves, threading our way along the waterfront streets, the last of the challengers to arrive. Here I was, John Bertrand, formerly of 22 Bristol Avenue, Chelsea, accompanied by my boys, hard on the heels of Sir Richard Sutton, the Earl of Dunraven, Sir Thomas Lipton, the aircraft tycoon Thomas Sopwith, and other distinguished chaps who attempted to wrest the "Auld Mug" from the New York Yacht Club. But in their time Newport had been a quiet, slightly seedy little seaport complete with tattoo parlors and coal docks. Today it is a symphony of fashionable boutiques, swinging bars, print and map shops, restaurants, and expensively converted buildings along the waterfront. Five nations were challenging for the Cup, and the entire place was bustling with people, talking excitedly, laughing and toasting.

Well, at long last, here we were. Newport. We pulled up outside our crew headquarters, Founders' Hall, a big, old wooden mansion on the outskirts of town where the crew had resided in 1980. It was a very companionable reunion, the first time we had all been together since we walloped *Challenge 12* in that final race for the Advance Australia Cup more than two months earlier. There was a lot of laughing and a torrent of information sharing.

And there was a major break in tradition for this Australian crew. I, with the help of Chink, had insisted that wives, children, and girl friends be allowed to join the team in Newport. The unmarried ones would stay in Founders' Hall—where I, too, would live for four weeks until Rasa and the kids arrived—while the rest would find independent accommodations for the families. The management of the syndicate had agreed to this revolutionary move, but as a kind of silent protest, they would not put one penny toward the expense of the others, nor would they assist in arranging for apartments. Anyone who wanted to live with his family could do so with the blessing of the management, but he must do so entirely on his own. Thus was born our little Australian colony in lovely Dennison Street, about 100 yards from the dock where *Australia II* would reside in secrecy and mystery for many a long month.

Dennison Street became a home away from home. I rented a little apartment for Rasa and the children, and Hughey and Dixie Treharne and their two children rented right below us in the same building. In a house almost opposite us were Chink and Jenny Longley, Tom Schnackenberg and Annie, and Skip Lissiman and his girl friend, Ginger. All the little families together, 12,000 miles from home, coping on a daily basis with the various problems such global dislocation can create. It is often awkward and sometimes frustrating, but nowhere near as flagrantly damaging as to have key men in a big-boat crew who are homesick, sad, and lonely, and whose hearts are back home in Perth or Melbourne rather than on the harsh, hectic deck of one of Benny Lexcen's fighting Twelves.

The night we arrived, we discovered that *Australia II* was safely at her dock. She had arrived on a container ship in New York City and was met there by Chink, Ya, Beasho, and a few of the boys. From the upper deck a huge crane lowered the 65-foot-long white hull, its winged keel still under tarpaulin wraps. Gently she slid into the water, and then the "skirt" was removed. A couple of the men from *Australia II* had stayed on board as she made her descent, and they quickly attached the lines from our launch, *Black Swan,* and began the long, 28-hour journey, under tow northward along the Atlantic coast to Newport, the familiar seagoing trek made by all the big Twelves that arrive in the U.S.A. to challenge for the America's Cup. Up the length of Long Island Sound they went, beyond North Point, buffeting through the waves where the fierce currents meet off New London, Connecticut, home of the U.S. nuclear submarines.

Australia II, her masts strapped down, sliced through the water like a sleek, white shark, with the boys on board wondering, wondering. Would she move with that effortless grace through the water when the big mainsail was hoisted in Newport and there was no *Black Swan* to haul her to her appointed destination? Shortly before the Brenton Reef tower, they left the Beavertail light flashing to port and entered the waters off Newport, finally coming to rest at the Australian dock at Newport Offshore. Her skirt, already in position, was lowered to shield Benny's keel from prying eyes, and, cloaked in mystery, *Australia II* was put away for the night, under guard, in the little seaport where her name would be forever remembered.

The following day they raised her mast. The shrouds were bolted into place and the halyards restored to their old positions. With her rig complete, they hauled up the mainsail on May 31, the day before I arrived, and took her for one trial run.

And now I was here to sail in the races for which I seemed to have been preparing all my life, since Great-Grandpa Tom Pearkes had shown me those big, dusty old books with their faded pictures of the giant *Shamrock*s, the huge English J-boats that had lost the America's Cup five times at the beginning of the century. I was awfully young at the time—I suppose about seven years old—but I remember it with immense clarity. He was a tough old guy, Tom Pearkes—until the day he died at about 94, he had a girl friend on the other side of Melbourne—and he never smiled when he showed me the pictures of the *Shamrock*s. I guess being involved in a losing America's Cup campaign is something you do not forget very quickly. I had been in three myself.

On the night before I first took the helm of *Australia II* in Newport, I recall being preoccupied with what we *knew* about our boat. It would have been far easier to make a proper assessment if we had realized that *Challenge 12* was *the best* of the foreign boats (not including us) at the time we arrived in the U.S.A. We could not have known that in terms of performance, she was just about the same as *Liberty* would be.

In Melbourne, on Port Phillip Bay, we were faster to windward in medium-fresh conditions and flat water. We pointed higher, went more slowly, but got there first. As soon as the bay developed a chop, from 6 to 14 knots, then *Challenge 12* got faster and faster than us to windward. Sometimes we held them, sometimes not. But when the chop was very severe, they would annihilate us. We put this down to the gyrations of the boat—our bow would ride up and down, chopping wood, as we say. This movement sometimes became so frequent that it would start to shake the wind out of the sails, slowing us down terribly. All this was associated with the wings underneath, and the turbulence and drag. She was a very critical boat to sail, and she required a lot more concentration than most Twelves, because she could get out of rhythm so quickly.

On the power reaches in Melbourne, we were *never* faster than *Challenge 12*. Usually she was between five and 10 seconds our superior, and we were swapping spinnakers with each other all the time, so the difference was in the hull. *Or the keel.* Square running, we were *never* faster than *Challenge*, and as soon as we hit a joggle, the other boat was clearly faster than us. She could gain large distances on us with very similar spinnakers. The wobble on *Australia II* was really unnerving, and sometimes when we swapped crews, the boys from *Challenge 12* could hardly stand up. I steered both boats and it was perfectly clear that *Challenge 12* was a much smoother boat through the water in any kind of a chop.

There were times when I had seriously considered changing and claiming *Challenge 12* for ourselves. But we wanted *Australia II* to be the best, because there was something special about her. She could always maneuver better than *Challenge*, and in the critical prestart maneuvers, she was a dream. She could also tack with superb economy, coming around in a glorious tight, smooth arc. I knew that if Dennis Conner wanted to tack with us, he would have to be very sharp indeed. And I also knew that if only we could get the boat to a normal *equal* performance through the water, our tacking ability could bring us home. But we could never overcome our downwind problem in a joggle, and when it was choppy to windward, we were in trouble in light to medium winds. When the wind got up, we were much better, probably because our keel held us more vertical, while *Challenge* was forced into a less economic heeling stance. But we never could really destroy them when we had equal sails.

And now I had to face the famous Newport slop, those short, chopping waves banging away at the bow. And in the races against the Americans, there would be a vast spectator fleet, thousands of propellers flailing away, removing almost every vestige of hope that we would ever find the flat water our beautiful white boat so enjoys.

The question of making quite sure that *Australia II* would go at least at the same speed as the American boat—and, indeed, the best of the foreign boats—still remained. It was our considered opinion that the solution rested firmly in the engine of the boat, the sails, the big motors that drive us forward. I keep talking about "equal sail" with *Challenge 12*. That is because whenever they were unequal, the difference was astounding. With a new, fast genoa, better than ours, she would draw away. Put the same sail on us and we would draw away. In my opinion, the key to the America's Cup is in the sails.

For all of those reasons, we arrived in Newport with the best sail-devel-

opment plan any foreign challenge has ever had in the history of
the America's Cup. It was also better than any American defender has
ever had—except perhaps *Courageous* in 1977. But now ours was better
than that of the *Freedom/Liberty* group of Dennis Conner. By the
time we were ready to race the Americans, we would have it nearly perfect, and to give us an even more important advantage, we would know
when and how to use them, a skill frequently missing among foreign challengers.

Most sail decisions in most crews are done by the top man, backing his
instinct. "I think we could stand a little more curve for light winds—let's
order another couple of genoas and see if we can improve a bit." That
type of stuff. That is not the way it was done on *Australia II*. We had a
superior decisionmaking team. As skipper and as managing director of
North Sails in Melbourne, I was on the team. Tom Schnackenberg, managing director of North Sails in Auckland, was in charge of our program.
The other member of the sail team was Hughey Treharne, managing director of Sobstad Sails in Sydney, and a vastly experienced ocean racer.
Three decisionmakers. Three sailmakers. Each man in tune with the scientific approach. And feeding these three minds was another fantastically
methodical brain—that of our young navigator, Grant ("Mad Dog") Simmer, whose quest for precise information was so intense he was reluctant
to say anything at all unless he was 1,000 percent certain that he was
1,000 percent right. His second nickname, "Mumbles," evolved from his
almost paranoid inability to express any form of an opinion in a normal
voice, on any subject, unless he *knew* beyond any doubt whatsoever that he
was copper-bottomed, gold-plated correct. As a result of this fanatical ad-
hesion to the truth, and nothing but the truth, he collected data about
boatspeed and recorded, known performance under racing conditions
that was awesome in its accuracy. It allowed our decisionmaking to be
almost error-free. And it improved the boat all the time—unlike any other
campaign in which I've ever been involved. Normally the decisionmaking
has been strictly the "seat-of-the-pants" variety, and thus far too vulnerable to mistakes.

Back in 1980, Benny was trying to coordinate both the sail program
and the boat-design program, and it was a hit-or-miss affair—similar, I
suspect, to the *Liberty* program, in which Dennis Conner's whim is almost
certainly law. As fine a sailor as Dennis is, he does not have an engineer's
brain. He is not a scientist, and his sail-development decisions would not
be as logical as those I insisted on for *Australia II*. I always felt that the
dominance of Dennis over his sail program would prove to be one of the
Liberty campaign's major undoings.

Tom Schnackenberg was just about the precise opposite to Dennis in every respect. He approached our task with the purity of science, beginning by looking back on every single sail used by race winners in Newport 1980. His data base was built up with extraordinary precision in the most methodical manner throughout all the sail testing we did in Melbourne and in Perth. He was the world's leading authority on the optimum sail shape of a 12-Meter, and by the time we arrived in Newport, he had put in two years of the most thorough and painstaking research. Back in Australia he had photographed us and *Challenge* at every stage of our trials, and all of this information—including 1980 photographs and 1983 pictures, right to the end of September—is still the exclusive property of our syndicate, confidential to the Australians and critical to our future campaigns.

Before we had settled into Founders' Hall, we had already arranged to rent an old fishing shed about 200 yards from our dock. We converted it into our own private sail loft and put down our own floor. It was some 3,000 square feet, and the contractors charged us a fortune to do it. In the loft we had a night staff of sailmakers working under Tom Schnackenberg's guidance. We brought them all from Australia. We also set up our own darkroom in the basement of Founders' Hall, with our own printing equipment, chemicals, and other paraphernalia. Our plan was to take cameras out on the water and photograph our sails, and those of our sailing companions or opponents, at every stage of every race. We would then rush the film into the darkroom and, after long conferences, we would start recutting and reshaping, working all night to have them ready for the following day, should we need them.

This worked brilliantly under Tom's overall supervision. We would come off the water and the film would go straight off for developing. Within an hour, we had 8-by-10-inch glossy photographs. Tom, Hughey, and I would go over them before dinner, and sometimes right through dinner. We would review with Mumbles the times during the day's racing when there appeared to have been a slackening of boatspeed. Usually my insights from behind the wheel coincided with the harsh facts that the navigator's computer printouts told us were unarguable. We would then pull out the appropriate pictures from that stage of the race and compare them, if necessary, with our opponent's sails. Tom would use a pen to mark in alterations to bring the sails back to optimum shape. On a typical evening, he would suggest ¾ inch off this seam, perhaps ¼ inch here, ⅛ inch there. The sails themselves, as soon as we knew we had to recut, had already been removed to the loft. Right after dinner, Tom and I would go down to see the cutters. Tom would mark the critical seams with a tailor's pen, and they would be split open in readiness for the precision surgery that would be performed throughout the night. When we radioed from the water that something major needed to be done on a certain genoa or spinnaker, or even the mainsail, Tom would try to catch a couple of hours of sleep in the early evening, because he knew he would be at the loft until perhaps 2 A.M. The other machinists would often be there until 4 or even 5 A.M. I used to ride over on my bike to see them—Ken O'Brien and Mike Quilter, Ted Silbereisen and David Rees—diligently performing the silent miracles that would make us faster, faster, faster. I just wanted to be there, to generate the feeling I knew would make them *feel* as vital as they were.

Everything was so refined and such was our team spirit that anyone would do anything to help. Laurie Hayden, our sports psychologist, used to take charge of the darkroom, spending hours down there developing prints. Our shore manager, Chink Longley—what a worker that man was!—would step in immediately and take over the developing if Laurie was busy. I've seen Chink so exhausted after a day out there on the water that he could not stay awake while we were towed home. This huge winch-grinder, sound asleep when we arrived at the dock, would drag himself up, jump off the boat with his pockets stuffed full of film, and pedal like a maniac up hill all the way to Founders' Hall. He would race down to the darkroom and work nonstop in the gloom until the photographs were ready, before dinner, before his last meeting with Warren Jones, before his last chat about the next day's sail with the Major, with me, before falling into bed, worn out, only to get up again at 5:45 A.M. and do it all over again. Week after week, month after month.

Tom Schnackenberg used to have a data base that recorded whether a new sail was less than its optimum shape or more; optimum shapes were his obsession and his specialty. Sometimes a new sail would work its way into its optimum shape with use, and Tom would have this recorded down to the tiniest detail. He would even rethink the optimum shape, review it, and update his data base. The moment it went beyond the optimum, Tom could see it in photographs, and by comparing it with the picture of the sail when it was at its best, he could restore it overnight with the help of the boys in the cutting loft. Now I'm a sailmaker, and I have a lot of inherent sail-design knowledge, but Schnackenberg in full cry is something to see.

The miracle Schnacks worked with our spinnakers was beyond anyone's hopes, because you can't define the parachute with numbers as you can do with a mainsail going to windward, which was Schnackenberg's real speciality. As soon as we hit Newport, he got to work on our Achilles heel, the fifth leg, and he told me that in two months' time we would be nearly unrecognizable from the floundering old tub we were when *Challenge 12* first walloped us downwind in Perth. He was right. Looking back, I know that without Schnacks, all of our efforts may very well have come to nothing.

But in the same way that we could not have reached our full potential without Tom, he could not have reached *his* without us. For instance, he could not have succeeded in the American camp, where he would have had to cope with Dennis's whim as well as the inevitable competition among the various sailmakers working as crew on the boat, each wanting his own product to be doing the driving. This kind of conflict has been evident in the American camp before—perhaps a reflection of the totally commercial way of life in the States—and I think it is counterproductive. It destroys quiet, methodical progress, and it produces emotion and a touch of self-interest.

Our arrival in Newport did not exactly set the town on fire. We were probably the least ostentatious of all the foreign crews, and we were always so busy or so tired in the evenings that it was difficult for us to have a smart identity. We were always moving fast, dressed in our green Aussie shirts. No one had any time for the gentle and refined art of shooting the breeze, so we seemed to fade quickly into the background. Except, of course, when the starting gun went off. The local press did not think much of us either, and most of the newspaper articles were a bit supercilious about our strange keel, still under wraps. They thought it was some kind of a joke, not to be taken seriously by our opponents. And they also ventured the opinion that Alan Bond had not been very sensible in selling the first *Australia* to the British. A top-class trial horse, this grand veteran of two campaigns, they reasoned, was lost to the Australians. What the scribes seemed to ignore, and what we were paranoid about, was the fact that *Australia* was a two-time loser, had won only one America's Cup race in nine starts, and had none of the modern design advantages.

Anyway, we were very satisfied with our preparation thus far, and now that we were finally here on the racecourse, we had to get down for the first time to the cold-blooded business of assessing the foreign competition. Since the British looked as if they had retaken Newport for the first time since the Revolutionary War, more than 200 years earlier, we might as well start with them.

Blue and yellow stripes were their colors, and a ludicrously smug-looking British bulldog named Winston was their symbol. They plastered Winston's image everywhere—on trucks, on boatsheds, on wire fencing. He was all over town. He was on parts of the sidewalk along Thames Street, the main thoroughfare. They even had a huge bulldog balloon on top of one of the buildings in the center of town, until some local marksman shot it down. Then there seemed to be hundreds of members of the British team, everyone running around in every direction. They were all over

Newport, and in their middle stood the chief, Peter de Savary, the cigar-smoking lord of all he surveyed, master of *Kalizma* (Richard Burton and Elizabeth Taylor's old 135-foot yacht). He was master of a veritable fleet of boats in Newport, including his lovely 55-footer, *Lisanola,* all painted dark blue and yellow. With his staff of about 100 souls, plus his Jaguars, Rovers, and who-knows-what-else, he was, as they say, keeping a high profile. It all cost him about $8 million, keeping the crew together for nearly two years and wintering in the Bahamas and all. But he loved it, at $60,000 a day, and he probably considered the whole thing rather inexpensive publicity. For I believe what he wanted was to place his own personal stamp on the world. Peter de Savary in 1983 was the 1974 edition of Alan Bond. But I still liked him very much, just as I have always liked the ferocious little demon of Perth. There's something about those bigger-than-life characters who flash around their money and their hasty opinions. It all has a certain charm, and it's good for the game and ultimately for everyone involved. Good on 'em both, I say.

The other fact about the British was that they had an extremely fast boat in *Victory '83,* and they had the wherewithal to tune her. They also had *Victory '82, Lionheart* (veteran of the 1980 campaign), and *Australia.* Four 12-Meter boats! It was a mammoth exercise just keeping them on the water. Peter de Savary, who was also operating his helicopter and a seaplane and his entire worldwide business from the dock or from his residence at The Towers, still had time to insist that *Victory '83* take off each morning at 10 sharp, when he was waiting on his balcony, puffing away. If they were five minutes late, he would roar at his helmsman. Every single problem they had was hit with a volley of grapeshot. If there were 10 possible solutions, they used every one, and their overall campaign was an object lesson in how not to do it. To make up for lost time, they had twice as many sails as we had. Since they did not have the technical experience, they tried to make up for it with a huge campaign, trying to crush their worries with money and effort and every conceivable type of help—such as submarine navigators and very sophisticated consultants for their state-of-the-art Apple computers. But you can't buy experience, and, in the end, such a vast operation must become unwieldy. Eventually, there is a buildup of rival factions. People who hardly know each other can scarcely be expected to pull together. PDS himself (everyone calls him PDS) made a substantial contribution to this lack of harmony by refusing to name a single skipper and thus wreaking havoc with the fragile egos of his afterguard. For example there was Harry Cudmore, a crack international match-racing helmsman who had won four of the previous five Royal Lymington Cups, Europe's top match-racing event. (He was not the reigning champion and holder of the Royal Lymington Cup, because in

1983 that honor belonged to my trusty tactician, Hughey Treharne, and me.) Harry was a top man and a very hard competitor. It was he who beat Hughey and me in a race in the New Zealand match-racing championship. Well, Harry had been with the *Victory '83* campaign for a very long time, and naturally he wanted the formal appointment as skipper. PDS would not agree to this, so Harry Cudmore packed his bags and went home to England. They lost the best man they had, in our opinion, and one of the three best match-racing skippers in Newport, particularly at the start. I was honestly glad to see him go! In fact, Hughey and I raised a surreptitious can of Swan Lager to the departure of one of our most aggressive rivals.

PDS used to love to keep his crew off balance, with no one quite knowing how they stood. He described this lunatic theory as "creative tension," whereby it is totally impossible for anyone to feel sure of himself. He thought that it kept everyone on their toes, which it probably did for a while. But you don't achieve famous team victories by making everyone nervous. You do that by making everyone *want* to lay down their lives for you because they believe in what you believe in, and what their entire team believes in. You might blunder along some of the way by using Peter's primitive psychology, but you will never go all the way, because your men will crack under the pressure, as his did.

But PDS was a wonderful addition. Down there on the British dock you could see a swarm of yellow-and-blue-striped men, diving this way and that like industrious hornets. Somewhere in the middle would be PDS, with a cigar about the size of a bazooka clamped between his teeth, bawling orders and instilling fear in riggers, winch-grinders, helmsmen, and tacticians—and clearly loving every minute of it. He was so like Bondy used to be, hiring and firing, shouting and yelling, demanding this, demanding that, expounding the most cringe-making opinions on the finer points of match racing these big boats, and generally having the time of his life.

Not only was he cast in the tradition of Bondy, he was cast in the tradition of many of the great America's Cup challengers. He was an educated man who understood the meaning of good manners, which he clearly had once been taught, but he was also a self-made man. The combination is rare and powerful, and it was fascinating to see him rule that enormous operation like an overbearing, slightly naughty Captain Bligh. PDS made his fortune in the Middle East during the oil-boom years, but, like Bondy, he is also heavily involved in real estate, including a large apartment complex in New York City's elegant Sutton Place.

I am not sure how PDS plans to cash in on the America's Cup should he one day manage to win it, but I have supreme confidence that he will

find a way to enrich himself further both monetarily and, in the broadest
sense, socially. He knows how to win and he knows how to lose. The departure of Harry Cudmore, which would have leveled a lesser man, fazed
PDS not one bit. He cheerfully recruited Chris Law, Britain's Finn Class
Gold Cup winner, to join the scramble for position among the potential
helmsmen: Rodney Pattison (the old Olympic Flying Dutchman king, with
two golds and one silver to his credit), Lawrie Smith, and Phil Crebbin.
This was largely hopeless. Law resigned and went home. Robin Fuger,
another vastly experienced English 12-Meter man, resigned and was instantly snapped up by Dennis Conner and placed in charge of *Liberty*'s
shore-based operations. Phil Crebbin, who believed that he would be
helmsman, was the next to go. Ultimately, Lawrie Smith, who had
won a 6-Meter world championship, became their number-one helmsman,
with Rodney Pattison as his tactician. Morale in the British camp was not
great.

I knew this, and because I had sailed with them, I knew the crew, too.
Their boat was fast, but that would not be good enough. My frank assessment of *Victory '83*'s chances of beating us? About 10 percent, because I
could not see how they could make up for the 10 years of campaigning we
had under our belts.

As for the French, I never considered them as serious opponents.
I'd probably have hanged myself from the yardarm and had the crew
keel-hauled if we had lost to them. Sadly, the imperious figure of Baron
Bich was missing in 1983, for he had recouped some of his $10 million
America's Cup losses by selling *France III* to the film producer Yves Rous-
set-Rouard, one of whose principal gifts to the world of art was the por-
nographic classic *Emmanuelle*. I considered it purely a matter of time
before *Australia II* delivered the French a sharp message, to one of those
parts of the human anatomy so fervently favored by his Gallic cameraman. I don't know what it is about French 12-Meter campaigns, but
they are never any good, and this time they lacked not only the correct
amount of time and the correct people, but also the Baron's money. Yves
did a good job of getting *France III* to Newport, but as his helmsman,
Bruno Trouble, was fond of saying, "Put eleven Americans on a boat and
you have a crew. Put eleven Frenchmen on a boat and you have eleven
Frenchmen." They never had a prayer. Because I did not need to assess
their potential in Newport, I shall not bother to do so here.

The Italians were rather a different story. They had a very beautiful
and very fast boat, *Azzurra*. She sailed under the flag of the Yacht Club
Costa Smeralda, the rugged piece of land on the northeast corner of the
island of Sardinia that the Aga Khan has converted into an idyllic holiday
resort favored by the very rich and famous. It also serves him as a kind of

manmade private kingdom. The Yacht Club Costa Smeralda is a lovely stone building along the dockside at Porto Cervo, where the Aga Khan has a house and where the international yacht-racing set tends to get together with ever-increasing regularity. Two of the principal backers of the Italian syndicate were the Aga Khan and Signor Gianni Agnelli, head of Fiat. *Azzurra,* named for the color of the glorious sea reflected from the crystalline blue sky over the Mediterranean, was designed by the naval architect Andrea Vallicelli at his Roman studio. The yacht was royal blue and boasted lovely lines—she always looked magnificent. She was, after all, floating on an ocean of money, for the not-inconsiderable bank accounts of the Aga Khan and Signor Agnelli were also supported by 17 major Italian corporations, including Alitalia (the country's national airline), a bank, the state telephone and telegraph company, Cinzano, and Barilla pasta. They were in Newport for a year before the races, and, although I did not think they could possibly beat us, I thought they might be quite good. I had sailed with them back in 1981, shortly after they bought the very fast American 12-Meter *Enterprise,* and I was impressed by their ambition. In 1983 they professed to want no more than to beat the French and learn a lot. That would disqualify them from having any chance against us. But I knew that *Azzurra* would be a good boat, and after I watched them for a while before the elimination races started, I considered, rather thoughtfully, that they had, potentially, the fastest boat in Newport. It was only a hunch at that stage, but I knew *Azzurra* was efficient and that we must not take her defeat for granted when we met.

The Canadians were also in Newport, and had been for several months. They were without hope. They did not have enough money, they did not have good sails, and they did not have enough experience. Also, there was a lot of drama in their camp—hiring and firing. Add to this the fact that they were about nine months behind our program, and their ultimate self-destruction was inevitable.

The only other boat to consider was the other Australian entry, *Advance,* from the Royal Sydney Yacht Club, but their boat was very tippy and difficult to maneuver, and their crew was too young and inexperienced. They had no chance whatsoever.

So that was it. As we went into the trials, *Challenge 12* was the boat we had to beat—with the prospect of one or two nasty moments from *Azzura* and *Victory '83.* My crew was confident, and *Australia II* was all that I hoped she would be at this early stage. The trials began on June 18, less than three weeks after I arrived in Newport. My worries at this stage were few. On the night of June 17, stretched out luxuriously in the skipper's room at Founders' Hall, I slept the deep and untroubled sleep of the righteous. Looking back, I hope that I made the most of it, because I did not have many such nights left.

12

The Summer Rampage of Australia II

I was charged up for this, spoiling for a fight, psyching myself up for the struggle. I was feeling total aggression, as you must before a battle. Nothing could get in my way, or I would destroy it.

I could not help feeling that the critical races we started in light winds on June 18, 1983, were nothing more than a dress rehearsal for the real thing. I realized that we *had* to win them, and I was sure that we would, but I could never get my thoughts entirely away from the American trials going on out on the America's Cup course—Conner struggling with *Liberty*, John Kolius struggling with his young crew on *Courageous*, and Blackaller struggling with the rating problems of *Defender*. I knew they were all good. In fact, I knew they were all very, very good. The question was, How fast are they?

For the moment, however, we had to concentrate on doing away with the French, the Italians, the British, the Canadians, and some of our fellow Aussies. Our plan was to come out like an enraged tiger—to go for them with total aggression before the start, to outmaneuver them as ruthlessly and with as many intimidating tactics as necessary before the gun. We planned to hit the line first, and then, if they were still close, to try to coax them into a tacking duel with us, to use *Australia II*'s super strength in this area and thus force them immediately into our wind-shadow. With a 12-Meter, that will give you about a 40-second lead. We then aimed to beat away to windward, using every lick of speed we could get out of our boat, with the object of gaining a one-minute lead, mini-mum, at the weather mark. This would give us a decent cushion to hold off the three boats we thought could run us down on the power reaches and the square run—*Azzurra, Victory '83,* and *Challenge 12.*

As plans go, this one certainly went. We lambasted our hapless oppo-nents. We frightened the French to death, demoralized the Canadians, clobbered the British twice in succession, ran all over the Italians, humili-ated *Advance,* and dealt with *Challenge 12* once. The trouble was, we also lost once to *Challenge 12,* in a chop and light winds, just as we had done so many times before. It was one of the days when *Australia II* was not very good, and we did not seem to be able to do very much about it in those conditions. However, we finished this first round-robin series with an 11-1 record. *Challenge* was improving, but we still had the same basic problems we always had had back in Australia. Our boat was outstandingly maneu-verable, but she still had those vices going downwind, and she was going to need all the help we could give her. Naturally, at the end of that series, with our nearly flawless record, the rumbling about the Superboat, which honestly had never occurred to us, began to take root. People began to talk about the fantastic boat from Down Under with the mysterious keel. We began to hear rumors from the American camp about the amazing speed of *Australia II.* From where we stood, it was hard to believe that they were all talking about the same boat—day after day, we felt that strange wobble in the chop and watched other boats come rolling up to us on the downwind legs, which form three of the six sections of the racecourse. Sure, we could outsail most of our opponents, and we could tack faster, and we could outmaneuver them at the start, and we were far more skill-ful with our sails, and our sail development and our crew work were be-coming superlative. But the press was not saying that. They were saying something quite different—that we had a fabulously fast boat that would carry us or anyone else to victory on pure boatspeed. That was not true. In fact, that was absolutely ridiculous. There were indeed some conditions in which we *could not win,* where we were plainly lousy against *Azzurra* and *Victory* and *Challenge 12.* Never mind the Americans.

However, from all of this I sensed an advantage. From all of my pre-vious experience, I knew there is nothing quite as offputting in a big race as to be up against an opponent whose boat was a bit of a mystery. It is psychologically harder to race something unknown than to race a known commodity. It has an unnerving effect, and here we were with what I perceived as a developing situation that was going to work powerfully for us. The world seemed to think that *Australia II* was a flying machine in all conditions. And the world did not know what was beneath our hull. That is the type of upsetting little scenario that can put the most stoic of skippers off their stride—a boat shrouded in mystery and believed by the press to be a seagoing rocketship. It was a lovely story for the newspapers, possessing the three advantages many sports journalists prize above everything: (1) It was dead easy to understand (not like the real issue, sails, which are wildly complicated and scientific and full of difficult connotations like aerodynamics); (2) it might even be true; and (3) even if it was not true, it was the type of thing we probably would not deny. Perfect.

There was, however, another aspect of what the press was beginning to accomplish that brought a very subtle smile of anticipation to my face. There was one man in the whole world who I knew would be most concerned and indeed affected by a piece of devious technical equipment he could not match. His name was Dennis Conner. And here I would like to tell a little story about Dennis—and I do not mean it to be in any way derogatory. I would like to express what we all know to be true about Dennis. He is a great helmsman, but what he likes most is to be better prepared than everyone else. And that is what he has often done, very successfully. At the same time, Dennis, like most world-class sportsmen—myself included—has an ego. Dennis has a championship-class ego, and it is most important to him to continue to assert his superiority. In 1979, when I was in San Francisco buying my Soling, which I hoped to race in the Moscow Olympics, I was at the yacht club watching the competitors prepare for the World Star Boat Championships and talking to my old friend Buddy Melges. Dennis came over to have a chat, and I will always remember him saying, "John, I will be very disappointed if I lose this regatta, because I have spent more time than anyone else preparing my boat and myself for it. I've spent three months preparing this boat." Now Buddy was listening to this, and he could not have cared two hoots what Dennis said—but the conversation was meant to intimidate him. Off they went for the first race, and Buddy walloped everyone, wiped Dennis off the map. And after the first race, Buddy recalls Dennis walking up to him and saying, "Buddy—it is Buddy, isn't it?—well done!" There is an example of subtle condescension—"welcome to the club," if you like (the idea of not quite knowing the name of a great yachtsman and an Olympic gold medalist!). So Buddy said, with heavily disguised sarcasm, "Oh, *thanks,* Dennis," pretending to be subservient, the underdog in the conversation.

Buddy thought that this unnerved Dennis, who in turn suspected that Buddy was playing with him. Anyway, they went out and Buddy won the regatta, no trouble at all. That may sound like a little bit of pure trivia, but in the world of international sport, major championships can be won and lost on seemingly insignificant confrontations like that. That's where the modern sports psychologists come in. They can help athletes who are going into combat to feel really good about themselves, sure and confident in their training. Mentally tough. Unshakable under pressure. "Just keep sailing, keep doing what you know is right. . . . Remember Montreal. . . ."

I believe Dennis had all kinds of hangups. He is just about as sensitive as anyone to those twin allies of the match racers—boatspeed and bullshit. Now, can you imagine what a man like that must have thought as he read daily in the papers that *Australia II* was the fastest 12-Meter in history, and that she had a keel that he not only was unable to match, but also was unable even to see? I am quite certain that *Australia II* was on his mind, more than it should have been and more than was good for him. I was also fairly certain that if Dennis was worried, then his immediate henchmen, Halsey Herreshoff and John Marshall, would also be affected. Our strategy was to ensure that the myth of *Australia II* caused their concern to become progressively worse.

I decided privately to do everything I could to perpetuate the powerful idea that our boat was "unbeatable." And my chief support in the glorious lie of the invincibility of *Australia II* would be the press. I resolved that no matter what happened, however badly we were beaten, I would take the blame personally—either that, or I would claim that we were testing sails or trying out new spinnakers. Anything I could think of to make our suspect downwind performance and our shaky performance to windward in a chop seem to be directly attributable to my own human error, or, alternatively, deliberate. I would *never* admit, till the day we all flew home, that *Australia II,* in certain conditions, had some serious flaws and that it was only the truly accomplished sailing of her crew and the ceaseless work of Schnackenberg on the sail wardrobe that kept us constantly ahead of our opponents technically and ahead of the less sophisticated foreign boats when we sailed so slowly downwind.

When you stay awake at night planning an elaborate labyrinth of real whoppers to inflict upon an unsuspecting world, I suppose there is an outside chance of some form of retribution from a power even higher than that of the New York Yacht Club. I had not considered the consequences of straying from the particular commandment that deals with bearing false witness, but anyway, in the middle of a soccer game just before the second trials began, I was singularly struck down. Not, I hasten to add, directly by the hand of God, but in fact by the left knee of Warren

Jones. We accidentally crashed into each other going for a high ball, and I landed on my head. My neck seemed a bit sore immediately afterward, but, like all athletes, I was certain I could "work it out" by ignoring it, so I played volleyball the next day and nearly ended up on a stretcher. A pinched nerve was diagnosed, and the local hospital put me into a neck brace. It hurt like hell, and it put me out of action on and off for about four weeks. It was traumatic for me, because I thought it might put me out of the America's Cup. However, right at that time, Rasa arrived like an angel of mercy with the children. With a huge sense of relief, I moved into the apartment on Dennison Street with my live-in nurse and constant savior from loneliness and pressure. Through a series of awful muscle spasms, she massaged my back, shoulders, and neck for arm-aching hours, and finally she got me right. I am afraid to pose the question, "What would I have done without her?" I honestly do not know.

But nothing is perfect and one evening Rasa let through the net one piece of trivia too many, a minor domestic request, and with a roar of fury, I slammed my right foot through the door of a bedroom cupboard, demolishing the wood and fracturing my big toe. It was incredibly painful, and it made me more furious than ever. At that moment I suppose that Rasa alone finally understood the monumental pressure with which I was trying to cope. I am a perfectionist by nature, and the frustration of trying to make perfect every aspect of the enormous *Australia II* campaign would have tested the qualities of Job himself. And Australia's Mr. Cool, as the press was inclined to call me, had blown his stack in spades—privately, but still I had blown it.

And I felt like an idiot the next day as I hobbled down Dennison Street with a broken neck and a broken foot. I looked like a refugee from the Battle of Waterloo. Benny, however, was a great help. It took him 10 minutes to stop laughing.

But the show had to go on. Sometimes I sailed and sometimes I couldn't do it because of the pain. On those days—I tried to be there for the tough ones—Jim Hardy stepped in for me at the helm and did a fantastic job. *Australia II* did her stuff as well, but it was the sailing that got us home in its early stages of the round robin. We tended to win all of our starts against the foreigners, just as we had planned, and we almost always got to the weather mark in very good order. Because of our terrific struggles back home with *Challenge,* we knew a lot more about match racing 12-Meters than our opponents in those early days. Also, we were far more advanced with our upwind sail selection and our knowledge of sail shapes. Our sails were quite superior going to windward because of our technology—always evolving, never remaining static. As a result, we were able to take the lead early on and tack quickly. The minute they tacked, we slapped the cover on.

On July 2 we faced up to the second round robin, and on the second day, with Jim Hardy helming for me, our luck ran out. *Victory '83* beat us. It was a long race with odd, shifting winds, and although Jim reached the fifth mark nearly 1½ minutes in the lead, he ran straight into a major hole in the wind and was almost completely becalmed at the bottom mark. The boys on *Victory* sailed very well and got the British boat moving up the final leg, upon which she gained five minutes 40 seconds, to win the race by the huge margin of three minutes 56 seconds. She took the lead on the big Louis Vuitton scoreboard on Thames Street for the first and only time. Back we came, handing out some severe beatings to everyone, but on July 13 we copped it again. I was at the helm, and we ran into *Azzurra* at her very best. We held a lead of about half a minute at the top mark, and then, dread of dreads, we just could not hold her, and she literally blew past us coming downwind on the square run.

I duly showed up at a press conference afterward and told them something about testing new spinnakers, that it had been all my fault, and that the Superboat would be right back on target forthwith. And just to confirm how straightforward and upright I am, we went out and delivered a monumental beating to the French two days later by nearly 6½ minutes.

The second round robin ended with *Australia II* sporting a 10–2 record. We had a total of 21 victories against three losses. *Challenge 12,* right behind us, had 17 wins and seven losses. *Victory '83* had 15 wins and nine losses. Ever since we annihilated the French, the press had been in a frenzy of excitement about the "unbeatable boat." And as that series of races ended, two fairly unorthodox events occurred. Halsey Herreshoff, the navigator on Dennis Conner's *Liberty,* made a public announcement. He said quite simply that *Australia II* was likely to win the America's Cup if she was allowed to race "as she is rated." This statement was unprecedented in living memory. In fact, it was probably unprecedented in the memory of anyone, alive or dead. An American navigator on a boat about to defend the America's Cup in her home waters, second officer to apparently the greatest living helmsman, coming out and saying they would probably be beaten! As far as I was concerned, that was tantamount to Admiral Horatio Nelson having hoisted his famous signal before the Battle of Trafalgar and adding a short rider: "England expects that every man will do his duty—and by the way, I don't like our chances much." I was staggered. The Americans were clearly terrified.

The next unorthodox occurrence was a formal letter from the chairman of the America's Cup Committee, Robert W. McCullough, to the American member of the three-man measuring committee. McCullough told him in no uncertain terms that, in his opinion, *Australia II,* with her winged keel, ought to be remeasured. In the opinion of the New York

Yacht Club, our rating was not fair—the keel gave us an unreasonable advantage.

This no longer fell under the general heading of a sporting altercation. This was out-and-out War. The measuring committee did not, it seems, agree with Mr. McCullough. But Halsey Herreshoff boldly demanded that the keel be unveiled and that all the other challengers and the defenders file a formal protest. He further demanded that Bondy and his men be given the opportunity to withdraw from the contest, or get those fins off the keel, or suffer a penalty for additional draft, gained when the boat heels. I thought Alan Bond might have apoplexy, but he didn't. He smiled the wickedly unpleasant snarl of the predator sensing a kill, and he liberated Warren Jones onto the battlefront. It was a scrap that feisty old Warren seemed to have been waiting for all his life. I was personally of the opinion that, having maimed the skipper on the soccer field, he ought to get busy in whatever way he could!

Warren began to prepare our defense—but I really do not mean *prepare*. He had done that months earlier. What I really mean is *refine*. He gathered his facts in that exemplary way of his, no stone left unturned, no base uncovered, sticking hard by his creed: "Only fight from high ground." Meanwhile, the world at large was amazed by this astonishing display by the New York Yacht Club. Now they were trying to change the rules after the competition had begun—a tactic that was not entirely foreign to them. People were outraged, and I saw the danger signal to my crew a long time before most did. I had to keep the crew separate. I could not let them become embroiled, whatever the outcome. At my breakfast speech a couple of days after this furor erupted, I said to them formally, "I do not know how long this row is going to go on, but I have total confidence that Warren will sort it out in our favor. We have to be legal, because otherwise Bondy and Ben would not have built the boat in the first place. But I would like to give you this brief warning. If you wish to spend one minute, one day, or one year thinking about the New York Yacht Club's protest, it will not do you one shred of good on the day we have to go out there for race number one. I ask you to forget it. Let Warren get on with it. Each night he will tell us what's happening. But right now, let's get back out there on the water and get those sails *right*."

I was deliberately not involving myself in this aspect of the matter. I was trying to keep myself and my crew as far away as possible from it, and while the free world went wild with accusations, the crew and I got on with the sailing. Our fellow competitors would not join the NYYC against us, and in broad terms, the measuring committee would not change its mind about the rating, so that particular door was summarily closed to the men in the straw hats. But they were tenacious about getting rid of us, I'll say that for them.

Next, the *Liberty* syndicate fired off a Telex to the head of design research at the Netherlands Ship Model Basin, where Ben had run the tank tests. A portion of the message read, "Understand you and your team are responsible for development and design of special keel of *Australia II*. We are fully convinced of her potential and would therefore like to build the same design under one of our boats. . . ." Now any damned fool could see that they were not serious. They just wanted an admission from the Dutch that they, rather than Benny, had designed the boat. Anyway, the Dutch, headed by our good friend Dr. Peter Van Oossanen, wired us back about the New York Yacht Club's request. That was the cannonball Warren had been waiting for, and he did not bother with a warning shot across the bows. He let 'em have it amidships in a vicious salvo that confirmed to the entire world that he had caught the Americans redhanded attempting to purchase a non-American Australian keel design, "in clear violation of the 1980 Resolution of the Board of Trustees of the NYYC."

It was clearly a devastating announcement, but frightened men have a tendency to lose their sense of proportion. Having found the going very tough in getting all the other challengers to support it in trying to force us out of the competition, the NYYC faced up, with the utmost bravery, to a positive outcry against it from the American public. We received bagloads of supportive mail from Americans who had never even been aboard a boat. But the men in the straw hats were determined to soldier on, despite casualties. By their own admission, they had not bothered to request permission, an opponent's prerogative, to attend our official measuring by the three-man committee in Cove Haven, Rhode Island, on June 16. Curiously, by late July their attitude had altered rather noticeably. Knowing their reputation for supreme sportsmanship, none of us considered for one moment that it had anything to do with the fact that on June 16 they thought we would probably be hopeless, and now we had won about 25 races and were cheerfully steamrolling our way toward the finals.

On July 23 there was an uproar down at our dock just as the crew was awakening. Our guards caught an underwater cameraman in a wet suit photographing the keel of *Australia II*. Phil Judge, our tender skipper, jumped into the water fully clothed, dragged him out, and turned him over to the Newport police. We dropped charges when the film was handed over and we had assurances that there was only one diver. But there were in fact two, and much later we found another film of our keel in the Canadian house. Jim Johnston, one of their boat drivers, was the man arrested, but we never found out for whom they were working.

By this time Newport seemed half crazed with the controversy. Some rather inaccurate pictures of the keel were being marketed in an art gallery, and accusations were flying everywhere. Benny, of course, was totally preoccupied with the New York Yacht Club's allegation that he had not designed the boat, and that it had been the work of the Dutch. Benny had previously been involved with winged keels and their possibilities, and I had seen his original drawings of *Australia II*. I had watched him at the test-tank facility, totally in charge of everything, with an enthusiastic team assisting him with the highly technical scientific aspects and drawings. One thing is absolutely certain: *Australia II* was Benny Lexcen's design, and since he was perfectly entitled to be at the Dutch testing tank, experimenting with his designs, he could scarcely be expected not to speak to the engineers who were helping him conduct the tests. As arguments go, this was a real nonstarter, but the men from the Yacht Club, with this nasty allegation, did manage to achieve one thing. They ended up giving poor old Benny a very frightening heart tremor. He has always had high blood pressure, and he had even spent some time in the hospital. I do not suppose they intended their allegations to give members of our team a heart attack, but, knowing them, I would not stake my life savings on that.

Although I tried to keep our crew separate from the controversy, it was nearly impossible. The mystery of the keel was on the front pages of just about every newspaper in the world. Television cameras were aimed permanently at us. I was very worried about the effect it would all have on the younger boys in the crew, and I did all I could to impress upon them that we could *not* become involved. We had to keep sailing and leave everything else to Warren and Bondy.

We raced almost daily, from the start of the third round robin on July 20, under the most insidious pressure. It was in the minds of the boys on the boat that all of this might be for nothing, that in the end they were not going to let us race, that ultimately the will of the New York Yacht Club would prevail, that somehow they would find a way to send us home. But I knew there was *some* good in this for us. I knew that we must have frightened the life out of the Americans—and I sensed the hand of Dennis Conner in the NYYC protest. I also knew that Halsey Herreshoff must be right in the thick of it somewhere. And John Marshall. I also recognized that they were burning up a lot of time worrying about us, expending their energy trying to figure out ways to get us thrown out.

The battle raged on, and out on the water we were beginning to sail beautifully. Day after day, through the last 11 days of July, we outclassed the opposition. No one seemed able to beat us, and we were so well forward with our sails that we appeared to be able to overcome the wiles of *Australia II*, improving on her weaknesses every day that we raced and developing her strength with every notch we put on our guns.

By lunchtime on August 2, we were unbeaten in this series of races. And in the afternoon we prepared once more to race against the Canadians, to whom we had never lost. I took *Australia II* back to the racecourse sometime before the 10-minute gun in a gusty wind, about 22 knots of it, and a lumpy sea. We were pitching into the waves with our bow, and I noticed that poor old Scotty McAllister was already soaked. We were wearing our foul-weather gear, and we had already had some trouble with our boom. We changed that to a different one, and then we were having trouble with the mast crane, 90 feet up, as we tried to raise the mainsail. We had had constant trouble with it for the previous few weeks, but now it seemed to be jammed. As we tried to get organized, the spray was breaking over our bow and we were rolling around in the sea. The wind was battering away at the sail, and we had to shout to be heard. The clock kept going and the crane stayed jammed. I had few alternatives, so I had to send a man up the mast, whether I liked it or not. There was only one choice—the man who had attended to the problem up there several times before, even back in 1980, when similar mainsail locks would not work. The thing was always going wrong. Shortly after two o'clock, I shouted to our veteran foredeck boss and my old pal, "Scotty! You'll have to go up— the bastard's jammed again." Scotty never hesitated. He buckled himself in the bosun's chair, and the Major and Ya hauled him to 90 feet with a wrench, a knife, and a screwdriver shoved in his belt. The noise was still deafening in the plastic Kevlar sails as I held *Australia II* into the wind, so no one heard that crane suddenly collapse on Scotty's arm, smashing it in two between the elbow and the wrist, trapping him completely. Scotty's scream was whipped away by the wind. It was amazing that he was not killed. Then he blacked out, and suddenly we all realized what had happened as we saw his head slump forward. Conditions up there were just terrible, the mast was swaying uncontrollably, and Scotty was held close to it mainly by his broken arm. We had no contingency plan to get him down and we had no way to get anyone else that high. I hated to ask anyone else to go up, but Colin Beashel, with immense heroism, stepped forward immediately and said, "Hitch me up. I'll go and get him." We knew we could pull Beasho only to 60 feet, and from there on, we were going to have to plan carefully. Beasho was prepared to shimmy up the last 30 feet and free Scotty, but I did not know if I could let him do it.

With 15 minutes to go before the start, Beasho set off, barefoot, up the mast, hanging on grimly as he swayed up to the 60-foot mark. We could hear him shouting at Scotty and we could see that our bow man at least was conscious. I cannot even explain how terrible I felt, and I knew that if Scotty could not get free, Beasho would go the rest of the way with no safety harness. But finally Scotty got his other hand on the crane, and, with what must have been superhuman effort, he pried that high-tensile-aluminum crane off his arm and freed himself. I will never know where he found the strength, but it is fantastic what a human being will do when in such danger. To this day, he does not remember anything about it.

At last we began to lower Scotty, and I believe he passed out once more. Colin grabbed him and held on as we lowered him to the 60-foot mark, and they set off together on this harrowing downward journey, with the mast swaying uncontrollably and Colin trying with all his strength, which was considerable, to hold them both close in to the mast. Thirty-five feet up the force broke Colin's grip, tearing his fingers loose, and the pair of them swung right out over the waves, 15 feet beyond the deck. Back they swung and crashed into the mast. Beasho was trying to shield Scotty from the impact, but Scotty screamed, and suddenly I realized that there were tears rolling down my own cheeks. It was like a nightmare, and I just could not stand to see my old mate hurt anymore. But Beasho did the rest, and he got them down onto the pitching, rolling deck of *Australia II*.

Then we were desperate to get help for Scotty. Suddenly, from nowhere came the speeding Magnum 55 of Peter de Savary, with the *Victory '83* boss himself in the cockpit. He had heard on the radio what was going on, and they had a doctor on their boat. They were very proficient, and they got Scotty off and looked after him, taking him at high speed across the water to the hospital in Newport. It was an amazing gesture. PDS did not have to do that. After all, we had just given his boys a couple of good beatings. But he is a generous, decent man, and that night I went back and wrote him a letter to thank him for his kindness and generosity.

But back to *Australia II*, where there was some chaos. We still could not raise the mainsail, we had no bow man, and I felt totally responsible for what had just happened. I asked for a postponement, and the committee granted us one, but it was a situation of high drama. If we beat the Canadians, it meant that *Challenge 12* could join us in the semifinal if they could beat either us or *Victory '83* in one of their next two races. Now we were on the verge of forfeiting the race to Canada, because our situation was impossible. We were drifting around out there, beating up the racing sails in the high wind, and beating up the boat. I was very upset and so were the boys. We did not have to worry about our place in the semifinal—we were winning the entire regatta easily, and I was well beyond caring about anyone else's problems. Poor Scotty had nearly been killed— he was in the hospital and I'd lost a top man from one of the key positions on the boat—my neck still hurt, and a bunch of maniacal octogenarians were trying to get us thrown out of the America's Cup. Bloody oath! Anyway, I'd had it, and we withdrew from the race against Canada, thus ending *Challenge 12*'s chances of progressing further. Imagine how popular that made us, particularly in a couple of certain publications in Melbourne. With a burst of excruciatingly ill-informed reporting, they accused us of dropping the race just to get rid of *Challenge 12*. They must have thought it was in the public interest to tell the Australian people that we had deliberately used Scotty's shocking injury to duck out of a possible repeat contest with *Challenge*. Little did they know that our entire mast-head crane had collapsed and there was no way we could hoist the main-sail, let alone race. And when they did find out, I did not notice a stampede of apology from the Fourth Estate.

The day after the accident, I went to the hospital to see Scotty, whose arm was now heavily plastered. On the way down to his room, I was think-ing how unfair it was that a tough, nice guy like Scotty McAllister had given so much for so long, and now he was out of it five weeks before the final. It was an emotional meeting. I told him how very sorry I was, and I told him how proud I had been of him, to watch him turn himself around and develop into one of the mainstays of our crew, how I thought he was as good as you can get at that demanding job of his on the foredeck. I also promised to do everything I could to help him. I knew in my soul that there was not a chance that he could recover in time to sail as bow man against the Americans. But he asked me to promise him that if he could get well, if he could exercise and build back that arm in time, I would keep his place open for him. I can hear him now. He said, "John, if I try with everything I have, would you give me that chance?" Before I left, I promised him.

The lights burned late that night on the dock of *Australia II* and early in the morning we were ready to fight again. That same day, Commodore Robert McCullough sent a 34-page document to George Andreadis, chair-man of the Keel Boat Technical Committee (KBTC) of the International Yacht Racing Union (IYRU), protesting the winged keel of *Australia II*.

This massive document contained the statement from Halsey Her-reshoff "that if the closely guarded keel design of *Australia II* is allowed to remain in competition, or is allowed to continue to be rated without penalty, the yacht will likely win the foreign trials and will be likely to win the America's Cup in September." It must have taken at least two weeks to prepare, and it was nothing short of a declaration of hostilities. We kept sailing and they kept arguing. Warren Jones replied to everything, argu-ing ferociously on our behalf. At the end of the week, Commodore Mc-Cullough and two of his henchmen went to Bondy's house for a meeting to try to calm the waters and get Bondy to back down and make the changes. I've heard of a waste of time, but that was ridiculous. Bondy, who is intimidated by nothing, let fly at them. He told them, in the most threatening manner, that he would drag the name of the New York Yacht Club through the gutter and embarrass them in every possible way. I was not there, but I know how Bondy looks when he gets cross or when he feels he is being given a hard time. I did not envy McCullough being on the wrong end of his tongue. It was said that no one had ever spoken to the commodore in quite that way before.

All through the month of August, the battle continued. We wound up winning 15 of our 16 races and forfeiting one in the third round robin to finish the three all-against-all series with a record of 36 wins, three losses, and one forfeit. And, of course, the press was in an uproar about the boat with the winged keel that could not be beaten. By this time, there were frequent charges that we were "sandbagging"—getting a big lead very fast and then not trying, in order to keep even our top speed a total secret, lulling the opposition into a false sense of security. Little did they know, we *had* to snatch a fast lead, and little did they know how grimly we had to sail the boat at times in order to hang on. There was *no* race in which *Australia II* did not sail as well as was humanly possible.

On August 22, Peter de Savary came to our aid for the second time in three weeks. It was interesting, because de Savary, like Bondy, is a man with a short fuse and a long memory. Perhaps that's why they are friends. Anyway, a couple of years back, PDS had paid $30,000 in design fees to Johan Valentijn, the Dutchman who designed *Liberty,* and then received a letter from the New York Yacht Club telling him he could use none of it because Valentijn had become a U.S. citizen and he was designing an American defender. PDS never got over that one, nor did he forget it. After watching, presumably with great glee, the NYYC people make complete fools of themselves in front of their own public, PDS rather spectacularly played his ace. He called a major press conference at the Newport Armory, and with the aid of some witheringly unkind cartoons depicting what he thought of the New York Yacht Club, he produced a letter from the KBTC of the IYRU, which confirmed that "tip wings are permitted so long as the static draft is not exceeded." In addition, Mark Vinbury, the official measurer of the NYYC, proceeded to give them formal clearance to use wings on their own keel, which had been specially drilled to accommodate them—"they would affect neither flotation nor draft"—and to all intents and purposes, this blew the jolly old straw hats right off the embattled committee. Four days later, the NYYC capitulated. The committee issued a statement that it was pleased to announce that the question relating to the keels of *Australia II* and *Victory '83,* and the design thereof, had been resolved.

But they were not yet finished with Benny, and for the next three weeks they did everything they could to try to prove we were in a Dutch boat. It was the most astonishing performance, because they were rowing against the massive tide of public opinion, the kind that drove Richard Nixon from office. My own view is that Americans are generally the best sports in the world. They know what's fair, and they have an innate sense of what's aboveboard and what's not, in the same way that the English and the Australians have this inbuilt sense of decency. I did not think the NYYC would have the stomach to announce that it was refusing to race us. There would have been an absolutely unbelievable uproar, one of the biggest rows in the history of sport. And the American public would have been on our side. I told the boys, "Those old bastards won't in the end have the guts to go through with it. Because that would be too much for anyone to face up to. They *have* to race us. And remember, they never objected to the keel until we started to win. This is a complete red herring, and we will get to race them, with our boat."

Meanwhile, in the middle of all this, we faced up to the semifinal round against *Victory '83, Canada,* and *Azzurra.* We walloped the last two boats three times each, and *Victory '83* twice. But we lost on August 18 to *Victory,* and it was very significant. In a light 4½-knot breeze, they romped away from us on the last beat home, winning by two minutes and 50 seconds. I busily stepped up and made up all kinds of reasons why the Superboat, the Wonder from Down Under, had not quite done her stuff on that day, explaining away the defeat and leaving intact the fearsome reputation of *Australia II.* However, down on our dock, things were less than serene. Benny was down in the dumps and Bondy was pacing around demanding to know what the hell was going on. The strain of the summer was beginning to show. I was in a rather difficult position, because I was trying to balance everyone's hopes and dreams with the hard facts. I did not want anyone to become disillusioned, and I was very mindful of the fact that by allowing the *Australia II* "invincibility" rumor to have progressed as far as it had, we had also allowed our own hierarchy to start believing our own publicity. By now Bondy and Warren and Benny believed that *Australia II was* the Wonder from Down Under. And they wanted to go on believing it. Most of my own crew also believed it, and the entire thing had been excellent for morale and fighting spirit.

But now Hughey and I were faced with a nervous, worried Alan Bond demanding to know why we had lost to *Victory '83* in a light wind. I followed my usual philosophy of dealing with Bondy—be progressive, fire solutions at him, and look as if you know precisely what you are talking about. I told him that we would have to rethink our light-air sails. I told him *Victory* was faster—anyone could see that. I told him I thought we needed a new light-wind sail to give us more speed. In particular, I thought we needed a new light-air *mainsail,* and that Schnacks should build it precisely to his exacting new specifications. "Well, get it," snapped Bond. *"Now."* That was it. $18,000. Crash! End of discussion.

What with my neck, the uproar in the Yacht Club, Scotty, and every other damned thing happening at the same time, I have omitted to mention the total demise of our old enemy, *Challenge 12*, whose hopes of getting to the semifinals ended at the moment the masthead crane crushed Scotty's arm. In fact, they then lost to *Victory '83* and to us in their next two races, so they would not have made it even if we had not given the Canadians those points. Theirs was a classic story of collapse. Like a couple of other crews, they improved rapidly when they got to Newport. Then, suddenly, they were required to go beyond their limitations. They did then what all beaten competitors start to do—they tried wild cards and made rash decisions, straining for the one great throw that would set them straight. They were overextended, because they did not have the technology, the organization, and the right compatibility within their group. When things got tight, they fell apart. We thus saw a crew that had steadily been getting better and better and then suddenly deteriorated almost overnight. In the second round robin they finished second to us. In the third round robin they finished last. Just like that. As a result of the enormous pressure, they did have a mutiny. Not like the *Bounty* or anything, but nevertheless a definite splinter group, led by the tactician, Frizzle Freeman. When things got tough, Frizzle and his men thought John Savage was not doing as well as he might, and Savage felt he was being seriously undermined. In the end, Savage said something that meant, "There's not room on this boat for both of us." Good-bye, Frizzle.

Anyway, as the *Challenge 12* campaign ended, we stepped in and recruited Mike Fletcher as our sailing coach, which took some of the strain off Hughey and me. And after that semifinal defeat by *Victory '83*, he observed that we were not trimming the mainsheet as hard as *Victory* did, and that we should be doing so. That was a critical observation, because it did improve us upwind in the joggle, a facet of the racing that was going to be vital when we faced the Americans, because the huge spectator fleet was going to ruffle up the flat water we loved.

So, not only were we going to have to go back to the drawing board on the light-wind sails, we were going to have to change our basic trim—all in the cause of getting some speed to windward for the boat with the winged keel. Not only was *Australia II* sometimes slower than *Victory* in these critical light winds, we were definitely slower than *Azzurra*, which I think was the fastest conventional Twelve in Newport all summer.

The other major problem was a replacement bow man. This highly visible and highly vulnerable position is one of the specialist places on the boat. The job calls for incredible experience. The bow man calls the overlaps in the prestart maneuvering, calls the line at the start, and is in charge of all headsail changes and spinnaker sets. He must connect the spinnaker pole to the opposite spinnaker guy when the boat jibes. He must swing out over the boat on the end of the pole and switch the guys when there is a spinnaker change. He also has to keep the foredeck clear and make sure there is always a halyard free for a sail change. And he has to be ready to go up the mast at a second's notice. It is a job that I have never done, have never wanted to do, and have no intention of ever attempting. And now we were considering facing up to the America's Cup without such a specialist.

Meanwhile, *Challenge 12* was packing up, and so was *Advance*. We decided to ask both of their bow men to come over for a trial. But, with dreadful irony, the man from *Advance* had gone out and gotten drunk the night Scotty ended up in the hospital—he was going home, after all, so it didn't seem to matter—and he contrived to fly straight over the handlebars of his bike and landed on his nose, which broke. With a bitter twist of fate, he then landed in the very next bed to Scotty in the hospital.

That left us with the bow man from *Challenge,* Damian Fewster. Young! He had not yet had his 21st birthday. But he came over to see me. He was a very quiet kid from Williamstown, just across the coast from Mum's house on Port Phillip Bay. I was national junior champion of Australia before he was born! I took a liking to him very quickly because of one factor. He was not in awe of the situation. I could not quite decide whether he was just totally without knowledge of the Americans, but he did not care a damn for them, and he thought we would *win.* He is a very determined, very likable kid, extremely fit, about five feet 11 inches, 176 pounds, well built, and very tough. He appeared to be afraid of nothing. He was younger than Scotty and he would do anything—go up the mast, go under the boat, go anywhere. We were just amazed at how good he was. So while poor Scotty struggled and strained in the gymnasium, pushing weights and hauling on pulleys, his replacement was working himself into the bow man's place. In one sense, I might have felt very divided about this situation, but I *knew* that whatever Scotty said, he was never going to be fit enough in four weeks to take his place in the crew, after an injury that always takes six weeks to heal. There's not much luck in this game, but we got our share this time, when our backs were to the wall, with this tough new kid who could fill Scotty's boots. He was the best man *Challenge 12* had.

With our expanded sail inventory and our ever-improving new bow man, we set off to face *Victory '83* in the final seven-race series for the right to face the Americans. None of the other points counted. It was them and us, starting from scratch, sudden death. First boat to win four races and that's the ball game, as they say. Now there were just two things standing between Dennis Conner and me—*Victory '83* and the Committee of the New York Yacht Club, which still was trying to put a sticker on our boat that would read, "Designed in Holland—Disqualified."

The day of the first race dawned. Medium fresh winds and very confused, choppy seas. Out on the water, everyone was revved up as we headed down to the killing ground, where we would begin the prestart maneuvers. I glanced up at the mainsheet and smiled at a little touch of humor from the sailmakers. Over the mainsail they had embroidered the five stars of the Southern Cross, the great, bright southern galaxy that can be seen so clearly back home in Australia and also adorns our national flag. Suddenly, across the water I saw a group of people hurtling toward us in our tender. They were doing about 100 miles an hour, and right in the middle was Bondy, yelling at the top of his lungs, "What the f--- is that on the sail for?" Benny was shouting, "Get it down, get it down. It's illegal." It was 15 minutes before the start, and there was no way I could start changing the mainsail. If we had tried, we would have missed the start by five minutes. So the discussion was irrelevant, right or wrong. I'd never heard anything more hysterical or more silly. But these guys had sent Alan wild with fury. They had effectively lost control of themselves— displaying the precise emotions I had been training the crew of *Australia II* *never* to give in to, no matter what.

Here I was at the helm, facing the combined talents of a world champion at the helm of *Victory '83* plus a tactician who has won *two* Olympic gold medals. I was charged up for this, spoiling for a fight, psyching myself up for the struggle. I was feeling total aggression, as you must before a battle. Nothing could get in my way, or I would destroy it. Hughey was feeling much the same, and everyone else was getting ready—the tension was fantastic. Suddenly I was faced with a group of people from my own team having collective hysterics. I looked down. Alan bawled again, "What the fuck is that doing on the sail?"

"FUCK OFF, ALAN!"

He started to come back at me. "FUCK OFF, ALAN, FUCK OFF!" I snapped. For two pins I could have hit him right in the mouth. Forget that. If I could have reached him, I would have knocked him flat on his back. That's how I felt, and that's what I would have done. But then Warren entered the fray, stoutly defending the honor of the man who pays him. "Who the hell do you think you are?" he asked, and he wanted to fight me right then, four minutes before the 10-minute gun. I told him, all five feet nine inches of him, precisely what I had told his boss a few seconds before.

Bondy, seeing the situation deteriorating, made the hard business decision and snapped to the powerboat skipper, "Get out of here right now. Take us back." The crew loved it. The Major flashed a wicked grin and

Grant looked up and said, "That was the greatest thing I've ever heard!" It was interesting. There was my own campaign's administrative chief wanting to punch his own helmsman on the chin just before we faced *Victory '83* in the *final* of the elimination races. I suppose that little altercation showed the profound emotion being felt by the hierarchy of our syndicate.

Anyway, we got back on track and, still shaking with anger, I blew the start and headed *Australia II* into the wind. We had now won 44 races and I was beginning to get the hang of it, but we had difficulty containing *Victory* upwind in the now deteriorating wind and the joggle. We tried everything, but we could not squeeze one ounce of extra speed out of *Australia II*, and *Victory* passed us and led at the first mark by 16 seconds. They still held us by 13 seconds at the gun. It was 1–0 to them.

When we returned to the dock, the atmosphere was despondent, but I knew we had not sailed our best in conditions that were against us. They had outsailed us, with a speed edge. All we could do was to work harder on our mainsail design and forget about boatspeed problems, which in the end probably were small enough to overcome.

The next day at breakfast, Bondy came over to me, grinned, put his hand on my shoulder, and said, "Forget it, John." I knew there would not be another altercation like the one on the previous day. Bondy had come too far for any more of that.

I had already managed to defend the towering reputation of the old Superboat to the press, and the first person I met from the *Victory* camp that day said, "You were obviously experimenting again yesterday." "Absolutely," I lied. Just throwing away a critical race while we tested a few sails!

The next day the troops rallied, and in a better breeze that was *all* we needed, we went out and leveled the score at 1–1. In the third race we sailed just beautifully. Hughey and I hit the windshifts perfectly, and we made hardly a mistake. *Australia II* put on one of her greatest-ever performances—in fact, that day she performed as the 1981 tank test had said she would. For some unknown reason, she went straight away from them to windward. She even felt differently drawing clear all the way up the first beat. We demoralized the British that day, winning easily and causing the press to thunder out the obvious message that we had been sandbagging in the first race. I just smiled slyly at the press conference, saying little and offering a little wink to the reporters, confirming their beliefs that *nothing* could beat the Superboat when we chose to let her go.

It was strange, that third race. *Australia II* found a lot of flat water almost as calm as that in which Benny's tests had been conducted. I assume it all had something to do with the laminar flow going around the keel, but the pity was that we could not get it to work very often. It only happened two or three times, but on those occasions she really did sail as Benny had predicted. In the meantime, however, we were always bothered by the fact that we hardly ever got her moving like that. She seemed to have a mind of her own, and she was without doubt the most capricious boat I had ever sailed. That tank test just about swore that we could win by 20 minutes in a strong breeze and that we would have a definite advantage in light air. Well, we never saw that, and although I am quite sure Benny is onto something major with this winged keel, *Australia II* still had her imperfections.

The British were never quite the same force after that third race. They missed some shifts while we more consistently found them, and there never was any doubt about either of the next two races, which would be the last *Victory '83* would sail in Newport 1983. Everything we had worked so hard on for so long was coming together. Schnacks's latest sails were proving to be a breakthrough in light winds—we were faster downwind than ever before, and the new light mainsail was a little masterpiece. Hughey's Sobstad spinnakers, recut, were the best we ever had. Morale was terrific. We took no prisoners. We crushed *Victory* 4–1 and entered the America's Cup as the 25th challenger against an opponent yet to be named—but it clearly would be Dennis Conner. We docked the boat that night, and I stood there by myself for a little while, thinking, "By Christ, it's been a long haul." But now, after all the years of trying, I was going to helm the Australian challenger in the America's Cup races in Newport. And finally it was going to be the match old D.C. had predicted nearly five years earlier. Australia (J. Bertrand) vs. America (D. Conner)—in 12-Meter yachts, on Rhode Island Sound, for the Holy Grail of our sport. I was not afraid. I had confidence that I had enough experience, that I had done so much down all the seasons since Lex and I first started racing the little Sabots nearly 30 years earlier. "Now," I said to myself, "it is time to stop practicing. The apprenticeship is over." Now it was time for me to deliver the goods.

13

Dennis Anyone?

"And he sang as he looked at his old billy boiling,
You'll come a-waltzing Matilda with me."
God help me if they're not singing that tomorrow night.

I t wasn't much fun in Newport if you happened to be sailing one of the American Twelves. The atmosphere started out awful and became worse. Tom Blackaller, the helmsman of the hideously slow *Defender,* could not bear Dennis Conner, and on the only occasion that Tom actually spoke to the New York Yacht Club Committee, he castigated them for their dreadful public image over their attack on our keel. They found it difficult to be united even in their dislike of us.

Blackaller's tactician, Gary Jobson, also hated Dennis, and he launched a furious public attack on him that grew so heated that both of them were lectured by the Committee. They have not, I believe, spoken to this day. Dennis, for his part, had no time for Blackaller or Jobson, and his autocratic bearing on the boat and on shore caused much unhappiness among his crew. David Hirsch, the *Liberty* sail coordinator, was so fed up with the backbiting that he came and rented a room on Dennison Street with Chink Longley and Tom Schnackenberg. "Hirschey Bar" ate with us, drank with us, and sat on our front porch at night having a beer and chatting with us. He was not exactly a "mole." It was just as though a ranking member of the Kremlin Politburo had taken a nice suite of rooms for the summer with Denis and Margaret Thatcher in Downing Street.

Oh yes, there was trouble in paradise all right, long before Conner and I actually threw down the gauntlet for Race 1 on September 13. In fact, just before the races started, the wife of a top *Liberty* crewman told Rasa, "I hope you win. I just cannot stand what's going on over there in the *Liberty* house." Whatever was going on was having a very upsetting effect. David Hirsch used to shake his head and say, "I just don't know. I don't know what's happening there . . . but the rival factions. Just leave me out of it." I surmised it was the old American problem of having in the crew sailmaking executives who wanted to promote their own product during the races. But whatever, I was delighted. For all we cared, they were welcome to fight another Civil War, because if they had their minds on screwing up each other, they might not have so much time to think about us.

There is no doubt that the American trial races were fought out in a cutthroat, acrimonious atmosphere, and it enabled them to develop their match-racing skills rather more intensely than we were able to do against the foreign boats. Early in the summer, there had been little difference among the U.S. Twelves, and they finished the first series of preliminary trials with close records: *Courageous*, 6–5; *Defender*, 5–6; *Liberty*, 5–5. But Dennis won four of his last five. In the observation trials, which began on July 16, *Defender* showed up after major surgery and turned out to be only marginally better. I noted that *Courageous* won only two of 15 races, but I also noted that she won more than her fair share of starts, and in one fantastically close race in which the boats were never more than 12 seconds apart, *Courageous* crossed the finish line first. The "invincible" D. Conner was having his problems.

By this time, however, it was obvious that the New York Yacht Club was determined to select *Liberty*. She was racing under a multiple-rating certificate, which permitted them to remove ballast from the keel and add more sail area, depending on the winds. She actually had three certificates—one for light air, one for medium air, and one for heavy air. All were legal, but what annoyed the boys from *Defender* and *Courageous* was the fact that they had not been informed of this advantageous position in which *Liberty* had placed herself. They were, after all, supposed to be on the same side. Not that you would have known it from the antics of their own selectors. I noticed that in one July race, *Defender* took 35 seconds off

Liberty at the start, and one minute later the Committee called off the race. Almost immediately, they raced again, and *Liberty* took 30 seconds off *Defender* at the start—and that race was allowed to go on.

I don't think *Defender* was ever allowed to sail over the full course. The American boats hardly ever did. The Committee kept them tight, match racing them hard against each other, counting on the fact that this toughness would bring us down to size. It was not a bad ploy, either, because we had inflicted many heavy defeats on our foreign opponents, and we rarely got into a fierce match-racing duel. I've explained our policy: Grab 40 seconds and hang on against the fast, downwind boats. The wily old devils of the New York Yacht Club were well aware of our potential weakness in a scrap, but they might not have been quite so sure if they had spent a few days watching the bloodletting that went on a few months earlier on Port Phillip Bay.

In race after race, they called off the action, recalling the American boats to fight against at close quarters. In the end, I thought it produced a lack of realism, with none of them being at home going all the way around the course. And these contrived trials were shielding a frightening fact from everyone—*Liberty* was a dog going downwind, and no one realized it. If they had been aware of this, they might have spent much more time correcting spinnakers and other downwind sails, but happily for us, they did not do this.

On August 27, the Committee of the New York Yacht Club formally excused Tom Blackaller from further duty. So *Defender* was out, and there would be eight more very close races between *Liberty* and *Courageous* before the defender of the Cup was named. Only two of these final trial races finished, and *Liberty* won them both—she had been in front in four of the others when they were called off. On Friday afternoon, September 2, John Kolius, skipper of *Courageous*, was told formally that his services were no longer required. Dennis Conner, skipper and helmsman of the ruby-red *Liberty*, would defend the America's Cup on behalf of the United States of America against *Australia II*.

Or, at least she *might*. The New York Yacht Club was still busily trying to get us disqualified because we were in a Dutch-designed boat. But as this tactic became more and more senseless, they were openly debating whether or not to refuse to race us. We were told that the club was just about divided on this issue. In those final days leading up to the first race on September 14, the New York Yacht Club's attorney, James Michael, prepared a three-page document called a Certificate of Compliance, an affidavit asking us Australians to state publicly—under penalty of perjury—that we had complied with conditions governing the races. Bondy, more out of devilment than anything else, suggested a rather exotic place in which they could store their affidavit. He just refused to sign it. And in total exasperation, Commodore McCullough went off to Bill Fesq, former commodore of the Royal Sydney Yacht Club, and asked him to supply another challenger. Fesq told him rather more politely what Bondy had been so poetically blunt about.

Once more McCullough retreated, reeling from the loss of battle after battle. The Committee met on board Bus Mosbacher's power yacht, *Summertime*, two days before the races were to begin, and, according to Victor Romagna, secretary of the America's Cup Committee, they were convinced the Australians had cheated in the design of *Australia II*. Now they had to decide either to have the courage of their convictions and refuse to race us and accept the uproar that would follow or to shut up and tell Dennis Conner to get out there and race us. According to Romagna, the majority of his Committee was in favor of pulling out of the America's Cup. But at that point, the enormity of their actions began to hit home. The possibility of this kind of confrontation with the whole world watching was just too great. Upon Romagna's own admission, "We did not have the guts to stand up and say we won't race. We just folded our tents and backed away." And that, essentially, was that. The politics had ended with a whimper, which was fitting, because that is all they ever were, anyway.

And now Dennis and I were slated to face each other out on those historic waters. I recall the question I was asked most during that week: "Would you rather race Dennis or John Kolius?" I always said I did not give a damn which one of them was my opponent. But deep in my soul, I was glad that it was Dennis. Kolius does not have the experience, but I think he may be a more naturally gifted yachtsman than the skipper from San Diego. Also, he does not have as many hangups as Dennis does. Kolius is a bit more like Buddy Melges in his approach. His attitude would be, "I don't give a damn about their goddam keel. Let's just get out there and race the boats."

Dennis had already announced that he would not get into a tacking duel with us if he could help it, but Kolius was nowhere near as intimidated as Dennis over the potential speed of *Australia II*. And since we all knew this was largely a myth anyway, well, I would rather face a man who is nervous than one who is not. As we approached the first race, there was no doubt that I'd rather be up against a worried Dennis Conner than a devil-may-care, nothing-to-lose John Kolius.

I have no wish to say anything unfair about Dennis, because I have the utmost respect for him as a skipper, but I know that he was disturbed about the 1983 defense. He knew he had not done all of his homework, he knew we could have a boatspeed edge, and he knew we could have more advanced sail development. And did not feel good about all that. For the first time, he was up against an opponent who had done as much as or more work than he had. He had no technical advantage, and he was unsure how much of a crew advantage he possessed.

As for his forthcoming personal battle with me, well, this is a matter so private, so deep for him, that I would not presume to intrude upon those most closely guarded of his thoughts. But I doubt that he thought I'd be a pushover. Dennis was vulnerable because he had fallen victim to the mystique of the keel. Both he and his navigator had given plenty of indication of being nervous. Halsey Herreshoff had made that notorious defeatist statement, and then there was the other historic phrase that came out of the *Liberty* camp: "We have boat trouble, and her name is *Australia II.*" Add to that Dennis's public announcement that he could not afford to get into a tacking duel with us, and his statement that we had been "sandbagging" against *Victory '83,* and you begin to see a picture of a man who is not quite as sure of himself as he would like to be.

I do not believe we sailed one yard throughout that summer without two men from *Liberty* watching us from a powerboat, timing us, even photographing us. We, of course, watched *them* from time to time, but not with the ferocious neurosis they displayed. Once Dennis was out there himself watching us tack, timing the arc through the wind of *Australia II*— and the speed with which we performed this function frightened him. Their subsequent remarks proved that. We had scared the Americans, and I think they thought they could lose to us. I'd go one step further than that. I do not think Dennis Conner, or his henchmen Halsey Herreshoff, Tom Whidden, and John Marshall, *wanted* to race us. I do not think that the men on the Committee wanted to be the men who organized the Defense that Lost the Cup. None of them could stand the thought of defeat. And my deepest sympathies were entirely with them. Neither could I.

The atmosphere in the *Liberty* house was not good—I was getting some high-quality feedback from my American friends. Very little happened in that American outfit about which I did not know. The tension was beginning to show in the *Liberty* camp. Just a few days before the first race, Dennis decided to change all of the instruments on his boat. He elected to use the same equipment we had on *Australia II,* and it must have been like changing the very heart of the yacht in which they had raced for so long. We found out about it from the service people, and since the two boats had not yet confronted each other, I thought it a rather extravagant decision.

Sometime during the three days before we were due to meet for the first time, I spent an afternoon in the outer reaches of the harbor, fishing with Lucas and Andre from one of the Boston Whalers. At one point as I sat there, with my feet up, trying to catch a fish, *Liberty* came swishing by, very close, testing her new instruments. I shoved back my hat, looked up at them with a large grin, and shouted, "Hi, guys! Having a nice day?"

It was clear that their morale was nowhere near as good as ours, for by now the men of *Australia II* were reaching a kind of peak of arrogance. One morning they surpassed themselves for pure brashness. Led by the Major, they set off on their morning run, and as they approached the big gates at the driveway to the *Liberty* house, the Australian Army officer made a decision to vary the usual routine. Instead of running straight by, he turned sharply left and led the crew straight into the gardens of the palatial mansion in which the *Liberty* crew lived. This was tantamount to the rape of your grandmother. They all got down on the lawn. Suddenly the Americans broke from their pushups and set off for *their* run, and to their amazement, they jogged right into the middle of the *Australia II* crew on their property. Tight-lipped, they ran on past the men from Down Under, and the incident might have ended there. However, Chink Longley, flushed with the success of the adventure thus far, suddenly hurled himself forward and rugby-tackled his opposite number on the *Liberty* crew. The pair of them went rolling into the rhododendrons, howling with laughter, but the rest of the American crew, including Conner, Whidden, Herreshoff, and Marshall, did not consider it very amusing. When they got back to Founders' Hall, my boys could hardly contain their delight at this childish, undignified behavior. I joined them in their laughter, but I was not laughing at the same thing. I was just overwhelmingly pleased at one aspect of this: For the first time, I was going to be in an Australian crew that was categorically not afraid of the Americans.

In fact, judging by the statements that kept being attributed to the defenders of the Cup, I would say they were rather more afraid of us. It was almost as if they were preparing an excuse to use in the event of losing the trophy to Australia. They never stopped going on about our boat and her keel. The message they were trying to impart was simple: If *Australia II* won the America's Cup, it would be because of the fast, unfair boat, and the very most the locals could expect from *Liberty* was gallantry against overwhelming odds. They picked no lesser man than the one with the most famous name in yacht design, Herreshoff, to assert, continually, that *Australia II* was not a 12-Meter but a 12.4-Meter, and thus had no right to be in the race. All this in spite of the categoric rulings in our favor by the America's Cup Measuring Committee. They knew the Committee would not back down, but they kept saying we were cheating for the perfectly obvious reason that they would always have an excuse. When we beat a foreign boat easily, we were the Superboat, when we just won, we were "sandbagging," and when we lost, we were "experimenting." In the end the Americans, particularly Conner and Herreshoff, had carefully laid the groundwork to be able to claim, in defeat, that there was *nothing* they could do. "We sailed as well as it is humanly possible to sail, but *Australia II* was unbeatable, and it was nothing short of a miracle that we did as well as we did. No 11 men on this planet could have matched our achievement in holding the Australians at bay for so long."

The reputation of Dennis Conner, which means so much to him, is the result of a propaganda machine. The myth is built up by people like John Marshall, with the aid of the press, and the more people talk about "the greatest helmsman in the world," the greater the aura of the man becomes. As we prepared for our showdown on Tuesday, September 13, when *Australia II* would finally face *Liberty,* this aura did not bother me, and that also applied to the crew of *Australia II.* In summary, I would say we went into the races with the following mental attitudes:

Hughey Treharne, Tactician. Very thoughtful. Believed we could win, and that if we sailed our best, we would win. Needed a little reassurance from me.

Grant Simmer, Navigator. A winner through and through. Just a little bit stagestruck, but believed we could beat the Americans.

Colin Beashel, Mainsheet Hand. A winner. Believed implicitly that we would win, and particularly that I could bring us home.

Skip Lissiman, Trimmer. Caught up in the crowd, susceptible to the prevailing mood.

Kenny Judge, Trimmer. A winner. Believed he was the world's best at his job, and that *Australia II* would crush the Americans 4–0.

Chink Longley, Winch-Grinder. Been beaten in three previous America's Cups, subconscious doubts. But desperately *wanted* to win and would work until he dropped to do so.

Brian Richardson, Winch-Grinder. Not a man of powerful spoken opinions, but a tough, hard Olympic oarsman who wanted to win badly and knew the taste of victory.

Phil Smidmore, Mastman. Old Ya. Little leadership and not much ambition, but a real professional who would hang in there.

Peter Costello, Sewerman. The Major believed 1,000 percent that we would destroy the Americans. There was no doubt in his mind. Ever.

Damian Fewster, Bow Man. Too young to appreciate the history or the power of our opponents. Also did not care. A winner. Believed in us totally.

Ben Lexcen, Designer. Was afraid to believe it would happen. Hoping all the time.

Warren Jones, Chief Executive. Had great respect for Dennis Conner. Hoping, hoping, hoping, and working.

Alan Bond, Syndicate Chief. Tough man, Bondy. Believed we could win and was not in awe of the Americans. Had a lot of faith in me.

As I looked at the men who would come with me into battle, I was sure we could do it. In my calmest moments, I could not imagine *Liberty* beating us. I could not visualize *anyone* beating us. We were too good and we'd come too far. In terms of pure boatspeed, in most conditions, we were one of the four fastest Twelves in Newport. We had our problems downwind particularly early on, but we had spent a lot of time improving, recutting sails and tuning the boat so that she was almost unrecognizable from her early days. The keel? Well, that never did do much for our straight-line boatspeed, but there was a priceless spinoff. It made *Australia II* highly maneuverable and gave us an advantage at the start and in tacking duels. She was very quick to spin around in the water, and, assuming that her driver knew more or less what he was about, we should go into every race against the Americans with a good shot at laying up with *Liberty.* If we sailed well enough, we would win. If we made a lot of mistakes, we would lose. It was just about as simple as that.

In one of our warmup races with *Challenge 12,* just before we faced the Americans, I thought the whole thing was put into perspective. *Challenge* flew a new genoa and she just steamed away from us. We swapped genoas and we immediately steamed away from them. That says most of it. The correct selection of sails is the total difference between winning and losing. I was confident that our team was the equal or superior of the *Liberty* sail men. In my opinion, to borrow a phrase from a well-known U.S. helmsman, we would have "no excuse to lose."

Morale in our camp had been extremely high all summer. Our principal problems involved, of all things, social functions and the distribution of invitations. Peter de Savary's glorious extravaganza at Beechwood, the old Astor mansion, was probably the highlight of the summer for those whose interests lay beyond the business of racing yachts. It was the British America's Cup Ball, and it featured Prince Andrew and the band of the Irish Guards. People flew in from all over the world for it, and it was probably the main social event in the world in 1983. Each syndicate was given six tickets. De Savary specified that they were for the syndicate chief and his wife and the helmsman and the tactician and their wives. Well, the tickets were not offered to Hughey and me, and we were the only skipper and helmsman in Newport not in attendance. *Australia II* was represented in our places by Mr. and Mrs. Warren Jones and Sir James and Lady Hardy. In Rasa's opinion, this was the most shocking embarrassment. She and Dixie Treharne felt awful about it in front of all their friends, and my feisty wife considered the entire thing a total humiliation. However, as it happened, something far worse happened on the very day of the ball. I received a cable from Melbourne telling me that one of my biggest life-long supporters, my grandma, Nan Cull, had died. I was terribly upset, and I had this strange feeling that a piece of my heritage, a real link with the past and the sea that was in my blood, had been taken away, that Nan could never turn on the television and see "her Johnny" at the helm of the Australian challenger, that somehow her proudest moment had been snatched away. She and Bant had both gone, and I found the whole thing nearly overpowering. I would not have gone to the ball if I'd had 20 tickets, but when our friends asked why we were not there, Rasa was able to explain that it was because of the death of my grandmother, not because we were not invited. Still, the beer was nice and cool that night on the porch of Founders' Hall.

Things were not much better in our camp for the America's Cup Ball, which was run by the Americans at the historic Italianate palace called The Breakers, built for the railroad tycoon Cornelius Vanderbilt III in 1895. There were more than 2,500 people at this little bash, and lines of limousines crawled up the driveway depositing America's finest before a massed guard of the Artillery Company of Newport, sabers raised. Cornelius Vanderbilt's granddaughter is Countess Szapary—she still lives in a 14-room apartment on the third floor of the house—and the Countess and her guests would dance to Viennese waltzes until dawn.

However, the ticket problem again reared its ugly head. As I recall, there were tickets for the Bertrands and the Treharnes, and some of the crew managed to buy tickets. But there was an awful fuss on Dennison Street because the tireless workhorse of *Australia II*, Chink Longley, and the deft little genius of the sail loft, Tom Schnackenberg, were not included. Jenny Longley was so upset she could not speak, Annie

Schnackenberg was in tears. Rasa, veteran of three previous America's Cups and thus a kind of "mother superior" to the girls, did what she always did. She stepped in to try to calm the waters—anything to remove unrest and emotional upset from my crew. I'm not sure how it happened, but somehow or other Bondy was coerced into buying tickets for his main winch-grinder and his chief sail coordinator so they could go to the ball. But a lot of others could not go. Big Will Ballieu never made it, nor did Kenny Beashel and his wife, nor did any of the sailmakers, the guys who used to work all night on the sewing machines.

Now I do not think I am a particularly petty person, but it is nearly impossible to describe the depth of unrest created by this type of discrimination. As a basic rule, if there is a ball or a major party, you have to make sure you invite *everyone*. If I were syndicate chief, it would be a simple matter—either we all go, or no one goes. If there is a kind of pecking order among the hierarchy, it's at the other end of the scale where the trouble begins, where someone is so upset that he just does not want to put out 100 percent for Alan Bond and Warren Jones, because he feels he has been humiliated. God knows what would have happened if Tom Schnackenberg, unable to cope with his distraught wife, Annie, had said, "To hell with this, we're going home." *Australia II* would have been in dead trouble, that's what. Each man in our small, tightly knit group performed a crucial task, and this ticket business was taking us to the brink of that graceless and subversive situation that I call "internal hemorrhaging."

For the America's Cup Ball at The Breakers, Rasa and I would gladly have given up our own tickets just to let *all* of the others go, the maintenance men, the boat drivers, the sailmakers and all, just to keep our superb morale high. But after much discussion they all got together and arranged to have their own party at home. The rest of us went to The Breakers and Rasa and I stayed until after midnight. I think she knew I was still very concerned about the rest of the team, because I remember as we danced one final Viennese waltz across the vast deserted marble-floored foyer together, she whispered to me, "Don't you worry, John, I bet they all had a lovely time."

It was, in a sense, a curious irony that a crew with as few social ambitions as that of *Australia II* should have been irritated by the allocation of tickets for a couple of dances. But that is the way things are in this world. You never know what little tsetse fly lurks around the corner, and whether the minute sting will turn into sleeping sickness. But on occasions such as those I have just described, I always made sure that my crew talks contained the words that would help us keep a proper sense of proportion. I would say to them repeatedly, "We have a once-in-a-lifetime opportunity to create history, history that will be remembered 100 years hence, as long as men talk about the racing of big yachts. We must take care to let nothing stand in the way of our single, unshakable ambition. We must remain totally focused on this ambition to win."

Out on the water the big countdown had begun. With just days to go, Dennis Conner and his men were out tuning *Liberty*, practicing for hour after hour on the racecourse with her trial horse, the royal-blue *Freedom*. We had a terrific group helping us, a combination of the boys from the departed *Advance* crew and from *Challenge*. Jim Hardy and Iain Murray used to take the helm of *Challenge 12*, and once more we all raced together, slogging it out for mile after mile, tuning, tuning, tuning.

Some people think 12-Meter racing yachts just happen. Someone like Benny makes a drawing, a bunch of shipwrights builds it, up go the sails, and that's the ball game. Good morning, Superboat. Well, it is not like that. Great racing boats do not just happen. They are developed, through months and months of testing, refining sail shapes, adjusting the rig, learning to sail her. When someone like Dennis or me says, "We have boat speed over them," we mean that one boat will go for instance 1,000 yards in 1,000 seconds. The other boat will go 1,000 yards in 993 seconds. That means you may pick up 10 seconds in a mile. Over the full America's Cup course you will thus pick up 240 seconds, or four minutes, which constitutes a regular thrashing. However, if you should jibe 10 times when the others do not, you will lose 30 feet a time, which equals 300 feet, or six boatlengths, and there goes 1½ minutes. The wrong mainsail could cost you a minimum of a minute over the full course. One mistake in the setting of a spinnaker, a genoa, one mistake going to the wrong side of the course, missing the wind, misjudging the start, just about anything that represents lack of perfection in racing, and you can kiss the Cup good-bye. Great races are won by great crews and great tactics and great sail selection and endless tuning. No keel has ever been built, or ever will be, that will carry a bunch of incompetents to victory. I doubt whether any keel would carry a bunch of world champions to victory against a top opponent if a couple of mistakes were made.

And so we went at it, Dennis and I, each in our separate time and practicing capsules, he against *Freedom*, we against *Challenge*. The first race was to be on Tuesday, September 13, and on the Friday before, I felt we had all had enough. Rasa and I went to New York for the weekend and the rest of the boys were given the weekend off. The tension was growing, as well it might have, and my instinct told me that we all needed to break free for a couple of days, to clear our minds, to remember our lessons, to arrive on that starting line on Tuesday morning whip sharp and ready for anything.

On that Saturday Rasa and I went to Flushing Meadows in New York to see the U.S. Open Tennis Championships, and we saw an inspiring match between Jimmy Connors and Jimmy Arias. (Our tickets had very kindly and very thoughtfully been arranged for us by Alan Bond. What a gigantic puzzle and contradiction he is.) It was a typical Connors game. There he was, as usual, dragging himself back into the lead by the bootstraps, chasing, retrieving, struggling, and then pouncing when he scented blood. He was a study in the art of hanging in there against all odds, and I felt that his example was a little scenario I was meant to see. As we left the stadium, I fell into conversation with a bunch of black American athletes from the Seattle Seahawks, who, like me, were rhapsodizing about Connors. One of them, a huge linebacker who I believe was named Shelton Robinson, asked me what I was doing in the U.S. I told him I was skipper of *Australia II*, and he and a couple of his pals knew all about that "fast white mother" from Down Under. We chatted for a while about fighting the odds, giving it all you've got, and they told me that they were going to the Super Bowl (in fact, they had their best-ever season and reached the playoffs, narrowly beating the champion Los Angeles Raiders twice). Just before we parted, big Shelton (I'm sure that was his name) pointed his finger at me sternly and said, "Don't you forget, man. Just make sure you give it your very best shot."

I kept thinking about what he had said. He had put his finger on the very crux of the matter. The worst thing of all would be to fail to sail the boat as well as we could—to be beaten and somehow have ourselves to blame. That would have been unthinkable. "Don't you forget, man. Just make sure you give it your very best shot."

With thoughts of my warning from the big Seattle Seahawk and of the gritty example of Connors still fresh in my mind, we returned to Dennison Street, to face what sleep I could manage and a critical Monday on which *Australia II* and the minds of her crew would be finally prepared for the combat to come. In the morning we had a meeting with Peter Lawson, the man cleared by the New York Yacht Club to be our rules adviser, our go-between to the Club who would help to forestall any misunderstandings between *Australia II* and *Liberty*. He was a very nice man and extremely helpful. Hughey and I spent a lot of time with him, going over the ground rules.

We also took *Challenge 12* out onto the water to test some spinnakers. We went out under the bridge and flew our various parachutes, which had been recut. We were still worried about the fifth leg, the downwind square run, which had been our weakest point against the foreign boats. We thought this was where we could be vulnerable to *Liberty*, and we were still cutting, curling up the upper edges of the chutes, looking for stability, reworking them, searching for more improvement. We were making sure that the leading edge of the spinnaker was rolling evenly from top to bottom. Aesthetically, they looked pretty good, so finally we signaled *Black Swan* to tow us home. The next time we left the dock would be on the morrow, when we would face *Liberty* for the first time.

It is a strange business, the final hours before a race such as this. For all the watching, all the observing, we still had no idea how fast we would be against each other. For all we knew, *Liberty* would sail right away from us. We had never even gone up against a boat that had raced them. Nor, of course, had they gone up against a boat that had raced us, and for all they knew, we would sail right away from them.

Late on Monday afternoon a formal edict was issued from our head-quarters that John Bertrand, skipper of *Australia II,* was henceforth forbidden to ride his flashy 10-speed blue Shogun racing bike through the streets of Newport after dark. The fact that I pedaled almost everywhere was beginning to get to everyone, including Rasa. We had been under constant surveillance for many weeks, and someone had thought it worthwhile to have frogmen under our boat. Should the administration take for granted the safety of their helmsman? In the opinion of Warren Jones, absolutely not, and Chink Longley was his most vociferous supporter in this. Chink's view was simply stated. "Right in front of the whole world, those bastards were debating whether to call off the whole thing altogether. In my opinion, we should take nothing for granted, including an 'accident' to John." Rasa was greatly relieved, and so, apparently, was everyone else. I was pretty relaxed personally, so I let them have their own way. Hughey was charged with the responsibility of getting me to Founders' Hall for the official team dinner, the last we would have before we faced *Liberty.*

The atmosphere was by now becoming very tense. Most of the boys were having trouble sleeping, and we were in a sense living on our nerve ends. I was not sleeping very well myself, except for the first four hours, when pure exhaustion would put me out. But I was regularly waking up at 3 A.M. and finding it nearly impossible to keep my mind from churning over and over. How fast would *Liberty* be? I used to dream that she was coming at us and I could not make *Australia II* go. It was like that feeling in a dream when you try to run away and you cannot move. I used to wake suddenly, sweating and feeling almost breathless. The dreadful old bed we had at 32 Dennison Street could not cope with much of that kind of violent activity. It was, after all, supported mainly on Rasa's side by our binoculars. This rather matched the decor, particularly the television set, which was set elegantly on an old cardboard fruit box at the end of the bed.

Hughey and I drove up to Founders' Hall that evening in his aged, secondhand Chevrolet. Everyone was there, including the rest of the team, Warren, Bondy, and the maintenance men. No wives or girl friends. I had decided that in my last formal speech to them before the first race, I would try to play down the nationalistic aspect of our quest, because this would do nothing more than put more weight on their shoulders, more strain on their nerves. I knew that my task was nearly impossible, because we all knew that we were ultimately sailing for faraway Australia and the land we all loved—the little nation of which we were so proud, the land of the kangaroo and the wallaby and the Stone Age men, the Aboriginals. The land that was so far from everything, so remote down there in the South Pacific, and yet a land of boisterous men, a nation with a personality as big as the Empire State Building, a nation whose armies had fought with the best of 'em in two world wars, with the Americans in Vietnam. A land virtually uninhabited for thousands and thousands of miles—just 15 million of us in a vast country bigger than the U.S.A. (if you forget Alaska and the water in the Great Lakes). A country with its own culture, its own tough heritage, its own folklore, its own sound from the very heart of the land, beyond the Great Dividing Range. "You'll come a-waltzing, Matilda, with me. . . ." God help me if they're not singing that tomorrow night.

We all knew what we represented. We represented the whole of that nation—each and every one of the people who lived there. We represented the great city of Sydney, the capital of New South Wales, Australia's largest city with three million people, six of whom—Hughey, Grant, Beasho, Skippy, Robbie, and Ya—had honed their sailing on the beautiful waters below the world-famous Harbor Bridge in the shadow of the Opera House. We represented Melbourne, the seaport capital of Victoria. "Splash" Richardson, Damian, Will, and I were from there. From Perth, 2,000 miles away to the west, came Chink and Scoop and Scotty. From Brisbane, the former penal colony that lies in the heat to the north of Sydney, came Major Peter Costello. We did not have anyone from Alice Springs, but the residents of that burning desert city were with us to a man.

First I told the crew that we had received a touching message of encouragement from Bob Hawke, the Prime Minister of Australia. It read: "Congratulations on winning through to be the final challenger for the America's Cup. All Down Under will be sailing with *Australia II* when the final series begins. Our hopes are high that you will sail into history and bring back that elusive Cup. Whatever the outcome, yours has been a magnificent venture. All Australians are very proud of you."

You could feel the tension in the air as I spoke. Many of the boys had seen *Liberty* come in from her final practice that day, and we were all keenly aware that we had no idea how we would go together. She had sailed her path and we ours, and the unknown factor almost doubled the tension.

I said to them, "We have come a long way together, thousands and thousands of miles, and throughout this, the strong have helped those with not as much experience. We were together when we started and tomorrow we will fight together against the red boat. We are not here because of luck or because of some failing on the part of others. We are here because we deserve it, because we have worked together to be here. No crew has ever worked harder than we have, and no crew has ever deserved to race for the America's Cup more than we do. We are probably the greatest boat crew ever to challenge for this historic trophy. And in that I include every last one of us. We will win if we are good enough ourselves, and it is up to each of us as individuals. It's up to us, the men who will sail *Australia II,* to go out and do it. The important thing is for us to do it for each other, for each one of us, to make the others proud to have been on the same team. That we can at the end of it hold our heads high, sure that we have done our very best, that we have not let anyone down."

I mentioned my new pal, the linebacker from the Seattle Seahawks, admirer of the "fast white mother from Down Under." "Don't you forget, man, just make sure you give it your very best shot." I reminded them of the psychological lesson Laurie Hayden and I had perfected—that all we were asking from each individual was to do what he has already trained to do, what he has done a thousand times before. Not to do anything outrageous or even different. "Just keep doing what we have trained to do."

I told them about 1970, how *Gretel* had sailed out so ill prepared to face *Intrepid.* It had been blowing hard that day, and we hoisted a new genoa, one we had never used before. What a disaster that was. Mistake number one. Then we rounded the top mark and set our first spinnaker. The trouble was, we stopped it differently than we had ever stopped it before (the amount of wool wrapped around it to stop it from breaking out was a different geometrical pattern), and what a disaster that was. That spinnaker was all over the place. The reason for these twin catastrophes was simple. The crew was so excited, trying so hard to improve our performance, that we just broke out and did new and rash things, going beyond our limitations, looking for the one shot that would throw us an advantage. It never works.

I said to them, "All we have to do is to reproduce our known winning form. Nothing different. Just the moves we *know* will be successful." I reminded them of the day I invented this wonderful brand-new shortcut around a mark that would take me clean away from an East German named Jochen Schumann in the 1976 Olympics. And I added, "No one is asking any more of you than what you have already produced a thousand times before."

My last words, before Hughey and I left, were, "Gentlemen, we have come a very long way together. But we have miles to go before we sleep. Thank you very much for all that you have done so far. I know that none of you will let me down tomorrow when battle commences, and I shall try very hard not to let you down. Good night."

Everyone was still petrified that my lightning-fast Shogun bike was suddenly going to materialize, and I noted that both Warren and Chink saw me safely into Hughey's car, protected from lurking fanatics. At our front door, Hughey and I parted, and I went upstairs to the apartment, where the children were by now asleep.

On this most poignant of nights, even Dennison Street had a strangeness about it. It suddenly felt totally foreign to me, as did everything about Newport. Some of the girls had been looking for inspiration from a little book about the stars and horoscopes, and I must admit that they had come up with very little of an encouraging nature. I took a look at the pictures of the Milky Way in the book and found no great sign of assistance from on high. I did know for sure that if I looked into the night sky, south toward the sea from Dennison Street, I would definitely not see Australia's home stars, which form the Southern Cross. But the book also told me that before I had slept for long, the brightest stars of the northern heavens would rise silently over sleepy Newport, just to the east, as if over the racecourse—the constellation of Orion the Hunter.

Eagerly aligning myself with this particular heavenly body, I swiftly rejoined another, more familiar one in the form of Nurse Rasa Bertrand. She greeted me with a glass of hot milk and gave me a mild tranquilizer to help me sleep and try to rid my dreams of the apparition of the hated red boat pursuing me. She used to come to bed with me for a little while until I slept, and then she would retreat to the tiny living room and curl up under a blanket on the sofa to give me more room and to make the night a bit more comfortable for me in this tiny double bed. She gave me my headphones so I could hear my favorite John Denver songs, like "Rocky Mountain High," as I dozed off, and she handed me my copy of *Jonathan Livingston Seagull* to try to purify my competitive instincts before I became unconscious. "I've left a little message in the front for you," she said, "just reminding you of the piece on page 60 that you love so much." ("For each of them, the most important thing in living was to reach out and touch perfection in that which they most loved to do and that was to fly.")

I lay there for just a few minutes, trying to wrestle from my mind the thoughts of the sails of *Australia II*, trying to cast aside the haunting image of *Liberty* sailing out from under us. And I drifted off to sleep, clutching Rasa's hand, as I prepared to meet the great unknown, thinking of the words she had written to me inside the cover of the book about the sea-gull.

"To John, just before your greatest challenge. I think Jonathan Livingston Seagull may have a few hints for you. I think page 60 is close to your heart. I hope you pull off this next set of races, not for any of the usual reasons, but just so you reach out and touch your perfection. You were given the initial talent, but you have dreamed your dream and worked often against tough odds, and still you continued. Newport '83 has shown me a new aspect of you. I love and admire you. Rasa."

14

One for the Red Boat

It was like David and Goliath, the little Aussies against the might of the U.S.A. But it's still a bit of a shock when Goliath unloads a backhander and catches you squarely in the mouth.

It was a crisp, clear September morning and the sun rose early, devil's red, from out of the Atlantic Ocean. At about the same time, I too rose from my slumbers, thinking for no good reason how that same sun could just be seen back home in Melbourne, sinking slowly now to the west of Port Phillip Bay, the color of spent fire. Tuesday, September 13, had ended for them, and I had a sudden, utterly irrational thought that as an Australian it ought to have ended for me too. But that it had not.

I showered and shaved calmly—always look sharp before the men at morning parade—and I met Hughey at the front door at 6 A.M. We spoke quietly in the soft morning light. Newport, still half asleep but neverthe-less half crazed with excitement, was only just stirring, and we stood there for a few moments looking at the leaves, not yet turning into their golden autumn finery, and furthermore not rustling on the branches. "Shit!" observed Hughey. "That wind's real light, it's going to be f-----g tricky out there today." No two hearts in Dennison Street, or even Thames Street, were pounding like mine and Hughey's, and all about us it was quiet beneath the rose-colored sky. It was nearly impossible to believe that just around the corner along the docks, the biggest oceangoing armada since Queen Victoria's Spithead Review off the Isle of Wight in 1897 was preparing to put to sea.

The Newport Coast Guard was already busy, making ready a show of strength that would have impressed Her Late Majesty herself: one high-endurance cutter, two medium-endurance cutters, one navy destroyer, two buoy tenders, three 82-foot patrol boats, and 28 utility boats. Various combat veterans of Vietnam were preparing to become airborne in 17 photographers' helicopters, which would fly clockwise in half-mile circles. Preparing to fly 500 feet above this lot was a fleet of fixed-wing aircraft carrying more newspaper, magazine, and television personnel. Below them all would be the gigantic Goodyear Blimp, the American airship that televises big U.S. sports events and to which massive international satellite hookups were being plotted even as Hughey and I spoke. Scientists and electronics experts were planning to straddle the stratosphere with vitally important, earth-shattering footage of, well . . . actually, a yacht race between the U.S.A. and Australia.

"One of the main tricks we have to pull off here, Hughey," I said, "is to convince the boys there is no need to get overexcited just because half the world seems to have gone berserk."

We wore our green track suits as we drove slowly through the deserted streets to Founders' Hall, and I noticed that Hughey was very pensive, quieter than usual. There was a knot in the stomach of one of the most experienced ocean racers in the world. God only knew how I would find the rest of them. I sat in the back seat, removed from the front by the baby chair, pondering my theme for the day, and the word I kept thinking of was *normal*. Everything had to be normal. I wanted no change in our routine. It had to be just another day. Steady, calm John. So we have to race the red boat, so what? Our crew has raced together hundreds of times, it's just another boat race, just another day, another dollar. (The crew was making $12.50 a day, which somehow made us all laugh, since we were about to entertain half a billion people.) My task, for the moment at least, was to try to diffuse the tension. There clearly would not be a · problem raising adrenaline. That would be pumping out of our eardrums. What I needed was calm, confidence. And so did the crew. We had raced 54 times in Newport, and on only five occasions had another boat crossed

the winning line in front of us. The America's Cup was, in my view, there
for the taking—just as long as the crew approached it with the poise and
easy arrogance that we had spent so many months cultivating.

There was no variation in our normal light exercise program. The
boys went for a brief run to loosen up, and we went through our calis-
thenics on the lawn. It was not until we sat down to breakfast that I began
to notice signs of the great tension we were under. We had all had our
hearts and blood pressure tested in the previous few days, and the doctors
assured us that no one was going to suffer a coronary thrombosis or anything, but I'm sure that lesser men could easily have had a heart attack
under this type of strain. Benny had already had one. But the little
giveaways were there at breakfast. I, of course, the "quiet, unsmiling, calm
Aussie," as the press was wont to call me, gave the outward appearance of
being exactly that. I rather hoped, however, that no one noticed I was not
able to eat my normal eggs and bacon. I was not even able to look at it. I
just had a piece of melon.

Hughey was terribly uptight, hardly ate anything. Grant Simmer, the
young navigator who had never been a navigator before, ate nothing, sat
there with a cup of coffee, very much within himself. He looked like just a
boy, but in the next 13 days he would become a man, right before my very
eyes. I watched Damian, the young carpenter from the Melbourne suburbs. He kept his head down and wolfed down a plate of eggs and bacon
as if it was his last meal on earth. But he said nothing. None of his normal
references to the "sheilahs me and my mate Blackie will be able to pick up
after we beat these bloody Yanks." Beasho, young Colin upon whose
shoulders so much depended, was also very quiet. He ate his breakfast,
but I could see he was steeling himself for the fray. The Major, God bless
him, was roaring around the house like a madman, back and forth, back
and forth, checking, checking, questioning, charging down to the dock in
the sail truck, back again. Breakfast? "No time, too much to do. Give me
some coffee." "Jesus Christ, it's calm, let's take another light-air spinnaker." That was his way of coping with the pressure.

Big Brian Richardson, veteran Olympic oarsman, a man accustomed to
holding his nerve, sat at the table with a sugar spoon in his coffee. As he
moved it, he kept flexing the muscle in his forearm, as if seeking some
assurance from his enormous strength.

Chink Longley tried to keep busy, but his extra task as shore manager
kept him in constant conversation with Warren Jones, who was as jumpy
as a cat. The two of them were on the edges of their nerves. And, not for
the first time, I thanked God for Scoop, suave Kenny Judge, brilliantly
confident, sure of himself, of me, of his crewmates. He just sat there buttering toast, eating his bacon and eggs, chatting away, laughing, as if noth-

ing were happening. He was a man who would take on anything. Old Ya, the mastman, hungry by nature, dead calm, ate two plates of bacon and eggs, same speed as usual, deceptively fast. Skippy Lissiman, lovely ingenuous Skippy, Rasa's favorite of them all ("Oh, hi, Ras, how are you? You look terrific. Anything I can do? How's the kids?")—he was a bit quiet today.

I made my talk brief, tried to be casual—nothing heavy, nothing formal. The only thing I stressed was the communications I *must have* when the gun goes. "Just remember, you guys, we've got to be loose. Keep alert, keep the information coming. Give me your thoughts, nice and easy. We're going to sail the boat, all together, relaxed, calm, confident. Now let's go and do our job." Briskly I went through the final sail selection with Schnacks, Skippy, Scoop, and Hughey. The winds would be light. We would take seven genoas and 10 spinnakers, all tailored for the mild breezes we would find today on Rhode Island Sound.

At quarter to eight, Warren Jones stood up and performed what may have been his greatest service of the day. "Order! Order!" he snapped, dead serious, knife ready to hit his orange-juice glass. Ding, ding, ding, ding, ding. "Order!

"Now it is 16 minutes to eight, and we all know we have an America's Cup race to sail today."

"Have we really? Oh, *thanks*, Warren."

"Christ, I'd forgotten all about that!"

"Oh shit, why didn't you tell us earlier? Who do we race?"

"And try to get the bloody time right, Warren. It's only 14 minutes to eight."

"Order! Order!"

"No, it isn't. It's at least 18 minutes to eight."

"What's that bloody race you mentioned? Who's in it?"

"Shut up!"

It's always funny, but today it was hysterical. We were all rocking with laughter as Warren, without a smile, soldiered on with the regular business of the day. "Right. We will now proceed to the dock."

"Oh, Warren," said someone wickedly. I think it was Scoop. "What time is it?"

"Er, nine minutes to eight."

"Rubbish. It's eight point two five minutes to eight."

"Don't be bloody silly. It's nine point one nine minutes to eight."

"It's like a damned sixth form in here," retorted our administrative chief, with blistering accuracy. I'm still not sure that he realized it, but Warren had diffused the tension in a way I can only describe as masterful.

My plan was to let the crew go down and prepare the boat without me.

I decided to let the tension build, especially since the Americans would leave their nearby dock 15 minutes before us. Then I would arrive, just two minutes before we were due to set off, and try to be a steadying influence, if I could. They pedaled away and Hughey dropped me back at the house, where I found Rasa coping with the kids and the rest of the women. I kissed Lucas, Andre, and Sunshine good-bye and left Rasa to deal with the rest. Poor Jenny Longley was beside herself, sick with nerves and worry, locked in the bathroom. Dixie Treharne was trembling with anxiety. And down at the dock, thousands of spectators were gathering, massed groups from Australia thronging around the wire pushing forward to catch a glimpse of the gladiators. Armed guards were already on duty, and out in the harbor more than a thousand boats were preparing to accompany us.

I kept my head well down, earphones on, listening to John Denver. At five to nine, I kissed Rasa good-bye, and she said what she would say to me every day when I left to face Dennis Conner. "Good luck, John, and have fun."

I struggled through the crowd and put my bike away, tossed my kitbag onto the boat, and at two minutes to nine, I stepped aboard *Australia II*. A light ripple of applause went through the crowd, but I did not acknowledge it. "Good morning, gentlemen," I said. The boat had been checked, double-checked, rechecked. Now I wanted to leave the dock in the slickest possible way. It was important for every member of the crew to feel superior at every aspect of sailing the boat. We did not just need to look good, we had to look bloody fantastic. All of our sails were in order, stored down below, our light-air mainsail ready on the boom. The lines were attached to *Black Swan,* which would tow us out to the racecourse. I signaled with a nod of my head to cast off. Damian ran up the big kangaroo flag and the breeze caught it. The crowd cheered. I nodded at Phil Judge, the tender driver, and Men at Work gave it all they'd got.

Do you come from a land Down Under,
Where women glow and men plunder?
Can't you hear, can't you hear the thunder?
You'd better run, you'd better take cover.

You could hear it on the top of Newport Bridge. You could hear our music everywhere. The crowd let out a roar as we set off. An Australian lady with tears streaming down her face shouted, "God be with you!" She was not the only one crying, either. It was as if we were going to war and never coming home. Australian flags seemed to bloom everywhere as we headed out into the harbor. People were yelling and screaming and cheering, we seemed to be the very hub of the universe, and the emotion of the moment was nearly unbearable. We had left the dock without one word being said among ourselves, and you cannot do it better than that. No one could take a boat off a dock like we could. No one.

Two-thirds of the way across the harbor, I called a crew meeting, a bit earlier than usual, before we had fetched the harbor wall. We went into a huddle, and I noticed that the Major was the last one to arrive as he was still down below, checking, checking, making sure those sails were precisely as he wanted them. And God help anyone who screwed it up. The wrath of the Major was not a pretty sight.

The spectator fleet was by now awe-inspiring, and the first thing I said was, "OK, guys, there are a lot of people out there watching us, and if anyone is interested, I want you to take a good look at them, right now, and then forget about it, because no one is going to help us. It's just ourselves now, and if you are feeling a bit nervous about a fight to the death, just think how those poor bastards on the red boat feel. They'll probably get sent to a penal colony when we beat them. Can you imagine racing with the America's Cup hanging around your neck, like they have?"

"Now let's concentrate on what we have to do. The only thing to remember is that each of you must just do his job. Nothing more is expected of you. Just do what we know, nice and cool, lots of poise. We do not want any stagefright and we want lots of communication—all the usual stuff we have done so many times before. Watch the target speeds, a bit faster, a bit slower, the position of the red boat. Watch the wind, feel our boat, all the things that are second nature to us."

"Gentlemen, we have a bloody good boat, we have great sails, we have a world-class tactician, every one of you is the best in the business. And, above all, we are ready for this. This is what we have come for. Now let's get down below and get some rest, and then we are going to whip those Americans once and for all."

We left our reserve, Robbie Brown, at the helm to steer us out. Splash stayed on deck because he gets seasick, Grant was too busy, and there was the usual unseemly scramble down the hatch by the rest of the mob to get the best places to sleep on the sails.

Just before 11, Robbie bangs hard on the deck with a winch handle—clack! clack! clack!—and we spring to life, heading up through the hatch. Out to weather is *Challenge 12*, towed out parallel to us. Our faithful warm-up companions are also making ready. I walk back to the cockpit. Each man moves into his right position.

"HOIST THE MAINSAIL!" The heavies start hauling away, Chink with the thin wire that is attached to the mast crane, delicately between his thumb and forefinger, waiting for the "clunk" from on high that will vi-

brate down and tell us she's locked in. I radio across to Jim Hardy at the
helm of *Challenge* to let him know which genoa I want him to use, because
for our trials before the gun, I want us to be pretty even. *Challenge* hauls
up her heavy-air main, and I call out for our code-one genoa—a deep,
round, very powerful sail designed to capture every possible breath of air.
"HOIST THE JIB!" *Challenge 12* and *Australia II* peel off in unison, going
to windward together, as we have nearly always done since those far-off
days on Port Phillip Bay.

The wind feels shifty, light, fickle. "Maximum input now, Ya," I call to
my diffident mastman. "Watch the wind, keep feeding me. Pay attention
now to the ripples. This is going to be damned tricky out here, and I
really need you." Up ahead I can see the red boat bowling along boldly
with *Freedom*. Their sails look very, very nice, but I say nothing. It's just
the red boat, and it's irrelevant to our own effort. The breeze keeps fad-
ing, and, as usual, *Challenge 12* and *Australia II* stay tight together. We
have a slight speed edge, as I knew we would, but after a few runs, we're
still together. Shortly after 11:30 A.M. we part, and we sail quietly down
toward the starting area. The red boat is now in the midst of the huge
fleet of spectator boats, Dennis waving to the crowd, absorbing the good
wishes of the thousands of spectators on this day, the day he has waited so
long for, when 250 million Americans are with him to a man. At least
that's what he claims. By my reckoning, about two-thirds of them are with
us to a man after that eccentric performance by the New York Yacht Club.
And anyway, even if I'm wrong, I know one thing. There are 500 Americans who are definitely *not* with him—the residents of Pewaukee, Wisconsin, who are with *me* to a man, and many of them have arrived to cheer on
their former lakeside neighbor.

Dennis, however, is loving this, grinning, holding his hand high in
greeting, getting topped up by the atmosphere. Back on *Australia II,* we
are trying our best to be nonchalant. I have won the toss and chosen the
port end of the line, and Hughey is quietly working me up into my most
aggressive mood. At 11:50, *Black Knight* hoists the course signals, I aim
Australia II downwind, and we come at the red boat from out of the ruck.
At high noon, the 10-minute gun fires, and *Liberty* and *Australia II* come
into close quarters for the first time. I glance over at Dennis and try to
look him in the eye. I do not smile and neither does he. But simultaneously we nod—curtly, formally. Then I go after him. You can almost
hear our crew stop breathing as I jibe around, hard on his tail. The red
boat tacks away, and back we come, hard on starboard. Conner tacks off
and we go after him again, circling, circling, feeling each other out. I am
oblivious to everything now, except the swirl of the water as I whip
Australia II around, trying to nail them, catch them off balance. But he's a

slippery bastard, and that big red boat of his keeps edging away. We lope on down to the line, but the wind is veering around terribly. It's almost impossible to set a course, and to no one's surprise, the Race Committee hauls up the red-and-white-striped postponement flag, with two minutes to go. The wind has just come around in a 40-degree shift and, with some relief, we lower the headsail.

Black Swan comes on over and we all wait for another two hours before we try to start for a second time.

Right now, I know we are more maneuverable, and this time we really go for them, locking in tight as soon as the 10-minute gun goes. The red boat circles away and we go right after him. Three times he tries to escape and then we have him—I stick the bow of *Australia II* right on his hip, forcing him away. There is nothing they can do—the Americans haul off to port trying to escape. I follow, or seem to, and just as the red boat jibes around, Hughey says quietly, "OK, John, let's go. Now." I balk away, catching them absolutely flat-footed, and I aim *Australia II* straight at the starting line in beautiful time. Hughey and I don't dare look at each other, in case we burst out laughing.

The invincible Americans had just mistimed it totally, and we headed for a start that could put us at least half a minute in front. We were at the right end, going the right way about twice as fast as our opponents. We had just made them look ridiculous. We were upwind of them at maximum speed and they were going slower and lower. We had them, and they knew it, and their only chance was that if this wind stayed at its shifting 7 knots, the race could become a crapshoot.

Since 132 years of history was hanging in the balance, the Committee did the prudent thing and called it off for the day with 90 seconds to go before the start. There were no complaints from us. You can't sail a big race in light, unstable winds like that. As we turned into the wind to await *Black Swan* and Bondy and all, there were smiles on the faces of the men on *Australia II*. First blood to us, no doubt about that. We must have shaken them up. No challenging crew in the history of the America's Cup had ever come out and gone after the defenders like that, and I don't think any American skipper had ever been caught so badly on the wrong foot on the first day as Dennis had. Later, he would say that his one regret was that he did not get *Liberty*'s sails down fast enough in order to disguise the big gap between the two boats. He was right about that, and I think he looked shell-shocked at the press conference.

As we came gliding to a halt out on the course, the atmosphere on our boat was terrific. We felt very good about ourselves, and that was important. Swiftly, I headed off any feeling of complacency. We stayed out there for another 90 minutes, and while *Liberty* headed straight home, we tested another mainsail and four spinnakers—the weather forecast said a cold front was heading toward our stretch of the East Coast, and tomorrow we might have to face a stiff breeze and a heavy sea. I told the boys not to get excited. We had done well, but we had not yet put a score on the board, and that's what we had to do, so we had to keep working. By the time we had carried out those tests, we were almost as tired as if we had raced. Damian hoisted the boxing kangaroo to shake his gloved fist at the world, and we all fell fast asleep on the sails as *Black Swan* towed us home.

Rasa and the children met me at the dock, and we all strolled up to the press conference, at which the traditional inanities were asked, and then we walked home. I was sorely tempted to stay home for dinner, but we had decided that it was critical for the crew to be all together that night, so I took Lucas up to Founders' Hall to watch television while I had a light-hearted dinner with the crew. Nothing serious. Just a couple of beers, a ghastly film, the identity of which I have mercifully forgotten, and home to bed at 9:30. After hot milk and a tranquilizer, I drifted off to sleep, John Denver accompanying me into oblivion.

I woke with a start before the 5:45 A.M. alarm and dived for the window. The front had arrived, and it was blowing out there. The skies were overcast—a gray, blustery day signaling the end of summer and the cooling approach of autumn.

The day was almost a replica of my first-ever America's Cup race, so many years ago, when *Gretel* was destroyed by *Intrepid*. I remember that sea, how everyone got sick on the way out to the start and how Paul Salmon, apparently in search of his ancestors, fell off the foredeck on the third leg. You have to be extremely careful on a racing Twelve in this kind of weather, and the prospect of all that stress, of the green water that will come crashing over the bow, causes the adrenaline to start pumping early.

Hughey and I arrived at Founders' Hall, and the routine was very much the same as always. There were still some very puny appetites, but this time it was more because of the natural trepidation that affects all seamen going out into rough water. There had to be 18 knots of breeze out there, so I had a careful little conference with Tom Schnackenberg— we discussed the new heavy-air mainsail we undoubtedly would use. We had never raced with it before, but it had been specially built for just such a day as this. We had used it and tested it and were all very happy with its shape—a little flatter than usual for this type of sail, but Schnackenberg had given it special attention. I had a lot of faith in it. Whether or not that faith would be justified would be known before this day was over.

I timed my arrival at the dock pretty much as I had done on the previous day. The tension was greatly reduced, because we had been out there once and delivered a message to Dennis Conner. The thought that occupied our minds as the boat was prepared to leave was the prospect of "Bennyurisms," as the weather would put huge strains on the boat and put the design to its stiffest test. Racing in this hard, cold wind is always harrowing, and sometimes it can be quite scary, especially if something breaks suddenly. And we were no strangers to breakages. When we lost to *Azzurra*, we had broken a halyard and a runner, in another race we broke a jib halyard and something on one of the running backstays, and in another race we broke a halyard lock and then the masthead crane. We also broke a boom, and once we snapped a jib halyard against *Challenge 12*. In fact, the only major breakage we had all summer, which was not a Bennyurism, was poor old Scotty's arm.

Another huge crowd was packed around the dock when I arrived, struggling my way past the guards, one of whom was a big, boisterous guy. When he saw me, he used to shout to the crowd, "All right, you guys, watch your backs, step aside, make way for the workers!"

I stopped to have a word with Phil Judge, the tender driver, about the weather, and then I stopped for a couple of minutes to talk to one of my great mentors and friends, Kenny Beashel, Colin's dad. I thought I did it just to be sociable, but there was more to it than that. I did it because I always knew he would know exactly the right thing to say to me, and he never let me down. "Just keep your eye on the water, Johnny, play the shifts and stay loose. We're going to do this. I know we are. I can feel it in my bones. Just keep watching the water and you're gonna bring us home." A real superstitious old seaman was Kenny. His presence in Newport meant a hell of a lot to me. We stood there together for a few seconds, grinning at each other. Neither of us mentioned the subject we both knew was utterly paramount today, the performance of his son, Colin, my mainsheet hand, on this day in this wind. He would be one of the most critical men on the boat, handling the big, flat, new mainsail. He was going to have his work cut out for him, that was for sure. But I didn't want to sound patronizing, and Kenny didn't want to say, "Look after him, Johnny," so we just left it unsaid.

I stepped aboard *Australia II*, said good morning to everyone, and casually patted Colin on the back as I passed him, head down checking his hydraulic controls. Everyone was in foul-weather gear—out beyond the harbor wall we were going to run into white water, no doubt about that. Damian, gloves on, was on the foredeck checking the towlines, and Grant had his head in the middle of his computer, mumbling away, checking, checking. The big new mainsail was on our carbon-fiber boom, and at nine o'clock sharp, I signaled for the castoff. Up went the flag, and Men at Work gave it their best shot at a truly massive decibel level:

"I come from a land Down Under,

"Where women glow and men plunder. . . ."

The crowd roared, but as *Black Swan* began to move forward, it was suddenly apparent that one of the lines that held the skirt around the keel was entangled in the keel, and the force of our departure was about to pull the entire skirt-holding structure down, causing God-knows-how-much damage. I was about to yell, "Hold it! Stop!" when there was a blur before my eyes. Colin Beashel leapt like a panther, his right hand unsheathing a vicious-looking seaman's knife. With a mighty slash, he severed the rope, freeing us in a fraction of a second.

Colin never even glanced up. He went straight back to his hydraulic controls without missing a beat. He didn't want to hear from me. I just smiled to myself, the smile of a man blissfully happy with those with whom he must go into battle.

Once more, a huge armada of spectator boats awaited us, and many of them hooted out greetings. Once more the Aussie flags went up, a great feeling of nationalistic pride somehow filling many an Australian chest. As the music came to an end, I called the crew into a huddle. Today my theme was different. I told them to forget yesterday and to forget tomorrow. Today was the day we were going to do it. I told them to remember that we had no score on the board, and that's what we were after today. It was Race 1, and we had to be really up for it, concentrating just as intensely as we had yesterday. I reminded them of something I had mentioned before—that I have a traditional flat spot in a seven-race regatta, that it took me years to figure out that I traditionally came out like a tiger, slacked off in races three, four, and five, and then finished with a rush for victory. I tried to impress on everyone that our concentration could never flag through these seven races—especially today. "Gentlemen, let's have a sleep and then get out there and put a score on the card."

It was a wet ride out. Water was crashing over the bow, and some of it was pouring down the mast into our below-deck quarters. The Major sat in the middle of it, not caring one way or another. By the time Robbie woke us, the wind was screaming, gusting to well over 20 knots. We answered the call of the winch handle, headed up on deck, and I radioed Jim Hardy to hoist the code-four genoa on *Challenge 12*.

"HOIST THE MAINSAIL!"—and up goes our new sail. Looks fine, and a hell of a lot better than the one we used against the foreign boats. I wished we had had the conditions to test it in a race, though. "Code-four genoa," I shout. "Ready!" roars the Major above the wind, which is now thundering into the eye of the Kevlar main, cracking and whacking, a terrible noise.

"HOIST THE JIB!"—and *Australia II* leans into the sea, straining with everything she has as we close with *Challenge 12*. For about a mile, we race neck and neck, and slowly but surely, she begins to eke out from under us. "Jesus Christ, this is all we need," Hughey says. "It's that jib. Let's get it down." "Good call," I say. "Break out the code-three genoa! Let's do this same run again." I thank my lucky stars we have arrived out here 15 minutes early, because we need all the time we can get. The foredeck boys execute the genoa switch brilliantly, and now we are set to deal with *Challenge 12*, which we do with some style. The sail change made the difference between defeat and victory. And the Superboat theory is not coming heavily into play in the real world out here in the wind.

What counts right now is the code-three genoa, and that is the one we will use to race *Liberty*. As we prepare to go down to the battleground, we are getting feedback from *Black Swan* on the wind velocity at heights of 10 feet, 20 feet, and 30 feet. Grant is logging the numbers, recording the density of the air at those various heights above the boat. This will affect how we shape the main. (In broad terms, you might have 18 knots of breeze at 40 feet up, but only 10 knots at deck level.) Peter van Oossanen, the Dutch test-tank genius, is aboard *Black Swan*, helping with this highly technical aspect of aiming a 12-Meter into the sea. The air velocity seems dense, but the sea is very, very choppy, and everything tells us that the code-three genoa will see us right all afternoon. Now Jim Hardy has to get *Challenge 12* off the course, the New York Yacht Club having been displeased yesterday with his presence so close to us. He calls out, "Goodbye, John. Good luck, boys," and wheels away.

I swing *Australia II* downwind and head for my long-awaited confrontation with Dennis Conner. We *still* do not know what will happen when the two warring hulls shape up against each other. "This is it, fellers," I announce. "Today we have a boat race. And there will be a result."

High above our heads, as others have observed, it looks like a scene from *Apocalypse Now*. The air is thick with helicopters and planes. It seems as if there are hundreds of them. Back home in Australia it is two o'clock in the morning, and I think briefly of Mum, and Lex and his family, all in their pajamas drinking coffee, and, by some modern miracle, watching me from halfway across the world in Chelsea.

Hughey checks the committee boat as we go by, "Still port end of the line?" And I head up to our rightful starting point. I feel very confident. "Just remember," I call, "we are going to be number one." I get a cheap burst of laughter when I turn toward *Liberty* and give the universal signal with forearm and fist which means stick it up your jumper, or thereabouts.

The sky is still very overcast and the wind remains steady at 18 knots. The spray is now banging over the side. Damian, already soaked, is up on the foredeck with Chink, standing in green water, holding onto the forestay as *Australia II* pitches up and down in the waves. Already she feels difficult to steer. Deep down below us, the winged keel is acting like a pendulum, playing havoc with our directional stability. I'm using a lot more rudder trying to keep her tracking in a straight line. But she will soon be free to do what she is good at, outmaneuver the red boat at the start. The tricky aspects of this boat mean that the mainsail has to be trimmed extremely delicately, and Colin is very much aware of his responsibility. He is already working overtime, his hands and eyes everywhere, watching, assessing, adjusting inch by inch.

At midday the 10-minute gun sounds. The Major hits the stopwatch. Because of the conditions, I do not want to get too close to Dennis, resplendent in his white crash helmet. We come off the port end of the line, content to stay on our own for four or five minutes. We delay our turn back until about 5½ minutes, and then *Australia II* comes charging out of that heaving sea, and I swing her right onto the tail of the red boat. You can nearly hear us growling with temper and aggression. Coming up to the starting line, we duck through on his leeward side, and the count goes into its final stages.

The Major is calling it, "50 . . . 45 . . . 40 . . . 35 . . .30 . . . 29 . . . 28 . . . 27 . . . ." "A little slower, John," says Hughey, and I head her up a fraction. "22 . . . 21 . . . 20 . . . ." "OK, guys," I say, "we're looking good, we're driving for it, driving for it now. . . ." "15 . . . 14 . . . 13 . . . 12 . . . ." *Liberty* tacks away. This is my time. I am ready for this. I have served my time, and I am ready to fight this battle. I am right in control. I am looking forward to it, and that's a great feeling. "9 . . . 8 . . . 7 . . . ." We're at full speed now, and we're going to be there first! The Major sends me a raw smile. "3 . . . 2 . . . 1 . . . Go!" he bellows. The gun crashes out simultaneously.

We're just a few feet from the line, and we hit it flying. You just can't do it better than that. "The American is three seconds back," says Hughey, with great calm, "and they're going slower. Let's tack over now and join 'em." I swing *Australia II* around to the right and slap a loose cover right on them. We now have the red boat safely to leeward. I look up and see the Major grinning from ear to ear. "Great start, John," he shouts. "Terrific, John," says Hughey. Now we have a boatspeed contest as we close with them . . . and we are holding the upper hand. "We've got good speed on them," says Hughey. "Speed?" I say, "we've got a rocketship on our hands. We're coming away from her." The atmosphere is fantastic. The boys, God bless 'em, are desperately trying to wear their busy-busy faces—but it is so exciting as we slip away from *Liberty,* banging through the waves. Damian up on the foredeck stands momentarily like a statue, his face a study in ecstasy, swept up with the sheer formal drama of the race.

But that feeling of joy is short-lived. As I head *Australia II* into the waves, the fierce chop under the bow begins to have an effect. I'm having a hard time steering the boat. Her stern is swinging around a lot. There's too much weather helm, and I call to Colin, "Ease the mainsheet!" He lets her out fractionally. "Too much!" I call, "come down." Colin winds her in another ¾ inch. "Better," I say. But I'm still having a very hard time holding her on track, and the fine-tuning on this boat is amazing. Remember, that sail is 95 feet high. We hit two successive waves hard, plowing in, green water rushing past Damian's knees. "Speed's off ⅓ knot," shouts Grant instantly, and to my horror, *Liberty* starts to come out from underneath us. This is trouble. We start to lose bearing, sagging down into the American's course, into the nightmare that has always haunted us in this boat—the short, choppy waves that no tank test can simulate. Momentarily the sea flattens out, and *Australia II* surges forward again, but *Liberty* is moving up on us. She is going slightly faster and, unfortunately, pointing higher. The blasted Superboat is not doing her stuff right now, and Red Dog has taken two full boatlengths off us. We have *never* seen that before in our races against the foreigners. We have always been able to hang on to our lead. "The Americans are going faster," says Hughey. "Yeah, I know," I say, ruefully. "They are pretty fast. We have a race on our hands. Let's just keep going."

Liberty tacks, heading right across our bow, and now for the first time I see the pressure on Hughey. He stands there uptight, uncertain whether to call for me to tack underneath her on starboard, going left to generate a safe lee-bow position, or to take her stern. At the last minute, Hughey calls, "Take her stern, John," but he's late and so am I. Colin does not have time to ease the mainsheet, and we slide across her stern, missing it by about 20 feet instead of by three. You just cannot afford to give away that type of distance, and I say, "Come on, Hughey, let's get our act together. Let's be more concise. That's too ragged and indecisive." Suddenly I realize that Hughey has been just a little bit stagestruck, and I am dealing with the razor edge of my tactician's confidence. I had *never* seen him like this. Quickly I say, "Come on, Hughey. There's no one better than you. Talk to me and let's be really clear about what we are doing."

We sail on for about another 50 yards, Hughey calls for a tack to the left, and we flop back on *Liberty's* weather quarter. *Australia II* accelerates very quickly out of the tack, but in a split second I realize that we may be underpowered. Could it be that this new, untested mainsail might be a little too flat in this kind of chop? Suddenly the wind shifts around, fractionally in our favor. I notice it immediately on the compass—five degrees—and Grant is saying, "We're up five, we're up five, it's looking good." He's quick, that Mad Dog. Now we are catching them, and suddenly we're blocking the way. Conner could not take our bow now if he wanted to. Hughey is saying, "We're looking good. Just keep going, keep going." Scoop is calling back, "We're going fine, just a little bit faster. We need 7.6 knots. Come on, John, just a little bit faster. Let's try for 7.7. That's our target speed."

By now, all the brains in the boat know that we may have a horsepower problem. And the speed calls are coming all the time. Skippy, down on the port side, has said, "We need 7.7." I'm holding *Australia II* on the knife edge known to all helmsmen—a fraction of an inch upwind to our right heading closer to the weather mark and our speed will drop to 7.3 or 7.4, a fraction of an inch the other way and we will dip down into *Liberty*, coming farther away from the mark at perhaps 7.8 knots. I'm happy at between 7.6 and 7.7, but the damned red boat is doing 7.8 knots and going parallel. For a split second we slip down a fraction and the dial suddenly reads 7.8. "Kill the speed! Kill the speed!" yells Scoop, "we're bearing off." Back we go to 7.7, and Hughey says coldly, "She still can't cross us, John." Whether or not he's right, we will soon know. *Liberty* tacks, roaring toward us. For a split second, I think Hughey is wrong, that she's going to take our bow. But those cool, blue seaman's eyes of his have not deceived him. At the last minute, *Liberty* ducks away underneath us, taking our stern. Hughey and I go for a plan that, if not pure daredevil, is certainly as bold as brass. We decide to slam-dunk the Americans, tacking on top of them and shutting off their option. It is the most aggressive move in yacht racing, and it has to be done with precision accuracy to about nine inches. One slight error and they will leave you.

The tension is incredible. Everyone senses what we are going to try. I can hear the slap, slap, slap of *Liberty*'s oncoming bow wave to leeward of us, but I cannot see her. Hughey is saying, "Not yet, not yet, not yet." Suddenly, he says, "Ready, John, *now!*" in a high-pitched yell. I know how nervous he is, and I wheel *Australia II* around.

Hughey's call was perfect, and I don't throw around that word much. We roll right over them in perhaps the most flawless slam-dunk I have ever seen—never mind executed. It is classic. The breeze dropped as we did it, and as Liberty eases along to our right, it is now impossible for her to eke up and get a safe position. If we had allowed her another 24 inches, she would have sliced up on our starboard side and we would have had to tack away. I turn to Hughey, grinning. "That was just terrific, Hughey. Well done." He doesn't even smile, just stands there, stooped under his boom with his eyes glued to the red boat. We had never been this close to Conner before.

Dennis ducks away in search of more speed. I go with him, trying to hold them. But *Liberty* has boatspeed on us in this chop. Our mainsail is clearly too flat, and Dennis seems to be able to roll up to 7.9 and 8 knots very quickly. He's in a fractionally faster combination, and we have to be very careful. We're locked together, and there's no way he can get away from us. For a mile and a half, hard on the wind, we sail almost as one, and Hughey and I drive them all the way down to the layline. Grant's calling it, "Two lengths to the layline . . . one length to the layline. . . ." Hughey says, "Let's make it a full layline." And we cross it completely. "OK, guys," I shout, "tacking the boat, tacking the boat!" *Liberty* tacks with us, and we decide to give her all the gas we have. I point *Australia II* higher as we hurtle toward the first weather mark. We have come away from that tack beautifully, and now we have *Liberty* right in our wind-shadow. We triple our lead right away because we have her in our back-wind.

Racing up toward the mark, there is now furious activity as we prepare for our first spinnaker set. The Major breaks it out of the pack down below and Damian starts feeding it out of the hatch. The Major rushes back on deck and grabs the halyard, hauling up the huge parachute. Ya hauls with him, still at his own pace but somehow keeping up with the Major. Now the whole world is looking at these lightning-fast boys from Down Under, yet in a sense they know so little about what is happening on *Australia II*. Skippy is scrambling along the weather side with the spin-naker sheet in his hand, after jamming off the genoa sheet. Scoop is madly getting the brace aft. Chink and Splash are furiously grinding the spinnaker pole aft. And Grant Simmer has bolted the length of the boat and is now up on the bow with the hoist, getting down the genoa. He looks as bloody awkward and uncoordinated as ever, and I can't help but think that it's a matter of time before he falls straight over the side. He hates it when I say anything to him about his agility, but I find it irresist-ible. "Careful now, Grant," I call, full of devilment. "Hang on to some-thing, and for Christ's sake, don't fall off." My young navigator finds time to glare ferociously at me. All this stuff is not tension. This is hyperten-sion. Rather like telling a joke as you are about to die. We hit the mark a full eight seconds in front of the red boat—just about a boatlength. Around we go, and as the stern clears the buoy, the spinnaker pops with superb precision. It's a lovely set, and I watch it for a few seconds. By now Grant is back at his instrument panel and everything is back in order. I let out a little "Yahoo!" Grant, startled for a moment, looks up, scowling, "Shut up, Bertrand, and sail the boat." I chuckle a bit at the tension packed into Mad Dog's whipcord frame, at his total concentration, at the fact that anything could irritate him, so totally focused are his thoughts as his eyes burn into the dials before him.

Now the pressure is *really* on. Everyone knew we were not strong going downwind, but we have tried for months to improve our performance on these reaching legs. *Liberty* is close, but her spinnaker set was not as fast as ours. How would we go against her downwind for the first time? Nobody knew that. In the frenzied rush back to positions, I see Hughey standing there, scratching the palms of his hands. He always does that when he's nervous; the more nervous he gets, the faster he scratches. Beasho eases out the mainsail, but Hughey is scratching like mad now, so I know that *Liberty* must be getting closer. I can hear that awful sound of her bow wave. I'm very uptight, but I can't let anyone know about the knot in my stomach. Now we can hear the shouting among the American crew, and the sound of her bow wave grows louder. She's in our wake up on our weather quarter, and Hughey is talking to me all the time. "He's up 10 feet on us." "Let's go up a little." "We've got it back." "Here he comes again." All I can do is work the boat through the waves, try to keep up our boatspeed, keep the spinnaker nice and firm. We hold them off all the way down the first power reach, and we jibe around the second mark 10 seconds in front. There is no question about one thing. *Liberty* is the toughest, fastest opponent we have ever had, just as I knew she would be. But she's not unbeatable. And we're still in front. *Liberty* takes the mark wider, and she's up to weather. "She's going very fast, John," says Hughey, "let's go higher." We begin to go higher and higher to try to block *Liberty*. Both boats are heeled over dramatically, the Americans more so than we are. I curse under my breath that we did not take that mark more aggressively and protect our position better. However, the only way she can pass us is to go over us. She cannot come underneath. Again I curse myself for misjudging the jibe mark. *Australia II* has never been in a race as tight as this one. *Liberty* is very, very competitive. It's going to be a long regatta.

And now she is trundling up to us, disproportionately fast. "What the hell is happening, Hughey?" I ask, my voice full of tension. I look around to check her out and call instantly for a staysail. The Major hurtles onto the deck with it and the boys haul it up inside the spinnaker in eight seconds flat. This speeds us up, and *Liberty* seems to slow down. She is still riding over us, but only half as fast as she was. The fact is, she is still faster and I just cannot believe it. *Liberty* eventually gets to us and takes our wind. She sails possibly a boatlength to weather of us. The Americans get ready to pass, and one of them shouts over in their familiar accent, the sickening sound, "Mast lahn!" (mast line or mast abeam). We pull away, back to our proper course, to mark number three, and the red boat comes through, causing our sails to sag. I wait till her stern is abeam of our bow and I swing up toward her, aggressively. Conner is not interested. He just keeps right on going, content with the fact that he is in a faster-reaching boat, a fact we now both know.

Eventually, with nothing short of pure hatred in my heart, I bite the bullet and come back down and fall in behind them to prepare for the rounding of the mark and the next leg to windward. She took 26 seconds off us on the second power-reaching leg, and I knew that it could not have been a fluke. Little did I know that on the next nine successive times *Liberty* and *Australia II* raced down these power-reach legs, we would *never* once gain even one second. For a bloke who is supposed to be in an unbeatable boat, I am beginning to form the opinion that things ought to be going a bit more smoothly, a bit more trouble-free, with the poor put-upon Americans gazing in exasperation as the Wonder from Down Under scoots away from them. No such luck. Mind you, I know power reaching is not our strong suit, but we certainly did not expect *Liberty* to be *that* quick.

I am determined not to get rattled. I have vast experience and I know that in some areas you have to give something away and in others you catch up. But it seems that once more we are going to be in a position where we have to grab the lead early and try to hang on downwind, just as we were forced to do against *Azzurra* and *Victory*, and earlier against *Challenge*. "So let's just hang in there, boys," I shout. "Keep doing our best, giving it our very best shot, as the old Seahawk said." In a second of irrelevant madness I wonder whether Shelton Robinson is watching us.

Down comes the spinnaker. We round the mark reasonably but not brilliantly. I am still fed up that I did not have a perfect angle at the last jibe mark, and now I've been less than perfect at mark three. *Liberty* made the biggest gain on us power reaching of any boat all summer. I glance at Hughey and he cannot believe it. He's just shaking his head. "That's OK, Hughey," I grin, "we're going to hang right in. That was just a little setback, all part of the deal. Let's get after 'em."

We head upwind and immediately initiate a vicious tacking duel, the area in which I know we are good. Tack after tack for mile after mile. Twenty-seven times we dive off to break free of them and every time they cover us, matching us, negating our efforts. That *Liberty* is a damned competitive boat upwind, which is very boring, since she seems to be fantastic downwind. Maybe it's just that heavy-air mainsail of ours. In any event, the big red boat rounds the top mark 28 seconds in front, and as the boys race into position to haul up the spinnaker for the second time, I can see *Liberty* heading off to the left for the run downhill to mark number five. I steel myself to deal with our traditionally weakest leg, but we're still hanging in there. Up pops our beautiful pure-white spinnaker. Ya calls back, "The best breeze is to the right, John," and I aim *Australia II* over to that side. Now we have to back our judgment. *Liberty* is on a port jibe, and we elect to stay on starboard jibe. Anxiously, I call out again to Ya, "What's the wind doing? How does it look?" I can see that Ya is still caught up in all the lines left over from the spinnaker set, and I turn to Hughey. "What do you think?" I ask. "Stay where you are," he says, without hesitation. I look over to Grant. "Let's stay in tune with the wind phasing," I mutter. "Do we have the right spinnaker up?" "Yes," says Grant, "We're all right." But I'm not sure. Again I ask, "Hughey, what d'you think? Is that spinnaker right?" "Leave it," he replied quietly. "OK," I say, "but keep watching. Let's not sail too far with the wrong chute." Again I call to Ya, "How does it look?" But suddenly there's a shift. Grant shouts, "Five degrees, John, up six, up seven. This is a big bastard." "We're right back in it," snaps Hughey. "*Liberty*'s in trouble." I can see her down on the left side. Dennis jibes back toward us to starboard, then almost immediately jibes back to port. All of a sudden we have a boat race again, and we are rolling up to them hand over fist. We're nearly even and we've gained back just about the whole 28 seconds. There's no question that they have not sailed downwind very well. They have been in less breeze, which is not a good idea, because that tends to be slow.

And now we are neck and neck. The red boat is still away to our left when suddenly Dennis swings over toward us. His bow man, Scott Vogel, seems to materialize from nowhere, and, after a wickedly fast dip-pole jibe, *Liberty* is coming at us on a collision course with full rights. This stuff is rough. (I later learned that Vogel had gone below and crawled forward to pop out of the hatch like a firecracker, so we would not know what they were doing. Sport? This was like the Cold War!) Hughey and I are faced with a very quick decision. Either we jibe instantly with the Americans and give them a guaranteed inside overlap—we're about 300 yards from the mark—or we lift up across their stern. *Liberty* has the right-of-way, and in 15 knots of breeze we have to decide what to do. The ever-aggressive Hughey wants to take their stern. I slam the wheel hard over, and from nowhere comes a sudden, near-deafening BANG! Christ, I think, the mast has broken! As I look to see what happened, I suddenly realize I have no steering. We careen crazily out of control, the spinnaker pole shoots into the sky, and I shout, "The f-----g steering's gone!" Hughey grabs rope. Beasho dives below, hammer, screwdriver, and knife at the ready. Hughey follows him down. No one knows what happened. I know that in this wind, now at around 15 knots, I have just put an enormous load on our gear. I grab for the trim tab and try to steer the boat, but it's hopeless. We jibe twice and somehow flounder around the mark. Beasho shouts up, "We've sheared a pulley right off the side of the hull. We can try to tie her up, but it doesn't look good."

Everyone had heard the thunderous clap of the breakage. It was like a cannon. In our hearts we know we are one down. There is no way we can fight *Liberty* upwind without proper steering. *Liberty* rounds the mark 35 seconds ahead, and we are just out of control. I am sure we have snapped the rudder right off, but Beasho yells up that it is only the steering cable. I am cursing roundly, not at anyone in particular, and finally Beasho has us back in some sort of jury-rigged shape. At least we can go forward. We round the mark like Jonathan with a broken wing, and we try our very best all the way home. But it is to no avail, and *Liberty*, which we let right off the hook, sails cheerfully across the line one minute and 10 seconds to the good. 1–0.

By the time we crossed the line, the exultation on *Liberty* was obvious. The vast crowd of American supporters was heading toward Dennis and the victorious red boat. He sailed into the fleet, his hand raised high, acknowledging the cheers, waving confidently at the Committee on *Black Knight,* tracked by a fleet of gigantic powerboats, the heavy-hitters of the American syndicate. There was something awesome about the American yacht-racing establishment in this mood—sure of their tactics, confident of their inevitable victory, the biggest and most powerful nation about to crush a small and rather woebegone challenger, which was limping, wounded, over the line, apparently unable to stand the heat of battle.

I looked at the boys, tired in defeat. You never feel this tired when you have won—even though you have done exactly the same amount of work—and I reflected on the afternoon. The most worrisome thought was that we had found for the first time a boat that had our measure to wind-ward in 15 to 18 knots of breeze. We had also found a boat that was a hell of a lot faster than we were on the power reaches. We had also run into a crew that was match-hard. I always knew that we had been in no scraps this tough with the foreign boats, as *Liberty* had with *Courageous,* and now we were paying the price. My violent move across *Liberty*'s stern was not the action of an ice-cool, match-trained helmsman. It was a slightly rash tactic of a chap who needed a bit more rough practice. Dennis had thrown a fast curve ball at us, and Hughey and I had been unable to whack it out of the way. Hughey desperately wanted to take their stern, and while I was not quite as sure, I agreed, and I flung the wheel around. Looking back, I realized that should not have done it. Dennis would not have done it. And the John Bertrand who had been so utterly match-hard eight summers earlier would not have done it either. I should have gone with him, jibed on starboard, let him have the overlap, and then tried to make a fight of it going upwind. But both Hughey and I knew that he had boatspeed on us going into the wind, and that our chances of catching him, with this main-sail, at least (we would not use it again in these conditions) were question-able. So we subconsciously decided to give it a go and try to jibe around him. It was now obvious to both of us that we should not have done this in that much breeze. There was no way it would have worked, and it was the first time we had ever been forced into using such a desperate tactic. The steering failure merely dramatized what was already doomed to failure. We now knew, beyond any doubt, that we were going to have to race the series of a lifetime to beat the Americans.

As we limped on toward *Black Swan*, I knew I had been quite badly shaken up. The boys on the red boat knew they had been in a fight, but in the end they had whacked us about the head and shoulders, smacked us back onto the ropes, and let us know what it was like to fight real men. People had frequently made the analogy that this was all like David and Goliath, the little Aussies against the might of the U.S.A. But it's still a bit of a shock when Goliath unloads a backhander and catches you squarely in the mouth. Also, our fabled tacking ability had not worked because we had stuck to long, loping tacks, allowing the boats to get up to speed. We made no gains tacking, which was tantamount to David dropping his hurling rocks in the middle of his backswing.

I knew that on the morrow we had to tack faster and more aggressively and not allow either boat to get above 7 knots before we tacked again. That could wear them down a bit. I also realized that I had been mentally stretched at some key moments, perhaps to a point where I lost a little bit of my judgment. I momentarily lost poise. When you think about it, it was not all that far removed from my performance in the 1976 Olympics against Schumann. I was stepping out of the area in which I had been trained, looking for the one thing that would put us right. Looking back, I realize that neither of those moves, played as they were seven years apart, was likely to have worked. But that's the beauty of hindsight. It's not quite the same when you're out there in the thick of it. As we headed back to the dock, I said to myself, "John, you have *got* to slow down a little bit. You have to generate a bit more poise." I said to my tactician, "Hughey, old pal, that was just a bit too much of a gamble. We should have known enough to back off." And he agreed with me immediately. There's no doubt that in the heat of battle we were stressed and did not maximize our own normally excellent powers of decisionmaking under pressure. And what a time we picked to get excited—right in the middle of the first race of the 1983 America's Cup, with the boats just about dead even.

I also returned to the dock rather worried about our communication. I was worried that young Grant was becoming a little bit "into himself." I was afraid I was not getting sufficient feedback from him. He was a bit too quiet for me, perhaps intimidated by the whole atmosphere of the America's Cup, and I had to stop that. I talked to him for a while and told him he had the maximum to offer here. Whatever he felt, I wanted to hear it. "If you think I've done something wrong," I said, "for Christ's sake, let me know. Have confidence in your own judgment, Grant." I knew that *anything* he said generally was worth listening to. I had to get that information out of him and encourage him to stay in touch with me always, and not to clam up.

One way or another, however, I felt very determined that we would do better the next day. I felt remarkably at peace with myself, because at least I knew where we must improve. I also felt at peace with the men I was sailing with. And I knew that when next we stepped aboard *Australia II,* I had to develop all the poise I possibly could—and try to lead this marvelous group of young men to a famous victory over the Americans.

15

Bennyurism Number Two

I hated it. We limped home, eleven somber men and a beautiful white boat, like a great seabird with a broken wing—all held together by one little line of Kevlar.

They towed us home across the cold, gray seas of Rhode Island Sound, and we did not hoist the kangaroo flag. We entered the harbor to a riotous cacophony of blaring horns and bursts of applause for the conquering American heroes. We did not play our music, and I suppose we must have looked like a very dejected little group, in contrast to the jubilant Americans laughing and waving to the crowd as they put their big, red, triumphant boat to bed for the night.

I stepped off the boat for a fast emergency meeting with Warren, Bondy, and the maintenance men before I went to the press conference. And to that meeting I took a truly shuddering little secret. Well, it was not quite a secret, but only I knew the full extent of its seriousness. Two days before, Kenny Beashel had told me he was not happy about the strength of those steering cables and the pulleys on which they ran, and the way they were welded to the hull. I immediately went to Benny and told him of Kenny's fears, and our designer went aboard *Australia II* to check them out. He returned to me and told me they were fine, so I let the matter drop. And now the pulley had broken in the middle of a race and to all intents and purposes tossed us out of the contest, and it was my fault. I am supposed to be the skipper of this boat, and I had let us go to sea for a violently competitive boat race against Dennis Conner in 18 knots of breeze with gear that I should have known was suspect. Christ! Kenny Beashel is one of the greatest boat men in the world. There is nothing he does not understand about them, there was nothing his champion-class father did not know, and there is precious little his 24-year-old son, Colin, does not know. They all have instincts about boats that are fantastic, and both Kenny and Colin can fix anything, anywhere, at any time. Kenny Beashel, transpacific sailor, championship yachtsman, shipwright, and boatbuilder, has no peer when it comes to judging the professional functioning of big racing yachts and the stress factors thereon. And I had ignored him. And now he was devastated. And it was my bloody fault.

When I faced Kenny, I just said, "Christ, I'm sorry, Beasho. I should have just told you to do it." Beasho was close to tears, and he stood there blaming himself, mentally berating himself for not insisting, for not telling me he didn't care what Benny said, but those pulleys had to be strengthened if we were going out in a big sea.

But we quickly sorted things out. Bondy now put Kenny in charge of everything to do with the maintenance. If he wanted something strengthened, then it would be strengthened, with no questions asked. Benny would be consulted on *how* it should be strengthened, but Beasho was in charge. I went to the press conference and very briefly explained the gear failure. Then I went straight down to the dock, where the arc lights were burning in the gathering gloom as Kenny and his men combed that boat for structural weakness. Most of the crew was still there. We broke for dinner and were all back down there before nine o'clock. Shortly thereafter, we all fell into bed—tired, shattered, and bitterly disappointed, but still fiercely determined that we would do better when we faced the red boat for the second time the next day. Down at the dock the arc light on *Australia II* burned all night. I don't think Kenny Beashel went to bed. And if he did retire for a couple of hours in the early part of the morning, I know he never slept. He was more upset that night than any member of the crew would ever be throughout all the trials and tribulations that would befall us. He was quietly, privately torturing himself, and I never felt as sorry for anyone in my life. What had happened was a straightforward Bennyurism.

This could never be allowed to happen again. We had to be totally strong, fail-safe. I was still cursing myself as I drifted off to sleep, clutching Rasa's hand, preparing myself to face Red Dog again in the morning.

The alarm rang angrily at the usual 5:45 A.M., and I pushed open the window, to be greeted by clearing blue skies with a stiff autumn breeze, which I guessed would blow as hard as or harder than the day before. It was cold at that dawn hour, extremely cold, the chill magnified by the sudden absence of the warm, misty days of late summer, which had given way before the cooling winds off the northeast Atlantic. The direction of the leaves told me we would face a wind out of the northeast, angled around slightly farther to the north. Unless conditions altered much during the day, we could look for some rough water.

But now we had come a long way. The men of *Australia II* were totally at home with high winds and heavy seas. We had dealt with them dozens of times and were extremely proficient at doing so. Today we would not use our heavy-air mainsail; instead, we would go to our medium-air equipment.

All I had to do before we set off was to make certain that the crew was at a peak of aggression and determination. This was particularly important on a day such as this would be. For it is not the same racing in light winds as it is in heavy ones. When the breeze is not strong and shifting, we sail like cats—very stealthy, delicate, and thoughtful, easing our way along with care and cunning. When the wind howls, we sail like tigers—full of aggression, like wild animals—because in such conditions a cat would be beaten around the ears, whereas a tiger would slash his way through it. Pure aggressiveness has a way of counteracting the forces, preventing surprises. It causes the crew to rise above the flying spray and the cracking of the great Kevlar sails, to force the boat forward into the elements, mentally on top of the situation, ready for anything, prepared to handle the huge forces that drive us, ready to ignore the tossing, pitching discomfort of the deck, to rush through the cold, flying spray. Oh, yes, we were ready for today all right.

I did not detect one vestige of defeatism as we got ready to go down to the dock that day. It was Thursday, September 15, and we arrived in full foul-weather gear, white with our green and yellow *Australia II* stripes. We could see the water tossing about in the harbor, the gathering fleet of spectator boats getting ready to batten down the hatches, just as we would have to do 3½ hours later. We were a little earlier than usual, for obvious reasons. Hughey and Beasho and I headed down below with Kenny to see how he had beefed up the welding that had wrenched off in Race 1. Naturally, he had done a careful, thorough job, and I was sure we would not experience such difficulty again. Kenny still felt awful, and he looked terribly tired after the long hours he had spent making certain *Australia II* would not fall apart again. I could not have expected him to attend to everything in the limited time he had, but he had done all that was humanly possible to strengthen us where we needed strengthening. Everything seemed fine, and the medium-air mainsail was already on the boom. Jim Hardy and his boys on *Challenge 12* were also ready for action, and at one minute to nine o'clock, I signaled Damian to run up the kangaroo to wave his boxing gloves once more at a world I trusted was not losing faith in us. The sight of the old kanga stirred all of us. Then Phil Judge hit the switch on *Black Swan,* and we heard the deafening strains of Men at Work singing our battle anthem.

> Can't you hear, can't you hear the thunder?
> You'd better run, you'd better take cover.

The lines slipped away, and amid a thunderous burst of applause from the massed ranks of the army of Australian supporters packed around our dock, we set off for the racecourse. Conditions were just about as I had assessed them, pretty tough, but we had raced in them many, many times before. We felt completely at home as soon as we broke free of the harbor wall, and I felt very confident that *Australia II* would whip Red Dog today and even the score.

One hour before the start, we had *Australia II* primed for our trial runs with *Challenge 12,* with whom we were enjoying the most fantastic cooperation. Jim Hardy was skippering an unbelievable hodgepodge of a crew assembled from *Advance* and from *Challenge.* Those kids have been giving it everything they have to help us to beat the Americans. *Challenge* has been flying her best sails and Jim has primed the crew before they set off with us. He has fantastic concentration both as a man and as a sailor, and I knew I was going to be able to put *Australia II* through her heavy-weather paces with a well-sailed boat, to give us a good insight into exactly what it would be like against the red boat 60 minutes later.

Australia II and *Challenge* headed off together, and we raced neck and neck for a good 10 minutes. We managed to gain a little, but not much, and Hughey and I felt our code-four genoa was not working quite as well as it should. I called for a jib change "Bag that code four and break out the code-three genoa," I yelled to the Major. He was ready. The code-three genoa was selected and ready for the changedown, which the boys on the foredeck performed in terrifically fast time, the Major's arms a mere blur as he hauled away. This sail's deeper curvature gave us a little more horsepower, and in this banging, chopping water, it would keep the air from being shaken from the sails.

Off we went to windward again with this very powerful sail. Sure enough, we were faster than before, and we began to draw away from *Challenge*. I liked our medium-air mainsail better as well. In fact, I was particularly happy with it as Beasho primed it into its precise optimum aerodynamic shape.

Suddenly, up ahead I saw *Freedom* working along with *Liberty*.

It's extraordinary how thrilling the sight of two Twelves can be, and I recall thinking at the time that it must be fantastic for the spectators to see perhaps the *four* greatest racing Twelves the world has ever seen bowling along in the wind, giving an exhibition of pure precision sailing. We originated from 12,000 miles apart, yet here were these four boats within yards of each other, demonstrating their superb action through the water and the magnificent seamanship of their crews. Surely, I thought, no one has ever seen anything like this before. Just from an engineering point of view, I thought our equality was nothing short of amazing. It also began to dawn on me for the first time that there would not be much difference between *Challenge 12* at her best and *Liberty*. Back in Melbourne, unbeknown to us, we had actually been racing the equivalent of Dennis Conner's Red Dog, and wouldn't it have been nice to have known that?

Each pair of boats was dueling out there, and *Challenge* and *Australia II* both ended up on port tack, steaming along together. Behind us, the spectator fleet began to break up and hundreds of boats began to fall in behind us so their passengers could photograph the four yachts, which were at this point only about 200 yards apart. Eventually, we turned around and headed back to the racecourse, waving good-bye to Jim and his boys, who in turn were heading off to the left-hand side of the course, keeping their mainsail up. They would be on a hard starboard tack as soon as the midday gun fired, and would thus give us a guide, way up the racecourse, as we set off. This may be illegal, but what the hell? We would know nothing about it, of course. The red boat will also see *Challenge,* but they will not know what Jim is doing, whether or not he is sailing flat-out. So away went *Challenge 12,* in the high, gusting wind, and we dropped our jib.

It is about 20 minutes to the start, and there is lots of chop as the spectator boats churn up the water. *Australia II* heads into the waves, and we quickly have green water crashing over the bow, and lots of spray breaking over the side, but we do not care. We are totally familiar with this environment and primed for battle.

I go through a brief little talk as we start our warm-up exercises. "We must win today, boys," I say. "We must level this at 1–1. We don't want to leave the racecourse without a victory." And as the Major and Chink lead the crew in the exercises, I give my own private warm-up signal toward the American boat, utilizing, as expressively as I know how, my right fist, forearm, and elbow. This always gets an easy laugh and eases the tension as we prepare to go once again to war. The Major starts chuckling at my antics, and I can feel that overwhelming tension beginning to ease off. But I know it will be there again as we head down toward the starting line.

We prepare for the 10-minute gun as we round into our starting area up near the committee boat. Chink Longley, my vastly experienced winch-grinder, is on the bow watching our distance. The stopwatch is taped to the center grinding pedestal of the mainsheet winch, and the Major is in charge. The stopwatch is checked. All systems are go. The gun fires and the Major has it. I wheel *Australia II* around and we go spearing down toward *Liberty*, aiming to meet her about halfway down the starting line. We make one fast circle together. WHACK! We lock into each other like two disagreeable predators. "Stay locked to the bastards, John," says Hughey quietly. And suddenly I realize that we are playing with them. However often they may have superior boatspeed, they cannot fence with us in the tight circles we perform at the prestart—the shining spinoff that Benny has bequeathed us. And Hughey and I know how to take advantage of this. We decide to trap *Liberty* when we have six minutes to go. It's too early right now, because if we trap her at nine minutes, we have to hold her for all that time, and we do not think we can hold Conner that long in a control position. The longer we wait, the better it will be. In my opinion, we can get control of *Liberty* anytime we feel like it. We can always turn inside them and stop them. We can achieve this sometimes with two circles, always within three. But if both boats come to a halt, we would drift onto them, because we tend to slip sideways through the water faster than they do. So we must be careful, and we decide to drive onto them with about six minutes to go. Now we make a couple of dummy circles to pass the time.

Coming down to about six minutes, we decide to make our move. I whack the boat around clockwise, and suddenly, to my utter horror, I hear a sound that literally chills my blood. A heartrending BANG from high up. It sounds like the Goodyear Blimp has burst. For a few seconds, every pulse in my body shuts down. All eyes are aimed skyward from the deck of *Australia II*. The explosion came from the top of the mast. I look around the boat, but nothing seems to be happening. Everyone on our boat and on *Liberty* is looking toward the heavens. Suddenly our mainsail starts to move down. Skippy spots it first. "John, John, the mainsail is falling down!" he cries above the wind. And sure enough, I can see it fluttering and slipping down the mast. I just cannot believe what is happening. Six minutes to go. We are 1–0 down. We must even the score.

And the bloody boat is falling apart. Again. We have sailed all summer, thousands of miles. We have a safety record pretty much second to none. And for the second time in less than 24 hours, we are having a major gear failure.

What had broken was a high-tensile lug on the upper edge of the mainsail headboard, right at the top of the mast. This lug attaches the headboard to the mast. That meant the headboard was being held only by the bottom lug, and it was only a matter of time before everything fell down—and that, of course, would be the ball game.

At this stage, however, we are not absolutely certain of what has happened. There is no possibility that anyone can go to the top of the mast— we are in a heavy sea and the mast is making hard circles in the sky. We are about to head upwind, which would make it impossible for any crew member to risk going up in the bosun's chair. The sail is looking very shaky now, and suddenly the boom starts to slip onto the deck. *Liberty*'s crew is staring at our masthead. I imagine they are gloating. This is a nightmare. The sail has slipped down about a foot and a half from the top of the mast. Our only chance is to rake the mast forward in order to lift the boom off the deck and to try to get some tightness into the sail. We keep circling while Beasho slogs away at his hydraulic controls and at the forestay, trying to adjust the mast.

Hughey suddenly has a brainstorm. "John," he says, "we might not be able to start if this thing is going to burst. Let's try to disqualify *Liberty* right now. Let's go for her and try to catch her with no right-of-way."

From where I stand, this sounds like our only hope. I fling *Australia II* into action. We wheel around and go after the red boat, churning up the water, jibing around, leaving a powerful wake behind us. This is total aggression, the desperate last effort of a crew who may not be able to start the race. *Liberty* senses our reckless assault and becomes defensive, backing away from our challenge, as indeed I would have done. They know we are in deep trouble, and they feel that they need only to play it carefully, not to get caught on a port tack as we lunge at them, and it will be a matter of time before *Australia II* falls apart for the second day in a row and they go ahead 2–0. Right now, the water in which we are dueling looks as if a bunch of sharks is thrashing around. The sea is boiling as we drive at them again and again, unleashing the most potent weapon we have—the super turning ability of this wounded white boat from Perth. I can see by their confident looks at close quarters that they believe we are in our death throes. It is hard to explain the effect of an American sneer on an Aussie with his back to the wall. But at this stage, neither they nor we know whether our sail will hold up and whether we can start the race. If the sail comes down, then we will have to pack it in. If it will just hold up till we round the first mark, then Beasho can go up and try to fix it, and we might yet have a chance. Whether or not *Australia II* can race with the sail in this condition is still a moot point. Right now we have only five minutes. Beasho is still wrestling with the problem of bringing the mast forward and then bending the top toward the bow with the forestay to try to get the boom off the deck, and to give us a semblance of a racing rig. Meanwhile, *Liberty* waits, gloating at us and at our plight.

As the count moves into the final stages, the strength of our crew begins to show. Every man is rallying round to help Beasho move that huge mast forward. Colin is pumping furiously with his bare hands, sweat pouring off him, as he forces the hydraulic controls.

The mainsail has not fallen any farther than it did in those first few seconds, principally because it is being held by the other high-tensile lug. What we could not know was that the sail was hanging on by a mere thread of Kevlar. Now Beasho has that 25-ton hydraulic ram in the bow working exactly right, and the mast is edging forward, reducing the length of the forestay. We are setting up the mast for the kind of rig we would normally use when we are square running. The whole rig is cocked over the bow, and it just might allow us to stay in this boat race.

It's now down to 30 seconds. "We're going to start this race," I call to the crew. "We're just going to keep racing and see what happens. But we are NOT GIVING UP!" I bawl the last three words at the top of my lungs, my fist clenched tight with pure frustration. We still cannot sheet the mainsail properly. In the last race, it was critical when Colin was adjusting the sail to within a half inch. It is another story entirely to have that big sail sagging 18 inches down the mast.

The gun fires. We are on starboard tack and *Liberty* cuts in underneath us. Officially, they are five seconds in front of us crossing the line. That's worth about 15 or 20 feet, but I'm pleased with our start. We are going slightly faster, but the mainsail is flagging and Colin is still working away at it. The situation looks pretty desperate, even to an optimist. Not surprisingly, we start to fall in on them. Hughey is calling it with icy accuracy, "We're falling in on them, John, we're falling in. Two more boatlengths and we'll have to tack."

Quickly we cover that much water, and I shout, "Tacking the boat, fellers." Beasho, still working on the hydraulic ram, trying to squeeze precious inches out of the controls, keeps his head down. We tack over. The big grinders, Chink and Splash, drive away on the winches; Skippy and Scoop, arms flailing, haul back the genoa lines. We're now on port tack, and the red boat follows as we head away to the right. There's not much wind now, and the Americans have a loose cover on us. Suddenly we start. feeding into a right-hand shift, and the mainsail leach is beginning to draw, despite the fact that the front half is blowing inside out. You just cannot race a 12-Meter like this, but we are doing it. Grant says quickly, "Five degrees, John," and I shout back, "This is one for the good guys!" I tack the boat hard, heading back. *Liberty* can't cross us, and they tack underneath us. We're bowling along now; miraculously, the leach of the mainsail is drawing. Beasho has done a fantastic job, and I have no idea how he has managed it, but he's playing those hydraulic controls like a Stradivarius violin.

We are very badly injured, our wing is not drawing 100 percent, and the rig is all over the place. I've got neutral, well, maybe a little bit of leeward, helm. *Liberty* is starting to suck into us, out to our left, underneath. Obviously they are a little bit faster than we are, and since they are only 30 yards away, we can get a pretty realistic feel for that. Now they are sucking into us fast, because we cannot point *Australia II* high enough without full use of a mainsail. So we tack back again, and *Liberty* follows. But once more we fall into a five-degree right shift, and it gives us some more breathing space. We are still going along, still fighting, but it's uphill all the way.

We tack back and I shout again, "Fellers, we're still in this. There's no way they can beat us if we just keep going, keep hanging in there. I have not even contemplated pulling out of this, and we are *not* going to throw in the sponge." Right now the crew is fantastic. There is not another word in the Australian language to describe them. They are working themselves to a standstill, racing back and forth, covering for each other, each man helping the others, all rallying around Beasho as he works the mainsail with wrists and forearms that on a lesser man would have given up 10 minutes ago. There's no way these boys are going to throw in the towel. About halfway up that first leg, I feel certain that I am watching a performance that will live in my mind and heart for the rest of my life. Deep down, these boys see themselves as the winners of this contest. I have never seen a crew so damned determined.

At this stage we must be driving Dennis and his boys nuts. We are sailing a boat that is crippled, but we are hitting the shifts almost perfectly, and every time their superior boatspeed gets them up to us, we tack off, hook into a new shift, and get back on top of them again. But Hughey and Grant are calling those windshifts clear and sure, and, although I am having a terribly hard time trying to keep this boat on track, we are still right there. It is all I can do to hold her on a straight line. We all owe a tremendous debt in this race to Hughey Treharne. He is standing right beside me, a really determined, silent character, grim-faced and unbending against these awful odds. His opposite number on *Liberty* is the international boss of Sobstad Sails, and Hughey is the managing director of

Sobstad in Sydney. I know he would dearly love to beat the hell out of Tom Whidden. And now he is calling the shots in what is, in retrospect, the finest hour of *Australia II*.

We are still on starboard tack, and we hook into a better shift with *Liberty* down to leeward. I tack back hard, and now they cannot cross us; in fact, they are going to cross our stern. We're up now to the left side of the course, getting close to the weather mark, and now Conner decides he had better do everything he can to smash *Australia II* once and for all. He initiates a wicked tacking duel, hoping that the colossal stress factors will cause our almost shattered equipment to break and put our mainsail on the deck and the race in his pocket. Everyone is poised at his position, waiting for the big red boat to try to obliterate us. On she comes, knifing through the water, looking for all the world as if she might cut us in half. Hughey called it. "Tack her, John, *now*," and *Australia II* wheeled round to cover *Liberty*. Back comes Dennis, time and again spearing toward our stern. Every time Hughey calls it, and every time we slap our cover back on them. Down on the winches, Chink, Splash, and the Major are pounding away with every ounce of their strength. After nine tries, back comes Conner for a 10th. The lines are whipping off the drums as the three heavyweights take the strain. The winches are screaming beneath their efforts as the sails seem to fly from side to side. Sweat is pouring off them, their lungs heaving as they struggle for breath like fighters coming up to the end of a particularly vicious round. "Shit," says Hughey, "here they come again." And on came *Liberty* to test us once more. I roar down to the grinders, "SPIT BLOOD! SPIT BLOOD! THIS IS WHAT YOU WERE BORN FOR!" And once more they hurl themselves into those winch handles, their aching, bandaged hands flying around in those murderous circles, their huge shoulders pumping away. After the 11th tack, Conner has had enough. He has lost 1½ to two boatlengths as a result of the duel, and he tacks away down toward the starboard layline. As they go, Chink Longley stands up, in a lather of sweat and anger, and turns toward *Liberty*, screaming out at them like a wild man, his teeth gleaming, "COME AND GET US, COME AND GET US, YOU BASTARDS!" It is a reflex action of pure defiance. Chink has not come through four America's Cup campaigns to give away races to anyone.

Those 11 tacks took four minutes, and we are now nearly three boatlengths in front, still crippled but still here. They have gone off by themselves and we, with some relief, are off by ourselves, because we have been worried that the mainsail may finally give up the ghost. Suddenly they head back to us, and Hughey, without missing a beat, says to me quietly, "Slam-dunk 'em, John, get ready." *Liberty* ducks under our stern and Hughey calls it right on the money, "NOW!" I wheel *Australia II* around hard. We settle, inch-perfect, right on top of her. Despite her clear boatspeed on us, she cannot escape, and we carry them to the mark with an utterly miraculous 45-second lead.

All the way to the mark she was trying to inch up on us, but we had them tight in our windshadow. They wallowed in our air and I loved it. They had no alternative but to follow us around. As we ran up to the mark, Grant called out, "CODE-ONE FOUR SPINNAKER!" and in a second the mighty figure of the Major could be seen manhandling the huge, soaking-wet chute into position. Damian clipped it up and the Major dived for the spinnaker halyard, his massive arms hauling away. "AAAAAR . . . AAAAAR . . . AAAR." He is roaring like a bull as he hoists it into place.

Down below the Major, in the birdbath up to his thighs in water, stands Phil Smidmore, old Ya, wearing big, rubber padded gloves. Faced with a Kevlar rope blazing off the winches, he never misses a beat as the wet spinnaker peels out, popping full in the most spectacular set in exactly eight seconds. This is not *Gretel II*, this is no amateur hour. This is professional sailing in its purest form. I had stolen a definition from a book about Ron Barassi, the greatest coach Australian football ever produced, and had read it to them a hundred times. "The difference between professionals and amateurs is that the professional is dedicated to the total eradication of errors. It has nothing to do with money."

And now we wheel around the first mark with our glorious green-and-gold parachute set like a symbol of Australia itself high out over the starboard side of the bow. It was out there as our stern rounded the mark. I feel us bound away from *Liberty* as the chute begins to draw. We have no right to be in the race, never mind winning it. For a moment, I find myself swept up in the heady feeling that a crew feels when sailing to within an inch of its life. I can think of no words to say to the boys, no phrase adequate to convey my admiration for what they are doing. I just feel very proud of them all, and perhaps most of all, I feel proud to be on the same boat with them.

And now I am jerked back to reality. Below the mast stands Beasho, strapping himself into the bosun's chair. Stuffed in Colin's belt are wrenches, a screwdriver, ropes, Kevlar line, a knife, and a marlinespike. For no reason, my mind flashes back to the final of the National Lightweight Sharpie Class in 1968. I remember Lex going forward and I remember saying to him, "We can't afford a mistake here. Set that spinnaker once and set it right." And now I decide to say something similar to Colin. As the Major begins to haul, I say to him quietly, "Colin, don't be in too much of a hurry. Take your time and fix it once, and fix it properly." I knew he would fix it better than anyone (with the possible exception of his dad, or perhaps his granddad). Colin sets off up the mast, the Major and

Chink hauling him to the hounds, at 60 feet, where he must unclip himself, hang on, and reclip himself onto the upper lanyard. Once more the Major and Chink haul away, and finally Beasho is at the top of the mast, after a 2½-minute journey. Conditions are getting lighter, but it is still pretty hair-raising up there. We're bowling along, sliding down the waves, which are rolling us toward the jibe mark nearly 100 feet below the place where Colin is working. As the wind eases off, I am delighted, because I know that *Liberty*, with her longer waterline, is much faster than we are on the power-reaching legs, and the harder the wind blows, the better she will go. But right now we are holding them, and we have given them quite a sailing lesson on the first leg. I doubt that even the inventive and self-protective minds of Conner and Herreshoff could come up with an acceptable way to explain why they came to miss all the windshifts, failed to take advantage of us at the start, got outtacked, slam-dunked, and windshadowed, and rounded the first mark 45 seconds down against a boat that could not hoist its mainsail and by any normal standards should have packed it all in before the starting gun.

And now the battle rages as we race down the first power-reaching leg. My crew has shaped up to take the attack of *Liberty*, which took a massive 26 seconds off us on the second power-reaching leg yesterday. Each crewman is working with a singleminded, cold fury, restrained and disciplined—each one of them is determined not to lose, each one of them is in complete control of his emotions.

I turned to Hughey and said, "We just need one break, one tiny bit of luck somewhere along the line, and we can still win this!" And here we were in what I believe must have been the most audacious performance ever by a challenging America's Cup boat, wounded, on the ropes and still punching, still in front.

High above us, Colin occasionally yells down, but it's hard to hear what he is saying. All we know is that he is using his marlinespike to try to punch a hole through the layers of Kevlar on the headboard. (For those who are unaware, Kevlar is fairly hard stuff, used for such things as bulletproof vests for President Ronald Reagan's bodyguards and armor plating on tanks.) Beasho keeps hammering away with his spike, and *Australia II* is whacking away down the reach, hitting 9½ knots at times and still holding *Liberty* at bay. Beasho is just about halfway through the headboard as we come racing up to the jibe mark, and there is no time to get him down. I yell up to him, "Hang on, Colin, we're jibing. Watch the sail as she comes across." Our mainsheet hand hangs on up there like a monkey as we steam toward the mark, with *Liberty* catching us fast, snatching back 14 seconds on the first reaching leg.

There are lots of boats waiting for us at the mark, including the New

York Yacht Club's committee boat, the vultures looking for the kill, waiting for us to fold up our wings and die. But that is what we are not going to do.

Damian is up on the foredeck, waiting to handle the switch of the spinnaker pole. The Major is on the trigger, and as we came barreling down to the mark, I call, "TRIP!" The pole drops away. Damian reclips as fast as he can, and we execute a perfect jibe.

Instinctively, I glance toward the top of the mast to see whether Colin is still there. He's safe, hanging on like grim death, still pounding away at the headboard with his free hand.

He's shouting down, but I can't hear him; the sounds are muffled by the wind and the sails and we just head on down the second reach. Hughey glances back. *Liberty* is round and she's still catching us. I call for a spinnaker change. "Break out the half-ounce spinnaker! And stand by for a peel." The Major hurtles down below, grabbing for the new chute, his huge hands ripping off the cover, struggling up the first steps. He is soaking wet with sea water and sweat, and he bears the weight of the great parachute entirely alone, and hurls it up onto the deck. Damian dives for the new spare halyard. Chink rushes up onto the foredeck to help. He is not only the best winch grinder I have ever seen, he's one of the best foredeck men in the world. Splash moves into the breach, trimming both the spinnaker sheet and the spinnaker brace at once, holding both winches down by himself. At times like this you can see why men become great Olympians, and you can see why Brian Richardson is one of the top Olympic oarsmen in the world. He just loves the pressure, glories in the drama of it. He has dreamed of this, the true heat of battle in the America's Cup and by Christ, he's in it right now.

Chink's huge hands are moving deftly as he helps with the clipping on of the new brace. Damian, this extraordinary young carpenter-cum-acrobat from Williamstown, is clipping his belt onto the halyard. The Major bounces out of the hatch and grabs the other end, swinging Damian out in a tight low arc beyond the bow wave until his fingers are locked tightly onto the end of the spinnaker pole, eight feet above the heaving waves, his right boot hooked over the black carbon-fiber pole. Damian clips over and the spinnaker is now flying out of the cockpit. The Major having cleated Damian off, is now hauling away on the other halyard, heaving the new spinnaker up inside the old one. "For Christ's sake be careful of that," I mutter under my breath. "This is a damned delicate piece of equipment. Don't rip it whatever you do." I know how easily it can happen in the heat of the moment, but now the breeze is dropping and we have to become like cats again, not pussycats, but precision cats, stealthy, careful, and cunning. Colin yells down that he is making gains. Apparently there is no way that he can get the sail back up to where it is supposed to be, but he can stop it from falling any farther. The marlinespike is almost through the headboard, and he is planning to lash the sail through that hole with a tough piece of Kevlar. If it slips another couple of inches before he can achieve this, and before we must again head upwind, I know we are finished. Beasho has been up there for nearly 40 minutes, and I pray that those steel wrists of his will hold out for us.

Damian swings in like Tarzan from the spinnaker pole, and hits the floor with both feet. He crashes backward onto the slippery deck and bounces up, all in one movement, unclipping his belt as he does so, diving for the old spinnaker, grabbing at it, helping Chink to haul it into order. The Major plunges back down into the sewer, dragging the spinnaker behind him. Chink and Damian feed it down, and the Major claws and grabs the huge, sopping-wet chute down on top of him, sweat and seawater pouring off, roaring his battle cry, "AAAARR . . . AAAARR . . . AAAARR," as he clears the foredeck.

But *Liberty* is catching up with us relentlessly. They are climbing up on us to weather and now we have to concentrate. The wind is still falling off. Now we are all boiling hot in our foul-weather gear, but we do not have one second to remove the heavy jackets and trousers, even as the sun begins to appear. The lighter conditions favor us, and I call to the crew, "Come on, boys! Let's get our act together!" Hughey has pulled himself out of his embroilment with the mechanics of the spinnaker change and the jibe, and now he is coolly facing aft, giving me exact range and bearing on *Liberty*, at all stages. "OK, John, just sail a little higher. That's good. Parallel, parallel. That's good."

"Have you got a good fix on the mark, Hughey?"

"Yes, it's OK. That's good, keep going. He's caught up a little bit, got a little bit of breeze. OK, it's our turn now, we've got a bit ourselves. We're about 3½ boatlengths in front."

We are now running down to the leeward mark, and we have to start easing down. Hughey calls it. "OK, Hughey, you're right, let's start easing down." I call out, "Make sure Colin knows when he has to come down. Stand by to get him."

Now we seem to be wobbling away from *Liberty*, the first time we have ever increased speed over them on a power reach. This little bit of lighter air continues to help us. We square up to get into the mark. The breeze has now gone aft. Colin is on his way down, and I'm sure he's fixed it. He has been up there throughout two legs. Now *Australia II*'s afterguard is in a deadly serious discussion about which genoa to hoist. "CODE TWO!" Grant finally shouts, as the boys prepare to haul in the spinnaker and hoist the jib. The breeze is dying pretty fast, and now the sun is out. Lots

of things are changing, and the breeze is moving around. It's going to be
very, very tricky going up this next leg. That code-two call was critical. We
round the mark, the spinnaker floats down, and the jib goes up hard. We
turn into the wind and continue this unbelievable race. With the dying
winds, I have just about neutral helm, and our precisely shaped, aerodynamic mainsail, as one of the boys rather poetically remarks, "looks like
a bag of shit."

I have never felt the boat quite like this before, and we flounder forward, sail flopping. "If ever we needed a bit of poise and knowhow, it's
right about now," I say. "OK, Ya, what does it look like? Let's try to put
this jigsaw together."

The breeze, which earlier had been gusting at between 20 and 25
knots, was now down to about 6 and 7 knots, and we have lots of joggle,
lots of cross chop—conditions *Australia II* dislikes at the best of times.
Nevertheless, we are halfway through the race, our nose is still in front,
and we are going to do everything we can to win.

"She's starting to knock," says Hughey, as the red boat tacks over
toward us. It's a very, very light sea-breeze zephyr—my grandpa would
have spotted it 10 minutes ago—and *Liberty* has hooked into it. The
damned breeze we are seeking to protect is receding some more, and it is
beginning to look awfully tough for us. We keep going, keep going, struggling to stay in the wind. But it keeps receding. I feel like a man dying of
thirst in the desert, crawling forward to a mirage of cool water, and as I
advance three paces on all fours, the water moves three paces farther
away. I can't reach it. This is now so delicate, so brittle.

An hour earlier, I was standing there in the howling wind, bellowing,
"Spit blood, this is what you were born for!" as we crashed through the
waves. Now we hardly dare breathe for fear of upsetting the knife's edge
of wind that gently blows us forward. Sometimes. But now we have to get
back into it, back into contact. *Liberty* is now in front of us, and we have to
tack back to join them. It's still very close: We are hooking into a little bit
of left wind, she is hooking into a right movement. There is not much in
it, but *Liberty* is coming across toward us fast.

"They're going to slam-dunk us, Hughey!" I call. "No, they're not, but
it looks close," he says. "Christ, John! Yes, they are. Here they come! No!
They're not. Yes! Yes! They are. They can't. They're too close. They
would not dare at this range. But, by Christ! They are going to do it, the
bastards."

In a split-second decision, I tack the boat, narrowly missing them as
they tack on our bow. If I had not moved, we would have crashed into
them, of that I am certain. I cannot believe what they have just done.
They must have had complete confusion on their boat. A slam-dunk is not

done that way. I am sure that Conner, Whidden, or Herreshoff has made a royal mess of that. It seemed almost unplanned and recklessly dangerous—not just because we would have hit them, but because they might have gotten themselves disqualified. Now they are wide open for that. "Break out the protest flag," snaps Hughey, and he calls formally across the water, "We're protesting." Halsey Herreshoff calls back, very gentlemanly, "Acknowledge that!" We would probably have shot back some quaint old-world Aussie phrase, but Halsey showed that he has inherited, at the very least, the beautiful manners of his famous ancestor, Nathanael Herreshoff, about whom my great-grandpa would not hear an unkind word. I could hardly believe this formal decorum in the middle of this rough-and-tumble, brutally tough international competition.

Our protest flag flying, we head to port again. That's no good. We come back and the red boat is now a few more boatlengths in front. We tack back again, but we are going from bad to worse. Things are not good. In fact, they are ranging perilously close to that state of grace colloquially known as absolutely bloody diabolical. The sun grows warmer and there is no way that the land breeze is going to make it. The air is rising from the land and the sea breeze is building. We have picked the wrong side, and on top of every other damned thing, that is going to be expensive. We are already beginning to pay the price. *Liberty* is going from strength to strength, the breeze from the sea is coming in fast, and she's into it first. We have no choice but to go all the way down to the left and then head up to the weather mark, at which point *Liberty* is going to have 48 seconds on us, or about three boatlengths. I say to Hughey, "Now listen. Things are not going well for us, old mate, but we have to hang right in there. We must not make any rash decisions. And above all, we must stay in contact and not slip too far behind."

I shout out to the crew, "OK, boys, here we go! Let's get that spinnaker up in eight seconds flat and we're going to run down the bastards." We are all saturated, but I've found a second to pull off my heavy foul-weather jacket. I feel we have a chance to pull back some time on the square run, but, unfortunately, it is rather nondescript. We keep playing the windshifts and feel we are doing well, but at the bottom mark we have pulled back only 17 seconds.

Liberty, with all her boatspeed to windward, heads smartly off to protect the right-hand side of the course. I cannot go with her, because she will slap a hard cover on us and we will lose for sure. The only thing we can do is to head out to the left and pray for a couple of shifts that might get us back in. That is our only chance. I am just considering the difference between instant death and lingering death, with a remote shot at a reprieve. With our sail still looking like a bag of you-know-what, we come floundering home. The gun goes for Dennis a long time before we get there. (It was only one minute 33 seconds, but it seemed like about an hour.)

I watched Dennis throw a salute at the committee boat in celebration of his 2–0 lead. I have rarely felt so galled by anything. We were all thinking the same thing: We just did not deserve to be 2–0 down. There was not a sound on the boat, and we sailed up to the line in the powerful silence of total frustration. It was the longest 90 seconds I have ever sailed. I hated it. I remember Conner and his crew waving like gladiators. We limped home, eleven somber men and a beautiful white boat, like a great seabird with a broken wing—all held together by one little line of Kevlar. The fact was, this was indeed amateur hour all over again. And *still* Alan Bond, in 15 jousts with the Americans, had won but one race—in 1980, when we beat *Freedom*.

I called the boys to the cockpit area and spoke to them right from my heart. "What you have just done was the gutsiest thing I have ever seen in all of my life. And it was probably the gutsiest thing I ever will see. To have gotten this boat around the course like that, in the condition she was in, should be a lesson in courage and determination for any sports team in years to come. And I, for one, am proud of you. Thank you very much. It was a fabulous éffort."

Hughey and I hopped aboard our inflatable, the *Rubber Ducky*, with our gear, in turn to be transferred to *Black Swan* to start preparing our case against *Liberty* for the protest "court," to be heard probably on the morrow. Naturally Alan was itching to know what had happened. I told him of the breakage at the top of the mast, and he was incredulous. He found it difficult to accept that, after all we had done, the boat had fallen apart around our ears for the second time in two days. On the ride home, towing the boys behind us, we began to discuss the protest formalities. Tomorrow would be a lay day, and there was also a pretty savage dispute over that lay day. We considered *they* had called it, the Committee considered *we* had called it. Which one of us was to use up one of our allotted lay days? The same jury would decide whether we had been fouled and who would be charged with the lay day.

Back in Newport, we began to prepare the case we anticipated would have *Liberty*'s win thrown out. There was, in my view, a 75 percent chance of our winning this protest and evening the series. One thing was very clear in my mind, and that was the fact that *Australia II* would have rammed straight into the stern of *Liberty* if I had not tacked away when they slam-dunked us on the fourth leg. We immediately heard that there was television footage available from the studios of Channel 10, pictures taken from the Blimp. We telephoned and found out that the *Liberty* group had already been there, seen the footage, and left with copies. We went up to the studios and watched the sequence about four times. We made arrangements for our copies, but it was clear already that the Americans were involved in this protest on a totally professional basis. They have had a lot of practice at this down the years. (The U.S. is a litigious country, and Americans tend to go running to lawyers much as Bolivian peasants are apt to head for the priest.) We called in our rules adviser, Peter Lawson, a member of the New York Yacht Club and a very nice and helpful man. He worked with us on the case, and at 2:30 in the morning, we finally were satisfied that we had done our best.

It scarcely occurred to me that we would lose, because I knew how scrambled that slam-dunk had been. I considered that Dennis must have been at his wit's end to try such a tactic, and in my heart I knew he was vulnerable because of it. In my opinion, there was no question that *Liberty* had tacked recklessly, stupidly, and perilously close to us, endangering everyone. They must disqualify her. Damian reckoned there was about 24 inches between us as we crossed. I thought it might have been six inches, but Damian is a carpenter, and your average carpenter can spot a two-foot piece of wood within half an inch with his eye alone. He said it was 24 inches and I am certain he was right.

The following morning, we headed for the protest room, an office on nearby Goat Island, a former naval munitions factory. It was 13 years to the day since we had faced the jury after the collision between *Gretel II* and *Intrepid*. That day I had thought we were probably wrong. But not this day. I was sure we were right.

The Americans had a professional team working on this, and, rather than pack up at 2:30 A.M., as we had done, they had worked through the night. Their evidence was presented beautifully in bound folders—an object lesson in how it should be done if you want to impress a presiding jury. About 500 reporters and television people staked out Goat Island all day, clamoring to speak to Dennis or me as we went in to present our cases. I was in the room for about three hours, and it did not take long to see that things were beginning to go against us. The *Liberty* group called in Bob Bavier to testify on their behalf. This former helmsman and member of the NYYC Selection Committee had watched the race from the Goodyear Blimp. Before he began presenting his evidence, he talked with the men on the jury and even proceeded to arrange a golf game with one of them. This was right in front of me—I was thunderstruck. Once Mr. Bavier had arranged the time for his game, he proceeded to savage us by saying that the television pictures, which I believe proved we were in the right, should be ignored because they were taken with a telephoto lens, which made the boats seem closer together than they actually were.

Coolly accepting the evidence of an NYYC committeeman who watched the action from several hundred feet up—rather than the sworn statement of the carpenter who manned our bow, was inches away, and was certain the distance was 24 inches—the jury deliberated and then threw out our protest. "*Australia II* could have kept clear of *Liberty* either by maintaining her course or by tacking as she did to avoid *Liberty*'s covering tack. *Liberty* has satisfied the jury that she completed her tack in accordance with Rule 41." They considered that the distance between us was four feet. They also decided that we had called for a lay day *one second* before *Liberty* had done so, and therefore the Americans could keep their lay day in the bank. It was a double blow.

Obviously we had not prepared our case as well as our opponents, and, despite my clear feeling that we would have sunk them if I had not dived away into clear water, the jury decided in their wisdom to overrule our evidence.

In the middle of all this, I encountered yet another crisis—as if we did not already have enough. We went over to *Black Swan* for a drink with Alan, who was terribly uptight about everything and seemed to feel that our covering of *Liberty* had not been all that it could have been. When we were alone, Hughey told me that Alan had really gone for him in private, berating him for our tactics and generally blowing his stack at Hughey, blaming my vastly experienced, ice-cool tactician for our defeat. I was just girding myself to give Hughey a pep talk, to try to calm this rapidly developing storm system, when Hughey uttered eight words that made the hair on the back of my neck stand on end. "John," he said, "I am starting to lose my confidence."

All I needed now was to have my irreplaceable tactician afraid to make a decision in case Bondy would think it was wrong—Bondy, whose span of concentration at the helm of any boat is in the 30-second range at best. I said to Hughey very seriously, "Now listen to me. You and I are in this boat because we are the best in the country at what we do. Bondy has in effect bought our judgment for these races against America, and he and you and I are going to have to sink or swim with it. For whatever it means to you, I believe in you completely, I believe you are the best there is, and the only thing I want you to do is to back your own judgment. Make those calls just as you see them. No one else can do a better job than we can, and that's all there is to it." I told him to ignore Bondy, although I pointed out to him that Alan nevertheless did have rights. He did own the boat, and he had put up God-knows-how-many millions of dollars, and he had won only one race in 10 years. He had to be allowed to blast off every now and then. He was listening to all kinds of different opinions, both sports writers and his pals, and the fact is that he doesn't spend much time racing yachts. He spends time making money. He is under a lot of pressure and he needs an escape valve.

Unfortunately for Hughey, Bondy would not go for me, except through someone else. So the person he chose was my mild-mannered, immensely sensitive tactician. What Bondy was doing was telling ME, through Hughey, he wanted us to cover. Well, only a few people in the world know *anything* about covering and when it is reasonable and when it's not. And then there are the subtleties of light shifting winds, and the extreme difficulty in trying to put a cover on someone when they have you on boatspeed and you can't get your mainsail up—well, it's too silly to discuss. I told this to Hughey, who knows as well I do that the classic covering techniques become obsolete as conditions become lighter and more variable. The subtleties of this phenomenon are known and appreciated only by an elite group. It is virtually unexplainable to newspaper reporters and other armchair admirals.

Well, having lost both protests and only narrowly restored the morale of my right-hand man, I headed back down to the dock to see Kenny Beashel and the boys. The entire crew had been slaving away all day. Kenny had insisted on beefing up the rudder gear even more. They had strengthened several components in the bow. They had strengthened the entire headboard system. Nothing had been left unchecked or unstrengthened. For the first time in two days, I saw a smile light up the weatherbeaten features of the senior member of the legendary sailing Beashels of Sydney. "Johnny," said Kenny, "this boat will not fall apart again. You have nothing more to worry about. Don't even think about breakages tomorrow, because there will not be any. Just go out there and beat the hell out of them. I know you are going to."

My confidence restored, I indulged in what for me counted as a riotous act of celebration. I rejoined the real world and took Rasa and the kids for ice cream in a little shop near Dennison Street. And later I took Lucas up to Founders' Hall to have dinner with us all. It was a very relaxed evening, despite the 2–0 score, and we mainly discussed the running repairs and improvements to the boat. Kenny was confident, which meant we were all confident, and Hughey, Lucas, and I headed for home for what I considered to be a well-deserved early night.

Before we left, I had arranged with Alan that Lucas should go out on the official boat in the morning to see the race. When I got home, I took my tired little veteran of three America's Cups up to bed. I tucked him in and told him, "Tomorrow you are going out on Alan's boat, *Black Swan,* to watch the race." His face lit up with excitement (as only an 11-year-old's can). I kissed him good night and whispered very quietly, and very privately, into his ear, "You're going to see Daddy win."

CHAPTER

16

The Longest Weekend

We have the Americans on the ropes and we are pounding them. We are whacking our opponent around the ears, and he has a memory, hasn't he? He cannot erase this from his memory.

Saturday morning, September 17. The new day. DING DING DING DING DING. "Order, order, it's seven minutes to eight."

"Eight minutes to eight."

"Nine."

"Four."

"Six."

"SHUT UP! ALL OF YOU."

The traditional dignified start to a race day. Warren Jones, he of the serious, tense countenance, was in charge, whacking away on his orange-juice glass. Everyone was unaccountably having hysterics at the wit of the crew of *Australia II,* the type of stuff that closed music halls all over the world.

"Now, as you all know, we have an America's Cup race today. . . ."

"Why didn't someone say so before. . . ."

"Is that right, Warren? How did you find that out?"

"No? Against those bloody Americans again?"

"WILL YOU SHUT UP! I'M IN CHARGE HERE." DING DING DING DING! [Orange-juice glass close to splintering before Warren's on-slaught.] "Now, first of all, we will have Sir James Hardy to tell us about the weather. Over to you, Sir James. . . ."

Up got Jim. Very slowly. He's the type of chap who takes about 15 minutes to dry the toes of one foot. But he can get them both done in 25 minutes because he gets quicker at it. (That's a real in joke, one that absolutely breaks us all up however often it is told.)

Jim was finally on his size-12 feet, having taken God-knows-how-long to find out what the weather would be like. "Gentlemen," he says, "it is my profound honor to tell you the weather forecast this morning."

At this point, everyone howled with laughter. "Go get 'em, Sir James." "Give 'em hell, Sir James!" "That's it, Sir James, give it to 'em straight."

Sir James Hardy just stood there, a slight smile on his face, loving the formality he had created and the joyful good humor that he had brought to the table. He stood gazing benignly at us, as only, I suppose, a true Knight of the Realm could. "We are expecting winds from out of the south-southwest at 5 to 10 knots. Sunny skies. It is going to be a light day for you gentlemen. It's going to be different from the first two races. You should find some flat water, and the breeze should be a little more steady." He finished as he always did. "That is all I can tell you at this moment—and God be with you all." At this point, right on cue, Ya, our designated clapper for that morning, leaped to his feet and let out one single burst of applause, just one hand clap, as if only one person applauded a great Shakespearean speech in a packed theater. Sir James Hardy then sat down again. In bounced Bondy—tough, aggressive, bursting with energy, always a little off-key when addressing a group. "Boys, we've got to feel that the boat is part of us. We've got to feel as if . . . as if . . . well, I'm not sure what, but let's get out there and sail our arses off and drive the bastards mad, and I know it's all going to be terrific. Well done, John and Hughey and everyone. Keep punching. Terrific." And he bounded out of the door, feeling he had done his part as our leader.

And in a very great sense he had, because Bondy never looked "down." He could cope with adversity, and his tenaciousness was a very important asset to us. Bondy was a man who was no stranger to the blows of life. I believe he is the only person in the whole of Australia to have been booked by the police for having bald tires on a Rolls-Royce. Oh, Bondy knew what it was about to have his back to the wall. He reveled in difficult times. However grim things would look, you could count on

Bondy to be just rolling along, getting ready to hurl forward his next onslaught. As things got bad, Bondy got tougher than ever.

And now it was my turn. "I do not have to tell you anything more about the boat. You have all been through it with Kenny and we all know it is not going to fall apart again. So let's not even worry about that. We are going to go out there, regardless of the conditions, and we are going to sail the hell out of *Australia II* today. Our effort on Thursday was an incredible example of a crew with a cast-iron ability to hang in there against the odds. But we can and will do better. Chink, I know you have followed through and that we will improve those spinnaker sets and take-downs. One thing we do know is that we have to put in maximum concentration. It's going to be tough racing, and, by God, we're going to do it!"

As we headed down to the dock, it was perfectly obvious that Newport, and, from where I was standing, the entire East Coast of the U.S., had gone wild. Hundreds of thousands of people had besieged the town. You could not move. Thames Street was jammed. Every road into the town for miles around was jammed. You could not get into Newport and you sure as hell could not get out.

They were packed around the dock, 10 deep, trying to catch glimpses of us. Out in the harbor and beyond its walls there was a fleet estimated at 1,500 starting to rev up for the long drive out to the racecourse. High above, planes and choppers already were buzzing about. There were television cameras everywhere, hundreds of newspaper reporters and photographers. There were technicians, sound men, lighting men, prompters, producers, assistants, and God-knows-who-else milling around aiming cameras and microphones all over the place. This was American television preparing for prime-time sports all through this sunlit Saturday afternoon. Australian television was preparing to beam the race home by satellite into the small hours of Sunday morning. Right now it was about 10:30 at night in Melbourne. Mum and Lex and everyone would be getting ready to watch me try again.

I had my arm around Lucas as we struggled our way through the crowds. In my mind were Rasa's words, the last sentence she uttered as I kissed her good-bye—"Please don't come back without winning, John." The big guard on the gate bellowed his usual cry, "Watch out for the workers!" as we pushed our way through. I put our bikes away and saw Lucas safely onto *Black Swan*, a very proud little boy climbing up onto the deck, a veteran of the America's Cup at the age of 11. Pulled down over his forehead was a sailing hat, exactly the same as mine.

I stepped aboard *Australia II,* and there was some applause from the massed ranks of the Aussies gathered around the dock. The countdown to our setting-off had begun. We always left right on time—today it was

8:45. Ya turned around, nodded to me that we were in the final half minute. I nodded to Damian, and the kangaroo with the boxing gloves flew up the forestay. I nodded to the boys to cast off. Scoop was on the stern behind me, closest to the photographers, which was important to him—to be right there near the press and the High Commissioners and Prime Ministers and the rest. With 10 seconds to go, I nodded to Phil Judge on *Black Swan*. He hit the button and rammed up the loudspeaker volume to flat-out:

> Do you come from a land Down Under,
> Where women glow and men plunder?
> Can't you hear, can't you hear the thunder?
> You'd better run, you'd better take cover.

At exactly 8:45, we pulled away from the dock to a thunderous round of applause, Australians shouting, "God bless you, John," "God be with you," "We're with you all the way." Even a person with a heart of pure stone couldn't ignore that much emotion, especially with our Men at Work battle hymn blaring from the big speakers—loud enough to hear, I was told, at the top of the towering edifice of Newport Bridge. Alongside *Challenge 12*, we were hauled out into the harbor, making about 5 knots over this lovely sunlit water beneath cloudless skies, heading for the horizon, beyond which lay Red Dog, waiting for us.

So off we went, the battling Aussies, 2–0 down, and we carried the good wishes of very many people. The boys came to the back of the boat and I began my short talk to them. "This, fellers," I began, "might loosely be described as a situation known in the Outback as Balls-to-the-Wall. It's going to be a very tricky day. It's going to be light, probably similar conditions to those when we raced *Victory* and gave them a very comprehensive beating. As you know, we are fast learners, we're great students, and I have total confidence that today we are coming home."

At that point there was the usual wild scramble for the best places to sleep down below, and it was led, as usual, by a blond-haired lightning bolt named Scoop, flying for his favorite spot, the high pile of genoas, on top of which he would rest, completely dry, for the duration of the tow. He always ended up in the best place, to which he felt cheerfully entitled by some divine right. Damian dived forward into the bow of the boat, dry and undisturbed in the shadows—like a rat up a drainpipe, I told him. The Major was spreadeagled under the hatch, probably in a puddle of seawater. He didn't care, because he was soon going to be soaked anyway. On his headset he was listening to Mozart sonatas—to soothe him before the battle. Between Damian and the Major was Ya, one of Australia's great frustrated comics, lying back with his feet in the air, making a succession of particularly gross remarks, and eating a large sandwich he had somehow managed to grab from the food box en route to his allotted place. Chink was also up in the bow area, writing the letter that had gone on endlessly for the whole summer. Splash, who sometimes gets a bit seasick, was down there with us on this calm-water day. He sat aft of the mast, alternating sides, never quite figuring which side was the most dry, but he tended to favor the area right beneath his own main winch, five feet above his head. Splash had at least two sandwiches and a couple of oranges already clamped in his huge hands. Skippy was not far away from this area, lolling back on his part of the sail inventory, happy-go-lucky, laughing joyously when someone got wet—a pastime in which he invariably was joined by Scoop, who, of course, on his high perch, never got wet. When Beasho comes down, he usually goes straight to sleep, but this day he stayed on deck, still busy. Grant had no time to come below either, and he worked away at his electronics on deck. Robbie Brown, our reserve, steered. At the very back of the below-deck area was the tall, graceful figure of Hughey Treharne—quiet, contemplating, lying back on a genoa, eyes to the ceiling, wide open, thinking, thinking. This superb tactician, and terribly sensitive man, was still struggling mentally to come to terms with that senseless attack delivered by Alan Bond the day before. Hughey was quite alone with his thoughts as we prepared once more to go into battle.

At 10:30 Robbie banged on the deck with a winch handle. "WAKEY, WAKEY, CHILDREN!" he yelled, "TIME TO GET UP!" The Major was on his feet in a fraction of a second—he has the reflexes of a panther, doubtless honed in training as one of the elite officers of the Australian Army. He was on his way up the ladder before Robbie had finished his wake-up call, shouting back down to us, "It's calm—a great day for the Aussies!" That below-deck area, which is so often nothing less than a soaking-wet hell hole, is the personal domain of the Major's and he assumes a loose command when we are all down there, lying on *his* sails, *his* spinnakers, packed *his* way, in *his* big sail bags, in the order *he* wants them, in *his* rather gloomy area, where everything is operated according to *his* instructions.

We all reported to our respective battle stations. On deck were two gigantic mainsails, the light-air one and the one for medium air. Obviously, we wanted the light-air main for this day, so the *Rubber Ducky* came alongside to allow Splash and the Major to unload the other huge, blue-bagged sausage over the side. Beasho supervised the preparations for his light-air main, checking the rig.

"HOIST THE MAINSAIL!" I shouted, and Ya began to haul away.

She snagged halfway up, and I cursed the crooked track on our mast as the great Kevlar sail hovered, fluttering in the wind. Then Ya freed her and on she went, up to the 90-foot mark. Chink was waiting below, the thin wire from the mast crane pinched between his thumb and forefinger. He felt the little vibration from the "clunk" of the crane high above, and he shouted in his deep, rich, Western Australian drawl, *"Lock off!"* Beasho, barefooted as usual, was right there to take the main halyard from Ya, and he scrambled back to connect it behind me, where it would serve as the backstay from the top of the mast.

"CODE-ONE GENOA!" I called, and the Major singlehandedly hauled it out of the hatch and onto the deck. Chink and Damian pulled it into position, hooked it up to the halyard, and the Major hauled it up. I radioed over to *Challenge*: "Use your code-one genoa." I figured we would be faster than *Challenge*, because she was using a medium-air mainsail, and I wanted the boys to experience that immediate confidence that comes from pulling away from another boat. We glided off together on a long port tack and then switched to a long starboard one. The wind was all over the place, but those are the conditions in which we excelled against *Victory '83*.

Up ahead was *Liberty*, working away against *Freedom*. We turned, instinctively, to watch her. *"Forget about them,"* I snarled. "Let's just concentrate on our own boat. We *must* get a score on the board today. It's going to take all the concentration we have, by the look of these winds, for a long time as well." I was delighted by the look of this new light-air mainsail, all $18,000 worth. Schnackenberg had done a super job. This was his best mainsail ever. I liked both the twist and the depth of it. It was a real *Australia II* sail, with much of the design input provided by me and some of it by Beasho. Hours and hours were spent in perfecting it, and now it had to do what it was built for and drive us to victory over the Americans. I didn't know whether we could live with 3–0. Defeat was unthinkable.

We kept working with *Challenge 12*, upwind and downwind, getting the feel of the boat and the conditions. Finally, at 11:35, we shouted good-bye to the *Challenge* boys and headed on down to the racecourse. That morning we had received a memorandum from the New York Yacht Club telling us that *Challenge* must not encroach too far onto the racecourse. Obviously they were on to us. *Challenge* was planning to stay slightly farther away, but she still could give us a good guide about the wind up the track. On we went toward our meeting with *Liberty*, with whom we intended to hook up seven minutes before the start.

At noon, there was an atmosphere of pure chaos. The sky was scarcely visible for the aircraft roaring around above us. The mighty spectator armada, herded by the Coast Guard, was trying to spread out around the fringes of the course. Horns were sounding, Australian and American flags were blooming everywhere, a pall of diesel smoke hung over the big powerboats, the television film was already rolling. Not even the Olympic Games ever had such a concentrated feeling of international tension and attention quite like this seagoing uproar that stretched out before us, beside us, behind us, and above us.

The 10-minute gun fires. The Major hits the stopwatch. Chink is on the bow and the Major is hard by the mainsheet winch. Grant is glued to his controls, mumbling away, and Hughey is at my side, talking quietly. "OK, John, take your time. Just run down behind them, and don't do anything yet." We sail along easily, until the Major shouts, "Seven minutes, John!" And I drive *Australia II* across to meet the red boat.

We lock in quickly and make a couple of circles, and once more we are in a control position. Suddenly we spot the critical opening. I swing back behind the line and come around, at once forcing the red boat to tack and head for the port end. We are now free to go straight for the committee-boat end.

The Major counts on, "20 . . . 19 . . . 18 . . . 17. . . ." I tack to starboard hard, and we hit the line flying, our best start of the series. On a nice, lifting breeze, we cross a full 11 seconds in front of Conner, going about twice as fast. We head off on a starboard tack, and by the time *Liberty* crosses on the same tack, she is just about dead abeam, so we have her by about 40 yards.

Then the most diabolical thing begins to happen. For no reason at all, *Liberty* starts to catch us, sucking right in toward us, almost on a collision course, gaining, gaining, gaining. It is almost as if we have something around our keel, but we just cannot stay with them. You could have cut the atmosphere with a knife as our boys watched her take us apart for 10 minutes, our huge lead diminishing before our eyes. Everyone feels a rising tide of impending panic. "Christ, Hughey," I say, "what do you make of this?" "Different windstream," he says coldly. "The breeze is shifting, and we're catching the wrong end of it, but it shouldn't last long." I can feel the warmth in the air, a strange warmth that should not be there. This is a really fluky stream of air, and it is killing us, as *Liberty* continues to ride about 10 degrees higher. Suddenly, just as Hughey has forecast, the situation swings back into our favor. We held onto our nerves for what seemed like four hours, although it was just 10 minutes, when the wind changed and we got a beautiful shift and glided back into a decisive lead.

Liberty tacks away to the right, and we follow in control position. But we cannot get clear, and we cannot shake them off. First they get a gain, then we get one. Hughey is trying to call it, but the situation keeps changing. As we drive down to the layline, Hughey estimates that the distance between the two boats is about the same as it was at the start. We still cling grimly to that 40-yard advantage. Down on the layline, Hughey calls for us to tack at the top weather mark, and we face this final stage of the first windward leg knowing that the difference in boatspeed between *Australia II* and *Liberty* is nearly zero. In these conditions, the boats are identical. We outgunned them at the start and the rest is a matter of who hits the shifts correctly.

Now we head into some very shaky water caused by that vast spectator fleet. At the same time, I realize that the wind is hitting the fleet before it gets to us; it is sweeping off the top of the powerboats and making conditions even lighter as we head for the mark. Suddenly, Hughey says quietly, "John, we have damned near doubled our lead over *Liberty*." I glance back, and Hughey, as usual, is dead right. The big red boat seems glued to the water, wallowing, heavy, unable to cope with these terribly light conditions. In the half-mile at the end of the leg, we really opened up, and, according to Grant, we would round the mark about 1¼ minutes in front.

"BREAK OUT THE CODE-ZERO SPINNAKER, THE 40-FOOTER," I call. The Major hits the deck with it with an outrageous show of brute strength, and the boys give me a classic demonstration that they have done their homework. This is the first spinnaker set since I gave them a mild roasting at the end of the second race, and this one is entirely different. There is a cold-blooded brilliance about this one, and the spinnaker snaps open perfectly in exactly eight seconds. "Beautiful set!" I call. "Well done!" She is up and pulling as the stern passes the mark and Grant calls back the range.

Now we are going for it, wobbling down the reach on our winged keel, and making good time. We hit the wing mark two minutes in front. In these light airs all the vivid dreams of Benny's, as he stood beside the Dutch testing tank so long ago, are coming true. Even on the reach legs, our real nemeses, we are as fast as Benny dreamed.

On we go, down the third leg. There's nothing much in it here, and *Liberty* picks up a couple of seconds. As we go up the second upwind leg, the wind picks up a little, and *Liberty*'s boatspeed increases. She begins to move up on us, but we are all sailing the boat perfectly. I have not yet tackled the problem of whether the time might run out (each America's Cup race must be concluded in five hours and 15 minutes). But I know for certain that I don't care whether the race finishes in the legal time limit or not, because nothing is going to take this lead from us. This is a tremendous psychological plus for the boys from Down Under. We are clobbering them, and I don't care about wind speed, boatspeed, or anything else. We are going to sail this boat flat-out until the gun goes, one way or another. All that counts is that my boys complete this day having whacked the Americans. We hit the top mark one minute 46 seconds in front.

Grant calls for our little spinnaker, the one from *Challenge 12*—red, white, and blue, their colors—and the set is nothing short of awesome. Crack! Out she goes, and again it takes eight seconds flat. The afternoon breeze is dying and we are down to about 6 knots, but *Australia II* loves it, and she rolls away from *Liberty*.

For the first time, I realize we have nothing more to fear in light winds from what has been for so long our fifth-leg blues. We can never be as bad as *Liberty*. Her spinnaker looks unstable and they just do not have the power to sail as low and as fast as we do. The mood in our crew is fantastic as the race becomes a joke. I know that Dennis Conner and his merry men are devastated. He knows and I know that this was the turning point.

People would later say to me, "You must have been so disappointed that the race did not count." But I would say, "You must be kidding. This was the greatest thing that ever happened. The morale in our crew was sky high."

Liberty slips farther and farther behind, and by now we are all pretty sure that the race will be called off before we hit the finish line. But who cares? We have the Americans on the ropes and we are pounding them. We are not scoring points, but it doesn't matter. We are whacking our opponent around the ears, and he has a memory, hasn't he? He cannot erase this from his memory.

No boat in the history of the America's Cup has ever crunched the invincible Americans like this. With three minutes to go until time runs out, and knowing we are going to be halted in a moment, we decide to do something hysterical. We position our boat so that *Liberty* is dead in line, floundering along down near the horizon, and we all go and sit up on the boom. I summon Damian to captain the ship, and I summon Chink with his camera. We pose as if for an old Edwardian portrait, with our arms crossed, smiling politely, and Chink snaps one for posterity. It is an elegant study of the boys and me—in the process of utterly demoralizing old D.C. and the American crew. They would not be sailing into the crowd waving like gladiators tonight, that's for sure.

The Americans have been blitzed. Six whole minutes! And Chink's picture of us all sitting there smiling, Damian at the helm, with *Liberty* crossing our stern, miles behind, will remain my memory of the America's Cup of 1983.

But now the time is 5:25 P.M., and the time allocated to complete the course—five hours and fifteen minutes—will expire in one minute. So we decide to pack up in style. Every man is ready. Beasho is unclipping the mainsheet, the Major is on the foredeck with Damian, Ya is on his halyard, Chink is counting down. "Five . . . four . . . three . . . two . . . one. . . ."

The gun fired from the committee boat, signifying the end of the race, and in that very instant, the sails of *Australia II* fluttered down and the kangaroo with the boxing gloves rocketed to the top of the forestay, a defiant gesture for what everyone knew had just happened. We were not on the board yet, but we had become the only challenger in history to lead at all three jibe marks, and we had also led at *every* mark on this particular day. Our margin of superiority was the greatest seen in the America's Cup since 1871, when Sir James Ashbury's massive *Livonia,* which measured 106 feet at the waterline, took more than 15 minutes off *Columbia,* which had broached in a heavy sea and lost all of her steering. Her crew had been obliged to smash open the wheel box with axes to rig an emergency tiller.

Meanwhile, a fleet of boats is hurtling toward us, with *Black Swan* out in front, engines opened at full throttle, Bondy on the upper deck, fist raised high, Warren next to him with both fists raised high, visible for a very long way. I also saw Lucas, lucky Lucas, smiling and waving. If we had not seen them, we would have heard them, for Phil Judge had the pounding beat of Men at Work at full volume:

> Can't you hear, can't you hear the thunder?
> You'd better run, you'd better take cover.

At the press conference that night, I was consistently asked, "Wasn't it very frustrating for the race not to count?" And I told the scribes of the world once and for all, "It was not in any way frustrating. We are in no hurry. We are here for as long as it takes to win the America's Cup. Today was a great victory for *Australia II.*" I remember Dennis Conner saying, "There was nothing we could do. We sailed our best, but there was nothing we could do." Actually, I could have made a few suggestions. They could have refigured their ballasting, they could have refigured their light-air sails, and they certainly could have done something about that spinnaker. But maybe they just had not done their homework.

That evening I had dinner with Rasa and the children, and then I went up to the crew house for a chat and one last conference with Schnacks. We had a beer and looked at the photographs. Conditions were forecast to be the same on the morrow, when we would race *Liberty* again, so we decided to have a couple of recuts made overnight. Again the lights in our sail loft burned until nearly 3 A.M., as Kenny and Mike worked away on the machines, doing their part toward helping *Australia II* keep driving through the water, no matter how light the breeze.

*   *   *

Sunday morning, September 18. There was not a single breath of air in the whole of Newport. The leaves on the big ash tree on Dennison Street were motionless. No sail flaps in the harbor. But it felt warm as Hughey and I set off for Founders' Hall, and we both thought there would be a light breeze in the afternoon as the land heated up and the air rose, and new air was sucked in from the ocean. At breakfast, I told the boys, "This is easy. We are going to wallop them today, and no error. If I were they, I'd be scared to death, and I expect they are. Yesterday was a disaster for them. I hope they remember it. Meanwhile, we must forget yesterday. Don't even have it on your minds. We achieved what we did because we concentrated totally, and that is what we must do again today. I would like us all to come home tonight with thumping headaches because we have been thinking so hard for hour after hour. Today I ask of you a totally disciplined and thorough job."

We arrived at the racecourse in the middle of another gigantic fleet of spectator boats—estimated by some at nearly 2,000—on this bright, sunny Sunday morning. But the wind was still very light, and it was touch-and-go whether we could start the race.

The keynote of our attack was total aggression, and we proceeded to tie *Liberty* in knots. We did a few circles. She did one extra one—unnecessary, in my opinion—and we came in right underneath her and had her pinned tight above the weather end of the starting line. It was very like the situation in 1970, when *Gretel* had *Intrepid* pinned too high with nowhere to go. But this time there would be no gap left by the Aussies. We had the red boat trapped, but with 30 seconds to go, the Race Committee postponed the race. If they had let it begin, *Liberty* would have been locked out and would have been forced to jibe around and come in behind us. They would have had no alternative. We would have beaten them by about 1½ minutes. As we temporarily packed up, I could not resist an impulse. I looked across the water to Dennis, smiled, and nodded, intimating that he was a very lucky boy. He just looked away.

We took a break. I headed off to the big power launch *Southern Cross* to see Rasa, and some of the boys went over to *Black Swan*. The race had been postponed because of a massive switch in the wind direction, and we had to wait until it settled. At one o'clock it seemed better, more or less steady at 220 degrees, 7 knots, water fairly flat—conditions that would be fine for us, and, judging by the situation of the day before, not great for *Liberty*. The Coast Guard began the titanic task of clearing the boats away from the course. We reboarded *Australia II,* and at 1:40 P.M., the committee boat hoisted the course signals. A semblance of order was restored, and everyone prepared for a grim fight to the death on these warm, calm, sunlit waters.

*   *   *

The wind has come around about 115 degrees from the time of our earlier start, and now it may be increasing. I can see those telltale little cat's-paws making indentations and patterns on the surface—a sure sign of a light, gusting breeze. At 1:50, the 10-minute gun goes, and very soon afterward, we are involved in some circling with *Liberty*. We have her up to weather and we work to the leeward side of *Liberty*, since we believe the leeward end of the starting line is heavily favored. We force *Liberty* to tack away, and she just makes the wrong end of the starting line, while we are going full bore. *Liberty* has to head right up into the wind, her sails luffing as she narrowly misses the committee boat. She is almost dead in the water, and she crosses the line eight seconds ahead of us, but she is wallowing as we come crashing across at the leeward end, driving beautifully. Hughey says cheerfully, "We're looking good, John. Correct that. We're looking damned good." The red boat takes another half minute to get up speed, and all the while we are bowling along at 7 knots. The breeze is dying down to the right, and by our reckoning, *Liberty* is in big trouble. And I doubt whether their morale is all that wonderful. We are in great shape, sailing along in these light conditions that Benny's creation seems to love. Hughey says, "We've just lifted out 1½ boatlengths." Grant looks up, "big lift coming, John, five degrees, six degrees . . . seven . . . eight . . . we're 10 degrees up on them. Lifting out, lifting out."

Liberty goes plowing on down to the right, where we think the wind is not. "She's hitting the spectator-boat chop," says Hughey. "Now she's tacking, coming back to us. Has to be a good 50 yards behind us." That is a lot, and we decide to tack on top of her, protecting our left side. *Liberty* is rolling along fine, but we are lifting into new air, and we are in the best place in the flat water we like. *Australia II* is being sailed as well as a 12-Meter can be sailed. Mistakes so far: zero.

The duel goes on. *Liberty* catches a bit of wind, gains a small amount. We catch a breeze, gain it back. Generally speaking, we are hitting the wind better than the Americans are doing—Grant is beginning to look like a veteran in his first America's Cup. He keeps calling out those crucial shifts, deadly accurate every time. It is a truly brilliant performance in his first major regatta as a navigator.

Grant keeps calling, "Up seven. The breeze is still moving to the left. Up eight degrees, averaging nine degrees. A full 10 degrees, John." Down at the mast, Ya calls back—laconic, relaxed, easy Ya, the old boat painter with salt water in his blood—"No sweat, John, the breeze still looks better to the left. The right side looks a bit sick to me. Christ knows what the red boat is doing down there." I agree with him, *Liberty* looks as though she might be sailing into oblivion down there, struggling with the spectator chop. This is not one of those wondrous days for *Australia II*, but we probably have a fraction of speed edge, though not much, until we get into the confused wobble up near the top mark, when I expect us to draw away. Like Ya, I don't know what Conner is doing down on the right. According to every instinct and piece of information we have, the left side is the place to be. But Dennis seems not to want to tack with *Australia II*, and that thought, which I think has some merit, but not that much, is turning his boat into a lame duck. If I were driving *Liberty*, I would come right back and lock horns with us in this better water and better breeze. Anyway, we hit the chop up near the mark and come whipping round the buoy one minute 14 seconds in front. On the two following power reaches, the Americans are, as always in any breeze over 8 knots, faster than we are, and by the time we reach the wing mark, they are catching us quite briskly. They caught up 22 seconds on the first reach; on the second reach, which became more square with medium winds, they got another 10 seconds, and we turned up the second windward leg just 42 seconds to the good.

Hughey says quietly, "Slap a hard cover on the bastards, John." As the red boat rounds the mark, we slip into phase with them, and once more we see the ferocity of the American skipper. Dennis decides to try a tacking duel to see if he can break us. His boys are ready to take the strain, and aboard *Australia II* we can see it coming. "They are going to start throwing tacks at us," says Hughey. And I say to the boys on the lower deck, "This is it, stand by to hold off the bastards." On comes Conner, tacking hard underneath us. "Tack the boat, John," calls Hughey. "TACKING!" And the heavies go to work down below, pounding away at the winches. By the time we both have tacked 16 times, the sweat is pouring off the boys—Chink and Splash heading up the main winches, the Major helping Splash, and Damian down helping Chink. The strain is enormous, and as they thunder away in the heat—muscles aching, lungs gasping for breath—I can hear them egging each other on. "Come on now, Longley, let's see what you're made of." "Righto, Major Costello, let's see something now." Again and again they lean into the winches, their arms blurring, precision, precision, never missing a beat. "TACKING!" I call for the 20th time, and the four of them go at it once more. Now I know that they are in the "red zone," where the pain is becoming so intense that it can no longer be tolerated, except by the trained athlete. Soon they will go through the pain barrier—a phenomenon that Olympic oarsmen and runners often experience in the final stages of their effort. Splash, the big Olympic oarsman, is no stranger to this condition, and I can hear him urging the others on. Back comes Conner. He has some big, tough guys on that boat of his—no doubt about that—but my boys are their equal. Again we tack, and again, now for the 25th time. "TACK-

ING!" I shout again, and the blur of activity down there is awe-inspiring. I begin to wonder how much more of this we can take. Now I hear Chink gasp out their plan to deal with total exhaustion when they suspect someone might pass out. "This one's for Benny," shouts Chink, "make it the best ever." And with a new, frenzied effort, they shoulder their way into the grinders, each one of them with thoughts focused on a mental picture of our great, grinning bear of a designer, whom we all love. Conner tacks again. "TACKING!" I yell once more. Chink shouts again, "This one is for Schnacks—let's all be perfect." And again they wind away at the merciless steel winches. It seems as if the boys only have seconds to catch their breath when *Liberty* comes at us again. "We're coming away from them," says Hughey. "Tack her again, John." "TACKING!" I bawl for the 28th time. "This one's for Hughey!" roars the Major, with a kind of mad, superhuman strength rising from his huge shoulders. *Liberty* sails on, but within seconds she wheels about, trying to break our cover for the 29th time. "TACKING!" I order yet again. And Chink, still going powerfully, his dark, curly hair lank with sweat, his mighty chest heaving, bellows, "ONE FOR THE SKIPPER, BOYS—AND LET'S MAKE IT OUR BEST!" Four colossally tired grinders flail away once more with a kind of madness. This time the Americans have had enough, and they track us up to the mark, where we round 1¼ minutes in front, our biggest margin in the race so far. In the light winds, where brains count for everything, we have them. And in that titanic struggle on the winches, we still won't give them best. What Chink once said very loudly, I now say to myself very quietly, "Come and get us, you bastards." And I glance down to see the Major, nearly breathless with exhaustion, sweat pouring into his eyes, grinning roundly as he furiously helps to haul up the spinnaker.

Up at the top mark, the crew performed yet another perfect spinnaker set. Again we used the little one from *Challenge 12*, and she cracked out beautifully. We were romping away down the fifth leg before *Liberty* could get around to join us. Her spinnaker set was not as good as ours, and when it did go up, it did not look as stable as ours. Halfway down the legs we changed spinnakers to get a little more speed, and we hit the bottom mark two minutes 47 seconds in the lead. Just before we got to that mark, I called Chink back. "Just take a look at them Chink," I said. "Doesn't it make you feel good?" And this huge man, still pouring sweat after that duel up leg four, reflected with me for a few seconds on the debacles we had both been in on board *Southern Cross* and then on *Australia I*. Then he smiled at me, patted me on the shoulder, and went back to his post.

Down comes the spinnaker as we set the jib to sail for home up the final leg. *Liberty* is too far behind for us to care now, and we sail like fury all the way, hitting the shifts when we can and finally rolling up to the line to victory.

As we crossed the Race Committee boat, the gun fired, and up on the bow Damian's fist shot into the air. We had beaten *Liberty* by three minutes 14 seconds, the largest margin of any challenger since 1958, when 12-Meter yachts first started racing for this elusive trophy. It was only the ninth win by any challenger in 103 years, and only the fourth since 1934. I glanced around the boat. Every man on board had a fist raised high in the air. It looked like a reunion of a prewar Fascist training school.

"By Christ, we've done it, John," shouted Hughey. "About time!" But our voices were already being drowned out by the maelstrom of noise coming from all around us. *Black Swan,* with Bondy on the bridge, was charging toward us; the helicopters with their cameramen seemed to be perched on top of the mast; and out there in the fleet, three enormous boatloads of Aussies were trying to get into harmony.

Suddenly we could all hear it, for the first time out there on the water, the rising notes of the strident yet mournful sounds of the great Australian anthem written in the Outback beyond the Great Dividing Range, by the immortal Aussie folk poet, Banjo Paterson.

> WALTZING MATILDA, WALTZING MATILDA,
> You'll come a-waltzing Matilda with me.
> And he sang as he looked at his old billy boiling,
> You'll come a-waltzing Matilda with me.

The sound sent chills down the spine of every member of the crew. This touching song, which cradles the very soul of Australia in its lilting melody, seemed to be coming now from the great stock routes of our homeland, from the land of cattle camps, walleroos, and wombats, from the land of Ned Kelly, of Clancy of the Overflow, of the man from Snowy River. From the land of Banjo Paterson and the Snakebite River. And now it was soaring into the air above these strange, hostile waters, so far from home.

> And he sang as he stowed him away into his tucker bag,
> You'll come a-waltzing Matilda with me.
> WALTZING MATILDA, WALTZING MATILDA . . .

They sang it at the top of their voices, at once full of pathos and jubilation. They sang it as only Australians can after a great battle. And now they were singing it for us. Hundreds of them, on boats out on Rhode Island Sound, sang for a proud little nation whose heart rested firmly on board a boat called *Australia II*. It was now Monday morning in Sydney, and half the population would have been up all through the night, watching us live on television. It was later reported that traffic had been the lightest in living memory during the Monday-morning rush hour on the Harbor Bridge.

Australia had become a nation of yachting converts. People who had never even been on a boat were reading up on the herculean struggle taking place off Newport, Rhode Island. The fascinating thing about their interest, however, is that it revolved around a total myth—that we had this boat that was about twice as fast as the Americans' *Liberty,* and that she was secretly powered by a mysterious keel with wings, and that essentially all we had to do was to sit on her and she would carry us to victory.

However, in the real world of wind, sea, spinnakers, mainsails, and genoas, where every second is crucial, where a four-second mistake can nearly cost you a race, the myth amounts to almost total drivel. But the myth, however lacking in truth it may have been, happened to suit everyone perfectly. The press, of course, loved it because it was easy to understand, such a marvelously simple concept that saved them the trouble of having to understand the almost unfathomable complications that surround 12-Meter racing yachts.

It also suited Dennis Conner and his henchmen, because it provided for them a perfect excuse for losing the America's Cup, should it come to that.

The third myth-lover was me. I knew that *Australia II* was not in any way unbeatable, and I also knew that the boat had the Americans rattled when they really should not have been. After four races, three of which counted, a few facts already were clear. In medium winds, going to windward, *Liberty* had a speed edge on us—a very small but definite speed edge, especially in a joggle. On the two power reaches, *Liberty* was faster (on the six power reaches so far sailed—that counted on the scoreboard—we had gained only two seconds—in Race 1.) On the square run, we had a speed edge on them, mainly because we had improved steadily with our sails and techniques.

In very light winds—under 7 knots, which is rare—*Australia II* had a speed edge. In high winds, and the confused seas of Newport, I would put the boats about even going upwind, with perhaps a slight speed edge to *Liberty*. When it really blew, very occasionally above 20 knots, I would say that we got back that edge.

In fast tacking duels, I would estimate that *Australia II* could take about one second per tack, no more. Thus, in 15 or 16 tacks, we might get two boatlengths. On long, loping tacks, the regular ones that happen throughout a race, the boats were exactly equal. At the start, we were more mobile, and I was able to maneuver *Liberty* into very unfavorable positions.

But in the end this would come down to a sailing contest, and victory would go to the crew who made the fewest mistakes, who sailed nearly perfectly, who judged the wind best, and, in the end, who wanted it most.

There was very little between *Australia II* and *Liberty* that could not be turned around by superior sail techniques, better crew work, and afterguard cunning. But, after all, the myth suited everyone. And so, at the press conference that evening, I again intimated that it was pure joy to be at the helm of the Great White Pointer.

Not long married, Rasa and I arrive in Newport for the 1970 America's Cup. As port trimmer I'm carrying the genoa sheets for Sir Frank Packer's *Gretel II*.

Canada, 1976. Receiving my Olympic Bronze medal. Above me stands the East German who out-psyched me and whose example would affect me profoundly for years to come. *(Modern Boating)*

En route to the old Leather Medal, working myself to death at the 1972 Olympic Games in Germany, Finn class. The Russian Potapov just beat me for the Bronze.

Australian V.J. and Sharpie champions, me (left) with brother
Lex.

Waiting for the postponed start, race three. "I'll just sit here. And I'll sit here for three months if I have to. But I'm not going home without it."

Rasa, photographed as we struggled back from the brink on the first beat to windward, race five, still 3–1 down to *Liberty*.

Bondy and me at the White House. President Reagan walked up to me and his handshake was strong. "John Bertrand," he said, "congratulations." And he sent me this picture, personally signed. (Jack Kightlinger)

The old firm—Bondy and me, skipper and owner, in our moment of supreme triumph after our victory. On board *Black Swan* with wife, Rasa, son, Lucas, and Eileen Bond. (Pamela Price, *Journal-Bulletin*)

A cuddle from little Sunshine, the light of my life, on the dock at Newport, after we had been beaten by the Americans to go 3–1 down. (Laurie Sullivan)

The Bertrand family arrived in Newport in 1980 (left to right): Lucas, Rasa, Andre, Sunshine. All together for another Aussie debacle.

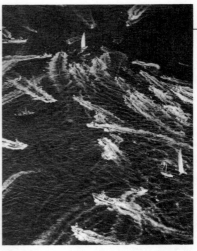

Rolling up to the finish line, with the America's Cup just about in the old tucker bag. "Try not to hit the committee boat," said my faithful, battle-scarred tactician, Hughey Treharne. (Richard Benjamin, *Journal-Bulletin*)

Race seven, immediately after the finish. Dennis Conner and his Americans are finally vanquished. Said Benny: "You've done it, you bastard, you've done it." (Richard Benjamin, *Journal-Bulletin*)

Australia II heels over while I gaze through my dark glasses at Chink, Ya, and the Major working away during practice on Port Phillip Bay, the waters on which I first learned to sail.

Outside the Chelsea Yacht Club with Andre. My grandpa, a fisherman by trade, was vice-commodore. And while I might be champion of the world, I'm still only a half cadet in there. (Greg Noakes)

Wedding day, 1969.

At the presentation of the America's Cup. Happy? I was bloody ecstatic.

Founders Hall, the Australian bastion in Newport, and our headquarters throughout the long summer of 1983.

A nostalgic return to Newport in 1984. I walked out on the headland and looked again out to the former America's Cup course, where, in a way, my very destiny had been decided.

O'Brien's pub, a bit unfashionable, just off the beaten track for the Newport tourists, but it was the little Aussie bar in Newport, round the corner from our sail loft. Our kangaroo flag still hangs in there.

A plaque on the wall of Number 32 Dennison Street now reads JOHN BERTRAND HOUSE.

We won the America's Cup in here. The old fishing hut we converted into our sail loft, right near our dock. They restitched and recut the engines of *Australia II* night after night in here, silently working away, to make us faster, faster, faster.

Robinson and Bertrand, co-authors and pals, fishing off Cape Cod from a sailing dinghy designed by Captain Nathanael Herreshoff. One can sail, the other can write, neither has a clue about fishing.

17

Humiliation

At nine minutes 45 seconds past midday on Tuesday, September 20, Dennis Conner, skipper of Liberty, *sails the big red defender, audaciously, arrogantly, and spectacularly, clean across the bow of* Australia II.

Dennis Conner called a lay day for Monday, September 19, presumably hoping that stronger breezes would arrive on the following day. A Monday morning when you do not have to go to work is, I suppose, welcome in any country, but on this day I was assailed by a most uneasy, slightly restless feeling. The previous evening had been a real high for all of us. After our great victory, the boys were justifiably feeling delighted with a job unquestionably well done. Alan Bond was full of bounce and exuberance, and all around the periphery of our camp were well-wishers congratulating us on winning the race. Everyone was making a very big deal out of it—a bit too big a deal, in my opinion. I had not come here to win a race. I had come here to win the America's Cup, nothing less.

Now I was well accustomed to hitting a low point in the middle of a regatta. As I have mentioned, that had always been a problem for me. And now we were approaching the middle of this one, and I feared that we might lose our intensity. It seemed to have taken us forever to win that one race, and suddenly I had a dim and vague vision of complacency rearing its ugly head. On the previous evening, my tigers had looked well fed, a bit too well fed for a crew that was still 2–1 down and for whom one sudden defeat would be just about catastrophic.

But by Tuesday morning, September 20, the heroes from Down Under seemed ready to go out and even the score. I spoke to the boys briefly, exhorting them to forget Sunday completely. I told them we were now in a position to level with *Liberty*, but that it would be no simpler than it had been before. If we did not keep up our momentum and all our skills, they would beat us. We could afford no mistakes.

The wind was gusting well above 10 knots when we arrived at the racecourse at 11 A.M. The sea was developing a real chop, and the foredeck was wet as we prepared to warm up with *Challenge*. I called for our code-four genoa, and we lined up for our first beat to weather. Within a couple of minutes, *Challenge* started to edge away from us, and then suddenly she was blowing us away! "We've got the wrong genoa up," said Hughey, "let's swing her around and change." "FETCH UP THE CODE-THREE GENOA AND GET READY TO CHANGE!" I shouted, dimly aware that maybe my fears about the complacency of the crew may have had something to do with me. I had chosen the wrong sail. Soon, with the change, we were much better, matching pace with *Challenge* as always. Out in front of us, *Liberty* was being burned off by *Freedom* so badly that Dennis, I later learned, decided to use *Freedom*'s genoa, a sail that had once belonged to *Courageous* and that he had *never* used before. This was a seat-of-the-pants gamble—gutsy, but without control—and if I had *my* worries, God knows what he must have been feeling like. If he lost today, he would be the first skipper since 1934 to lose two races in the America's Cup. I would not have wanted to trade places with him.

The wind was steady at about 10 knots out of the west-southwest (235 degrees). The course signals were hoisted at 11:50 A.M. under sunny skies. *Liberty* had hauled up that new genoa, a beautiful crosscut sail that they had never tested. In these conditions, I estimated that *Liberty* would have two advantages on *Australia II*. She would be highly competitive on all three upwind legs, and, as ever, faster on the two power reaches. That meant we would have our work cut out, because the forecast suggested that the wind would build during the afternoon, and *Australia II* was only as fast as or faster than *Liberty* on the beats when the wind was below 8 knots or above 16 or 18 knots. What I did not know was that *Liberty*'s new genoa would give her real boatspeed on us, so much so that we would be able to calculate it most of the way around.

Above our heads was the usual pandemonium of helicopters and planes recording our every movement. The spectator fleet had thinned a little from the weekend mob scene, but the big American boats out in front, in the privileged positions, were as numerous as usual, waiting for Mr. Conner to slap us into a position from which recovery would be almost impossible. Alternately, all of Australia waited anxiously in the small hours of their Wednesday morning for us to even the score.

The 10-minute gun goes. The Major hits the stopwatch. The two boats are quite far apart, and it is clear that *Liberty* is very much into the time-on-distance start. We head over to try to catch them on the wrong foot, but they do not want to play. We make a few circles, but she tacks away on her own. With 2½ minutes to go, we go off on port tack and begin to set ourselves up for a closehauled run up to the line, hitting it on starboard tack near the committee-boat end. Things are looking fantastic as we head inside the two-minute call from the Major.

Beasho is poised at the mainsheet, ready to haul the sail as soon as I shout. Scoop and Skippy, hearts pounding in their little cockpits, are hanging on to the genoa sheets. Chink and Damian are up on the bow, the Major and Splash are on the winches. The Major is counting every five seconds now. "100 . . . 95 . . . 90 . . . 85 . . . 80. . . ." "TIGHTEN THE MAINSHEET!" I call, and the sails harden. *Australia II* moves forward into battle. Way out to the left, *Liberty* is already coming across to meet us on a port tack, but we have the right-of-way on starboard, and she will have to duck under our stern, with precious little room, near the committee boat.

The count goes on, now faster. "35 . . . 34 . . . 33 . . . 32 . . . 31. . . ." "This is going to be bloody close, Hughey," I say, as we race toward the line. Our timing looks good, and *Liberty* is still on a collision course with us. We're running hard at the line now, and so is she. Hughey is stooped beside me, looking under the boom, his fists clenched tightly, teeth gritted, saying nothing. "27 . . . 26 . . . 25 . . . 24. . . ." "Hughey, this is really tight. She's headed right up. You don't think she's going to cross our bow, do you?" Hughey still says nothing, but now all eyes are on *Liberty,* as the big red boat continues to make no move toward cutting our stern. She's still on a collision course. Hughey lifts his hand in a futile gesture, as though to stop the red boat from doing the unthinkable and crossing our bow. The Major counts, "23 . . . 22 . . . 21 . . . 20. . . ." This is ghastly. I have blown it. I have called for the sails too late by at least 10 seconds. Up on the bow, Damian turns around, white-faced, and shouts impulsively what by now we all know. "She's going to cross us, John!" There is nothing I can do about it. I would give everything I have to urge more speed from *Australia II,* but it is too late. The count goes on, and at nine minutes 45 seconds past midday on Tuesday, September 20, Dennis Conner, skipper of *Liberty,* sails the big red defender, audaciously, arrogantly, and spectacularly, clean across the bow of *Australia II.* I have never felt quite so humiliated in my entire life. I should have pulled on the sails when the count was at "90" rather than at "80." If I had done so, *Liberty* would not have been in time and would have been forced to drive under our stern or tack to leeward, leaving us in the control position. Whatever, I had royally screwed up everyone's day—as they say about a collision at sea.

Now *Australia II* is flying for the line, grotesquely astern of *Liberty.* She hits the line first, six seconds ahead of us. It's as though we have been in a time capsule for about 15 seconds—no one on *Australia II* dared to breathe as I held on to the wheel, berating myself loudly, mercilessly, and publicly. The error, in normal terms and total context, was minuscule, but to me it was life and death. Suddenly, Hughey says just the right thing, without mentioning the foulup. "*Liberty* stays on port tack. Her bearing's good, she makes just under 8 knots through the water. She has about one boatlength on us." He hasn't looked around and our eyes haven't met, but I sense that he is doing everything he can to help me, to get me back on the rails. Again he calls, "I think she's a shade faster through the water than we are right now. We should tack over and join her quite soon. But she's moving very fast." "OK, John, let's go. Tack her now." It is a performance that is at once pure steel and immensely sensitive, and I gain great new security from standing there alongside Hughey Treharne. It is the first time I have ever felt so close and so reassured by the mere presence of a fellow yacht racer.

I tack the boat, and the sudden flurry of activity brings more relief to the crew. We are easing back into the swing of things now.

"She points exactly the same height as we do," says Hughey, "but she is edging out—not a hell of a lot, but enough. Now she is 1½ boatlengths in front. She's slipping out from under us, John."

"She's increased her bearing again, John, another five feet on us. No change in height. But every now and then she slips away." Now we have *Australia II* traveling all out, and we are running into the same problems in this joggle and medium winds that we always have. In exactly these conditions, we would be chained to *Challenge 12.* And now Grant calls it, "We are 30 seconds behind her, John."

I sense that we have a desperate struggle on our hands. The apparition of 3–1 down is too awful to think about. But right now we are strapped for tactics. If we tack away, the red boat will not come with us.

She is determined to stay down here to the right and play the windshifts, hoping for a lift. It is hard for me to do anything else except tag along and hope to outsail her, or perhaps get a couple of lifts to get us back into the hunt. But as we slide along, up toward the first weather mark, it is *Liberty* that gets a couple of shifts. Their crew is sailing beautifully, and they are making their boat go as fast as she can. This is developing into a real afterguard's race. Everything is dependent upon the decisions of tacticians, skippers, and navigators. It is very clinical and very quiet. I can see the weather mark up ahead, and Hughey again calls, "She's increased her bearing again, another half a boatlength." Grant looks up, only marginally holding back his ice-cold anger at being behind. "She's going around about 30 seconds in front, John," he snaps. He is angry at the world. Rarely have I seen anyone who hates to lose as much as Grant ("Mad Dog") Simmer. Except, perhaps, myself.

Hughey and I are discussing changing the genoa, despite the fact that we *know* this is the right one for us. But we have to get some boatspeed. Every time I look at *Liberty,* her new genoa looks terrific. Dennis's random decision to take a sail he had never even tried, just because he was being battered badly by *Freedom,* had paid off in spades. They would not change it all day, and there is no question that the sail gave them extra horsepower, and they were taking every possible advantage of it by sailing their boat superbly.

This is a classic boatspeed race, and we are not winning it. Dennis is sailing that boat brilliantly. I've been told often enough that this guy is the best 12-Meter sailor in the world, and he certainly looks like it right now.

Hope, however, springs eternal, and the wind begins to drop as we come up to the fourth mark. With spinnakers set once more, we head down the leg in wind dropping to around 10 knots, sometimes a little less. It is possible we could roll over them if this continues. But it does not. The wind stays quite strong enough for *Liberty,* and we take only 11 seconds off them all the way down the run. *Liberty* turns for home still dictating the tactics, still 35 seconds in front, exactly as she had been at the first mark.

The breeze freshens as we head upwind for the last time, and quite early on there are a couple of good windshifts. *Liberty* gets them both, and in sullen outrage, the men of *Australia II* cross the line 43 seconds behind.

As the cannon fired and the *Liberty* crew set off on their triumphant tour through the spectator fleet, I noticed Commodore Robert Mc-Cullough, our old antagonist, leaning out over the side of *Black Knight,* a huge smile on his face, his fist raised in a victory salute to Dennis. That night they would order up the champagne for their victory party, scheduled to take place after the next race. Neither of us was interested in a lay day.

They had sailed magnificently, as well as we had done during the weekend. On balance, they deserved to win this time. Dennis made two brilliant gambles—one by using an unfamiliar sail and the other by crashing across our bow. Even his mainsheet hand, John Marshall, was heard to comment as they powered toward us at the start, "Dennis, if this goes wrong, don't try to take me into the protest room with you!" But it did not go wrong. Dennis demonstrated a crucial factor in winning any major competition—he backed his own judgment.

Before I left for the press conference, Hughey gave me a nice little sendoff. He said, "John, listen, they were faster than we were today. There was nothing we could do about it. So forget it. When the wind got up to 15 knots on the second beat to windward, they were even faster. *No one* could have pegged them back in *Australia II.*"

I knew that was true, but I would never say it and risk damaging the glorious reputation of the Superboat. When I arrived at the Newport Armory for the conference, the atmosphere was rather different. Instead of just Dennis Conner and perhaps Tom Whidden in the audience, they were all there—all the key men on *Liberty,* with their wives, laughing and talking—full of arrogance toward the battered Aussies. Just inside the doorway, there was a very interesting little exchange. I had not yet signed my contract with North Sails to take over the Australian operations in Sydney—largely because I had not had time to think about it—and John Marshall, the American head of North Sails, greeted Rasa with a large smile and the words, "John should have signed that North Sails contract." The implication of my diminishing importance was perfectly clear, and the large, smiling, successful figure of John Marshall, my boss, was a fairly daunting sight, particularly since he was surrounded by his large entourage. Rasa turned to face them all, bravely I thought, and I heard her say quietly, "I shouldn't count on anything if I were you, John. We're not finished yet." The feeling was only just short of outright hostility.

And then I was up at the table speaking to the reporters. I took the full blame and responsibility for the defeat, putting it down to a judgmental error. I never once mentioned the real truth, boatspeed, because it was not in our interests to do so. I did not want Dennis to gain even a glimmer of confidence about his boat.

I then made the remark that I understand virtually silenced the Australian nation. As millions of people who had been up all night sat glued to the television back home, waiting, wondering if we could still pull it off, I said, "Basically, nothing has changed. After Sunday afternoon, we had to win three boat races. Today we still have to win three boat races. Nothing has changed." Months later, people still remembered my saying that, although I never gave it another thought. And at a dinner in Australia in 1984, one of the speakers brought it up again. He said, "That morning when they were 3–1 down, about a dozen of us had been up all night, and when John Bertrand said, 'Nothing has changed,' I just remember the room went totally silent. I suppose we were stunned by the guts and the backbone of that Australian boat crew."

Well, I was right in one sense. Nothing *had* changed. We still needed to win three races. But, in another sense, something had changed fairly drastically. The feeling of complacency, if it had ever existed, was now gone, and it would never return. Each member of this crew, in his own way, was seized by a near-manic desire never to lose again. It began to build as we packed up for the evening, and it remained with us indefinitely.

By the time I arrived home, I was burning with indignation and determination. "We will not lose," I kept telling myself, "we will not lose." I was a forbidding sight as I entered our tiny, seedy apartment, and Rasa said something that, under the circumstances, struck me as quite funny. "You and Grant Simmer are both very much the same in defeat," she said. "Just two plain, ordinary, everyday, highly unpleasant, nasty people."

We both laughed, and I did reflect that I had very little to be nasty about. Rasa still thought we would win—of that I was in no doubt. Not one member of my crew had made a single reference to my mistake. Alan Bond had been tough and determined, and had said not one word against me. No one had. And tonight we would all meet together at the crew house, for what would inevitably become a council of war. We knew how to celebrate and we knew how to close ranks.

Every member of the Australian camp understood the peril that we faced. There was a very peculiar atmosphere as we prepared to go to Founders' Hall. We never even discussed whether I would go alone or whether Rasa should come. We just all got ready—Lucas, Andre, Sunshine, all of us. We had a powerful compulsion that somehow we all had to be together on this evening. Everyone felt it, and everyone was doing the same thing. Every single member of the camp—men, women and children—was preparing to go to Founders' Hall. I suppose it was a return to the old herding instinct, primeval in origin, but there is no question that we were driven together that night like a flock of migrating birds. And if I was not careful tomorrow, we would soon be migrating, south by southwest, to Sydney, New South Wales.

But only one thing beat us today. It was boat speed. We could not catch them. That new genoa of theirs made them very fast. Our code-three genoa had to be improved. Tonight the photographs were critical, as were the brains of Schnacks and Hughey. It was a high-tech puzzle. And when it was solved it had to be explained to all of the boys in the most simple terms, so that they understood quite clearly what we were doing and what we must do on the following day.

I had a lot of very diverse personalities to cope with, and in turn, each of them had to cope with things in his own way. As we sat there on the very brink of extinction, after more than two years of murderously hard work, and thousands and thousands of hours of dedication, all of our hopes and all of our dreams of glory and a place in history were about to be obliterated. It was not a very easy night. Each man had to grapple with that, emotionally and realistically, in his own way. Of course, there was also some despondency. Poor Dixie Treharne, so sensitive to it and to what it meant to Hughey, just wept quietly by herself, talking only to her husband, and sometimes to Rasa.

The Major was blasting around the house, yelling and roaring about what we were going to do to them tomorrow. But his was blind faith, an unreasonable and obdurate obsession with victory. All that roaring was just his way of handling his overpowering frustration. Rumor has it that he went home that night and knocked down a door, then fell sobbing into his wife's arms. And Sheila just put him to bed. He was a big man, in every sense of the word, driven nearly insane by blighted hopes.

Grant scowled his way through dinner and then spent ages with his head buried in his computer printouts, muttering, checking, and grumbling, very snarly, typical Mad Dog. He was trying to pinpoint the exact strength and direction of the wind at the exact moments *Liberty* slipped away from us. He pretended that his anger was directed purely at some kind of minor inefficiency. But he was more vulnerable than that. He used to sleep at the crew house, and his girl friend, Alex, lived over at Alan Bond's house. But on this night, Grant could not stand to be alone with the demons that haunted us both. He left quietly, quite late, and slept that night with Alex.

Colin Beashel had dinner at the main table with his mother and father. He talked little, smiled not once, and was very much into himself. He was an ace racing yachtsman brought up in a family of ace racing yachtsmen. He knew everything about winning and losing. All his life he had known the pressure and frustration of this game at an international level. He was weaned on stories of the great victories of his grandfather, and he lived with the victories and defeats of his father. He knew that you could be right there one day and gone the next. This style of competition was second nature to him, but tonight was a real shaker. Beasho packed up much earlier than usual and went off to bed, shutting himself away with a book and his thoughts. He felt better able to cope with it on his own, and he stayed there, wrestling throughout the night, no doubt, with the massive

95-foot-high mainsail of *Australia II* that he must trim to perfection the next day.

Skippy was worried. But his natural sunny disposition came through, and he talked very happily to Rasa for a while. Whichever way you looked at it, it was important to him, but it was not life and death. Ya was rather the same, but he did not feel like cracking many jokes that night. Damian had not been with us long enough to comprehend the full shattering effect that our situation was having on some of us. He would never feel the total joy of triumph, but neither would he feel the pain of defeat.

Chink Longley was bullish on the surface, but, in truth, he was a three-time loser in this competition, and I sensed he was aware that right now we were in the same position as *Australia I* had been in 1980—but better than he had ever experienced on *Southern Cross,* or on the old *Australia* in 1977. There was just a little touch of acceptance in Chink's soul that was not in mine or Grant's or Colin's or the Major's. And not in the soul of old Scoop, either. Scoop was ice-cool throughout the evening, viciously determined to win the next race. But he understood very clearly that the problem was technical, that he could not really help. And then he did what he *never* did. At about nine o'clock, he went out to a bar in Newport and sat in a corner and nursed a beer and his thoughts very privately for two whole hours.

Alan Bond was very good. He had been so all along during the heat of the competition. That afternoon, he had bounded onto the boat to talk to me and Hughey. I told him straight out that I had screwed up the start. He absorbed the technical problem in one breath. Then he snapped back, "Right, John, what about tomorrow, do we race?" "I don't know why not," I said. "We have nothing to gain by sitting around. Fuck it. Let's get into it." Bondy grinned and said, "Right. Fuck it. Let's get into it." Good, hard guy, Bondy, when the chips are down.

I felt rather sorry for Warren. He had much to do, and he was trying desperately hard to do anything he possibly could to help us. If I had said to Warren, "Go and jump in the Atlantic and swim to Australia, and then we can win," he would have done it. He tried and tried that evening—anything he could contribute, anything at all, he would do. But inside, I think he must have been nearly at his wit's end. To any man as coldly logical and methodical as Warren, our position must have seemed appalling. I guessed, quite correctly, that Warren Jones would not sleep this night. The visions of the previous defeats posed stark and gruesome in his darkened room.

At the conclusion of dinner there were four principal characters still at the table: Kenny, Schnacks, Hughey, and me. Before us were the photographs that had been snapped off during the race by Scoop and Skippy.

The problem we faced was how to get more horsepower out of that jib, and we sat there for three hours. Finally, our conclusions were complete and Schnacks and the sailmakers headed off down to the sail loft in which the lights would again burn all night.

I took Rasa and the children home, and then I went down to the loft. I did what I could down there to encourage the boys, and I stayed there for a little while. But I had to get some sleep. I left them slicing at the seams of the code-three genoa, Schnacks making his marks, the machines humming, ready to stitch us back together to sail against the Americans the next day.

Newport was half asleep, although many of the bars were still packed with Aussies drowning their sorrows. Out over the racecourse, the constellation of Orion the Hunter would soon rise in the heavens. As I made my lonely way back up the steep hill of Dennison Street, I muttered in tune with the revolutions of the pedals on my bike, "I'm not going to lose . . . I'm not going to lose . . . I'm not going to lose."

For some unaccountable reason, perhaps exhaustion, I slept like a baby that night. The following morning, when I bounded out of bed, I knew I was going to win. Actually, it was a bit more basic than that. I knew I could not face defeat, elimination, being sent home. So I presumed that I would either win or die—either way, I would not be required to face humiliation from my peers. I had to get up to Founders' Hall to make my breakfast speech, but there was a bit more activity on Dennison Street that morning. Lucas was not going to school, he was going out on *Black Swan*. Bondy had arrived at the obvious conclusion that we had lost on all three occasions when Lucas was *not* out there. On the two occasions he had watched us, we had won (once when the race was called off). So my little boy, at the age of 11, was made the official mascot of *Australia II,* and that morning, while his classmates prepared for school, Lucas Bertrand packed his foul-weather gear in his little kitbag and set off for *Black Swan,* like a little soldier going to battle.

On top of this, Rasa uncorked a zinger at me when I left to go down to the dock. She said, "John, just remember that you have so far proved nothing. You are just the same as all the rest of them. The skipper of an Australian boat getting badly beaten by the Americans. I know you have always considered yourself better than Jim Hardy, which is why you have dragged us all around the world while you proved it. But essentially, you are not better. You are just the same. You are both three-time losers."

If I ever needed firing up, that did it. I was like a caged lion that morning. I set off for the dock with murder in my heart. "We are going to win today," I kept saying. "We are going to crush them today." I did not, of course, know that another interesting conversation would take place at just about the time I was setting out across Newport Harbor. Rasa helped to organize babysitters at the time, and one of the things that was on the minds of some of the wives was the possibility of staging this evening a riotous loser's party—for which we were justifiably famous. Cathy, our babysitter, said to Rasa, "I could stay all night tonight if you like, Mrs. Bertrand." "All night? What for?" asked Rasa. "Well, I just thought you might be having a party tonight." And Rasa, who had just delivered such a psychological bombshell to me, an hour before, just smiled and said, "No, Cathy, that will not be necessary. There will not be a party tonight."

The dock, as usual, was jammed. But the atmosphere was unlike the previous days. There was no feeling of jubilation and expectancy, of impending victory. It was very restrained. On board *Australia II,* we had a brief council of war. The kangaroo shot up the mast, and then there was a truly devastating occurrence. Instead of our regular battle anthem, which we wanted to hear on this day above all others, a ridiculous song suddenly started to burst from our loudspeakers. Some meaningless rubbish that we were unfamiliar with. Bondy had decided he wanted a change, and he told the men on *Black Swan* to play a different song. Now he is not a sensitive man at best, but there are times when words more or less fail me. We were absolutely flabbergasted as we stood there, aghast, our routine broken. The sight and the sounds that for us signified victory, which we had used all summer—Men at Work, "Down Under"—the very soul of our feeling for this boat, were gone. You never know who will be most affected by something like that. Suddenly, I heard an enraged noise from the bow of the boat, and little Skippy, his face purple with fury, came out of his battle station like a rocket, trembling and screaming at the top of his lungs, "GET THAT SHIT OFF! GET IT OFF. GET IT OFF. GET IT OFF, I SAY!" The most inoffensive member of the crew—sunny, cheerful Skippy—had gone berserk. Never has a tape been turned off with greater haste. Phil Judge turned it down, ripped it out of the machine, and slapped on "Down Under" in less than five seconds. We had just seen the sudden crackup of an infantryman going into battle. Skippy knew what he had to do out there, and he wanted simple, careful, familiar instructions fed into his brain. He had a lot on his mind, and anything that was not usual was tantamount to the appearance of the enemy.

Just as I was about to go on board, Eileen Bond came up to me, saying nothing, tears in her eyes. I've always been a very close friend of Eileen's, and I just gave her a big hug and said, "Don't worry, Eileen, I won't let you down."

18

September 21, 12:56 P.M.

Once more I doff my cap raffishly to the world in general, and then I go back to work with the feverish devotion to duty of one who lately has returned from the dead.

We are now 46 minutes into Race 5, headed for the first mark. (Those earlier minutes, the most stupefying of my entire life, were already recounted in Chapter 1.)

All around me I have been watching a devastating performance in terms of crew work. I call for a medium-air spinnaker and it is hauled up onto the deck singlehandedly by the Major. Grant, foul-weather boots and all, leaves his post and rushes up onto the foredeck. Damian attaches the clips. Ya frees the genoa. Damian starts to feed out the spinnaker. Two-thirds of the way up, someone bellows, "N-O-O-O-O-W!" Ya drops the genoa, and the spinnaker—now free from the danger of sucking in behind the jib—cracks out magnificently. The Major and Grant haul it up the rest of the way. She clips on at the top. Grant dives for the half of the jib that is now in the water and starts hauling it out. Damian's arms are flailing as he grabs the genoa down the forestay until it is right on the deck. Grant's arms are still going as the Major hurtles down his hatch in one jump and bounds back up, holding our translucent Mylar staysail under one arm. He unfolds this delicate intermediate little sail, which weighs only ¼ ounce per square yard and will fit under the spinnaker, sheeted to the outboard end of the boom. Ya is there with a spare halyard and they haul it up the mast together, hand over hand. Precision timing. The Major shouts, "OK!" Grant takes over the rest of the cleanup operation on the code-three genoa. The Major dives back down the hatch, hauling the huge sail in on top of him, grabbing it, fighting it, stuffing hundreds of square feet of soaking-wet Kevlar into the sewer. Grant races back to his post, running along the weather edge of the boat. He hits the floor hard and picks up his computer readings instantly.

All of the above has happened in less than 40 seconds, and suddenly we are breathing clear air, out in front of *Liberty*.

I am nearly prostrate with emotion. But as *Liberty* slides around, now a couple of boatlengths behind us, I feel perhaps the most overwhelming relief I have ever known. The possibility of being 3–2 dances before my eyes. I feel ecstasy and admiration for everyone. I blow hard through my lips, making a noise like a ruptured trombone, with my cheeks like little balloons on either side of my face—the universal signal for a very close call. "You guys just hauled me back from the precipice," I say. Grant never looks up, just snaps out a phrase I am beginning to get used to, "Shut your mouth, Bertrand, and sail the boat." My mood is so buoyant that I look up with a huge grin and take my hat off to the crew in an extravagant gesture. Beasho glances up, glances down again, and says, "We haven't won it yet, and there's a damned long way to go. Sail the boat."

Those two grumpy little bastards could think what they like. Once more I doff my cap raffishly to the world in general, and then I go back to work with the feverish devotion to duty of one who lately has returned from the dead. I love the look of the staysail. We have been using it consistently ever since Race 1, when *Liberty* dealt us that harsh lesson by powering right over us. We have not let her batter us quite that badly again on the power reaches, and we sure as hell are not going to let her do so today.

Right now, she's about three boatlengths behind us, and now that I have completed my music-hall turn behind the wheel, I get right back into it with the rest of them. Grant shouts our compass bearing to the wing mark. I check it automatically, at the same time calling to Hughey, "Give me a fix on 'em." Hughey's got the stadometer already trained on *Liberty*, mentally recording their every move in case the Red Dog starts rolling down on us again. Hughey says calmly, "Three boatlengths, John. We're looking good." I look down to Scoop in the tailer's tiny cockpit to weather, on my right side. "Kenny, keep your eyes peeled for stronger winds on our weather side. Let's keep tuned in. If necessary, I'll zigzag a bit to find the fresher breeze." Ya can't help much at the moment. He has his head down, cleaning up the hundreds of feet of line all over the deck as a result of the spinnaker, genoa, and staysail maneuvers. Beasho now has the mainsail loosed out over the weather side, and I call to him, "Watch for a breeze now, keep your eyes wide open."

Hughey says again, "No change, John. *Liberty* matches us for speed, but we hold them. No gain. We still have three boatlengths." By now the breeze is gusting at up to 15 knots. The sea is choppy, but we don't notice it as much going downwind. This is the first time in our races against the Americans that we have been sailing in these conditions and not contending with broken equipment. Now it is the turn of the red boat to deal with that, and Hughey reports that they seem to be preparing to send a man back up the mast to try to do something with that jumper strut. There is no doubt it does affect them a bit on starboard tack, but it does not affect them on port, and they are nothing like as gutsy as we were when we raced the bastards with a mainsail that would not go up. *And* we took them on in a long, brutally hard tacking duel.

"OK, boys," I shout, "we're looking real good right now. It's our turn to be settled and their turn to cope with trouble. Let's not let 'em off the hook. Let's just sail this boat really accurately." The wind is really going at it now, and the water's getting turbulent. We're all in our foul-weather gear, protected from the cold, sailing our little white boat as hard as we can.

To maximize our performance down this power reach, to try to keep them at bay, we are now going to have to employ some ferocious small-boat techniques, the kind I used to apply in my halcyon days in the Finn Class when I was acknowledged as one of the best downwind sailors in the world. As you come to the top of the waves in those little boats, you haul in the sail, squeezing out the air and shoving the boat down the wave, pulling yourself down the face of the water, just diagonal to the flow in the trough of the wave. That, however, is a rather more difficult ploy to perform successfully in a 23-ton 12-Meter. Now we are making about 9½ knots, and still *Liberty* does not gain. Now the Major comes back onto the mainsheet grinder, working in close harmony with Beasho. Chink and Splash are down on the main winch, which controls the spinnaker, the port coffee-grinder drum. The staysail is trimmed to the boom, so what the mainsail does, the staysail does.

Up the first big wave we go. *Australia II* plows through the top. I head her off a fraction. "STAND BY!" yells Beasho. "PUMP!" The Major roars away at the mainsheet grinder, singlehandedly forcing the giant mainsail and the staysail to come in just six feet. Chink and Splash flail away at their winch, literally wrenching the spinnaker in until the seams are at breaking point—in effect, hauling the boat down the wave. We hit the trough at the bottom, split the next wave in half, shouldering the water off to the side, as I straighten the boat. All of our eyes are glued to the sea as we assess the next big oncoming wave. "Here she comes," I mutter. "STAND BY!" yells Beasho. "PU-U-U-MP!" Away go the Major, Chink, and Splash once more. I head *Australia II* off just a fraction as we drive down the wave, straightening her into the trough, smashing the next wave apart as we blaze down the second leg.

This is real seat-of-the-pants stuff. Grant is calling out our course and bearing, and I am trying to gauge the increase in speed against the loss of yards this zigzagging, highly instinctive power-reaching technique is gaining for us. All we know for sure is that *Liberty* is not sailing like this—she's too absorbed in her other problems—and we are definitely holding them off. The might of the American 12-Meter empire, with all of its millions, is right now being held at bay by Beasho, Mad Dog, and me—three hotshot dinghy sailors from little old Australia, working our arses off.

"WE'RE HOLDING 'EM, BOYS, WE'RE HOLDING THEM!" I shout down to the grinders, who are by now just about exhausted in their heavy foul-weather gear. Behind us, *Liberty* rolls on, and, unaccountably, Rasa's words run through my mind. "John, just remember that you have so far proved nothing. You are just the same as all the rest of them." Incensed by this piece of pure sacrilege, I tighten my grip on the wheel, aim *Australia II* hard down the next wave, and peer ahead through the spray to try to spot the jibe mark.

We've been racing down this leg for about 17 minutes now, and I can see the mark up ahead, closer than I thought it would be. "STAND BY TO LOWER THE STAYSAIL!" I shout, as I try to position *Australia II* perfectly for this tricky maneuver—one at which I have not been consistently brilliant. I head her up a fraction, aiming our bow at such an angle that we will sweep into the buoy on a nice, wide arc and then cut it tight as we come out, like a racing car on one of those tight turns in Monaco—except that this racing car weighs 23 tons and is 65 feet long. We are 50 yards from the mark now. "DROP THE STAYSAIL!" I yell, and Ya sends it fluttering to the foredeck. The Major is waiting, and he grabs it, stopping the tissuelike fabric from being seized by the voracious wind across our bow and being whipped into the sea. He makes no mistake. He thrusts it down the hatch into the safety of the sewer, all ready to be hauled up again in less than a minute's time. Damian unclips it just before it disappears, leaving the air clear for the spinnaker pole to come through.

We are coming into the mark very fast now. This is absolutely critical. Damian is up on the bow. Scoop is on the starboard side, Skippy on the port side controlling the angles of the spinnaker. Beasho is back in command of the mainsail, which is about to jibe right across the deck. "Heads down, boys. We're coming in now, still very fast." Beasho flails away on the grinder, hauling the mainsail over, doing it all himself now. We are into the mark still clocking 9½ knots. "POLE AFT! POLE AFT!" I bellow. I can see the Major up there, his mighty thumb on the trigger that will release the spinnaker pole. The winds are whipping my commands away, but the Major is watching me, reading my lips. "T-R-I-P!" I bawl into the wind, as I twist the wheel over. The Major releases the trigger right on time. The big, black carbon pole drops down into the bow. Damian is right there with the old "lazy sheet," which will now become the new brace. Like lightning, he clips the pole on, screaming at the top of his lungs, "P-O-O-O-O-LE!" so that everyone can hear. Chink and Splash lean into their grinder, hauling away at it, powering the spinnaker into its new set on the other side of the boat as we go across the wind. I'm just about in the middle of the turn right now. Beasho dives from the winch handles back to the coffee-grinder, releasing the main to swing right across to the port side with the wind. "JIBING!" I yell, releasing the steering wheel and grabbing the twin wheel on the port side as the boom comes over. The mainsail sets firm, as Colin still grapples with his controls. We have lost only a fraction of a knot, and the whole exercise has taken just about five seconds. "RAISE THE STAYSAIL!" I call, rather unnecessarily, because the Major is already flying out of the sewer with that light, critical piece of Mylar under his arm.

Another flurry of activity up on the foredeck and the staysail tightens. We are set fair for the third leg. Hughey is facing aft again, watching for the Americans to round. We were good, damned good, but here comes *Liberty*, and she's better. *Liberty*'s foredeck crew gets her around in fantastic shape. They must have gained a couple of seconds on us on that jibe. I glance back at them, noting their course, again thinking that I could have steered a slightly better course myself. Dennis has a marginal edge there, just a slicker bit of steering.

Grant confirms it. "They caught 10 feet there." "Clean up your act, Bertrand," I say to myself, before one of those impertinent characters says it for me. "She rounded still 23 seconds behind," says Hughey, "but they're a bit closer now."

Liberty has a man up the mast again at the level of that port spreader. There is no doubt they are still in some trouble, but I do not feel sorry for them, and on we sail, down the third leg, the big grinders again hauling in the sails every 20 or 30 seconds, whenever Beasho calls a big wave. Flashing through my mind are a hundred little pictures of those far-distant days when I used to race little boats using these same techniques. For one insane moment, I imagined looking over the side and seeing myself as I once was, leaning out over the water in a little Finn, planing past both *Liberty* and *Australia II,* with Conner, Whidden, Marshall, Hughey, Chink, and Scoop all speechless with admiration. Another thought comes to my mind as well. "John, just remember that you have so far proved nothing. You are just the same as the rest of them."

I put aside my fleeting daydreams and just keep sailing. I need every instinct I have to keep us rolling along at top speed. A big Twelve does not plane like the Finn. It surges through the water as you come off the wave, and the angle you need is very subtle indeed. However the wave breaks, you cannot go too far off your original course in order to maximize your speed; otherwise, the extra distance makes it not worth doing. There is no computer known to us to clarify the matter, either, and the only arbiter we have is my intuition, developed from years and years of planing top racing dinghies down the power reaches in international regattas.

These are conditions where we can work the boat hard, and we are like a bunch of wild men, hurling her through the water, surfing, shouting, using our best judgment, as we drive on to what we pray will be victory. It is at once exhilarating, nerve-racking, and very, very tough. No stealth and catlike cunning is required here—just daring, a touch of recklessness, and a sure hand on the wheel. As the boys haul the sails tight, I watch the bow, steely-eyed, spotting the vast tonnage of water as it threatens to break over the foredeck. We do not need that much weight and drag right now, so I kick her up a few degrees, skidding her away from the waves, driving into the trough at a slight angle, spearing most of the water to one side. At this high speed, *Australia II* steers beautifully with her big rudder, and I can just thread her like a needle through the most gentle slopes of the waters.

The boat has so little bustle (stern weight) that I can whip her along perfectly at 9 + knots, but when we develop a funny quarter wave under the stern going to windward, she can be a bitchy boat to steer, with a marked tendency to corkscrew. But on a fast-tracking power reach, *Australia II* is a very easy boat to move around.

We race on toward the next mark. Grant calls out our bearing. Hughey estimates we will hit the mark with a lead of 18 seconds. We have lost five seconds on this leg, but most of it came on the jibe. Essentially, we have held them, which is excellent performance, because they are longer on the waterline, so *Liberty* is subsequently a much faster power-reaching boat. In our first three races, she took an average of about 27 seconds off us on the second and third legs. The five seconds today suggests we continue to improve.

Now we are bowling on down to the third mark, before we turn once more into the wind. I shout for the crew to check everything—every line, halyard, and clip. "We're not having any screwups here, you guys," I yell, and the boys hustle around, making sure we are in top shape for the change. "OK! DROP THE STAYSAIL!" Ya looses her. The big code-three genoa is already in place on the foredeck, clipped up to the halyard by Damian. The Major grabs the staysail, hauls it out of the water with his tremendous strength, and packs it away down the hatch. He spins around, joins Ya on the jib halyard, and the two of them haul it up, hand over hand. I swing *Australia II* into her arc, once more like a racing car, aiming for the tight, hard turn around the buoy that will save us yards and seconds. "DROP THE SPINNAKER!" And down comes the big green-and-gold parachute, the Major and Damian clawing her in, dropping the pole, and unclipping the sheet. The Major jumps down in the hatch, dragging the sail behind him, landing on a dripping swamp of seawater and sails. He stays down there for a while, sorting it all out. Hughey calls, "Jibe onto a port tack, John." We both know this will coax *Liberty* onto starboard tack, her slower tack, as she rounds the mark. We will be waiting for her. Around comes *Liberty*, 18 seconds behind, as Grant forecast. Just a couple of boatlengths. Dennis throws her straight onto a starboard tack. Hughey says calmly, "There she goes, John. Tack the boat NOW!" Around we go, tacking on top of the red enemy, on her slow side. We have her now, and there's nothing they can do about it. At least not on this upwind leg. This is a classic covering situation, a nice little lesson for the armchair admirals. When *Liberty* tacks, we tack, and our hard cover stays slapped on them, Hughey calling it dead right every time.

This second upwind leg often proves vital in an America's Cup race, and now *Liberty* is trying everything. She changes her genoas twice, to no avail. Soon we notice that her lightweight medium-air mainsail is starting to deteriorate as the wind starts gusting to more than 20 knots. This probably has something to do with their wounded jumper strut, but I notice another aspect that should be considered. Our own genoas, vertically cut by the brilliant Schnacks, seem to have more range than the American ones. When the breeze changes, the optimum shape of the jib on *Australia II* is retained for a far longer time than that of our opponent. In fact, *Liberty* has been using a lot of crosscut sails, and it appears to us that she has had to change them much more often than we have.

Whatever, Dennis Conner and his boys have tried everything in their power to reel us in closer to them—but not today. We are driving *Australia II* farther and farther ahead. After we have been racing upwind for about a half hour, Grant Simmer makes a brilliant call. "We're approaching the layline, John," he calls. "Three boatlengths . . . two boatlengths . . . one boat length . . . NOW." Hughey calls, "TACK!" and I echo him. We swing onto the most superb starboard tack and sail to the mark in one go. It takes 13 minutes, and Grant must have been accurate to about two feet, considering the wind and tide. We are now one minute 11 seconds in the lead.

I call for our biggest spinnaker to drag us down the square run. "CODE FOUR, MAJOR!" I yell, and the boys pull off yet another super change. Now we face a power run, and I mention to Hughey that I will not be surprised if *Liberty,* with her longer waterline, grabs back a bit of time from us here. Any longer-waterline boat would be better on this square run with the high velocity, so all we can do is keep sailing, keep trying our best.

And now *Liberty* starts to roll up toward us. After eight minutes, Grant says, "She's caught five seconds." Hughey confirms, "Twenty feet, John." And the vision of our lead evaporating momentarily crosses my mind. Grant says, "Even if she improves like that all the way down here, we should not lose more than a boatlength." Hughey is inclined to agree with that, but I do not want to lose a foot—never mind a boatlength.

"John, just remember that you have so far proved nothing. You are just the same as the rest of them."

We have covered them all the way down here, and they have grabbed back 19 seconds, fairly predictably, but I am still very glad when the square run is over and we turn into the wind for the last time, still a handy 52 seconds in front. I decide to let the crew know they must stay on their toes, so I shout, "Facts, facts. Give me facts, not opinion!"

"If we don't screw this up," I disclose to Hughey, very quietly, "we've got 'em." "Yeah," says my tactician, "let's just cover the bastards tight." They change their genoas again, and then again. But it is like watching a fly in a spider's web. We have them now, and that is all there is to it. On the first beat to windward we had, on the book, a minute off them—more realistically, 50 seconds; on the second beat, we had 53 seconds; on this last one, we will have 55 seconds, which suggests a degree of consistency.

Grant again does a superb job of calling the final layline. He is saying, "Three boatlengths . . . two boatlengths . . . one boatlength. OK, we can conservatively make the line right now." I glance down at *Liberty,* about 100 yards to leeward, and I tack the boat for home. Hughey says, nonchalantly, "Hope their celebration champagne holds up all right. They might not need it tonight." We bowl along closehauled for the rest of the way, in no danger from our opponents.

The gun fires, and we all feel the same fantastic sense of relief that we have broken the back of this regatta. The difference between 3–1 and 3–2 is as wide as the Nullarbor Desert. We have turned the tide, stopped the rot, improved the boat—choose your metaphor. We have fought for it, all the way, and we all feel the most tremendous feeling of self-satisfaction. We have proved that we could do it—proved we could come back against all odds. Let's face it, if we can win this one after my antics at the start, we can probably win anything.

The kangaroo with the boxing gloves flew up the mast, and all around us, thousands of well-wishers on boats were going wild with celebration. The Major looked up at me without a smile and just said, "Great job, John." And somehow that meant a hell of a lot to me. I stared out at the onrushing fleet, looking for Rasa. Finally, I spotted her on a boat in the middle of a huge sea of waving arms. A great friend of ours from home, Noel Simmens, was standing next to her, his fist in the air, openly weeping at the wonder of our achievement. I wanted to yell out to Rasa, "I'M NOT JUST LIKE THE BLOODY OTHERS, AM I?" But from 50 yards away, I knew that she was aware of my every thought. She was not waving at me, nor was she saying anything. She was just leaning out over the bow, gazing at me, with a little smile on her face. I have rarely felt so close to her.

Almost half a century had passed since a challenging skipper had taken two races in *Endeavour* from Mike Vanderbilt's *Rainbow*. The time before that was in 1920, when Sir Thomas Lipton's *Shamrock IV,* which my great-grandpa helped to prepare in England, had the first two races off the great Charles Adams's *Resolute.*

Now the whole world seemed to be arriving around our boat, but none of us felt like being congratulated. The last thing I wanted was to have my back slapped. We felt that we were in the middle of a fight, not at the end of it. Bondy, in much the same mood I was in, rushed up to me. Very tough, steely, and determined. "What about tomorrow, John?" he asked. "Do you wanna race?" "Hell, yes," I said. "Let's not screw around. Let's stay right in it. Keep going." "OK, let's race," he said. "Hoist the flag." The Americans now had crossed the line, and soon they acknowledged that they, too, would race. It was thus on for the next day, *Australia II* vs. *Liberty,* in Race 6 of America's 25th Defense of the Cup. The date would be September 22, and we would either even the score at 3–3 or they would send us home in defeat.

We decided to ride back on the boat together, but first I found Lucas, standing on the upper deck of *Black Swan*, wearing what his mother describes as "that huge Bertrand grin." I got him on board *Australia II* for the long ride back to the harbor, but I am afraid Dad went below to join the rest of the exhausted crew for an hour's sleep on the sopping-wet sails. *Australia II* was escorted by a churning fleet of spectator boats and flanked by two big Coast Guard launches, their huge blue lights flashing brightly as we headed for the dock. Just before I went below, I did remember that members of the press were always griping that I never smiled and waved at them for photographs, so I turned and smiled and waved.

It was not until we approached the first landfall, Castle Hill, that it dawned on me what we had done. We were dozing, rather unattractively hot in our gear in the wet, musty atmosphere of the Major's hell hole, when someone yelled down, "You guys, come up here and see this." Massed on the Castle Hill lawn, and all along the shore to Hammersmith Farm, were thousands and thousands of supporters of *Australia II*. Some of them were Americans, embarrassed by the antics of the New York Yacht Club, whose celebration we had summarily wrecked out there today. As the sun went down over the ocean, leaving a blood-red reflection on the waves, we left behind a legacy of determination and achievement. The NYYC left behind a trail of colored balloons, which had been intended to help in the festivities but now trailed pitifully, forlornly in the water. The action was right now at Castle Hill, and before we could even emerge from the hatch, we could hear the huge noise rising from the shore as we drew near. It was a mighty, swelling sound, the sound of the Australian Outback, the breathtaking sounds of a massive impromptu choir sending the words of Banjo Paterson roaring across the water and to the heavens and beyond.

WALTZING MATILDA, WALTZING MATILDA,
YOU'LL COME A-WALTZING MATILDA WITH ME.
AND HE SANG AS HE LOOKED AT HIS OLD BILLY BOILING,
WHO'LL COME A-WALTZING MATILDA WITH ME?

But we did not feel we had done anything to warrant this ecstasy. We had come to make real history. Not mini-history.

Back at the dock, an enormous flotilla of boats bobbed alongside us— big boats, little boats, Fiberglas boats, rubber boats, motorboats, rowing boats, canoes, windsurfers, rafts, dinghies—stopping and stalling, bumping and boring. People were waving the Australian flag, shouting, cheering, drinking, singing, and falling into the harbor. The spectators packed on Bondy's *Southern Cross* were loudly massacring Banjo's haunting melody. And Bondy, in a moment of overwhelming goodwill, had thrown open our doors and let the press on our dock, which was listing precariously as we arrived. There must have been more than a thousand television, newspaper, and magazine men standing there. I'm mildly surprised that half of them did not slip off and drown. Everywhere there were cameras, microphones, recorders, lights, cables, men with notebooks, men with cassettes, men with big control boxes bursting with electronics. There were people shouting, complaining, demanding, panicking, cheering, questioning, questioning. "John, John, how do you feel?" "John, is this the biggest moment of your life?" "John, how did you feel at the start?" "Did you think you had lost it?" "Did you know you're the first skipper to win two races in half a century?" In the gathering gloom and burgeoning bedlam, I could see but two things of any importance. Rasa was at the gate trying to drag Rupert Murdoch, Australia's newspaper tycoon, past the guards— "Let him in, he's my friend"—and Cathy, our babysitter, was standing next to the boat with our two youngest children, Andre and Sunshine. Through all of this chaos, I walked over to Andre past a forest of microphones. "JOHN! JOHN! HOW DID IT FEEL WHEN YOU BLEW THE START?" "JOHN! HOW DOES IT FEEL TO HAVE MADE HISTORY?" "JOHN! JOHN! JOHN!" All I cared about was shy little Andre standing there in the middle of this mob. I leaned over and said to him, very softly, as I always did when he came home from school, "Hello, Andre, tell Daddy how school went today. What was the best thing you did?" The next day a couple of the reporters told me that just about blew everyone away, but we all have to do what is important to us. Then Rasa finally pushed her way through the crowd. We had already said a thousand words to each other across the water, without speaking, two hours before. I gave her a hug and asked her if she "would go and talk to the damned press" while I talked to Andre and Sunshine.

This may have been my second major tactical error of the afternoon, for Rasa was at the time feeling rather cheerful after a couple of fairly substantial glasses of champagne, a brew that is inclined to make her just a bit carefree. Apparently about 40 journalists, practically in unison, asked her how she felt, and Rasa used a rather graphic old Australian expression that, broadly interpreted, meant that she did not particularly care about the future of *Liberty*. It seems that she had not so much uttered this phrase as shouted it, and she rushed up to me 10 minutes later, full of remorse. "John! John! I've done something awful. I've said something dreadful on television—there were about a hundred different 'bleeps' going off at once to blank me out." When she told me the actual phrase she had used, I told her that was not too bad to be used either on television or in the papers. Later, however, I did dispatch a member of the *Australia II* press office and resident diplomatic corps, just to make sure. This was largely at

Skippy's insistence. He came rushing up to me about the incident, torn between hysterical laughter and genuine concern for Rasa's dignity. The two of them are great pals, and he managed to say to me very seriously, "I think we should tell someone in P.R., just in case they have a real go at her." "What exactly did she say?" I asked, eager for a second opinion. "Well . . ." he said, and then he just collapsed with laughter. He was laughing so hard that I had to help him off the boat.

I found Schnacks and Kenny Beashel and talked to Hughey. The new recut genoa had been superb, and we all thought that when the pictures came up from the darkroom in an hour's time, they would show that we were in very good shape. That night, for the very first time in months and months, we would not recut *one* of *Australia II*'s sails.

I gathered up the family, arranged for them all to meet me at the house, and went off with Rasa and Bondy for the press conference. It had been a very brilliant tactical race for us, and I looked around for Hughey to join us, but then I could not find him. We struggled through the crowd and into the Armory, where about a thousand of the media's finest awaited us. I joined Bondy and Warren at the official table and let them field the questions. Attendance from the *Liberty* camp was off about 95 percent. The image of the Superboat remained intact, and the problem with *Liberty*'s broken jumper strut was high on their priority list. I did tell them that I blew the start and that the crew got me out of it. "They did a superhuman job," I said.

It is strange how you remember certain things about major events. But I recall glancing up toward the rear of the hall, where a large mob of lesser journalists and hangers-on was standing. And amid this crowd, toward the back, stood the tall, unsmiling figure of Hughey Treharne, with his baby, Robbie, in his arms. He was too shy to come up to the official table, where he belonged. When I thought of all the people grabbing and clawing for the reflected vicarious glory that our victory had provided, it seemed somehow incongruous that there should be such total obscurity for my richly talented tactician, who had given so much.

Now the press would go off and record that the crippled *Liberty* had been unable to contain the Wonder from Down Under. And secure in the knowledge that the crew would be given little or no credit, I headed for Dennison Street, up the old white staircase, past the torn wallpaper, to help get the kids into their pajamas and give them their supper before Rasa and I went off to Founders' Hall.

It was, as always, a rather formal dinner that night. We always dressed properly, falling somewhere short of dinner jackets but a long way up from ordinary sailing gear. That night, Warren Jones made an excellent speech to the boys, telling them how greatly he and Bondy appreciated their titanic efforts that day, and bringing them back to earth steadily, reminding them of the ensuing battle, that our struggle was not yet over, that there was so much to be done before we left this place.

I was very brief. I thanked everyone formally and reiterated the "win today" theme I had extolled that morning. "We must continue to take each day as it comes. I do not want anyone to start thinking that if we win tomorrow the score will be 3–3. If we lose tomorrow, they will send us home. Gentlemen, let us just go out and win the boat race tomorrow."

The atmosphere had changed somewhat from the previous evening. There was a mood of optimism, and the boys clearly felt that this trophy was within their grasp. Rasa told me on the way home, "I think they believe they are unbeatable." Rasa's opinions about the thoughts of the crew were always worth listening to, because she was a real friend to them. I had noticed that when we docked that afternoon, she went up to every one of them and kissed them and said they had done a "totally fantastic job." In so many ways, she was an extension of me, and, for the boys, *her* delight and congratulations were mine. During our preparations in Melbourne, many of them had stayed with us for weeks at a time. We were a tightly knit fighting unit, and the job that Rasa did for us in Newport, keeping this spirit strong among us, was a unique achievement. None of the men in our administration could possibly have acted as the friend and confidante that Rasa was to this crew. With people like Grant Simmer, she was nothing short of wonderful. Young Grant, with the cares of the world upon his shoulders, his mind churning away throughout all of his waking hours and probably his sleeping ones too, had much responsibility. Not one of them cared. But Rasa did, and I remember thinking, as we arrived at Founders' Hall that night, that Newport '83 was probably Rasa's finest hour. Her contribution was priceless, and she kept that *Australia II* "family" together throughout our stay. She always had time to talk to the boys, and somehow they would talk to her and discuss their problems. As for the girls, well, I think some of them *would* have had nervous breakdowns without her.

Before dinner that night, I noticed Rasa circulating among the crew, telling them the things that I had said. Telling them that I thought they were the best ever. Making each one of them feel as I had felt when Major Peter Costello turned to me at the end of the race and just said, "Great job, John." Each of these iron-willed men on the boat had the same amount of sensitivity and need for praise as the rest of us. Sometimes it was very difficult for me to do this as their skipper, the man charged with the responsibility of preparing them for battle, getting them charged up. But Rasa, quietly and subtly, could do it, conveying to them my appreciation for their efforts, treating them as members of the Bertrand family—

which, in a very powerful way, they all very much were. And because of that momentous struggle we fought together, in a sense they always will be.

We returned home, and Rasa made me hot milk and gave me a mild tranquilizer, as was usual these days. I listened to John Denver for a while, but before we went to sleep, Rasa reminded me once more that she had been thinking about me fiercely out there that afternoon. She had been thinking of all of the lessons of Jonathan Livingston Seagull, how I had strived for so long, like him, to find perfection, to have this boat sailed as it would be in the year 2000—as perhaps Lucas or Andre would one day expect to sail. She said that she was concentrating so hard on what she knew I had to do out there that she felt almost as if she were in a trance, as if there were no other people in the world except the two of us. She was concentrating so hard, trying to let me know, as Jonathan had done, that there are no limits, that perfection does not recognize limits, in speed or anything else. It was as if Rasa herself were The Great Gull, trying to help me expand my mind and my horizons to where I knew there were no limits, that our boat could slide away to its destiny, if only I could feel free to sail as I had practiced for such a terribly long time.

C H A P T E R

19

"We Are the Best in the World"

Hughey shouts, "Take her stern!" We duck underneath, gasping for clean air. At that moment, Dennis Conner should have slapped that cover hard on us again, but he was late. "She's late, she's late. Thank God, she's late."

Septenber 22. A bright, sunny Thursday morning. DING DING DING DING! "ORDER, ORDER!" Warren Jones steeled himself for the normal schoolboyish outburst from the crew of *Australia II*. "Gentlemen, it is now 17½ minutes to eight o'clock, and as you know, we have an America's Cup race to sail today."

He glanced down at his notes, poised for the morning torrent of abuse and derision that traditionally greeted these pedantic facts. But there was only silence, except perhaps for the steady munching of Splash and Ya, heavily into their second plates of bacon and eggs. Grant Simmer was too preoccupied to listen. He had his diagrams spread out before him in preparation for a couple of new computer fittings he had to attach before we sailed.

Today Warren Jones faced a group of men who had collectively aged several years since first he ran into those good-humored Aussie jesters happily yelling, "Rubbish, Warren!" "Can't you even tell the time?" "What do you mean, America's Cup? Who's in it?" Personally, I had aged about 10 years since the previous week. Together these superbly fit yachtsmen from Down Under had been to the precipice, slipped over the edge, and clawed and scrambled their way back up from the very fires of hell. They had coped with the highs and the lows. They had taken the most staggering setbacks, body blow after body blow. Yet we were still here—knocked about, shaken, and, in many ways, the most battle-hardened America's Cup crew there has ever been. From the triumph of the day before, through all of the exultation of our supporters, we really felt only one emotion. We were damned glad to be alive, to still have a chance. I don't care who you are—when you have been through something like this, so very publicly, you are not the same. It changes you terribly, I suspect forever.

On this day, as Warren read out the morning's order of business, there was not much flippancy. We were, each of us, deadly serious. Today, September 22, was not a day for laughter, or complacency, or even self-pride. This was the day when we must stand up and be counted.

We sat there, unsmiling, each man grappling with his own thoughts, waiting to hear the weather forecast of Sir James Hardy, to whom Warren relinquished the floor with his customary flourish. "Over to you, Sir James. . . ." The knight from South Australia stood up slowly, wished us all a formal good morning, and then revealed to us precisely what I did not wish to hear. "It will probably be overcast today," he said, "and there will be an offshore breeze of some 12 to 16 knots." Those are the most tricky conditions in Newport, with the breeze gusting off the land, shifty, sometimes moderating, sometimes not. For a start, it meant the course would move around so that we would have to face the same water through which the vast spectator fleet had just plowed. *Australia II* hates that Newport slop, and today it would probably be like sailing in a bloody dishwasher out there. Second, the winds were forecast to be medium, which meant that *Liberty* would be at her best on all three of the upwind legs, and certainly on the two power reaches. Third, in these conditions there is a large element of fickleness and luck, and we would have our share of the bad as well as the good. But it is always a terribly emotional race in conditions where the wind keeps shifting. Through no fault of your own, you can suddenly find yourself slipping behind, watching an opponent who has done nothing whatsoever to deserve a lead suddenly get one, while you fall behind helplessly.

I rose to my feet, conscious that there could be no repeat of that disastrous slump that had followed our victory on the previous weekend. I was not worried, because I sensed the hard, determined professionalism around me. "Gentlemen," I said, "we are the best in the world. Everyone here is the very best at what he does. There is no reason for anyone to question himself or his worth or his ability to deliver the goods today. We are going to level the score at 3–3."

I arrived at the Australian dock before 8:30 that morning. There were already hundreds of people milling around. It occurred to me that newsrooms and television stations around the world must be very nearly deserted, since every journalist on earth seemed to be watching the impending departure of *Australia II*. Still, I suppose most wars get fairly extensive coverage. As I arrived, I saw a well-known Australian yachtsman, Gordon Ingate, the owner of *Gretel II*. As usual he was wearing his natty American boater, around which was the hated colored ribbon of the New York Yacht Club—of which he is, I believe, the only Australian member. I cannot describe how his inflammatory headgear irritated the boys on *Australia II*. To us it was a symbol of high treason—suggesting, in a way, that not all Australians really were for us. He is a strange man, Ingate, but we hated him for that bloody boater of his. I was surprised to see him walking past our dock en route to join his friends, to watch us from an American boat on which there would be *Liberty* syndicate members. Because a few days earlier there had been an interesting confrontation at the very spot I now observed him walking. Bondy, muttering something like "You treasonous bastard," had marched up to him, ripped the offensive boater from his head, flung it into a puddle, and jumped up and down on it three times, before picking it up and banging it back on the Aussie's head, battered and dripping muddy water down his face. That is how high feelings were running right now, and here he was again, walking past the dock, in a brand-new New York Yacht Club boater, in my opinion taking his life in his hands.

I walked on through the crowd. An Australian lady, with a handkerchief held to her eyes, said, "Godspeed, John," as I walked past. I smiled at her, but said nothing.

I spoke to Hughey, Schnacks, and Kenny Beashel on the dock about the wind. It was already gusting from the land, nearly directly from the north, cool, right out of Canada. This was going to be a real test, because it would certainly moderate, and a dying breeze has more shifts, more fluctuations, and many more variables in direction. We have to be prepared for anything, for any shocks. And we have to be like granite emotionally, because things are going to happen out there, suddenly, unpredictably, and probably unreasonably. We have to be prepared to accept it all—the changes and the setbacks—and rebound again hard, striking back as soon as the opportunity presents itself.

The Major was on deck preparing the two massive mainsails, our me-dium- and heavy-air "engines," for a fair bit of breeze. Our final sail selec-tion was made, and he had much to do, packing up our inventory of eight spinnakers, making ready the huge genoas, unloading the sails we would not need. Grant had been on board for ages, surrounded by his computer-repairing tools and instruments. Chink, our great strength in the middle of the boat, was helping the Major—checking the winches, the lines, and the coffee-grinders, telling people what to do in a voice that suggested that any second opinion was essentially inapplicable. Scoop and Skippy were chuckling about the Führer as they checked their sheets over and over. Beasho, with a winch handle in his hands, was testing each and every one of his myriad of hydraulic controls, checking over the areas that take the massive stresses, the very same ones his own father had passed as A-1 earlier that morning. Up on the foredeck, Damian, within a few hours of his 21st birthday, was tidying his little area, checking clips, guys, and the spinnaker pole. Ya worked away at his own steady speed in the bird-bath, hauling on halyards, making sure there could never be even the semblance of a tangle. Every inch of *Australia II*, every working part, was checked again and again. Every inch would be fail-safe before we cleared the dock this morning. Hughey and I, meanwhile, stood watching the water, discussing the wind, and chatting about a nasty little robbery we had suffered during the night. Someone had stolen two hand-held radios, the walkie-talkies we used to contact our spies up the course, to find out about the wind before the start. These had been replaced, but there were also reports of a frogman having been sighted underneath our boat in the small hours. He had escaped, and, of course, the Americans were denying any knowledge of such an outrage.

Hughey stepped on board just before I did. Kenny Beashel pulled me aside, gave me a big wink, and, almost under his breath, surreptitiously, said in a confiding voice, "Johnny, you're going to do it today. I've got the feeling in my bones. Now just get out there and whip 'em. Keep your eyes on the water, play the shifts, and we'll be all square when you come home tonight." That, from one of Australia's greatest natural seat-of-the-pants sailing champions, set me up for the battle. I slapped him on the shoulder and stepped on board *Australia II*. It was no time for me to be jittery, for the quirky conditions out there would require nerves of steel. I was sure we could do it, if we could just get this temperamental boat going in the slop out there beyond the Brenton Reef Light.

All around us, we could feel the good wishes of our supporters as we prepared to cast off. The crowd was grim as they clapped us away, almost as if they, too, had arrived at the conclusion we had reached on the pre-vious joyous evening. That we were in the middle of a fight, not at the end of it. The kangaroo with the boxing gloves hit the high point of the forestay. Men at Work gave it their all, and, as we were towed out into the harbor behind *Black Swan,* there was a steady, deep-throated symphony of boat horns. We were on our way. As we reached the harbor wall off Fort Adams, I called a crew meeting, and we all sat around the wheel in a small, tight circle. Scoop was steering, ever alert for a chance meeting with 20th Century-Fox, and I began my little speech by saying, "*Australia II* is not just sailed by the afterguard—Hughey, Grant, and myself. She is sailed by every one of you. And I want every one of you totally involved from the time the 10-minute gun goes to the moment the gun goes, for us, as we cross the winning line. If any day has ever been sent to test us, this is the one; no one on board has ever sailed a more important race and the breeze is going to be a bitch. It will be random and variable. It will test what we are made of, how strong we are, how mentally tough, and whether we have the ability to hit back. Conditions are the same as they were in Race 2, when each of you performed fantastically, nothing less. Today that offshore wind may be a little stronger, but we are also a little stronger, and, if necessary, I will require an effort from everyone that may have to surpass even those supreme hours of sailing you produced when we could not hoist the mainsail. We are capable of being quicker than they are, and more flexible, and I must have those trained eyes of some of you. Of course I mean Ya and Beasho, Skippy and Scoop, watching the water for me, spotting the wind. Eleven minds will always outthink one, so I must have total concentration. And remember, as usual, give me facts, not opinions. If there is a windshift, it is no less the responsibility of Damian to see it than it is Ya's or Hughey's or Grant's or mine. Feedback. Feedback. Feedback. We are a total democracy on this boat, and no one is any less important than anyone else. If any one of you falters, or loses interest, however briefly, that could quite easily see the whole lot of us on the 3:45 afternoon plane for Sydney tomorrow. If we sail as I know we can, then those fellows who sail the red boat are going to be feeling suicidal by around five o'clock tonight. Someone once made a very telling remark about sportsmen and soldiers and statesmen. I forget who it was, but the words are clear in my mind, 'Great men and great teams do great things at great moments.' Gentlemen, one day someone will say that, and the team he will have in mind will be this one."

Most of us slept down below on the way out to the racecourse, and at a quarter to eleven, I radioed to *Challenge 12* to hoist her code-three genoa. We hoisted the identical sail and set off together for our final warm-up before Race 6. The chop was just as bad as I had suspected it would be. In fact, it was probably worse—very confused, short, mismatched waves churned up by the big powerboats that had already arrived to watch us. I wondered if they knew how vulnerable this water made us. It was exactly like a washing machine, with waves swiping us at all angles. Crash! Bang! Bump! All the way. *Australia II* was corkscrewing her way along, that light shallow stern of hers swinging back and forth against the quarter waves. She was now very difficult to sail, I didn't have a lot of tracking ability, the water was whipping the boat around, and I was using a lot of corrective helm. Whenever this happens and I have to keep pushing her back on course, it means we are out of tune and we are going slowly. It happened constantly on Port Phillip Bay in these conditions. And sure enough, *Challenge 12* immediately blew us away. I called to Colin, "I really need your help here. That mainsail cannot be overtrimmed. Let's just twist the sail a bit more and de-power it. I'm using way too much helm and trim tab to correct it." I shouted down to Scoop and Skippy on the genoa, "You guys, we really have to work our way through the water, because I can tell you the damned boat is really difficult to steer today." Crash! Bang! Bump! *Australia II* was at her worst, swinging around at the stern. *Challenge* was leaving us for dead, because she is a conventional boat with more bustle behind and much more directional stability. I fought with the helm to keep her straight in the sea, and again I yelled above the wind, "Look, you guys, I'm relying on you to get this boat through the water. Ease the trim, get more twist to the sail. Let's ease the jib and the mainsail in unison, working the sails together. Let's try to get into a real rhythm here . . . EASE! RETRIM! REBALANCE! Just so she starts to track in a straight line."

Meanwhile, *Challenge* blew us away again. Badly. *Challenge 12*, with just a hack, makeshift crew, was faster, just when we absolutely knew that *Liberty* was going to be very, very competitive. The jubilation of the previous night was rapidly retreating into a distant corner of my mind. This was down-to-the-wire stuff, and I knew better than anyone that we were in dangerous waters. We started to work the sails as we made our final runs before the race began. Slowly we began to get to *Challenge*, to hold her and finally to draw away. The turnaround was dramatic, a bit too dramatic, and it flashed through my mind that Jim Hardy was going a little easy on us, skillfully instilling some extra confidence in us before the battle. To this day, I do not know whether or not that was so. I have never wanted to ask, but I was suspicious then, and I always will be. On our very last run, we blew *Challenge* away. I wondered to myself again, would I have done the same? I think I would, because if I had been in Jim's place, I would have been doing anything I could to help, and no one on earth wanted us to beat *Liberty* more than Sir James Hardy. He was for us all the way, and in particular, he was for me. I trust he does not think I missed that secret little smile he threw me before we peeled off to face *Liberty* without him.

Challenge 12 sailed closehauled up the left-hand side of the course to "weathercock" the route for us. We were not yet certain which way we would race, but by now our spies in the little boats, led by the effervescent Robbie Brown—he of the deafening wake-up winch handle—were firing back information on our private radio-wave band. Our sign calls and codes were straight out of some sheep-shearing station. Robbie sounded like Saltbush Bill, King of the Overland, when he hit the airwaves, "Jabberoo, Jabberoo, Jabberoo to Snakebite. From where I'm camped, she blows steady out to the right, 335 degrees." In our code for the day, this meant the breeze was stronger on the left at 350 degrees. Grant would come in, the jackeroo of the cockpit, "Snakebite, Snakebite to Jabberoo, we have your message. Didjeridu, camped a quarter of a mile to your port beam, agrees with you." Then we would hear crackling away from another whaler, "Didjeridu, Didjeridu to Snakebite. We like the breeze to the right."

It was clear to us that the breeze was coming in bands, and, judging by the way *Challenge* had just seen us off, we were sure it was going to be the left. Then Jabberoo and Didjeridu came in again, swearing it was better to the left, and Ya was inclined to agree, so the only conclusion we could arrive at was that the breeze was coming in waves of air across Rhode Island Sound. *Tricky* was no longer the word for this day—it was going to be bloody treacherous. What was right at this point would be utterly incorrect five minutes later. I called to the boys, "It is going to be difficult out here, and we have to sail with our heads right out of the boat, watching that wind every second in case she shifts."

I called to Ya and said to him, "Ya, old mate, this is it. If you were born for any reason whatsoever, and that reason should include sailing on *Australia II* today, then your role in life was preordained. You *must* find the wind for us today. I want your eyeballs locked to the horizon for hour after hour, searching for the wind." He looked at me and replied, slowly, "Ya . . . ya." Then he smiled and laconically stuck his two thumbs in the air. That was his signal for "mission understood and will proceed optimistically." He also spoke again. "Ya," he added. He could never be described as verbally demonstrative, except when making a string of daft remarks in more unpressured moments. But at this point, he was thinking carefully. At his own pace, of course. Very deliberate, very reliable.

Beasho by now was so locked into his own hydraulic controls that he was almost in a private trance. He was shouldering a huge responsibility, and if I was not careful, he would become too preoccupied to speak. "Beasho," I said quietly, "I want you firing back information to me as you think of it. I want the same thoughts from you that you would be giving to yourself if you were sailing that Laser of yours on the first beat of the

Australian Nationals." Today's race had nothing to do with instrumentation. This was purely a matter of figuring the wind on the water and figuring out short-term and long-term plans for where we should have our little boat placed on the racetrack. This was a seat-of-the-pants day, and the boat with the best natural sailors was going to win it. There was a breeze trying to make from the sea, and there was also some land breeze from the right. It was as erratic as it could get.

Hughey stood beside me—quiet, reflective, a study in calmness, the supreme racing strategist. Behind that silent, expressionless face was a yachtsman's brain, and I always knew that at moments like this, it was whirring at about 100 miles an hour. His eyes, as fierce as those of a hawk, were fixed on the waves.

Soon we were down at the killing ground, preparing to face *Liberty*. We could see her out to weather. We trimmed the sails, down at the leeward end, and I headed *Australia II* up to meet *Liberty*. Dennis swung the American boat down toward us. There were still five minutes to go before the 10-minute gun, and we ran on down toward each other. Just as we crossed, I glance over at Dennis, and he looked directly at me. Neither of us smiled, and neither of us nodded. I raised my right hand in a formal wave to him. He did the same. It was too cold and impersonal to represent a declaration of war. It was more of a battle signal, purely to acknowledge impending combat. The tension between us was no less than atomic. Both boats were silent as we passed, and we were careful not to display a hint of intimidation. Perhaps three of the boys who happened to be facing that way looked over at *Liberty;* the others just had their backs to her, and kept them there.

High above us, there seemed once more to be hundreds of press helicopters and low-flying planes making the most desperate noise in the sky. Cameras from all over the world were whirring in our direction. There were more than 1,500 boats churning around, jockeying for position. The television audience was hovering somewhere near the 500-million mark. Back home at Mum's house, my little family would be huddled around the television, drinking coffee, or, if they had any brains, something stronger, listening to Mum telling everyone that it will be all right. "John'll win today, don't you worry." I could just hear her. The little house on Bristol Avenue, number 22, swathed in moonlight on the shores of Port Phillip Bay, behind the old bathing hut where Lex and I first put to sea. It is absolutely amazing, the fleeting thoughts that flash through your mind when the pressure you face seems too great for a normal person to bear.

The 10-minute gun crashes out over the pandemonium of the choppers above. The Major hits the stopwatch. "Got it, John," he calls, and I glance up to the bow to see Chink and Damian standing up there like two sentinels. I wheel *Australia II* around and head down toward *Liberty*. Dennis does the same, and we come at each other like two disagreeable predators. I come snarling in at them on starboard tack, quivering with aggression. Right now, I'll fight anybody. Dennis swings away, jibes, circles. "Steady, John," says Hughey, as we drive at them again. *Liberty* slips away, tacks, and circles again, and I round on them once more, slightly misjudge it, tack away, and come back at them again. With about three minutes to go, I suddenly realize that I'm too aggressive, too hot, my adrenaline has just bubbled over. I'm not thinking clearly enough, I'm too uptight, and I am in a situation in which we no longer control the start, even though we have the more maneuverable boat. This is ridiculous, but *Liberty* has the control position, and for the *third* race in a row, I have not dominated the start. In Race 4, I misjudged it and gave it away. In Race 5, I misjudged it and gave it away. In Race 6, I have now somehow contrived to give it away again.

Dennis and I are worthy opponents by international standards, but at this particular moment, I still feel like a complete fool. It might be worth remembering, however, that in this kind of boat race, Dennis is so good that he could probably stop 99 percent of all big-boat racers from ever crossing the starting line—never mind staying with him competitively. "Christ, Hughey," I said, "I have just made fools of us again."

Australia II is on port tack, and *Liberty* is blocking our way to the line. I know that if we stay on this port tack behind *Liberty,* we might not even fetch the line. Hughey, still expressionless, says, "Tack the boat, John, we're better on starboard. He'll cover us, but we can't stay here like this." So we tack with him all the way to the line, clipping his stern every time by about three feet. It is not a bad bit of precision tacking, as a matter of fact, but the circumstances are lousy, and eventually we hit the starting line about 10 feet behind them, with the red boat battering her way into the wind, closehauled on starboard tack.

We tack back onto starboard, right onto his weather hip. One of the boys calls out, "He had seven seconds on us there, John," but not one of the experienced sailors on *Australia II* seems to care about this small amount of distance. But I do. I care terribly. Dennis Conner has done a superb job, outgunning me totally. Perhaps only he really understands how decisive that clash was, but right now he is probably too busy to give the matter much serious thought.

For someone as unashamedly in search of personal perfection as I am, right now I need a fair amount of improvement, and I curse myself roundly for my moderate performance. Then I jerk back to reality and say, "OK, boys, this is really tricky now. Let's just get it together." Beasho, without even glancing up, says quietly, "About time, too." You cannot beat democracy on a big racing boat, and the remark was timed perfectly, but I still thought it was a bit bloody rude from someone who is only 24 years old. Wait till he gets it wrong.

And now, after that sobering blast of cold air from one of the most impertinent mainsheet hands in the business, I aim *Australia II* into this short choppy sea. BANG! THUMP! CRASH! On we go, our stern swinging around, Beasho working the controls fiercely. Dennis starts to tack back toward us. "He'll cross our bow about a boatlength in front," calls Hughey. *Liberty* sails on, cleaving her way through the sea, a big red machine being sailed very beautifully. Then she tacks again, right on top of us, crossing us again, the same distance in front, with a tight cover on us. Suddenly Ya calls out slowly, "The breeze freshens out to the left, John." Hughey glances over. "Tack her onto starboard, John," he shouts, "and take her stern." I wheel *Australia II* right across the wind and we duck underneath, gasping for clean air. At that moment, Dennis Conner should have slapped that cover hard on us again, but he was late. He sails on for another 120 feet, while Hughey and the boys and I hoof it for the breeze Ya has spotted out to the left. The red boat tacks in a vain search for a safe weather position on us, but she's late, she's late. Thank God, she's late. "COME ON, BOYS," I roar. "LET'S GO! WORK THOSE SAILS. GIVE IT EVERYTHING YOU HAVE. EASE! RETRIM! RE-BALANCE!"

We are now separated by about 130 feet—*Liberty* up to weather and aft of us—and slowly, inexorably, we start to eke out from underneath them, kicking along on this high starboard-tack lift. To our absolute amazement, we are faster, which is impossible, since we hate the conditions and we have just been burned off by *Challenge.* Either they are doing something appalling or we are doing something wonderful, I'm not sure which. In a fleeting second I understand what is happening. *Australia II* is being sailed perfectly by this crew. Every single one of them is using precisely 100 percent of his ability—hitting the straps, as we say. It is categorically not possible to sail a Twelve better than the boys are doing at this moment. Ecstatically, in these tricky conditions, we head over to the left, gaining, gaining, losing a bit, gaining again. It is like watching a miracle right before my eyes. It would not even surprise me if Splash jumped over the side and walked on the water without making a ripple. What cannot happen is actually happening. *Australia II*, in this wind, is slower than *Liberty,* and in this sea she is even slower. Those are facts, indisputable. Winged keels do not suddenly start working halfway through a race right out of the blue, in the kind of wicked joggle that this boat has always detested.

There is but one explanation—crew work, seamanship, nothing more, nothing less.

"Am I seeing things or are we actually blowing the bastards out of the water?" I ask Hughey. "We are actually blowing the bastards out of the water," he confirms, and we're doing it in conditions we have never before been able to handle. Into the joggle we crash. I'm just about to say, "We're corkscrewing again," but Beasho feels it, eases the mainsail an inch and a half; Skippy feels it, eases the genoa in unison. We slide back on track, and Beasho, Skippy, and Splash haul in the big sails an inch and a half. This is poetry, pure poetry. If Jonathan Livingston Seagull had swooped low above us, he would probably have nosedived in disbelief. We are totally unrecognizable from the crew that practiced in Australia, unrecognizable from the men who arrived in Newport nearly four months ago.

And the glory of it, as we slide away, watching the Americans slip behind on our weather hip, gives us a psychological boost nearly unprecedented in my experience. "We continue to increase bearing on her," calls Hughey. I glance back. Less than 30 feet between us as we power our way forward inch by inch, a gain of about half a boatlength in 10 minutes—a massive amount in a straight-line drag race such as this. *Liberty*, heavier as she is, should have clobbered us in this sea, just as *Challenge* did. But she cannot do it, not against this crew. On we go into that sea, the spray flying as we crash across the water, Skippy's right hand, out to the side, signaling tiny fractions with his fingers; Splash, his great sausagelike pinkies wrapped around the winch handle, doing precisely as Skippy commands. Not a word between them: a great bear and a study in obedience. Nor does Beasho speak as we struggle forward. There is but one sound on the boat above the CRASH! THUMP! BANG! of the sea. "Seven point six, seven point six, seven point five, up point two, John, up point two, John."

Now we hit some flatter water. "She's tracking better now," I call, and simultaneously Beasho grinds in the sail, Skippy signals, and I head her up a fraction. We're all steering the boat together. Now there are waves again. Beasho and Skippy ease her off, get her moving, giving her air, letting me come up 1½ tenths of a knot. "Seven point six five, seven point six five, seven point seven. That's good, John. Seven point seven." I mutter to Hughey, "This crew is hot." Our speed is explosive.

I know what is happening on the red boat. They are all getting jittery, and I can see them watching us. Marshall and Whidden, agitated, are staring at *Australia II*. Soon they will make a move, take a gamble, and Hughey and I will take them by the jugular. Dennis has lost his control position, because we have neutralized it by superb sailing. "They can't stay there for long," says Hughey. "Any minute now, they'll leave us." We sail on, the two boats strung together, *Australia II* still gaining fractions, fractions. Suddenly *Liberty* seems to falter. "She's going, John, she's going," says Hughey, fighting back his excitement. I glance over, and there I see Dennis Conner on the wrong end of a psychological battering from us. *Liberty* tacks away to port. "She's gone, she's gone, we've cracked 'em." What a moment! What a breakthrough! We are ecstatic. *Liberty* tacked away because she could not stay where she was, being outsailed that comprehensively.

"Where's the wind?" I shout.

Beasho says slowly, "I think . . . it . . . it looks better to the left." Hughey turns around and says, "I think the center, slightly left." I "smell" wind to the left as well. And I wait a few seconds for Ya. We all do. It is no use to yell, "Hurry up, for Christ's sake," because Ya does not increase speed. Suddenly, he calls out, "MORE BREEZE TO THE LEFT, JOHN." That confirms it. Ya speaks only when he knows something is correct. But at that moment, I sense the sails shivering just a touch, and the boat stands up a bit. "It's a knock, it's a knock," I snap. Grant says instantly, "Five degrees, John, a solid five down." "This is for us," I say to Hughey, as we both feel the breeze freshen. "Let's go down a bit deeper into it." This is slightly unorthodox. The textbook on match racing says, when the wind knocks, tack. But all my experience tells me that may or may not be appropriate. "We're going into it," I call, and I head *Australia II* deeper into the wind, slicing into the knock. After 50 yards, we have put 100 yards between us and *Liberty*. The breeze is still strong, and I wheel her around. "TACKING, GUYS," I call. We feel the breeze freshening again from the left and hook into it. So does *Liberty*, and we batter our separate ways forward again, parallel, fighting for yards, every step of the way. Suddenly, the breeze that we have all forecast starts to gust. Up ahead I can see *Challenge 12* heeling right over. "Here she, comes," says Hughey, and *Australia II* heels over too, as the windshift blows in, lifting us, lifting us. Grant says, "John, nine up, ten up, eleven up, 12 degrees, John, now 14, 15." This is massive, and we're chugging along. I can't see a thing down to leeward where the red boat sails, but Hughey has ducked under the boom to get a fix on them. "What's happening?" I call. "What the fuck's happening? Don't keep it a secret. What's going on down there?" Hughey yells back above the wind, "We sail five degrees higher than the Americans. And we have more breeze. Five higher, five higher! Looking good, John, real solid, keep going."

From nowhere, Ya yells back, "SHE'S STILL SOLID TO THE MIDDLE AND LEFT!" "Five higher!" calls Hughey, as our bow dips under and Scoop and Beasho ease the sails, tightening them on the waves. Green water rolls over the foredeck. "We're still five higher, still five higher!" Beasho and Splash are working the big winches. "Seven point seven, seven point seven, seven point seven," calls Skippy. (On this tack he and Scoop have changed places, of course.) "Seven point seven, seven point six, up point one, John, up point one, John, up point one, John, seven point seven, seven point seven, seven point seven."

"Five higher, five higher!" We're hanging on the edge of wind. *Liberty* is wallowing in lighter air. Now I know we are taking distance from *Liberty,* but I also know we have to consolidate and get into a control position. If this wind shifts and lifts, that's fine, but if she knocks and *Liberty* tacks, we are vulnerable. I call to Hughey, "Let's get closer to them and get into control in this boat race." "We're increasing speed," I shout, "looking for seven eight, seven nine. We want full numbers low and fast." Skippy sticks his thumb in the air and again, the breeze the boys had predicted lifts us. Now we are bowling past the Americans, who are about 75 yards down to leeward of us. Not only have we sailed the boat perfectly, we have called the wind perfectly, as well.

This is just fantastic, and right now Hughey calls out, "Red Dog sails dead abeam, John." If I knew I had to die today, I'd die right now and I'd die happy. This turnaround has been amazing. "Seven point eight, seven point nine, seven point nine, that's good, John, that's real good, seven point nine, seven point nine." Now we are dominating the race, banging along, coping with this treacherous sea, reading the wind, and piling on the pressure. *Australia II* is well in the lead, and then *Liberty* tacks, giving up the ill-advised struggle to make for the right, where we are sure the wind is not. She heads back toward us. "Here she comes, John," calls Hughey. "Steady, steady, wait till she's dead to leeward. Not yet, not yet, not yet, not yet. . . ." I still cannot see Hughey under the mainsail, and we are all *completely* in his hands. "Not yet . . . not yet . . . STAND BY TO TACK THE BOAT, JOHN!" I squeeze the wheel, white-knuckling it. "This is it, John," I mutter, "this is bloody well it." "TACK THE BOAT!" roars Hughey, and blindly I swing *Australia II* across the wind, seeing for the first time how far behind *Liberty* is. Hughey has called it dead right. We have tacked slap on top of her, precise to a half inch. She's right in our windshadow.

We glance back to see *Liberty* in the worst possible place on the racecourse. She is underneath us, right in our slipstream, her mainsail billowing as we fling back disturbed air onto them. She cannot possibly stand that for long, and she soon tacks away to the right. We crash on for a bit, back in the left shift, and then we tack on her again as we batter our way up toward the first mark. For the second day in a row we have overcome a shaky start and come from behind to nail the Americans on this difficult upwind leg. It would not surprise me if they were getting a bit demoralized by this, because they must be becoming accustomed to our getting the better of them. I suspect they are spending too much time locked into us and what we are doing, rather than concentrating on their own boat.

By now we are nearly 100 yards out in front, banging up toward the mark. Grant calls out, "We'll round the mark better than two minutes in front." (It turned out to be two minutes 29 seconds.) Right now the wind is screaming, and we are heeled right over, with green water cascading over the foredeck. And here we are with a spinnaker to fly! "CLOSE-REACHING SPINNAKER!" I call, as I feel the wind veer around to the left even more. "MAJOR! THE 1½-OUNCER. DROP THE GENOA!" And the huge sail, soaking wet at the bottom, flops onto the deck, hundreds of square feet, some of it cascading over the side into the angry sea. Chink grabs for the heavy, soaking Kevlar, his huge arms just a blur as the mighty winch-grinder heaves the sail, hand over hand, back onto the boat. Below the mast, the Major and Grant are hanging on to the spinnaker halyard as Damian finishes the final clips. "NOW!" he roars, and the Major and Mad Dog leap into the air together, like a cross between an orangutan and Rudolf Nureyev, slamming back to the deck, hauling up the big green-and-gold chute, leaping into the air in a graceless ballet, their arms working, one over the other, thumping back down again, as we pass the mark.

We broadside around the top mark, the sea engulfing the port side of the bow as Chink and Damian struggle with the rushing water and the big genoa, trying desperately to get the bloody thing down the hatch. The Major rushes over to help, almost falling back down into the sewer, where there's water everywhere. Now he's pulling down the big code-three genoa, wrestling it, fighting the Kevlar, dragging it down on top of him, hand over hand. Twelve seconds. Not too bad, under the circumstances, and now we start romping away from *Liberty* as we head down this power reach. Grant rushes back along the weather side, slipping and blundering, then jumps back into the cockpit, looks back at our opponents, and snaps, "Two minutes 29 seconds, John."

Now the parachute flies fiercely out on the port side as I aim *Australia II* down the middle of the runway toward the wing mark. The wind is blowing and the stresses are colossal. Twelves break equipment in this type of stuff. We are screaming along, working away in this potential death trap—every sheet, every line stretched rigid. The carbon-fiber spinnaker pole is rammed against the forestay, massive strains everywhere.

Now we are feeding into some new breeze, and the wind is gusting up to 22 knots. *Liberty* slips farther behind in this classic situation where she has lost contact. We hit new wind and she misses it altogether. "I just can't believe this," I say, "I truly cannot believe it." We are annihilating them, our lead nearly up to four minutes. I wonder how many times in his dreams Dennis Conner will curse the moment when he let us off the hook by tacking late right after the start of Race 6. But luck has been with us all the way.

Then, steadily, the wind drops. At least it drops where we are, although it keeps going where *Liberty* is. Hughey and I spin around to see them, and they are rolling down on us, with a bloody great bow wave, making about 20 knots. We are nearly becalmed. "Now what's happening?" I ask. "It's their turn now," says Hughey, as the red boat slices into our huge lead. She's cutting it back, hand over fist, still with a bow wave in front of her. We round the mark, now only two minutes and 28 seconds in the lead.

With the wind veering left, the second power reach has turned into a square run, with the wind dead astern. *Liberty* belts around the mark, sailed beautifully, and I aim *Australia II* out to the left to stay on top of her. Then Dennis runs into the hole in the wind through which we have just floundered. We hit some new breeze from the left, and away we go again. Scoop is up on the weather side, working the spinnaker, calling the shots like a champion. "Little too low, John, come up a bit, up a bit. Come up five . . . come up 10. . . . That's good. That's fine. Up a bit more . . . OK, that's good. . . . Pressure now, good pressure." I'm holding *Australia II* on that feather edge of the wind, searching for that groove, carefully stopping her spinnaker from turning into jelly, holding her exactly where the wind pressure is maximum. If you sail too close to the wind on these square runs, you are sailing too big a distance, and you don't optimize your speed. (It's called "velocity made good," or VMG.) The skipper and the trimmer must get into tight harmony and keep her balanced, like threading a needle, getting the most "pull" out of that parachute.

"That's good, John, no, too far, too far, up three degrees, make it five. That's good." The monologue never stops, as we plot and scheme our way forward, too busy to worry about the personal strain on our nerves, too hyped up to realize most of us are hovering somewhere near breaking point. God knows what they feel like on Red Dog.

And now it is the turn of Hughey Treharne to excel yet again. Twice the wind shifts. Both times Hughey spots it. Both times he calls it beautifully. And both times I jibe as close to perfectly as you can get, hitting the shifts downstream, sliding farther and farther away from our opponents. We roll on down to the mark and round it a gigantic three minutes 46 seconds in front. We hear the "BEEP BEEP BEEP" from the committee boat's horn signifying a course change. It's 295 degrees, and they signal us with code flags. "Get that?" I say to Grant. "Got it," he mumbles, and we head upwind, with the breeze swinging to the southwest. "Let's just cover them," says Hughey, "nice and conservative. No mistakes."

By planting ourselves right between the Americans and the mark, we did nothing daring or rash all the way up to the top, and we dropped about 24 seconds as they fought their way along behind us, trying to find the shifts.

But now the breeze is getting up again, and as we head into the America's Cup buoy, I call for our biggest spinnaker, the 47-footer, pure white and a staggeringly beautiful piece of symmetry. Immediately we feed into some new air and are again bowling along.

Liberty is on a port tack, and she is still not going to fetch the mark. At that moment, Hughey speaks in a strange voice. "I would not be surprised if they try to ram us, John," he says. "Be very careful. I'll watch the bastards." And then it happens. Dennis tacks, and *Liberty* sets off toward us like a big red torpedo. "Here he comes," growls Beasho. "Well, it's his only hope of beating us," says Hughey, "just to collide." The upwind boat has the right-of-way, and it is our responsibility to stay clear of him. "We are dealing with a bloody animal here," I say, as *Liberty* comes on, closehauled into the wind, straight at us. And now we can all see what's happening. "BE PREPARED TO DROP THE SPINNAKER," Hughey yells to Chink. "Right!" he shouts, not batting an eyelid. And still *Liberty* comes on, aimed right at us.

Back on *Black Swan,* Sir James Hardy was utterly outraged at this appalling sportsmanship—well, neither I nor Hughey nor any of the men on our boat had ever done such a thing—and Jim rounded on the New York Yacht Club committee boat, *Fox Hunter.* He yelled at the top of his lungs, "This is the worst sportsmanship I have ever seen. It's a disgrace!" He screamed at McCullough, using language that might have made your average staff sergeant blanch. No one had ever seen Sir James that angry. Benny Lexcen clapped him on the shoulder and said, "Sir James, Sir James, really! I thought you had to sign a piece of paper saying you would never use that kind of language once you become a knight."

On *Australia II* we change course. I head her up 20 degrees, and there's no way he can hit us now. We surge straight across his bow, missing him by about 80 feet. Chink Longley says what most of us are thinking. He bounds to the port side, stares at the men on *Liberty,* and roars an obscenity very slowly and very, very loudly: "FUUUKYOO!" I am obliged to say that we all cracked up laughing. And Chink, flushed with this oratorical success, adds, "MOST UNSPORTSMANLIKE. YOU OUGHT TO BE ASHAMED OF YOURSELVES!" We all crack up again. But at that moment we feel nothing but scorn and derision for the men on the red boat, who could not even commit a foul properly. I finally say, "Piss off, you arrogant bastards, I'm going to grind you into the dirt." It is not exactly a garden party out here.

We swing around the bottom mark with another 46 seconds under our belts—a grand total of four minutes eight seconds in the lead. Now all we must do is sail conservatively up the last windward leg, and we will level the score at 3–3.

Just as we set off upwind, something pretty interesting happens. The Americans come driving down to the mark and totally mistime their approach, missing it by about 30 yards, the spinnaker ludicrously late. They must be completely shell-shocked and frustrated, with tempers frayed and some angry words being exchanged among the crew. Three days ago, they were 3–1 up. Now they are nearly all square and the celebration champagne is still on ice. Their timing in the stiff, 22-knot breeze is all over the place, nothing like the cold precision my boys have displayed in rough conditions, in which we are naturally very good. Right now the American jib is *still* fluttering, really ragged stuff. (We later learned that there was indeed a fierce altercation on the boat, the tempers of Conner's merry men boiling over.)

As we race through the last mile or so, *Liberty* gets a couple of nice shifts, which even I do not begrudge them, and finally we hit the winning line three minutes 25 seconds in front, the biggest margin of victory against the United States in the history of 12-Meter sailing in the America's Cup. The gun fires for us, and the score is: America 3–Australia 3.

We were the only crew ever to win three races from the U. S. A. in 132 years. No wonder they decided to try to ram us, after we messed up their record like that. And no wonder they got into such a mess at the fifth mark. They had probably recalled a couple of their boys from the foredeck to help with the press release explaining how no one in the entire world could possibly have beaten the Winged Superboat, not even with their perfect crew and their invincible skipper.

Soon Bondy arrived. So did Benny. And Warren. And Scotty. And Robbie. And Will. And Schnacks. Our ecstatic little army, so far from home, so irredeemably happy. I wanted to join them, to be part of this overpowering sunburst of joy, but it was not possible. I felt unaccountably removed, and so did the rest of the boys who had sailed *Australia II* across the line that day. I had never seen them so quiet, so reserved after a victory. The boat was nearly silent as we all tried to wind down, feeling almost crushed beneath the all-encompassing thought that weighed so heavily, so totally on each one of us—on the nearly exhausted Major Costello; on the sweat- and saltwater-soaked Chink; on Damian and Splash; on Ya, whose eyes were smarting as he groped for his dark glasses; on

Scoop and Skippy, worn out with the concentration; on Grant, sitting with his head in his hands; and on poor, tired Beasho, who had wrestled with that great mainsail on his own for nearly four hours. The thought that oppressed me was very simple: "Just one more time. Can this just happen one more time? I will never ask for anything, ever again, if today could just happen one more time."

CHAPTER

20

The Final
Assault

Could it be like that? Could we throw off all limitations and make the great white hull of Australia II *move with that same speed and control? "We've come to take you higher, John, to take you home."*

We decided to sail home that evening, without a tow, and we were mildly amused to discover that our natural course to the harbor, toward the Brenton Reef tower, would take us to within about 75 yards of *Liberty,* whose crew was still flogging away up the final beat. Benny Lexcen took the helm of *Australia II,* and the rest of us sat slumped on the weather side of the boat and gazed at Dennis and the All-American Rammers as we passed. We gave no hint of recognition, no smiles, no waves. We just watched them stonily, and I was wondering if they had any idea of how close they had come to a seven-minute beating rather than one of a mere record-breaking 3¼ minutes. A couple of good windshifts on the last windward leg had essentially saved them from the humiliation of the most shattering defeat of an American boat since 1871.

Flanked by an enormous escort, we blew back to Newport Harbor in excellent time under the most beautiful rig you have ever seen. Tom Schnackenberg had really done it. After thousands and thousands of miles of tuning, months and months of refining, and hundreds of hours of re-cutting, we very nearly had perfection stretched out from our mast. And in these blustery conditions, I believed we would be very, very difficult to defeat as long as this amazing crew stayed right at the top of their game in our sacred boat, and that the gods who ordain the direction of the breezes remained sympathetic to our cause. They might not need to move in with us, as they had done today, but it would be useful if they could stay more or less in constant touch.

Bondy and I decided not to race the next day, Friday, September 23. The boys were probably in need of a rest and a break, the boat needed checking over, and the forecast was for light-to-medium winds. Bondy was pretty damned excited, determined to savor this moment, just in case it turned out to be the best one of all. It would have been fun for all of us to have joined him in this feeling of achievement and celebration, as the most successful challengers ever to come to Newport. But we felt only the powerful contentment of mountaineers, who have faced death in a couple of avalanches, and struggled through two or three blizzards, before find-ing respite from the cold and danger on a ledge on the frozen rockface, which would keep us safe for a few hours. Death, we knew, could still await us on the final assault upon the mountain's uppermost peak this weekend.

However, there was a further reason why we decided to abandon our proven powerful momentum in favor of calling a lay day. The leader of our little expedition was having a bit of trouble with his time-on-distance judgment at the start. And when you are this far up the mountain, it would be nice to eliminate all forms of weakness. Generally speaking, it's too far to fall. I told Alan that I did not feel that I lacked confidence, but my judgment was off. I had had three bad starts in a row, and I wanted to take some time off to improve my sensitivity to this most precarious of moments in a big yacht race. So we called the lay day.

My first call that evening was to Harold Cudmore, the crack Irish sailor and former helmsman of *Victory '83,* whose ability in a start I respect nearly as much as that of Conner himself. And I asked him, "Harry, would you take the helm of *Challenge 12* tomorrow and give me and the boys a really hard workout, with starts and short races, before I screw it up again?" He is a grand old pal of mine, and, after suffering a few min-utes of general leg-pulling and light abuse, I was happy to welcome him on board, and I looked forward to his assistance on the following day.

Meanwhile, Newport was a scene of pure pandemonium. Hundreds and hundreds of people remained around our dock long after Rasa and Lucas and I had left. Journalists and television people were everywhere, and by now the CIA and the FBI were beginning to infiltrate the dock area. We were told that they were there to hold back any moves by a fanatic fringe that might decide to make a name for itself by blowing up a couple of America's Cup crews. Our executive staff felt that our own security should also be beefed up, and in the past 24 hours we had recruited two armed guards to patrol Founders' Hall around the clock, and we had four men, armed to the teeth, on duty on *Australia II*. There were, after all, plenty of people in Newport who stood to lose large sums of money should the America's Cup be lost to the town, and you never know who might do what these days, do you?

I thought it all rather a shame that these extreme safety measures had to be taken, because I was very conscious of a solid base of affection for the Australians from a large section of the American public. The Americans really love a contest, and they knew that we had turned this normally lopsided little upper-class scenario into a real battle, with the eyes of the entire world focused upon us all with rapt fascination. The sheer volume of publicity brought home to us, on a daily basis, just how mammoth this struggle had become.

Early that evening, I decided to join a few of the boys for a couple of drinks at O'Brien's, the little bar off the beaten track that we had adopted as our "local." And as I made my way there, I reflected that in a sense it was a pity we had not reveled in our victories and celebrated them, as anyone else would have done. This might have been the last time we would sail *Australia II* to victory, and in a way, it would have been a bit sad to think that we never even had a laugh and a shout together. But as I approached the pub, I quickly shook myself out of that mood. Haunted as I was by the fact that a 4–3 defeat would be just as bad as, if not worse than, a 4–0 defeat, I said to myself, for the 100th time, "Just give us one half a chance, and we will win this damned thing outright—never mind 3–3."

I stepped inside the bar to what I remember as a thunderous round of applause. I had not counted on this. For some daft reason, I thought that I was just going to have a couple of quiet drinks with the boys. But this was chaos—backslapping, congratulations, and accolades. It was just too rich for me to handle. I finished about half a glass of beer and left. I just could not cope with that.

Up at Founders' Hall at dinner that night, I told the boys that we would sail early the following day with Harry Cudmore at the helm of *Challenge 12,* and shortly after dinner I went home and collapsed with tiredness and, I suppose, the emotion of the day. As I slept, every afternoon newspaper in Australia gave us front-page headlines, and our little nation stood transfixed with excitement over the impending contest.

I awoke early on the morning of the lay day, September 23. It was, as always, before six o'clock, and the long, pink ribbons of the Newport dawn were creeping across the sky. There was little wind, and down at the sail loft, Tom Schnackenberg and his boys had just crashed, exhausted, on a pile of genoas. They had worked throughout the night, reshaping spinnakers and adding the final cuts and tucks to the big Kevlar "motor" we hoped would bring us to victory in the showdown that Dennis Conner had called, the previous evening, "The Race of the Century."

After breakfast, we made our way back down to the docks, where Harry Cudmore awaited, finding his way around *Challenge 12*. He and Hughey and I went over the starting tactics we expected Dennis to employ on *Liberty* the next day. We told him how wary Dennis was, how he tried to avoid close confrontation if he could, what a slippery devil he could be on the defensive, and how brilliantly calculating was his time-on-distance clock.

By 10 o'clock we were out there, and Harry had assured us he would be as tough and aggressive as Dennis was. Actually, in match racing I would not put a hell of a lot between them—and I remember how glad Hughey and I were when Harry had a disagreement with Peter de Savary and left the British challenge.

Anyway, we began the exercise, and it took a couple of go-arounds before Harry quite got the hang of things on *Challenge*. After that, he came at us like a madman. I thought it was Dennis for a minute. For one brief spell, Hughey and I were all over the place, not quite ready to cope with this kind of aggression, but soon we shaped up, and it became a hard contest out there, with Harry sailing his tail off to beat us. At one point, it became quite tense. I was still getting my time-on-distance wrong, and I was calling for the sails late. Hughey was starting to get uptight with me, and I wondered if I was haunted still by the specter of the day I hit the line too early in Race 5 and damned near lost the America's Cup. But I found it difficult to be confident of how long it would take *Australia II* to cross a given stretch of water to a given point. I'm not talking about being five minutes adrift—I'm talking about three or four seconds. But that is what we were dealing with here. And Hughey got crosser. "Come on, John, GO! GO! GO!" Fists clenched with anxiety.

Finally I had to slow it all down. I said, "Now look, Hughey, let's just cool it. I have to get my confidence back. It's no good my getting it right a couple of times and beating Harry if I'm still not sure of myself. I have to keep trying, keep practicing until I am dead sure of what I am doing. It's no good trying to rush it. We have a lot of time, and I'm quite prepared to stay out here and practice all night under floodlights if I have to. I'm not going back until I am quite sure I can confidently hit that starting line, right on the button."

Finally, as the afternoon wore on, I got it. Again and again we came flying up to the line, the Major counting, "5 . . . 4 . . . 3 . . . 2 . . . 1 . . . GO!" And there we were, right where we were supposed to be. The last two starts I did were terrific. We were right in there, and for the first time in a week, I felt happy about starting *Australia II* against Dennis Conner. I thanked Harry profusely for what he had done, and we sailed back to the dock, feeling very pleased with our performance—a very productive day.

While all of this was going on, the Americans had towed *Liberty* around to Cove Haven Marina, at Barrington, north of Newport, to have her ballasting changed. We were told they removed 920 pounds of lead from the keel and added 22 square feet of sail in a last-ditch effort to beat us. She had those three multiple-rating certificates, which permitted her to change her weight and mainsail area according to the conditions. She was thus a boat for all seasons—light air, medium air, and heavy air. This had certainly irritated her American opponents during the trials, because they had not been told, and it gave the big red boat an advantage. And from Blackaller's and Kolius's points of view, it was a rather unfair one. I, too, was totally irritated about it, but not for the same reasons. I just wished *we* had thought of it. Anyway, we sent Benny around to watch the remeasuring, and he reported back to us at dinner that night at Founders' Hall.

The circumstances surrounding what could very well have been our last supper together prompt me once more to mention the extraordinary role that Rasa played in all this. Before dinner, she was fielding phone calls, keeping people out of my way, dealing with the children, getting them ready for bed, cleaning up the bathroom after Lucas and Andre had swamped it, talking to Jenny Longley and Dixie Treharne and Annie Schnacks. She also calmed some troubled waters in the girls' camp. Above all, the skipper's wife did something else for which I will be forever grateful. She never once bothered me with any of the little domestic upsets that occurred. She dealt with them as best she could, as an adviser, counselor, friend, and, in some cases, guardian. She never even reported their existence to me, figuring for some reason that I might be a bit too preoccupied to care. It is hard for me to stress how vital all of this was. If a couple of these girls had folded, I could have had a couple of key guys on the boat with other things occupying their minds. And with the pressure under which we were sailing, a mistake by one of them could have cost us the race—and in the past week the Cup, never mind a race.

Dinner that night was a very quiet, formal affair as we prepared, hopefully, to face the red boat once more, to put the lid on the longest America's Cup competition ever sailed. The atmosphere in Newport was vibrant as the battle lines were drawn for the last race. We did not have any speeches—just a general talk among the crew about potential problems on the boat—and all the time I was trying to defuse that atmosphere.

When I returned to Dennison Street, Rasa and I had a long talk about sailing, and we stayed up until quite late. Finally I had my trusty glass of warm milk and my tranquilizer and drifted off to sleep at about 11:30. And 12,000 miles away, on a sunlit spring afternoon in Melbourne, 125,000 people, packed into the old Olympic stadium for the Grand Final of Australian Rules Football, were on their feet looking at a picture of *Australia II* flashing on the huge scoreboard. And they were all roaring, chanting, "AUSTRALIA GO! AUSTRALIA GO! AUSTRALIA GO!" No one had ever heard anything quite like that. They say the sound could be heard five miles away across the city.

Melbourne was not the only place in which there was fierce activity surrounding *Australia II*. At 2 A.M. Saturday, the unmistakable bubbles of a scuba diver were spotted by the guards, and they were coming from down by the keel. The guards raised an unholy alarm, stopping only just short of firing shots into the water. The intruder displayed not only courage and ingenuity, but also judgment, and headed out into the harbor.

We all slept as best we could while all of this was going on, and on Saturday morning, September 24, after a rather nervous breakfast, we set out for the racecourse. We were confident of our boat, and I was confident about the starting maneuvers, but the wind was shifting all over the place. It was clear to us, and I am sure to the men on *Liberty,* that we might not be able to start. The wind just kept veering around, and the Race Committee was trying to work out the starting line and the direction we had to take on that first beat. But it was just about impossible. Finally, they set a course, and both 12-Meters went boring into the attack. However, a couple of minutes before the starting gun, the Race Committee hoisted the postponement flag because of yet another huge shift in the wind direction. The massive fleet of spectator boats and the swarm of choppers and planes circled for a while, but time was running out, and a fair race was nearly out of the question. So the Committee called it off for the day, and we headed home once more. To our amazement, *Liberty* then called for a lay day—officially, since the 10-minute gun had gone, we had started Race 7, and officially it had been postponed.

As things turned out, the boys of *Liberty* had a rather disruptive weekend, because on Sunday they had to cope with the six-hour ordeal of towing the boat back up to Cove Haven, where they had to pile all the lead back in, then the weather forecast changed and it all had to come back out again. Then they towed her back to Newport weighing exactly the same as she weighed after they removed the lead on Friday. Dennis was not a major participant in all of these technical shenanigans; in fact, he was playing golf during some of the reballasting.

We returned to the dock to a very big crowd, which dispersed fairly quickly. I guess people were extending their reservations for tickets and hotels, since now we would not race the final showdown until Monday. Rasa and I spent a cheerful Saturday night with Robbie Doyle, the old pal who had introduced me to Finn racing so long ago.

On Sunday we spent another quiet family day. I took Rasa and the kids for a bicycle ride around town, threading our way through the traffic. Little Sunshine was on the handlebars of Dad's bike, Lucas was right behind, then Andre on his new bike, and Rasa was bringing up the rear. Mum and Dad and the three little ducks.

There was yet another fuss about my riding that terrific 10-speed bike when I whipped up to Founders' Hall on it Sunday night. I loved the bike. It made me feel free. When I was on it, no one could get at me, and I used to hurtle along Newport's back roads on it. No one knew where I was. I felt a bit like a naughty boy, to tell the truth. Anyway, that night at dinner I was formally banned by Warren, upon strict orders from Bondy, not to get on the thing again.

Monday we would race, of that I was very sure. The forecast was for lightish winds, but we thought they would probably be steadier than they had been on Saturday. Thus we sat down to a very formal dinner, the last we would have as a racing crew together facing the prospect of a major contest the following day. We had all had a nice break, and I could sense the adrenaline rising in the room. Bondy was very quiet and serious and told us how proud he was. And I reminded the boys once more that they all had done the most fantastic job in the last race, on Thursday, and that I felt another such impeccable example of big-boat racing would be bound to get us home tomorrow.

I went home quite early—by car—but I was not tired. I was wide awake, ready to race Conner right then if necessary. The children were all asleep, and Rasa could tell I was on the very edge of my nerve ends. She had seen me through the defeats, she had comforted me through my darkest moments, and, like Kenny Beashel, who knew me so well, she always knew what to say. I telephoned Mum, who was very concerned about me. (Apparently that day the name John Bertrand was mentioned about every seven seconds on the television, and she was afraid to keep it on in case something happened to me.)

But then Rasa started to say something very appropriate, the same thought she had been trying to communicate to me when she had watched us batter our way back from 3–1 down. "John," she said thoughtfully, "no one has ever found it very easy to beat you. I've followed you all over the world and as a general rule, you tend to win. I know that if you will just let your natural talent flow, you can win this race. Because when all the rubbish is over with, it will finally come down to the wind, and the water, and the sails, and you will be called upon to do what you know best, just to do what you are good at: to sail, to race, to make *Australia II* go."

Rasa and I talked about the little boats that I had sailed and won with. And how Rasa had watched me when I was about a thousand years younger, winning in Finland, winning the Olympic trials in Australia on all of the three occasions that I had entered. We talked about how we had gone to New Orleans together when I won the American Nationals, how I had struggled so damned hard in the Olympic Games. Now it seemed that it was just the two of us again, here in this dingy little room in this tiny apartment, still with not much money. And once more she was holding my hand as I prepared to go out and take on the world again. It was a feeling that suddenly had a lot of loneliness in it, and it held us together.

Rasa went off to bring my good old hot milk and tranquilizer to see if it would send me to sleep for one last time. But I was too restless, and I just lay there listening to John Denver, trying to cast from my thoughts the monstrous possibility of defeat on Monday. I thought, deep in my subconscious, that I had noticed *Liberty* a bit sharper in the very few minutes we fenced together in her lighter mode on Saturday. But that may have been in my imagination. Rasa told me again to think only of my own search for perfection, which I believed we had in fact attained on the first beat to windward in Race 6.

I took my headset off and read some of my favorite passages of *Jonathan Livingston Seagull* over again. They were, as ever, hauntingly appropriate.

They came in the evening then, and found Jonathan gliding peaceful and alone through his beloved sky. The two gulls that appeared at his wings were as pure as starlight, and the glow from them was friendly in the high night air. But most lovely of all was the skill with which they flew, their wingtips moving a precise and constant inch from his own.

Without a word, Jonathan put them to his test, a test no gull had ever passed. He twisted his wings to a single mile-per-hour above stall. The two radiant birds slowed with him, smoothly, locked in position. They knew about slow flying.

He folded his wings, rolled and dropped in a dive to a hundred and ninety miles per hour. They dropped with him, streaking down in flawless formation. At last he turned that speed straight up into a long vertical slow-roll. They rolled with him, smiling.

Could it be like that out on the water tomorrow? Could we throw off all limitations and make the great white hull of *Australia II* move with that same speed and control? Could the ambition of the whole of my life perhaps come true after all the years of practice? I fell into a fitful sleep, hearing another voice talking to me from the little book. It was very clear, and the words were strong and calm and real, "We've come to take you higher, John, to take you home."

I awoke, sweating, shortly after five o'clock in the morning, my mind locking instantly onto the Race of the Century. I found myself only just capable of touching on the size of the event I was going, this day, to shape. I had no idea how any of the others were reacting, but I felt pretty queasy as soon as I rose from my bed.

Breakfast at Founders' Hall was about as tense as it is possible to imagine. Grant was off his food, could eat nothing. I was not a lot better, and the coffee made me feel sick. Hughey was worse than both of us. He ate nothing as he walked toward his lifelong dream. I looked around the table at them all, wondering what they were feeling. Hughey caught me watching him and half smiled, but we said nothing, and somehow he knew that I was thinking of him and his task today, and he was thinking of me and my task. I trust Hughey.

Across the table the performance of Ya and Damian was nearly horrifying as they blithely threw back two entire plates of bacon and eggs *each,* as if nothing was happening. When Ya actually went up for just one more egg and another bit of bacon, Hughey and I nearly had to go to the bathroom. Old Splash Richardson was not on what you might call "iron rations" either. But Chink was very quiet, endlessly stirring his coffee, trying to think of a word of encouragement to say. Colin Beashel, who I now believed was the finest natural yachtsman I had ever met, was terribly within himself, staring out of the window, very tense, saying nothing. Skippy was eating his breakfast and being cheerful, happy-go-lucky Skippy, very confident in that which he was going to do this day. But I could see the signs even in his permanently relaxed face. He did not feel carefree on this Monday morning. Kenny Judge remained Mr. Cool, the role the press believed that I always played. And while I wrestled with half a piece of toast and a teaspoonful of coffee, he was only just behind Ya and Damian, scoffing away on his bacon and eggs as if the America's Cup were over.

The last man to come for breakfast was Major Peter Costello, back after one final check to see that all sails were dry, packed, and in perfect order. He arrived, delicately closing the door behind him with a force that ought to have knocked out every window in the house, but in fact only cracked the foundations. I thought then that it was a pretty symbolic crash—barring, as it did, the outside world from our innermost sanctum. For we had now closed ranks more securely than most of us realized. By this time, any stranger was an enemy. Just the previous evening, our chase-boat skipper, Mark Reid, had told me, quietly, that the manager of one of the pubs along the waterfront had told him and a couple of the boys that they were no longer welcome to have a drink there. So Warren suggested at breakfast that it would be best for us not to venture into Newport again, because a lot of people had a great deal to lose if we won today.

The mornings were becoming darker now. And colder. And so was the atmosphere. A week earlier, I had estimated that about three-quarters of the American public was with us. That was no longer true. The Americans are good sports, and they do love a contest, but they are patriots like the rest of us when it comes down to what Dennis calls "the short strokes." And now we were essentially on our own, ranks closed behind the locked doors of Founders' Hall, our little boat under heavy armed guard in this foreign country, our opponents with their noses badly out of joint, a town turning slightly sour on us. And five hours from now, we would face the enemy in open combat.

I stood up and wished everyone a formal good morning. I told them that this was a time that would test our mental discipline. I went over with them one of our great maxims—when the moment comes, we will do what great teams always do. We will call upon our proven capacity to slip into overdrive as soon as our backs are pushed to the wall. "We have discussed it long and often, and today we are going to be required to do it. To hit the switch and raise our game, like great champions, like men who deserve to be recognized as the best in the world. We are going to sail our boat as it has *never* been sailed before. Nothing is going to stop us. Now let's go, gentlemen, and win the America's Cup."

I was deliberately late for the boat that morning. I knew that the tension on the dock would be electric, that the crowds would be enormous and the well-wishers plentiful, and I decided to stay home for an extra 15 minutes and listen to John Denver. Then I would arrive at 9 A.M. sharp, in time to cast off straightaway. I had not misjudged things, either. The place was like a nuthouse. Cruising beyond the dock were huge powerboats, including a big white one belonging to the Aga Khan. The crowd cheered as I threw my gear on board and stepped onto the deck of *Australia II*. At the end of the dock, American television networks had built huge scaffolds with cameras perched on gantries above the boat. Helicopters were circling above, with men hanging out of them, strapped onto the sides and holding huge cameras. Girls were in tears as they clapped and cheered the Australian warriors. I resolved not to look up.

People were shouting, "God bless you, John," all along the dock. Cries of "Godspeed" could be heard everywhere. It was a departure absolutely chockful of emotion, as though we were leading the little armada of private ships that crossed the English Channel to Dunkirk to bring home the embattled British soldiers trapped on the beach. But I found myself completely aloof, on an entirely different plateau. I was in battle mode.

Damian ran up the kangaroo with the boxing gloves. We played the music at full volume, casting off the lines for the last time. *Australia II* was on her way to the wars.

> Do you come from a land down under,
> Where women glow and men plunder?
> Can't you hear, can't you hear the thunder?
> You'd better run, you'd better take cover.

This was reality, the earthy tones of our familiar battle hymn, and the crowd clapped and cheered us all the way along the shore. We were veterans of many harsh and uncompromising struggles. We had lost and we had won. And today was our chance to batter the anvil of history with one final victory for the 11 men on board the white boat from Perth, sailing together for the very last time in their lives. "Godspeed, John!" "God bless you all!" I could still hear them shouting at us as we slapped along behind *Black Swan*. We were sitting quietly, men with a lot on our minds. Some of the veterans—like Chink, the Major, Scoop, Ya, and perhaps myself—betrayed no emotion. But as for Grant and Hughey and Beasho, their inner turmoil was more obvious. We stood there, all together in a tight group, our tanned faces serious, apparently calm, but shielding so much inner emotion. There was a dreadful beauty about that last departure from Newport.

They towed us out into cooler air. The summer season was coming to an end—and the commercial bonanza of the America's Cup with it.

We kept the routine below deck pretty much static. Damian shot into the bow, Scoop sped smoothly to the best spot on the boat, and the others crashed in their usual places. The Major played Chopin on his little tape recorder and sat against the mast with his eyes half closed, a great bull of a man entranced by the beautifully contrived scherzos of Poland's most beloved composer. Ya actually managed to get his hands on a sandwich, and Hughey and I sat quietly, discussing the light, shifting winds and the possibility of a more "slippery" *Liberty* than we had ever met before.

Our warm-up with *Challenge* before the start was pretty satisfactory, but by now we were all becoming concerned that the wind kept veering around. It would be a great shame if the "Race of the Century" should turn out to be just a crapshoot decided on the pure luck of which boat landed the best of an unequal wind. What worried Hughey and me was that the Committee might decide that, given our record in light air, *Liberty*'s best shot might just *be* a crapshoot, and they would let the race go on with the Americans having a 50–50 chance of winning. But they did no such thing, and, much to our relief, they postponed the race seven minutes after the 10-minute gun.

Liberty ran into the VIP fleet and we stayed distant. *Black Swan* pulled alongside, and suddenly we noticed the sea breeze started to fill in. I said to Hughey, "This is it. Let's go for a couple of runs with *Challenge*." Grant hit the radio, and I called down to the foredeck, "HOIST THE GENOA!" And we worked to windward with Sir James and his boys two or three times before the course signals were hauled up again on the aft halyard of *Black Knight* at 12:45 P.M.

More than 1,500 boats were out there watching as we waited for the 10-minute gun. The breeze was filling in nicely, and I knew that this was it. We were now going to race *Liberty* for the America's Cup. High above us buzzed the biggest fleet of helicopters I had ever seen. Above them were fixed-wing aircraft, and below them was the mighty Goodyear Blimp, with its full television crew on board. I could see huge cameras out over the sides of the choppers, men in straps manning them. And all this was linked mysteriously to those satellites far above.

It is exactly 2:55 Tuesday morning back home on Bristol Avenue when the 10-minute gun blasts off here on Rhode Island Sound. And I bring *Australia II* loping downwind to meet the red boat. The conditions still seem a little tricky, and I can feel the air going warm for two or three minutes, then cool across my face. There is instability out there, with warm pockets of air wafting across the water, but I know these conditions. We have faced them a couple of times against *Liberty,* and usually the breeze will veer to the left, so the port end of the starting line is where we want to be. Dennis seems cautious behind the wheel of *Liberty*, and we slide by each other, wary, suspicious. Less than five minutes to the starting gun, and I wheel *Australia II* around, making for *Liberty*'s stern—the most aggressive move by either of us so far. Up on the bow I can see Chink. I know he is rigid with nerves, and he has my total sympathy. Now I am working us into the right place, and suddenly we are precisely where we want to be. I'm right under *Liberty*'s hip as we race bow to bow toward the line. We're inside the 100-second mark now, and the Major is counting. This is pure time-on-distance, just as I practiced with Harry Cudmore, and *Liberty* is not in good shape. She cannot stay up on our weather hip for much longer, or we can squeeze her out and stop her. But Conner just hangs in there, hangs in there, as the Major counts down, "95 . . . 90 . . . 85 . . . 80. . . ." Hughey speaks methodically, "She's going, John, *Liberty*'s tacking." The red boat tacks away, down to the unfavored end of the line, and I know we are in beautiful shape. I start nudging up again as the count continues, "20 . . . 19 . . . 18 . . .17. . . ." "Head her down!" calls Chink. "GO DOWN! GO DOWN! NO CLOSER! NO CLOSER!" On our bow is a man who does not want to take us over the line early, not in this historic race. I can't find it within myself to berate him, and I nudge closer. "NO, NO, NO!" shouts Chink. "We're close, we're close," calls Chink. But I know we're not that close, and we are in fact a full boatlength from the line when the gun goes. *Liberty* crosses eight seconds before us, but we are at the favored end, nearest the mark and going a lot faster.

We head off to port, going as fast as we can in search of what we always called "the old *Australia II* lift," the breeze we have so often found out here in the early part of the afternoon. We have good speed and have won the start, but slowly we begin to knock. Grant calls out, "It's a header, John. Down three, down three, down three degrees." And Hughey says, "Let's tack, John, and join *Liberty*." I wheel *Australia II* through the wind, bringing her about onto a parallel course. Hughey ducks under the boom and starts to take an accurate fix on her with the stadometer. "No change in bearing! No change!" he calls to me. But a minute later, he says, quietly, "We've fallen in a touch. We're falling in on them just a touch."

Now I know the game has changed. *Liberty* is supposed to be 1,000 pounds lighter, but we had heard that they may have removed closer to 1,500 pounds of lead from her keel. She has more sail area, and the fact is, she is now very competitive. We're losing bearing against her. At this point in time she has fractional boatspeed on us. "We have a real race on our hands here," I say to Hughey, who says nothing. He never does when he's really nervous, but both of us know now that *Liberty* is going very well. We must keep going and keep trying to track the wind. In fact, the only thing that is saving us at the present is a sudden beautiful lift, the one we have been seeking, and Grant calls, "Up five degrees, John. Up five, up five!"

We are racing a different boat that is faster than she was. I call to Hughey, "Let's try to run over her. We've got to get our boatspeed up and hit the higher numbers. Then we can slide down to them and try to get across them. But we've got to get the numbers up."

We are bumping along at about 7.3 knots, and Scoop is calling the speed. I yell out to him, "I'm looking for full numbers, heading her down a fraction." Scoop never misses a beat. "Seven point three, John, seven point three, seven point four, seven point four, seven point four. That's good. Up one more, John. Seven point four, up point one, John, up point one, John. Seven point five, John, seven point five, seven point five, now seven point six. That's good, John. Seven point six, seven point six, seven point six."

Skippy eases the jib half an inch. That's good. Then Colin eases the mainsail one inch. That's better, but I'm having trouble steering in this swell. We are right on the razor edge of the wind, and we are still trying to get over, to get across *Liberty*. It is very tense on the boat, and I know that we are only just hanging in there, on the inside of this lift, by the grace of the gods of the wind. If the breeze starts to knock, it will not be good. In fact, it will be bloody awful. One way or another, this is going to be a long boat race. There is about 10 knots of true breeze right now, which should be super for us, but it isn't, and I sense we are doing no more than just hanging on. Hughey is still under the boom when *Liberty* comes about and heads right back toward us. "How do we look?" I mutter, and Hughey responds, "I'd say we'll have about two boatlengths on them when we cross." Now we will find out. Hughey is right, and, as he predicted, *Liberty* takes our stern a couple of boatlengths away, a big, angry, dark-red shape smacking her way through the water, bent on the destruction of all our hopes and dreams.

We tack right on top of her, forcing her away back to the right. "Stay on top of her, John," growls Hughey, and we tack again immediately. Once more the Americans cannot stay there, so they come about again, heading out to the left. We are short of wind pressure, and Hughey and I are sure that the wind now will feed around to the right. Ya is calling out that it will swing right. We decide to protect that side, and we head down there. But this time we are wrong. I'm already having a hard time steering the boat in the spectator chop, which swings us around, and the breeze, unfortunately for us, swings farther left. *Liberty* feeds into it, and the next time we converge, we are dead even, our lead gone. She ducks under our stern. There is nothing in the race at this stage, and we head back to the right side of the course once more.

Hughey keeps watching the red boat. With two more tacks, she is up on our weather hip. To our horror, the breeze starts to veer farther to the left. "Hughey, this is trouble!" Red Dog is extremely competitive now—of that none of us is in any doubt. In bleak contrast to the glorious Race 6, it is we who are now uncomfortable. Our eyes dart around for a way out of this predicament. At this stage we are emotionally ready to make a rash move. This is the time when competitors start to stretch beyond themselves and look for a throw of the dice that will get them out. I snap to Hughey, "Let's not do anything rash now. Let's just hang in, stay close, keep focused, stay in contact with this character. We'll get our chance."

But the breeze continues to go wrong for us—left, left, left—and we are obliged to stick hard to the course the American dictates, all the way over to the layline. We head up to the first weather mark nearly half a minute behind, about four boatlengths. The boat is very quiet. The boys have worked damned hard all the way up that first leg, and no one feels the need to enunciate our precarious position. I call for the code-two reaching spinnaker, and the Major, Damian, Chink, and Ya crack it up in eight seconds flat, a superb set with the little staysail flying underneath.

Down the first reach we go, still hanging on. Sometimes we get a little gust, sometimes they get it. Just when we think we have clawed a few seconds back from them, they grab it back from us.

The breeze goes more left. We can see up ahead a huge armada of powerboats packed around the wing mark, causing "wind umbrella," which prevents the full force of the wind from hitting us. It is going to be terribly light around there as the air ricochets over the boats. "We're going to sail this closer to the wind than normal to keep our speed up," I mutter to Hughey. We go a little deeper coming to the mark, but at this point the breeze is backing farther to the left, so we come in a little bit too close and have burned off a little speed. Hughey confirms that *Liberty* got time off us on that first power reach, and we come jibing around 45 seconds behind. As good luck goes, ours certainly has gone.

The breeze has in fact shifted around so far that the second power reach is now a square run, so I call for our little code-one spinnaker, the green-and-gold Sobstad, made by Hughey's company. We execute another super change, with the Major and the foredeck boys working furiously to salvage these precious seconds. And now at last we start to gain, to pull back the yards. I can feel the mood tightening on *Australia II*, and down in front of me I can see Chink, his knuckles ivory-white on his grinder, and Skippy and Scoop, their brains working overtime, as the chute stretches out in perfect formation above the bow. Scoop is calling, "Come on, John, up five degrees, up five, John. Keep her in the groove." Suddenly Grant looks up, his eyes irritated. "No," he says, "we're going too high. We should not have to go this high." In his opinion, based on his computer calculations, we are veering too far away from the mark. For the first time I step in and say, "Come on, guys, steady, steady. Let's just take it easy. We are going to catch them. Don't worry about that." And I yell out to the crew to ease the tension, "WE ARE GOING TO NAIL THESE BAS-TARDS! JUST HANG IN THERE!" I say to Grant, "This is real seat-of-the-pants stuff right now, because of the tricky, unstable wind. But the boat feels right, and I'm sure we must push on and keep sailing these angles."

The wind is now so mushy that it is probably skewing around at the top of the mast, and I know that right now is the time to discount our instruments a little. Secretly, I am amazed at the speed with which Grant has spotted the deviation from normal sailing procedures. But on we go, snatching back the yards as best we can. Scoop is calling the pressure on the spinnaker and we are making some big gains. We almost have back that 16 seconds we lost on the second leg. Now the breeze is freshening, and we are able to slide down about 20 degrees. We come rolling straight up to the mark, picking up six more seconds, and we turn up the second windward leg—the fourth leg of the race—only 23 seconds behind, about two boatlengths. We are right back in the ball game, and we decide to use our trusty code-two genoa and head closehauled into the loose cover that *Liberty* has now slapped on us. Within two minutes, Hughey is telling me the disagreeable news that *Liberty* has a touch of speed on us, as she has had at so many of the wrong times in this regatta.

"No change in height," he calls. "We point the same. But she has a slight edge again." Our options are limited now. We cannot get to them by boatspeed, but there is no sense in getting excited, because Dennis sure as hell is not going to join us in a tacking duel that he didn't believe he could win. The only tactic I can employ is the one that wins Olympic gold medals: Keep hanging in there, do what we have been trained to do, don't give up, don't panic, and don't do anything rash.

"HANG IN THERE, BOYS," I bawl. "JUST KEEP ON SAILING THE BOAT." We sail on, hard on this port tack, and when the breeze hardens to the right, we tack immediately. Conner ignores us totally, just going forward and then tacking in his own sweet time, gaining a little bit of ground on us. Quite obviously, he is not interested in sparring with us.

We have only one choice, I tell my tactician. We just have to play the shifts and try to outwit them all the way up this leg and forget all about them as opponents. We can't let them put us off our game plan. I call down to Ya, "We just have to play the shifts and sail the boat as we know best." I know that if they make one mistake, we will have them, but right now things look very difficult for us.

Slowly the breeze starts to moderate, dropping down to about 8 knots. Grant calls, "GENOA CHANGE! DROPPING DOWN TO OUR CODE ONE." The activity on the bow is swift and certain. Damian and the Major are moving around effortlessly, clipping, hauling, and pulling. The switch of these two big, heavy sails takes exactly 50 seconds. It is a superb piece of seamanship, and I long to get back into this fight, just to give the boys a chance to show their stuff to erase their frustrations. Halfway up the leg, we still cannot see the mark in the mist ahead, but now the breeze has softened and we are beginning to go very well again. A week ago, before the Americans changed their boat, we would have annhilated them in this.

But not now. We tack underneath them and *Liberty* sails on for a long while before tacking hard onto our weather hip. Slowly we start to suck right in toward them, but in these new conditions, we are now faster. Our turn. Hughey says, "We've halved her lead, John. Keep going." I guessed that we are within 15 seconds of her. The feeling on *Australia II* is one of high anticipation.

We claw our way along for almost 10 minutes, and we are sucking into her. The boys are working the sails like men possessed—Scoop easing the genoa, Colin easing the mainsail, then trimming it, both of them masklike in their concentration. Skippy is calling it, "That's beautiful, John, just ease her along, ease her along. That's real nice." And up above, that big code-one genoa is doing a great job for us.

Then it happens. Some gusting new air starts to feed across the racecourse. Ya calls it. We could all see it coming, and there is nothing we can do as it hits *Liberty*, filling her sails and sending her leaping away from us yet again. We all stand there in helpless agony. "She's sailing five to 10 degrees higher than us," says Hughey. And I cannot believe it. After all that work, *Liberty* has negated it entirely in no time by catching that one gust. I look around at Hughey, and he is just standing there, saying, over and over again, "I just cannot believe this. I just cannot believe this. I just cannot believe this . . . ." We're losing contact with her, a terrible feeling. Grant is calling, "Three minutes to the layline . . . one minute to the layline. . . . We are on the lay line."

We have been whacked right on the chin. But that's yacht racing. I curse the world in general, and we follow the red boat up to the mark. I watch in frustration and fury as she sets her spinnaker beautifully, about 75 yards ahead of us. Too far. She's getting away. The American horns are blaring and baying their approval as Dennis moves in for the kill. I call for the same code-one spinnaker that hauled us down the second reach, and once more the boys execute a perfect eight-second set. Grant calls, "We are 57 seconds behind." The conditions are awful for the "Race of the Century," a nightmare in this wafty breeze. The sky is full of loud, buzzing insects with rotors clattering away overhead as the world prepares to watch us set off down that fateful fifth leg.

But those nine words of Sir Winston, speaking at Harrow, ring clearly in my mind: "Never give in. Never give in. Never give in."

21

To Take You Home

Liberty jibes. Dennis Conner swings the big red bow toward us, and in the light wind I can hear her winches as her great sails are adjusted. "Here she comes, John," calls Hughey.

We whiplashed around the top mark in Race 7 shortly after 5:30 in the morning. The sun was struggling into the sky over Port Phillip Bay, casting a rosy light over the south-western suburbs of the city of Melbourne. Someone estimated that 75 percent of all the television sets in this metropolis of three million souls were switched on. The capital of the State of Victoria watched in unabated horror as Dennis Conner, on an elegant starboard tack, aimed the American defender to the left-hand side of the runway.

There was an unearthly silence among all the houses down the little streets that flanked the waterside along the reach from Mordialloc to Frankston. But it was broken in one waterfront room by the words of my mum, who kept repeating, over and over again, "John'll catch them, don't you worry. John'll catch them, don't you worry.

Six hundred miles to the northeast, the great city of Sydney was still. No early morning traffic crossed the Harbor Bridge. No one was going to work. The international airport, normally buzzing with activity ready for the 6 A.M. arrival of the first intercontinental flights, was paralyzed. Passengers, staff, crew, and air traffic control—all were glued to radios and televisions sited around the complex. A few miles to the north, along the estuary of the Hawkesbury River, home of Colin Beashel and his family, no house was unlighted. The entire city of Brisbane, still farther north, watched the TV transfixed, hoping for a glimpse of their new favorite son, the mighty Major Peter Costello. They watched us in the government city of Canberra, in Darwin, in Alice Springs, and in the tiny sheep stations dotted all along the dry, lonely acres of the Great Dividing Range. Everyone sat hypnotized by the pictures arriving live by satellite from Rhode Island Sound. They watched us up in the Northern Territory—in Newcastle Waters and Powell Creek. And they watched us all along the endless railway that crosses the Nullarbor Desert from Adelaide, calling at all stations—Tarcoola, Deakin, Forrest, Rawlinna, Kalgoorlie, and Coolgardie— stations for which the young Alan Bond painted signs years ago, names that Geoff and Lex and I gazed at more than 20 years ago as we rumbled along toward my first National Junior Championship in the sleek and lovely *Triad*.

But perhaps most of all they were watching us in the great Western Australian city of Perth, birthplace of *Australia II*, home of Alan Bond, 60 miles south along the shores of the Indian Ocean from Yanchep, Sun City ("Home of the Twelves"), where in a sense it all began. Heartbroken may be too strong a word, but it's close. And millions of unshed tears were held back that morning, as Australia prepared to mourn the sorrowful end of a truly titanic effort. On shore in Newport, a waiter at a little breakfast bar used by yachtsmen was high up a ladder attaching a painted sign, "Welcome home, Dennis and the Boys." A Melbourne reporter, passing by, told me later that his heart sank.

Even Benny Lexcen had lost faith, retreating below on board *Black Swan*, curling up on a bunk and closing his eyes tightly, pretending it was all a ghastly dream, that somehow we would survive to fight again tomorrow. That it was not about to end. Not like this. Alan Bond looked as if he had seen a ghost. Despair was nearly total.

"This is it," I decide. "WE'RE GOING TO RUN THESE BASTARDS DOWN!" Our spinnaker set is magical. Our sails are balanced perfectly, and with the light wind dead astern, we set off down the run. It is not yet 3:35 P.M. There is no feeling of panic on the boat. We have 57 seconds to find but we don't think it is beyond us. Every man is ready.

I speak briefly to Beasho, imploring him once more to keep his eyes on the water, all of the time. I speak again to Ya, telling him that the purpose of his entire life is to spend the next 40 minutes finding the wind. After that, it may very well be oblivion, but if he can just find the wind, right now, everything will have been worth it. And once more we set off in pursuit of Red Dog.

The very instant we head downwind, I know we are sailing in that helmsman's paradise known as "The Groove." We are cutting along a knife edge—between "too low," when the spinnaker becomes like a sheet of jelly and you have to come up, and "too high," when the speed numbers go off the chart and the spinnaker gets too hard. The Groove is a subtle no-man's-land in which you walk a tightrope of pure efficiency, and in which, in a Shangri-la of communication with the trimmers, you always have a split-second warning before you slip down too low and fall off the cliff into that grotesque area where you look up and see the parachute unstable, wobbly, and slowing you down yard by yard.

Right now, *Australia II* is the beneficiary of the thousands of hours of honed concentration we have gone through together on this fifth leg, the former home of our "fifth-leg blues," during which the foreign boats used to run us down again and again in those early elimination trials—the area where those halfwits used to say we were sandbagging.

We are not great down here even now, but we have improved and improved. The dozens of recuts on our spinnakers have brought us up to a pitch of perfection. And while *Australia II* will never be a great downwind boat, we can sail her on this square run at precisely 100 percent of her potential. And we are doing exactly that, each man running over the key lessons we have all learned about her.

Now we are rolling downwind, and the boat feels better than she has ever felt before on this leg. She is very nearly mystical in her excellence as we began to race along, with *Liberty* still out there 75 yards ahead, slightly to port, her spinnaker to my eye a bit wobbly, rocking around. Within the first minute of that square run I know we are doing brilliantly.

"OK, Ya!" I call to my careful and deliberate mastman up on the foredeck. "Which side? What do you think?" Ya continues to deliberate. Hughey calls, "The wind looks better to the left." Ya finally speaks. "The left side looks stronger, John. Hold this course," he says.

And now Skippy, the port trimmer and round-the-world sailor, takes over the calls, locking into my mind so that we can think and speak and feel the boat as one. He is doing the best job he has ever done since I have sailed with him. "Up two, John, up two, up three, up three. That's good. Down a fraction, bit more. That's good, good. Dead right." High above us, a beating swarm of helicopters is threatening to drown out Skippy's clear voice: ". . . up two, up three. That's good, that's perfect. Beautiful, John, that's great."

Suddenly Hughey calls, "We're gaining, John, just about a boatlength." I find myself gripping the wheel harder, then forcing myself to relax, until the wheel feels like a silken thread, and we race on. It feels like perfection.

"We've come to take you higher, John, to take you home."

Then Grant says, with mounting excitement, "Their heads are swiveling, John! We're giving them the heebie-jeebies!" I glance over at *Liberty*. They are sailing lower than we are, but too slowly, and Grant is right—their heads are rotating toward us. He says again, "John, we are right back in this race." And we can all see *Liberty*'s spinnaker dancing around. She sails too low, just off the edge. Still the heads rotate, and it is obvious that they know they will have a hard time containing us. Hughey calls again, "She's jibing away, John." I snap to Ya, "Come on, Ya, what would you do now?" The three seconds longer that it takes Ya to answer, three seconds longer than with any human being I know, seem like an eternity. Then he calls it. "The breeze is stronger to the left, John. Stay where you are." The Americans and the Australians have agreed to differ. Hughey goes with Ya, "Let's stay here." And I say to Grant, "Let's make sure we track the shifts downwind. Keep watching the compass bearing."

Right then Conner jibes again, placing *Liberty* dead parallel with us, just aft of abeam, but if we cross, she still will have us by a couple of boatlengths. *Australia II* is still right in that magical groove of perfection—you can always tell, because there is no disagreement from the trimmers. You never hear, "Get her up," then, "Get her down!" It is very smooth when everything is right. And one thing is certain—Skippy Lissiman is doing the most fantastic job of helping to balance the boat. I mutter to him, "Keep it up, Skippy, for Christ's sake. Let me keep hearing your voice. Keep telling me." It is almost as though my lifeblood, my very oxygen, is coming from Skippy's words. "We have definite boatspeed on them," calls Hughey. "In fact, we're catching them fast."

The wind veers right and *Liberty* jibes again. I know we should go, too. "JIBING THE BOAT," I call, as we sail higher and faster than they do. Hughey swings around, his cool eyes gleaming, and he blurts out, uncharacteristically, "We're back in it, John, we're back in it!"

I call down to the middle of the boat, "Chink, old son, we are right back in it!" He turns around briefly, too afraid to smile, and just gets a tighter grip on the winch handles.

I hold *Australia II* on this long port tack, and to our left we can see *Liberty,* some of her crew still staring, mesmerized by us. Conner jibes again, then again, and now we are almost neck and neck, sailing parallel, with only about a boatlength between us. The unthinkable is happening.

We are preparing to take them, and I think my pulse must be hitting nearly 200 as we veer off, slightly to my right, gaining, gaining.

Here is the result of another lesson learned in Newport. In that first race, where we smashed our steering gear trying to take *Liberty*'s stern, we realized we should have squared up and kept going, eking out to leeward. Hughey and I, on those long, sleepy journeys out to the racecourse, had gone over it a hundred times. And now it was happening again, just as we had planned.

We keep going, eking out to leeward, going just a little faster, a little lower toward the mark. For 10 minutes we roll along, still just behind them, with Scoop calling the shots. "Up a bit, John, that's nice, looks good, looks really good. Up a bit more. That's good, John, real nice. Down a shade. Beautiful, that's beautiful, John." And now the breeze is going lighter, and we have caught up another half a boatlength. We are running through her, and soon we will face the moment of truth. *Liberty* must jibe over toward us, because she clearly cannot stay where she is, being overtaken. Right now we are just about level, and Hughey is saying, "She'll come over in a minute, John." In that split second my entire life passed before me. Everything I have ever worked for, everything I have ever wanted, is about to be placed within my grasp. My heritage of the sea, my very destiny dances before my eyes. Twelve thousand miles away, a nation is holding its breath. And now it is deathly quiet on *Australia II*.

When *Liberty* jibes, the only thing that matters is that she cross behind us. If she hits us, *we* get disqualified. We all stand there, the tension beyond anyone's comprehension, almost afraid to breathe, afraid that our own heartbeats will somehow rock the boat.

Liberty jibes. Dennis Conner swings the big red bow toward us, and in the light wind I can hear her winches as her great sails are adjusted. "Here she comes, John," calls Hughey. And Scoop keeps calling the shots, "We're looking good, John, up a bit. That's good, that's very good. Keep going along. That's great. Looking good, John, looking real good." And on comes *Liberty*. I have *Australia II* up to our fastest course, and now we can hear the American crew calling to each other. "She's going to cross our stern, John," says Hughey, uttering words I can hardly believe I am hearing. "We have about half a boatlength on them," he adds. And Grant is saying to me quietly, "OK, John, we're moving forward on bearing. We're in good shape, moving forward on bearing." I glance left. *Liberty* is on us. "She takes our stern, John," says Hughey, quietly. And I hear her light bow wave as she slides by behind us. Scoop calls out again, a bit cheekily, "We are actually looking very nice indeed. That John is real good."

Right about now, the waiter at the breakfast bar in Newport was back up the ladder, and the same Melbourne reporter, Bob McDonald, walking past, said to him, "What's going on up there now?" "Just patching the names," he said. "For 'Dennis,' read 'John.'"

I estimate that we have about half a knot of boatspeed on *Liberty* at this minute, and I turn around and look over my right shoulder at the enemy. They have frozen up, panicked. And I know the feeling. Dennis is sailing that boat artificially low, doing what we used to do when *Azzurra* put us in a flat spin a couple of times. His spinnaker pole is much farther aft than it should be, his mainsail and spinnaker have much less pressure on them than they should have.

Now we have passed them, and we are out in front in the race. There is a lot of action on board *Australia II*. These boys are real professionals by now, and one thing we do know how to do is to get in front and then stay there. "Damian, get up on the bow and be prepared for a jibe!" For all we know, Dennis might want to lure us into a jibing duel, but somehow I doubt it, although I am pleased that we are ready. My hands are sweaty, but I know that *Australia II* prefers a light grip downwind. Let it flow, Bertrand, let it flow.

Hughey believes we should sail on, to go farther into some fresh breeze he has spotted on the water. But I will not take that chance. "No," I tell him, "we must stay in contact." Just about when *Liberty* jibes, we do the same, and once more we are on a collision course. This time we sail across her bow, and we jibe hard back onto a port tack about 1½ boatlengths in front. On we go, down toward the fifth mark. Dennis takes our stern once more, jibing just aft of us. Then he jibes again, and again, as he runs toward the mark. We jibe just once onto starboard tack as we head up to the red buoy, the America's Cup buoy. I decide then to pull off one of our most daring and tricky maneuvers, the "float drop," which will gain us a few more seconds if it works but will be a total catastrophe if we make a mistake. We are about 20 seconds in front, and I know that's not enough to be safe. Hughey calls out the difficult sail change: "PREPARE FOR A FLOAT DROP, YA!" Very, very concise, no confusion. Ya makes a major speech. "Ya," he replies, thumbs up. "FLOAT DROP CON-FIRMED," I call.

By now the Major is fighting his way out of the sewer with the big code-one genoa slung over his huge shoulders. He dumps it on the deck in its bag, and Damian seizes the top of the sail and clips it to the forestay feeder. I'm coming in now very fast toward the mark, a little bit high, looking for a racing-car turn.

After the Major dives across the foredeck to clip on the genoa, we are ready, ready to drop the beloved green-and-gold spinnaker of *Australia II* for the last time. Ya gets ready to release her. The Major has slipped back to seize the halyard for the hoist. I watch the operation with mounting concern. I remember that day in Melbourne when we floundered through this maneuver and came around the mark with no genoa up at all. Please, God, don't let there be a foulup.

Now Chink's nerves are getting the better of him. He has assumed command in the center of the boat, and he shouts out, "Come on, John, let's go, let's go!" But I'm hanging on to the wheel as we drive up to the mark, and I snap, "NO! NO! HOLD IT! HOLD IT! YOU'LL COLLAPSE THE CHUTE! EASY DOES IT." I wait a few seconds, and then call, "HOIST THE GENOA!" And with a nuclear outpouring of pure pent-up fury, the Major heaves at the halyard, running up the genoa with spellbinding speed. Up she goes, and I'm thinking, "Don't rip that genoa. Careful, careful." I snap, "If that develops even a slight kink, it'll tear the luff tape. Make sure he doesn't pull it up too hard."

And now the spinnaker is set to come down. "POLE AFT," I shout, "POLE AFT! POLE AFT!" The pole swings back, and I yell, "TRIP!" The pole crashes onto the deck. Ya hits the quick-release button to ease the halyard and let the spinnaker go floating to the deck. I shout again, "JIBING THE BOAT!" and we glide around the mark, the boom swinging over, as close to perfection as you can get. And now the Major is back down the starboard hatch dragging the lazy sheet with him. The line is screaming off the winch at about 100 m.p.h. and the spinnaker is collapsing on the leeward side of the boat, hitting the water before the Major can stop it. But it only skims the surface, and deep in the hold of the boat, his mighty arms are flailing, left-right, left-right, as he drags and wrenches the big, wet parachute in on top of him. The last time we shall ever see it in action.

Now Scoop is down on the starboard side, taking his spinnaker sheet off his major drum and transferring his genoa sheet onto it. And all the while Chink and Splash are battering away at the winches, trimming the genoa while I'm still turning the boat. Beasho is going like crazy, winding in the mainsheet, and I come in hard, as if we are on a monorail. I think I'm getting the hang of this, so I risk a glance behind, to see what I hope is the red boat in her death throes. Our "float drop" was executed under the most terrible pressure. Any one of the boys could have been excused if he had quietly fainted.

We have picked up a few seconds, so we head up the final windward leg 21 seconds in front. This means of course that we took one minute 18 seconds off the Americans on the fifth leg—principally because Dennis Conner jibed 11 times to our five. Since you lose about 30 feet every time you jibe, well, there's 60 yards. All that jibing, which I put down to panic, cost them 30 seconds. Also, they were on the wrong side of the racecourse and missed both of the major windshifts. I thought they sailed that leg very moderately indeed, and their spinnaker did not appear to be set very well. The angle was wrong. They were off-key. We had significant boatspeed on them, no doubt—perhaps 20 seconds on the run—but not 78 seconds. We had bided our time and they had made the mistakes.

The other key point is the timing of our jibes. We did it at exactly the right time, every time, taking advantage of the shifts.

Right now the battle is still very much on, and we round on a port tack, knowing we have no time to make two more jibes before the red boat comes sliding around on the attack. Our spinnaker pole crashes onto the deck completely as Ya releases the inboard end. Now the jib is drawing, and we are squeezing up onto the wind, waiting for the full force of the American 12-Meter war machine to be launched against us as we attempt to hold a tight cover on them all the way to the finish line.

I can hardly believe all this is happening, but I do know that it is not over yet—not by a long way. We hang on to the port tack, and Hughey and I decide just to wait for them and tack when they tack. And now she's coming at us. Hughey is facing aft, and I am leaving the calls to him. The next few minutes will probably have an element of blood and guts, so I shout down to Chink and Splash and the Major and Damian to stand by for what we are sure will be the most vicious tacking duel we have yet been asked to withstand. In fact, we are on the verge of perhaps the greatest tacking duel in history.

Like many really bloody scraps, this one starts off a bit tamely. Dennis knows he can probably boatspeed us upwind, and as soon as they have *Liberty* closehauled, they start off in a straight line. We go with them for a short distance, and when they find out pretty quickly that this is not going to do the job for them, they throw a tack at us immediately. Hughey calls it, and we tack on top of them again. After six more, we begin to eke out a little, because we do have an advantage when it gets down to a series of these quick, aggressive maneuvers. Then Dennis starts to intersperse his real tacks with a few dummies (i.e., pretending to go and then luffing up and not going, hoping to cause us to go the wrong way, rather like a slow-motion feint by a soccer or football player). Again and again he tacks, every time Hughey calls it right, and every time I plant *Australia II* right between the red boat and the distant finish line.

At around the 24th tack, we are beginning to get a little uptight. A touch of nervous anxiety is beginning to creep into Hughey's voice as he calls out the shots. Now Dennis is throwing in a few extra "dummies." From where I am standing, it is beginning to get a bit hair-raising, as the Americans keep charging—still behind, but flailing away with both fists in an attempt to get away from us. All I can hear is, "TACK!" "TACK IT AGAIN!" "TACK!" "NO! SHE'S LUFFING, DON'T GO!" "TACK!"

"TACK IT AGAIN!" I am being asked to tack again before I have even gotten her going off the last one. We are beginning to lose boatspeed as well as sweat and energy, as the heavies flog away on the grinders. I know we are beginning to slow down, and I know we are getting a bit rattled. I also know that in a similar situation in Race 2, Dennis got by, despite our cover, so there is no question that he knows how to do it. My job is to stop him, and stop him I will. There's no way he is going to get by us today. And I say to myself again, "I'm not practicing anymore. This is it." And I say to Hughey, "Steady now. Let's settle down. We must have more speed from the boat before we tack. We just cannot tack instantly with them. Let's not get sucked into their plan. Let's just sail this our own way."

And with that, we start to loosen our cover in order to keep up our boatspeed. We have to do that, because the Americans are doing a better job than we are at this minute. Dennis is tacking that big red boat more sharply and keeping up his speed better. He is a bit more accomplished at this than I am, because he has had so much experience with this type of 12-Meter match racing. He and Blackaller and Kolius were going at each other like this for months on end, all summer, while I was trying to hang on to big leads against the foreign boats. And now *Liberty*'s expertise is showing. We have a technically superior tacking boat, but we are not doing such a good job, and danger threatens with every gust of this light, moderating wind.

"Right, Hughey," I say, "let's just relax a bit and get that boatspeed up." This is a major philosophical change, and we decide to try to consolidate, staying on top of *Liberty* but not matching them every time they flex their muscles. Speed is the key, and I know that we have been going into tacks at about 6 knots and coming out at about 4½ knots. "We need 6½ knots before we tack," I estimate, and immediately we begin to hold them at bay.

Dennis keeps throwing them at us. Now we are well into the 30s, and the boys down on the winches are getting tired for sure, although none of them will ever admit it. As we lean into the 41st tack, I can see young Damian charging away with big Splash, our very own Hercules in his bright-yellow rubber boots, in nothing short of heroic fashion. I am pretty sure that they are either in, or entering, the "red zone" now, and the pain must be beginning to recede a bit as they come through it. I can see Splash talking to Damian, and now I can suddenly hear them start to. "dedicate" the tacks—not loudly, but loudly enough for me to know how fantastically hard they all are trying. Conner brings *Liberty* slicing along underneath us. We smooth back up to our optimum speed, and now Hughey calls again, his voice calm, the anxiety gone, "TACK THE BOAT, JOHN." I shout down to the boys, "TACKING!" The Major says, grimly,

"This one's for Hughey." And on they go, their huge shoulders churning, their gloved hands, gripped tight, racing around as they whip the genoa lines back.

We are now well into this final, last-ditch struggle, and the consequences of its outcome are clear to everyone. We are fighting for our lives again, but I know that the real danger to us—perhaps even more so than Dennis—is the possibility of 11th-hour stagefright seizing me and my boys. We cannot even think of the result of this race, or what it will mean, because that is just too overwhelming. And all of my lessons in sports psychology are clambering into my mind as if I am suddenly a mere spectator. I know that none of us can think, even for a fleeting second, of what might happen if we should win, or if we should lose, or if we should make a mistake. Dimly I am aware that whatever does happen to us in the next half hour is going to live with us, or grotesquely haunt us, for the rest of our lives.

I could see Hughey tightening up. Hughey, five-time veteran of the Admiral's Cup, former world 18-foot champion, is the one man in all of the five hundred million people watching this contest, who *must not* take his eyes off the red boat. And his voice is betraying the colossal pressure he is under, and I can feel that dreadful tightening of nerve ends becoming infectious. I found my own mind racing, groping back through the years, searching through a thousand memories of big international competition for the moments when I had coped with anything like this before. And of course there were none. All I could do was to fall back on the words Rasa had spoken to me: "You can win this race, John, if you will let your natural talents flow." I know what to do. All I must remember is to relax, relax, let it flow, let it flow.

But yet again, I find myself gripping the wheel, and yet again I will myself to find the velvet touch when I seem to be holding *Australia II* on reins of silken thread.

"We've come to take you higher, John, to take you home."

But right now that big red son of a bitch is right behind us, and I can hear them shouting. I glance around and see that *Liberty* has about halved our lead. They are now within about 1½ boatlengths, nipping at our heels. I can hear their winches going now about as clearly as I can hear our own.

Suddenly a voice from *Liberty* shouts, "We're getting closer, guys!" All the boys hear that American voice, but it is Chink who decides to reply. He swings around from his grinder, sweat pouring down his face, and bellows, "COME AND GET US! COME AND BLOODY GET US!" Now there is a frenzy of activity around us, and I am thinking to myself, "Come on, John, just hang loose. Don't get excited. Just keep sailing. This is no time to practice. This is it. Just deliver the America's Cup to Australia."

And now *Liberty* comes at us for the 45th time. The sweat is pouring off the boys and their muscles are throbbing, heartbeats as high as any top athlete ever wants them. "Tack her, John," says Hughey, and again I shout, "TACKING!" to the boys. And once more I hear Chink shout, "WHAT ABOUT ONE FOR SCOTTY!" And they grind away, with what looks like murderous fury, in honor of our stricken bow man, who helped for so long to get us to this final showdown with *Liberty*, and whose quest for the America's Cup ended so very tragically high on the mast of *Australia II*.

Boatspeed back to normal, we prepare to withstand the 46th tack, and *Liberty* wheels around underneath us very fast. Hughey says, urgently, "Tack her now," and I call out, "TACKING!" just in time to hear the Major gasp, "COME ON, BOYS, THIS ONE'S FOR JOHN. LET'S MAKE IT THE BEST EVER!" I am not sure how much more of this anyone can stand, and, sure enough, the 47th tack is the last. Chink calls it for Beasho, and the red boat does not try the maneuver again.

I immediately call out to Ya to watch the wind carefully, because now we are going to start playing the shifts. We still lead by two or three boatlengths, and up above us, past this giant fleet of spectator boats, we can just see the finish line. Now *Liberty* starts to move through to leeward alarmingly, and the angles are getting pretty wide. We are both on port tack, but Dennis swings the red boat back, the breeze is dropping, and they are almost sailing in their own wake. We tack on top of them, and then we do the same thing. "This is tricky," I say to Hughey. "One gust of breeze could make a major difference to either of us right now." And I call to Beasho, "You are doing a fantastic job, Colin, but please keep your head out of the boat and watch for the breeze. Let me have feedback if you spot anything."

At that moment, Ya calls out from his area, "Here's some breeze for us," and immediately we surge forward and start to increase our lead for the first time in half an hour. *Liberty* tacks back on a long port beat over to the spectator fleet, with the intent of dragging us into the chop, and we cover her from our high position. Together we drive into the fleet, with hundreds and hundreds of boats slamming their engines into reverse to make room, like a big ocean wall on the move.

I call to Hughey, "We just want to make one big, full tack to the line from here. I don't want to make any more tacks than we absolutely need." Grant suddenly says, "We're on the layline right now. We can tack if you like." I say, "No, no, let's just keep going." Hughey agrees. "We keep going." Grant looks up and says, "It's not a problem. We could tack and run right up to the line, no trouble." But I insist, "Forget it, we're staying right between *Liberty* and the finish, and there is no way they are going to pass us." On we go, right into the fleet, weaving around in the Superboat.

Hughey then says, "John, we are a good 10 to 15 degrees above the line. We could go now and take her home." Finally I agree, trying not to be mesmerized by the colossal number of people out there, packed on the bows of the boats, all panicking and trying to back out of our way, churning the water into a giant washing machine. I swing the boat around very smoothly, and we head up toward the line.

Now Hughey is facing aft again, calling, "Red Dog sucks into some new air. She increases bearing on us." But we are sailing 15 degrees above the line, and sooner or later we are going to have to sail so low that the wind might shift behind us. Grant calls out, "There might be a situation for a spinnaker here in a few minutes." And I call down to Damian, "GET THE SPINNAKER READY. CODE TWO, THE LIGHT-AIR CHUTE." Now we can see *Liberty* getting a pole ready. Everything is assembled on our boat, and I call out, "HOLD IT! Let's not do anything right now." But Hughey then calls that *Liberty* is lifting up a little bit on our weather stern. "Are we parallel?" I ask. "Yes," he says, "but sail a little higher. Let's get right in front of her." I ease her up, higher and higher, until Hughey says, "OK, fine. Hold this course." Now we have *Liberty* in a near-impossible position, and unless something absolutely diabolical happens, we are about to record the biggest upset in sporting history.

The entire world right now is in a frenzy of anticipation, as Dennis Conner and his afterguard, Tom Whidden and Halsey ("I Think We're Going to Lose") Herreshoff, face the prospect of being the men who finally lost the America's Cup after 132 years. The tension on *Australia II* is nothing short of staggering. No one speaks. Most of us can't, with pulses racing at about 160 instead of 80. Suddenly Chink blurts out what no one dares to say, "I THINK WE'RE GOING TO WIN THE AMERICA'S CUP!" About four of the boys pounce on him in unison. "SHUT UP, CHINK!" We still have about half a mile to go, and each of us is coping with the pressure and the tension as best he can. I'm calmly expecting the mast to fall down or something, since I find the entire concept of victory just a fraction beyond my current imaginative process. Also, I'm busy.

In fact, as I hang on to the wheel, on the verge of making history, I remember a moment 13 years ago on *Gretel II* in the final race against France. We were out in front, and one of our boys said, "I think we are going to beat the French." At that moment, the bow fitting broke and the jib shot straight up the forestay, flapping like a broken wing. We just managed to limp across the line about 10 seconds in front of the French boat. Holy *merde*! We sailors tend to be a bit superstitious.

Chink goes stone silent. He knows what he has done, because anything can still happen, any kind of gear failure could rob us of our rightful spoils. We are not totally in control of our destiny, because on a big racing boat you can never be totally sure you are going to hold up. The air is supercharged. Suddenly I see about six faces staring back at *Liberty,* and I call out, "Could someone just tell us where we are going, rather than where we have just been?" But I suppose the excitement is nearly overpowering.

Hughey says reassuringly, "We're in good shape, John, right in front of them. We are 40 seconds in front of them. We're in good shape." Hughey never loses concentration once, all the way to the line, and I do not think I have, either. Not on this day, the day for which I have been waiting since I was big enough to sail an old converted motor launch on Port Phillip Bay.

Now we are coming nearer to the line. Damian is up on the bow, and I can hear someone calling, "Four boatlengths . . . three boatlengths. . . ." Up ahead I can see that half of the New York Yacht Club Committee is not on deck to watch us cross the line. They must be thunderstruck, locked away in a cabin below, probably with very large glasses full of something powerful, not wanting to watch John Bertrand and his bloody Aussies come rolling home. "Two boatlengths . . . one boatlength. . . ." My battle-scarred friend Hughey says, dryly, "Try not to hit the committee boat." AND THERE'S THE GUN!

Damian's left fist flew into the air. I glanced up and saw a couple of the New York Yacht Club Committee men giving us the famous Australian fly-swatting salute in a gesture of sportsmanship. "Well done!" they called.

I let go of the wheel for the first time in 4½ hours and sat down. I felt the most overpowering sense of relief—not contentment, just relief—that the huge responsibility I had been shouldering for as long as I could remember had suddenly been lifted. Perhaps this was peace, true peace, the first I had ever known. For a minute I thought I was dead. The boat was silent, but I looked up at Hughey, and he was standing there as if he had just been frightened to death. He kept saying, "We've won . . . we've won . . . we've won . . . we've won!"

I put my head into my hands and, unaccountably, felt tears welling into my eyes. I looked up at Hughey, and he was looking at me and shaking his head. Then he said, "John . . . you're the best. . . . You *are* the best!" For some reason, that completely overcame me, and I flung my arms around my faithful tactician and wept shamelessly. I was not alone, either. I looked over to Beasho, and he was still standing by himself next to the hydraulic controls upon which he had imposed such killing concentration for so long. Great tears were rolling down his cheeks. Chink, who had been trying for so long, was hugging both Skippy and Splash, and they were all in tears, while the Major was leaping up and down like a madman, punching the air and roaring. Grant was standing beside

Hughey and me, laughing and laughing, and I remember Damian running back shouting, "John, John, do you think someone could phone my mum to tell her we've won?"

I wasn't able to say anything to anybody, but I remember saying to myself, "Thank God! Thank God!" It had been such a terribly long time. I had been dreaming about this moment since old Tom Pearkes first showed me his big America's Cup scrapbooks back on Bristol Avenue. God knows what he would have said if he could have seen me now. And what about Bant, and Nan and Dad? Could they see me? I had so many tears to shed that I didn't know where to start.

Everyone was hugging everyone. Chink and the Major were like two great dancing bears. I went over to every member of the crew and hugged him and thanked him for everything. At this stage, no one was steering the boat or, indeed, doing anything. We were all in shock, as an avalanche of powerboats hurtled toward us. After what seemed an eternity, *Liberty* was now over the line, and Hughey made his last call, "John, JOHN! They're waving at us." I turned around and waved, noticing that Dennis Conner was slumped in his cockpit, head bowed, a shattered man. The afterguard of *Liberty* was not waving, but most of the crew were.

Half the world now seemed to be upon us. *Black Swan* had arrived, and the guys were arriving on *Rubber Ducky*. The first man over the side rushed up to congratulate me, and I flung my arms around Scotty McAllister. Bondy was next over, bounding down the boat and throwing his arms around me and shouting, "We've done it! We've done it! We've done it!"

And done it we had. When all this riotous celebration has subsided—indeed, a hundred years hence—the history books will record formally that at precisely 45 seconds after 5:20 on the afternoon of September 26, 1983, Australia won the America's Cup. Their 12-Meter racing yacht, *Australia II*, designed by Ben Lexcen, built in Perth by Steve Ward, helmed by John Bertrand, assisted by Hugh Treharne (tactician) and Grant Simmer (navigator), defeated the American 12-Meter, *Liberty*, designed by Johan Valentijn, built by Newport Offshore, helmed by Dennis Conner, assisted by Tom Whidden (tactician) and Halsey Herreshoff (navigator), by a score of 3–4. Winning distance (seventh race): 41 seconds.

Now it was over, and with it had died 132 years of American yacht-racing supremacy. One hundred fifty miles south of Newport, they were ordering a Brink's truck to drive the "Holy Grail" of the world's oceans up to Newport, and ultimately into the hands of Bondy, who would take it home, at last, to Australia, to the land of Banjo Paterson, where the waters roll onto our gigantic coastline beneath the constellation of the Southern Cross.

And now they were singing Banjo's famous lines throughout the waterborne armada that floated all around us. They were singing on hundreds of boats laden with Aussies trying to catch a glimpse of us. Absolute pandemonium reigned out there on Rhode Island Sound—but the sound today was "Waltzing Matilda"! It was a joyful cry from the very heart of Australia that rent the cool evening air above *Australia II,* and slowly but surely urged home to us some of the magnitude of what we had achieved.

In one glorious moment of unrestrained exultation, I suddenly leaped into the air and punched the sky three times in quick succession, letting out a rebel yell that might have been envied at the Battle of Bull Run. It was the first time I had let myself go for months, and there I was, right up there yelling with the Major, the image of utterly unrestrained happiness. A couple of kids—probably Scoop and certainly Damian—yelled, "Go on, John, give 'em hell."

And now I was in Benny's arms. Like another huge bear—there were bears all over the place on this boat—he was saying over and over to me, "You've done it, you bastard, you've done it." The boats were now tightly packed against *Australia II,* and I was looking for Rasa, but she was in the safest and most competent hands of all, being driven over to us through the other boats in a little Whaler, ducking and diving all over the place. At the helm, beside himself with joy, tears streaming down his face, was the great seaman who held *Australia II* together, Kenny Beashel.

As Rasa came on board, I noticed Robbie Brown up on the foredeck trying to get the kangaroo up the forestay. In the panic, we had forgotten that. Then Lucas showed up from *Black Swan.* Bondy was right again—he never saw us lose. I lifted him up high and he patted me on the back. I hugged Rasa, who was weeping as I had *never* seen her weep before. Right up to the end, she had never cracked, not even when Australia's toughest newspaper tycoon, Rupert Murdoch, broke down on the boat and wept, holding her hand, as we hit the finish line. After all of the months and months in which she had done so much to hold our little family together—the family of John Bertrand as well as the extended family of *Australia II*—she could contain it all no longer. I held her next to me and felt her sobbing uncontrollably. She had finally allowed 14 years of anxiety, devotion, and pure emotion to boil over. She had never done that before.

And now they were attaching the towlines to our bow. Benny was behind the wheel, the first and last man to take the helm of his creation in the campaign for the America's Cup. And at last we began the long tow home to Newport Harbor. We were flanked by two big Coast Guard boats, their blue lights swiveling, and hundreds more all around.

Men at Work were giving 'em hell from the mighty speakers on *Black*

Swan, and there was champagne all over the place. Some of the boys were sitting down, singing along. Skippy and Scoop, who only 90 minutes earlier had been nursing the boat along, trimming that spinnaker to within an inch of its life, their nerves stretched to a point beyond any reason, were now sitting with their feet on the winches, swallowing champagne and cheerfully giving Men at Work their complete concentration and assistance.

DO YOU COME FROM A LAND DOWN UNDER . . .
WHERE WOMEN GLOW AND MEN PLUNDER. . . .

The sun was setting as we were towed triumphantly into the outer waters of the harbor, the huge, red, fiery ball in the sky sinking below the long hills off to our left. From the vast crowd gathered along the foreshore of Castle Hill, a great swell of "Waltzing Matilda" rose into the air as we approached. Fireworks exploded overhead as darkness fell, and I thought of home, of how they could see that same sun back in Melbourne rising up above the bay. I did not know that even now there were still no rush-hour cars on Harbor Bridge in Sydney, that the entire country had ground to a complete standstill, that the Prime Minister, Bob Hawke, had gone on the television, glowing with excitement, and just about forbade any employer from firing anyone for not turning up for work after being up all night watching the white boat from Perth.

When we reached the harbor, the sight was unforgettable. It was full of boats. We could have gotten out and walked to shore. They hitched us up for the traditional lap of honor around the harbor, the first time any foreign boat had been eligible. The whistles and foghorns gave us a nearly deafening salute, and all around the docks were thousands and thousands of people, clapping and cheering beneath the skyrockets exploding above us. It was a scene the like of which I had never seen before and I don't expect I ever shall see again. It was a fiercely nautical moment, and one that I will never forget. Huge spotlights were trained upon us as we inched our way in. Searchlights lit up the sky. A hundred yards from our final destination, it was just about over. The place was just like a logjam. Somehow a path was made for us, but it took us about 40 minutes to cover the last 100 yards. Some of the huge boats were listing at dangerous angles as everyone rushed to one side to try to see us. As we reached the dock, Rasa told me that I had not stopped grinning for two hours, and I kissed her. What a private moment that turned out to be! We were now within the range of the dockside television cameras, and about half a billion people saw it. All around us were amazing colors as the rockets kept exploding and the flags and ribbons broke out all along the docks.

It's funny, but Rasa remembers nothing of this at all. She can scarcely remember anything whatsoever about the spectacular journey from the racecourse into the harbor—not the lights or the singing, the cheering or the horns, the huge crowds or the boats. She was, I believe, in total shock at what we had done. I mean this in the strictly medical sense. But her mental condition was nowhere near as severe as that of the crew, some of whom would take several months to recover from the psychological ordeal we had undergone.

Finally we made the dock, which was listing perilously under the weight of the crowds. There were reporters and television technicians everywhere, and beyond our dock gates were thousands and thousands of people, just ordinary people who had cascaded through Newport's streets to catch a glimpse of history. In the water around *Australia II* were dozens of boats—rowboats, Windsurfers, inflatables, Whalers, rafts, kayaks, and launches. Up on the deck of *Challenge* were Aussies drinking and spraying huge magnums of champagne. Sir James Hardy, the veteran helmsman who had lost so many times and who had been so utterly faithful to our cause throughout everything, stood for a while next to me with the most enormous smile on his face and tears streaming down his cheeks. He kept letting huge jets of Rheims's finest shoot across the deck, and then he would yell through his tears, "Don't waste it. DRINK IT!" Benny was aboard *Australia II*, dancing a little jig above the keel with which he had driven half the world mad. There was Benny, a world figure, made for life—and you cannot find a nicer fellow than Benny anywhere among the ranks of those who have suddenly been "made for life."

Then, seemingly from nowhere, the men from *Liberty* arrived in their red foul-weather gear. Dennis Conner was devastated, and he walked up to me with a red handkerchief to wipe away the tears from his cheeks. He could not manage much. I said to him, "Dennis, I do not know what to say." And he replied, "I did my best, John." I tried to be nonchalant, but it did not work. I said, rather awkwardly, "But it was some kind of a boat race, wasn't it?" And he just said again, "I did my best. I could not do any more than that." He wiped his eyes with his big red handkerchief, because by now the tears were just streaming down his face. He walked over to speak to the champagne-shooting Sir James, whom he had beaten in 1980, and as he went, I thought, "There is a man who wanted all the glory of victory, and now he is going to have to cope personally with all of the agony of defeat." The volume of the responsibility had been borne so individually by Dennis that in one sense it was less a personal matter for the others. Tom Whidden, the tactician, came over to me and said, with a great sporting smile, "Well done, John." Halsey Herreshoff, who presumably had been preparing for this moment for several weeks, came over and said, "Congratulations, John." John Marshall was in tears and did not speak to me. I have not yet decided whether he was crying over the loss of the America's Cup or over the prospect of what I might demand now to continue to work for North Sails. Anyway, he did not seem to be in a mood to mention the contract again, as he had done with such cheerfulness on that evening when Australia had been 3–1 down. Moods do change, of course.

The men from *Liberty* did not stay for long—about five minutes—but as they went, I noticed that Betsy Whidden was sobbing uncontrollably in Rasa's arms, saying, "I'm just so glad you won it, after all these years."

Bondy and I shortly left *Australia II* with our arms around each other's shoulders. We made our way through the mighty throng to *Black Swan*, where we had a few glasses of champagne. The noise and celebrations were now, if anything, more intense than they had been when we arrived. And now the crowd was chanting, "Show us the keel! Show us the keel!" Bondy orchestrated that moment, raising his arms like the conductor of a great symphony as *Australia II* was lifted slowly out of the water to show the world for the first time the keel and its wings. As she emerged from the waters of the harbor, a mighty cheer went up, and a chap on a Windsurfer, dressed in a tuxedo, eased alongside, poured himself a glass of champagne, plonked the bottle on the keel, and drank a ceremonial toast. I'm not sure who he was, but Rasa said he was a pal of Lucas's, who seemed to know everyone in the entire town.

And now it was time for us to make our way to the press conference at the Armory. As we arrived at the gates to our dock, there was a scene bordering on riot conditions. People were packed thousands deep, and policemen were trying to clear a way for us. At one stage, nightsticks were drawn, and in the midst of it all, about 200 photographers were battling for position to immortalize us in publications all over the world. The crowd was just extraordinary, as if someone had shouted, "Fire!" in the middle of the World Series and thousands of baseball fans were stampeding for the exits. Rasa's feet were not touching the ground as Bondy dragged her along. Then we lost Lucas, and it was impossible to try to look for him. I heard Rasa call back to a couple of the boys, "Please, please find Lucas and bring him here." And we pressed on through the mob trying to reach the conference. At one stage, in a moment of devilment, I jumped on the back of a policeman's motorbike, and he drove me the last few yards to the door. Once there, it was a diabolical scramble to get in. We sort of popped out of the crowd into the room, like seeds being squirted out of an orange. Then Eileen Bond was refused admission by the guards because she did not have the proper credentials. Bondy solved that in his usual direct way. "Either you let that lady in or there is not going to be a press conference," he said. Eileen made her entrance. Rasa then rushed over to the office and rang home to see if Lucas had arrived, but he had not done so, so she alerted the police to watch out for him. But just as she arrived back at the Armory, a few minutes before the conference started, in through the door came Skippy and Ginger, holding hands with Lucas. Dear old Skippy, rescuer of Lucas, could not understand what the fuss was about. As usual, he didn't miss a beat. "Oh, Hi, Ras, everything OK? I brought Lucas along, found him riding his bike out in the street."

God knows how Lucas managed to be riding his bike, since Thames Street was jammed with people. They were hanging out of every window, three stories high, shouting and cheering. They were on top of roofs, on top of cars, hanging on to lampposts and awnings. I have never seen anything even remotely like it. Inside the Armory, you could still hear the huge mob outside. Eileen lost a $50,000 diamond-studded watch in the uproar, but it was later found, and somehow or other we proceeded to the table, where Warren Jones introduced every single member of our group—right down to the most junior sailmaker. Even the press applauded and cheered us.

And then it was time for me to make some sort of statement. I told them that I felt very proud and very humble to have been able to sail with this extraordinary crew. "In my opinion, they are the best in the world. And I have been involved with the most incredible team spirit that any skipper could possibly wish for. I am very honored to have won the Cup for Australia. Thank you very much."

Dennis had appeared at the press conference before we arrived, and I did look at a transcript of his little statement. I understand that he was desperately upset, but I also noted that the theme that he and his henchmen had stuck to all summer, the excuse they had prepared even before we started, did not vary. He said, "Today *Australia II* was just a better boat. And they beat us. And we had no excuses. So I'd like at this point to congratulate Alan Bond and *Australia II* on their superb effort over the summer. They proved they were an outstanding boat and today was their day." I do not think it ought to have been beyond him to mention something about the Australian crew, particularly since he and I both knew that in *Liberty*'s light mode for that final race there was, boat for boat, very little difference in boatspeed.

Somehow we began to make our way home to Dennison Street, and very slowly the light of achievement began to shine for me. We had to stop down at the boat to get our gear, and I stepped on board by myself. The crowd was still celebrating, and some kids were now using the keel's wings as a water slide and were shooting off into the harbor. I just stood there, near the place where Colin had worked the hydraulics for so long, and smiled and smiled. As we wandered up Dennison Street, I remember saying to Rasa, "Do you realize what we have just done? We have won the America's Cup." Just the sound of the phrase was such sweet music. I kept saying it.

After I had showered and changed, Rasa came into the bedroom and said, "John, you have actually just won the America's Cup." We could not stop saying it. And neither, I soon realized, could the rest of the crew. Or their wives or girl friends. Or Bondy, or Warren, or Benny. It was almost as though we were all going mad.

Founders' Hall was in an uproar, and we did not like it. There were people everywhere, and Rasa and Annie were at the door to try to stop people from coming into the Australian bastion, which had been our fortress and our domain for such a terribly long time. Strangers had just about cleaned out the kitchen. Beasho was wandering around, saying, "What are all these people here for?" We were men who did not really belong anywhere, except with each other. The only light moment was provided by Damian, who was still charging around the building trying to get through to his mum to tell her we had won. What Damian did not know was that at that particular moment, his mum and dad were being chaired shoulder-high down the main street of his village of Williamstown by exultant neighbors. They were, after all, the parents of *Australia II*'s 21-year-old bow man, Damian Fewster—carpenter, pursuer of the local sheilahs, the first man over the winning line.

Basically, we felt confused by the intensity of the events unfolding around *Australia II*. We were all supposed to be on our way to a party at Alan Bond's house, and none of us realized how difficult it would be. But it was. Soon we found ourselves in little huddles together, and whenever a perfectly well-meaning, nice, friendly person would come up to talk to us, perhaps to offer congratulations, we tended to shy away. We were in close little groups all together. I was dimly aware that it was antisocial behavior. And then it began to dawn on me that we had nothing to say to anyone except each other. That no one could understand what had happened to us and what we had been through. We had forgotten how to go to a party, how to perform that social art that takes a bit of practice—to circulate, to talk to different people, to tell a few tales, to laugh at things that are not terribly funny, to be normal human beings, indulging in everyday social chitchat.

We would just keep saying, "Do you guys know what we have done? We have just won the America's Cup!" I think those were the only words we were capable of finding agreeable. But only from each other. Only we knew the true dimensions and the terrors of the Everest we had scaled together.

No one else knew how we had each held on to our nerves as the world watched us. How each of us had lived with the cold fear of making a mistake, of letting the others down. It was just not possible to understand how stretched-out we were. We were men who, without the aid of tranquilizers, would wake in the middle of the night, out of breath, sweating, grabbing for a winch handle, the wheel, or a line—anything to stop the red boat from coming by. Our ordeal, I concluded, was no different from that of soldiers who had been on active duty for four months. To us, the terror of failure was the equivalent of the soldier's terror of death. I doubt if our nervous systems could tell the difference. The strain must have been equal.

I suppose the measure of the trauma our respective psyches had gone through could be taken as we crossed the line. I, John Bertrand—acknowledged international competitor, veteran of four America's Cups, a yacht-racing champion since I was a mere child, a competitor who had faced up to the toughest contests in our sport, including two Olympics in which I had been out there with the leaders all the way—just collapsed, sobbing, into the arms of the tactician. It takes a lot of tension over a long time to reduce a world-ranking sportsman to that.

We went home at about 1 A.M., and on the way back I remember talking to Rasa about the possibility of the need for rehabilitation. And later, various psychologists agreed that we were as men who had been pulled out from behind enemy lines. They do not ask those returning soldiers to go off to a few parties. They debrief them and slowly let them assimilate to life in society, over a period of time.

That night, I was suddenly overcome with tiredness. We went to bed and I sank into a deep and peaceful sleep, at least for a while. But as another dawn began to approach Newport, I began to stir. And shortly after 5 A.M., I woke myself up, breathless, grabbing for the wheel of *Australia II* in what seemed like a totally futile gesture, trying to stop the red boat from coming by. I looked at the clock, where the compass bearing should have been, and it was 5:15 A.M. Reality came rushing back, and I smiled and turned over and went back to sleep for a long time.

Three months would pass before I could dismiss from my subconscious mind the nightly terror of the red boat going too fast for me to catch, as I struggled with the appalling dead weight of an *Australia II* that refused to obey my commands.

22

Return of the Milkman

This high-paneled Colonial room in the heart of this historic seafaring town would never rid itself of the ghosts of the men of Australia II. *Never.*

It was a perfect place for such a ceremony—Newport's Marble House. Here in these grand and elegant rooms were a hundred memories of American yachtsmen of another era, men who had plotted the downfall of Sir Thomas Lipton and Tommy Sopwith. Here, amid all of the refined splendor of this great summer "cottage," had once lived Mike Vanderbilt, the swashbuckling and fanatical America's Cup helmsman of the 1930s. Around the walls were great paintings of his mighty J-boats, *Enterprise, Rainbow,* and finally the massive 135-foot-long *Ranger.* For me, the rooms echoed with the cries and commands of the legendary sail trimmer Sherman Hoyt; of the old master of the monster-sized J-boat spinnakers, Frank Paine; of the young and dextrous big-boat racers Olin and Rod Stephens. What days those must have been, when they were all gathered in the palatial home of Mike Vanderbilt, brother of England's Duchess of Marlborough, great-grandson of the railroad tycoon Cornelius Vanderbilt. Here in this magnificent house in the early part of the century, Mike had learned the rudiments of yacht racing, perhaps in some quiet corner making the first notes toward his wonderful sailing book, *On the Wind's Highway*, of which my great-grandfather had a well-read copy, and which I, too, have read many times.

Marble House has so much glorious memorabilia of those bygone days of half a century ago, when superb U.S. yachtsmen fought off challenge after challenge from England's finest, in enormous boats that must have been the very devil to sail.

And there before me, against a stone wall—gleaming, brightly dramatic, on a plush velvet cloth—stood the America's Cup, for which I, too, had fought so long and so hard. And now, in a sense, it was mine. For no matter how much value men of finance, yacht club officials, and even boat designers may place their own personal claims to glory, it was I who now followed in the wake of John Cox Stevens, Captain Nathanael Herreshoff, Charlie Barr, Charles Francis Adams (The Deacon), Mike Vanderbilt, Briggs Cunningham, and Bus Mosbacher. I was I who, like them, had been at the helm, and steered *Australia II* over 200 miles of pure warfare against *Liberty*. And until the day I die, no one will ever be able to take that away from me.

I stood there before the gleaming trophy and wanted, like a child, to reach out and touch it. But it had not yet been handed over formally from its traditional owners, and it did not seem quite correct that I should do so. I just stood there for a few moments and beheld a very glorious sight with a deep and abiding personal reverence.

Actually, I had seen the trophy before. Back in 1970, after we had been defeated by *Intrepid*, I made a pilgrimage to New York and was given permission to see it. But my feelings were different then. In 1970, it seemed even more dramatic, with a mystique that belongs only to the truly unattainable. Now I had been involved with that great silver cup for so long that it was robbed of some of that mystery. I doubt whether Mount Everest looked quite as awesome from the top as it did from the bottom. But even though I had fought and conquered that which seemed to be impossible, the Cup still held for me dreams and fantasies untold. It was, I suppose, symbolism in its highest moment. A great, ornate, silver ewer for which men virtually had risked their lives, for which vast fortunes had been laid on the line, and for which acts of skill, heroism, and seamanship had been constant companions down through the years. If the America's Cup did not deserve everyone's respect and reverence, it certainly deserved mine.

For the presentation, we gathered on the terrace—nearly all of the men who had waged this gargantuan struggle on the waters of Rhode Island Sound. I say *nearly* because three fairly substantial characters were absent, and I believe their failure to turn up to see the presentation of the America's Cup to the victors should not go unrecorded.

First, we were without Dennis Conner, who had packed and was en route to California. I noted that there were some grumblings about poor sportsmanship, comments that the American skipper should have been present to witness the formal departure of the trophy for which he practically had laid down his life. I was not among those who criticized him. I am not at all sure that anyone had the right to say what Dennis should or should not have done at this moment. I knew what he was going through, and in my view, he should have been able to do anything he wanted. He earned privacy, or even seclusion, if that is what he required. I think it should be remembered that in 1980, that tough character Ted Turner was found wandering around, unsure of his whereabouts, after being eliminated from the competition. Dennis, too, had been completely lost for a few moments, bewildered in that vast crowd in Newport on the previous evening. The shock to his system had been total—a staggering psychological blow. No one had the right to expect anything more from him. He had given, in my opinion, everything he had.

The second missing person was the New York Yacht Club Commodore, Robert McCullough, who had escaped to New York as soon as the race was over and was preparing to leave for Europe, where he would stay for a month. The Commodore, who had been such a terrible antagonist in all the controversy over the keel and the legality of our design, did not bother to say good-bye to his own skipper, so he certainly was in no mood to say good-bye to the America's Cup. In fact, I thought this was not very sportsmanlike, and it did not show him in a particularly good light.

The other missing person was *Liberty*'s navigator, Halsey Herreshoff, a member of the family of the man who designed winning America's Cup defenders for six races between 1893 and 1920—*Vigilant, Defender, Columbia* (twice), *Reliance,* and *Resolute.* In all that time, those yachts lost only three races among them, and now the *Liberty* navigator, who bears the great Captain Nathanael's name, could not see his way clear to turn up for the formal departure of the trophy that his family had glorified for almost 100 years. Not for the first time in 1983, I thought Halsey's performance could have been better.

For myself, I was suddenly aware of a new and huge responsibility— that I, without all that much practice, must be able to present to the public the correct and proper image of the World Champion Australians. I wanted to project what I hoped was our true character—that of dignity and humility. I wanted to represent the men of *Australia II* as the quiet achievers who had never boasted, and who would not be seen to gloat in victory. I just wanted to present a public image of which all the people of our little nation would feel damned proud.

We stood there together, and Commodore Robert Stone handed over the America's Cup. He did it with grace and style and immense gallantry. The powers-that-be at the New York Yacht Club had done everything they could for 132 years to hang on to the Cup, but, having lost it, they behaved like true sportsmen. Commodore Stone was impeccable, commenting on the fierce brilliance of the competition and then presenting Ben Lexcen with a hubcap from an old Plymouth—in recognition of Benny's avowed desire to steamroller the Cup and then call it the America's Plate. It lent just the right touch of humor to a beautifully structured ceremony.

And then it was my turn to stand once more before the world's press and the assembled dignitaries. But before I did so, I did reach out and touch the Cup with my fingertips. I repeated how proud I was to have been a member of this tremendous Australian crew and how humble it all made me feel. Then Bondy and I held up the great trophy for the press, after which we passed it around among the boys, just so that they, too, could touch that piece of antique silver for which they had struggled and fought every yard of the way.

I am not entirely sure who would have been more amazed at the sight of us—the tyrannical old skipper of *Enterprise* or his British opponent's main engineer, Tom Pearkes, my great-grandpa.

The following morning, we sailed while a film crew put the finishing touches on a documentary about our victory in Newport. It felt rather hollow to put to sea in *Australia II* without the atmosphere of war in our bellies. By now the post mortems of the race were being printed all over America and, as we suspected, the party line of the *Liberty* group had remained pretty solid—that *Australia II* was the fastest boat ever built and that there was nothing that anyone could do about that. The miracle was that the superior Dennis Conner and his men had been able to run us so close, but basically they never had a chance. Benny's boat beat them and that was that. As we slid out beyond the harbor for the film, I found myself reflecting on a quotation from my old friend, Ron Barassi, a quote we had often read aloud in our crew meetings. It said, very simply: "Winners never blame anybody. It's only losers who try to blame other people for what went wrong. So never con yourself that your failures, and your weaknesses, are someone else's fault."

* * *

This seems as good a time as any to summarize what really happened on Rhode Island Sound in September of 1983—aside, of course, from the fact that, after sailing seven complete races and one almost complete race covering, in real-distance terms, over 200 miles, we defeated *Liberty* by 41 seconds, about three boatlengths. By any standards, that's pretty close. And by any standards, those boats were close. *Liberty* was terribly competitive upwind, except when the wind was light in the second Race 3 (in the first one, it took us so long we could not even finish in time). So there you have one shining fact that no member of either crew will dispute. Over the upwind legs of the regatta, *Australia II* and *Liberty* were just inseparable. Sometimes we had an edge, sometimes they had it. On the power reaches, we were not naturally fast, and *Liberty* was our superior. By the wing mark in Race 6, we had fought it out on 11 power reaches, and only on one of them had we picked up any time—and that was only two seconds. *In all of the other 10 legs, we had been decisively beaten or narrowly held them to a draw.* Our only major gain on any one of the 14 power reaches of the seven races was on the second one in Race 6—but that was when the wind came around and turned it into a square run.

Which brings us to the downwind leg—the fifth leg, where for so long we were inferior to *Azzurra, Challenge,* and *Victory '83.* We were superior to *Liberty* here, but not because of a mystical keel. We had, after all, exactly the same keel when we were worse than the foreigners as we had when we beat the Americans. In general terms, there was nothing much in it in Races 1, 2, 4, and 5—20 seconds or less, either way. In Race 3 we clobbered them in light wind, but in Race 6 they were getting spooked, and we had 46 seconds off them. In Race 7 they were all over the place, terribly incompetent, and we had 78 seconds off them, even with their new light mode. But we had improved our sails dramatically by then, and our sailing techniques. We just plain outsailed them in that most tricky area of racing these big yachts and they in turn had lost confidence in their boat. They had not done enough work on their sail inventory, or their spinnakers, and they were scared to death of us as well. Our keel had not changed; its help to us, running downwind, rested in its mystique.

We did have an advantage that the keel gave us, and that was in tacking duels, but these were—at Dennis Conner's insistence—restricted, and generally they resulted in a gain for us.

Was the keel, then, the architect of the American defeat, giving us, as it did, a turning advantage at the start? Well, scarcely. *Australia II* won the start in two of the three races the Americans won. And *Liberty* won the start in two of the four races that we won. Einstein himself would have had trouble turning that into a decisive anything.

In summary, I would say that *Australia II* had about a 10 percent edge on *Liberty* in general terms, boat for boat. Half of this 10 percent involved our often-superior sails and our ability to know when to use them. The other half of our 10 percent involved the keel, but a large part of that was its mystique, its capacity to torment the Americans. They were much more afraid of *Australia II* than they should have been.

Also, I believe that Dennis was much too preoccupied with the design of the hull of his yacht. I believe that the Americans did not spend enough time on their tuning and sails. The trim of their mainsail often looked old-fashioned to me. I am sure we outgunned them in this area, and I know we did so with our spinnakers, which we were forever recutting. And on the last spinnaker run, when the United States surrendered the America's Cup, I thought their chute was too flat up high and too unstable down below. Hughey, who built the spinnaker that we flew when we overtook them for the last time, was quite critical of the American downwind rig. Also, I thought that some of their crew work was surprisingly slack.

As a matter of fact, on that fifth leg, theirs was a bit of a lame-duck performance, and they gave it to us on a plate. If it had been Race 1 instead of Race 7, it would have been a damned sight harder, of that I am certain. But by now the Americans had psyched themselves into believing that we were so much faster than they were, and on their boat, as we began to catch up, there was a feeling of, "Uh-oh, here she comes." As Dennis said to his crew during the fifth leg, "Anyone got any ideas?" What they did *not* know was that we were stretched to the limit—everyone working away, thinking, helping, trimming, searching out the wind, taking bearings, sailing the boat as she had *never* been sailed before. Our pulses were racing, our hearts were pounding, but I think the public thought we were all sitting there having a drink and laughing as we rolled inevitably by on our winged keel.

What they also did not know was that we showed a fighting spirit under pressure that the Americans could not even have approached. They would have died if they had ever been 3–1 down, of that I am certain. Because they would have hemorrhaged internally. There is no question in my mind about that. There was not enough genuine compatibility in their camp.

Also, they did not appreciate how much we improved. We got tougher and tougher, particularly as the pressure increased. I doubt whether the Americans could make such a claim.

When the boys of *Australia II* had their first race against the French, I would have rated them, as a crew, at about 4 on a scale of 10. In the last race against the Americans, I would have rated them at 9½ out of 10. In the last two races, if I had been offered the 10-man all-star crew of *Liberty* instead of my own, I would not have accepted them. By that stage of the game, the Australians were sailing our little boat close to the way big racing yachts *will* be sailed in the year 2000.

Our organization, the men who backed the crew, was the best there has ever been. From the fanatical determination and guts of Bondy, and the fierce, dedicated executive administration of Warren Jones, right down to the boys who worked night after night, all night, on the sails—we made the Americans look inferior.

I am afraid that, even in this age of high technology, I am going to be forced into venturing the opinion that the America's Cup ultimately was won by the men who sailed *Australia II*. When it came right down to it, we held our nerve, we read the wind right at critical times, our general crew work was always equal and ultimately superior. We outworked them and we outsailed them. Our morale was better, our team spirit was better, and our sail inventory was better. And in the end it came down to 41 seconds. If I had to mark the two skippers I'd give Dennis Conner 8 out of 10, and myself . . . well, about the same—8 out of 10. We both made mistakes and we both had great moments. But I think my crew fought harder for me than his did for him.

I think Dennis, being essentially an autocrat, did not get the same help and feedback that I received from my boys. No one would have dared to shout, "SHUT UP, CONNER, AND SAIL THE BOAT." And the eager, helpful democracy of *Australia II* was missing in the American camp. Dennis places himself above other men, and many of the *Liberty* crew's decisions were made on his whim. Many of their sail selections were made on his whim. And when it came down to the winning and losing of the America's Cup, I am afraid that Dennis found himself a man alone, as well as a man apart. Even his own boss, big Robert McCullough, did not call him to thank him. All through that summer, Dennis, as always, stayed apart from his crew socially, and I believe that hurt him. My boys would have died for me, but I do not think his would have done so for him.

America did not lose the America's Cup, as so many newspapers and magazines and, indeed, books would have us believe. The Australians came and won the America's Cup. We came and took it away with brilliant crew work, seamanship, preparation, administration, and a very, very fast boat. And we won it because, in the end, we wanted it most. The Americans had a team of champions, but we were a champion team.

All of these thoughts filled my mind that morning as we worked the boat along, nice and easy, for the camera crew, before Hughey, Mad Dog, Chink, and I flew south with Warren and Bondy to meet the President of the United States, Ronald Reagan, in the Rose Garden of the White House, Washington, D.C.

When our private plane landed in Washington, we were met by limousines from the Australian Embassy. They drove us up Massachusetts Avenue and in through the great wrought-iron gates onto what is, under international law, Australian soil. When we walked into the foyer of this most imposing building, we all received a major shock. The entire staff of the embassy, about 100 people, had gathered to see us, and they clapped and cheered for nearly four minutes. I remember thinking that this was fantastic, this outburst of recognition from our own country, and that we must have caused some kind of a stir back home. But how big that particular stir was, none of us yet knew.

Accompanied by the Australian Ambassador, Sir Robert Cotton, we arrived at the gates of the White House at just about the same time as the men from *Liberty,* and we decided right there to swap ties, in the old tradition of sports antagonists all over the world. I swapped mine with the tactician, Tom Whidden, a good friend under different circumstances, and he said to me, "You guys did a hell of a job." It was the first time I had heard an American crewman depart from their party line.

But even as Tom uttered them, I knew that they were not the words of a defeated man. They were more like, "You guys did a hell of a job—welcome to the club." And in a way they echoed Dennis's last words at the press conference, "America is still Number One." And it demonstrated to me yet again, as if I needed any reinforcement, that there was the most incredible strength of character in that American crew. Tough, tough, tough. Those bastards were tough. I smiled at Tom, savoring the moment, and I also found myself picturing once more the sight of the men on *Liberty* at the end of the race, the afterguard slumped in the cockpit, these viciously competitive guys who had fought and fought and fought, all the way, experiencing what must have been a nightmare.

And now we were all together, before their president, at the White House. Ronald Reagan was advancing toward us wearing the shiniest shoes I had ever seen. He had the bearing of a statesman, the grace of a statesman, and the clear and obvious strength of a president. I would not mind looking like that when I'm his age. Also, he exuded a real presence and a wonderful sense of occasion. He walked up to me, and his handshake was strong. "John Bertrand," he said, "congratulations." I replied very formally, "Thank you, Mr. President." Just 132 years and five weeks earlier, Commodore John Cox Stevens had taken the hand of Queen Victoria on board the yacht *America* off the Isle of Wight. On reflection, I rather like the tidy, ordered traditions that history requires on occasions such as these.

President Reagan's speech to us all was superb, truly inspiring, with a few sharp reminders that we need not get too attached to that trophy. He said that people must now be questioning whether the term *Down Under* applies to Australians anymore, and he congratulated both crews on putting on such a superb race.

"You both did an outstanding job," he said. "You captured the imagination of the people, the world over.

"Skipper John Bertrand, you and the crew of *Australia II* have shown us the stuff of which you Australians are made. I know that your countrymen are very proud of you. And I want you to take this message back . . . that Americans are proud of you, too. We're proud to have Australians as our very dear friends. And we salute you in your moment of triumph. . . ."

He said, "Well done," to the crew of *Liberty* as well, and God knows they deserved it. And he did not forget the absent Dennis Conner either. He said, "I spoke with Dennis Conner after the race, and I am sorry he could not be with us today. But we should think of him not as the loser of this race, but as the man who successfully defended the America's Cup in 1980, and as a skipper who has had a brilliant yachting career."

He especially congratulated Bondy, saying, "Alan, you represent the kind of tenacity with which Americans and Australians identify. For 11 years and four challenges, and at heavy financial sacrifice, you have been trying to accomplish this feat. You just kept on coming. But don't relax now, Alan—and this is the other message to our friends in Australia—because the Americans are coming back . . . stronger than ever next time around." There was a burst of applause in the Rose Garden. Those Americans, from their deckhands to their head of state—they don't take kindly to defeat. And they *never* give up.

President Reagan referred to the race 132 years earlier, reminding us all of the fact that the old *America* was once 7½ miles in front of the British, and that when they passed the Royal Yacht, the skipper and crew doffed their caps and stood at attention as a salute to the Queen of England and to their opponents. And he mentioned the tribute we had been paid by Commodore Robert Stone and the NYYC members as we had passed *Black Knight* at the end of this America's Cup. And with immense style, he added, "I join them in that salute. And I might add that when we won that Cup in 1851, there were numerous comments about the *America*'s unique design. We had every innovation of the day—except, of course, for a winged keel!

"Let me just say that that was 132 years ago. This time, if we had to get beaten, we're glad it was by the Aussies. But I have one final piece of advice to the Perth Yacht Club—don't bolt that Cup down too tightly! Congratulations to all of you, both teams, and God bless you all."

I don't know what anyone else thought, but I thought that was magnificent. I had never seen Bondy nervous before, but he was now. He was
shaking as he prepared to reply to the President. But he stepped forward
and did his stuff, presenting President Reagan with a beautiful book about
the two decades of Australian challenges for the America's Cup, personally signed by us all. "I hope you will keep this as a memento," he said,
"not just to Australia's victory, but to the great friendship that exists between our two nations. Thank you, Mr. President."

And now we stood and chatted for a while with the men from *Liberty*.
It was an appropriate place for us to say good-bye, and we all stood reflectively in the twilight of our great battle campaign of 1983, here at the
headquarters of the government of the United States. It was indeed a
proper place. There must be both a winner and a loser, but at the end of
it, after all of the brutal competition, we still have to behave like civilized
people. I had not yet spoken to my boss, *Liberty*'s mainsheet hand, John
Marshall of North Sails, and I remember thinking, right out of the blue,
of a managers' meeting in Hawaii two years earlier. I had joked one evening with John—in the way two very competitive sporting men will—that
the main reason I wanted to win the America's Cup was "so that you will
have to call me 'Sir John.'" That made him laugh, and now he came up to
me and said for the first time, "Well done." Then we all said our farewells
and stepped back into the embassy limousines. But just as we pulled away,
I heard one last voice call out to me from the gates of the White House,
"Good-bye, Sir John!" It made me laugh all over again.

We returned to the Australian Embassy for tea, and Lady Cotton produced some of the famous little coconut-and-chocolate cakes we Aussies
call lamingtons. We really were on Australian soil. After our second cup of
tea, the ambassador's wife—they have a home near Sydney—admitted
that when we crossed the winning line, she and her daughter, with glasses
of champagne, ran out onto Massachusetts Avenue and danced in the
street. The press officer told me that in the three days since our victory,
there was more press coverage about Australia in the U.S. than there had
been in the previous 20 years. He said to me, "You cannot believe what
you have done for our nation."

We flew back to Newport, arriving late in the evening, and the next
day we started to pack up. By now I was being besieged with phone calls,
requests for appearances, offers, and God-knows-what. I had to get someone to represent me and to help me apportion my time. So I called my
new press-officer pal in the Australian Embassy and told him I wanted to
get in touch with John Newcombe, the Australian tennis player, whom I
had never met. Within a couple of hours, they called back with his phone
number, and I telephoned him in Australia. When he answered the
phone, I said, with some slight trepidation, "This is John Bertrand calling

from Newport." "Jesus, John," yelled "Newk," "this is bloody fantastic. I was up all through that night watching. It was the greatest thing that has ever happened. The whole country has gone bloody mad." He was ecstatic, and he gave the names of his agents. When I got off that phone, I thought again, "This is getting bigger by the minute."

What I did not know was that by now it was not possible to buy a bottle of champagne in all of Australia. There was none left. The same applied to gold and green ribbons. The whole country was decked out in the livery of *Australia II*—from Perth to Brisbane, from Adelaide to Darwin. No ribbons were left. They were all flying proudly from every available space. The government had declared a national holiday. Down on the Newport dock in our little office, the teleprinters had not stopped for one second, day or night, for nearly two weeks. Messages of goodwill and best wishes now became messages of congratulations—from corporations, officials, government departments, sailors, yacht clubs, and from just ordinary Australian people. Thousands and thousands of minutes were being logged on those two machines. At various times, we had to send staff down to change the tapes to keep up with the avalanche of intercontinental words of joy that were battering their way to us on these noisy little bearers of the delight of Australia. In the first three days after our win, there were about 7,000 minutes of messages. It was like a paper factory in that office.

But now it was time for us to think about leaving. I told a reporter that I was going to Hawaii, "to sit on the beach for a week and smile." But before we went to the sunny South Pacific, there was much to do. We began to pack up at Dennison Street on Thursday morning, but the day was heavily interrupted by a formal crew luncheon Alan Bond gave for us at the Newport restaurant Christie's. He presented us all with gleaming gold krugerrands worth $1,000 each. Actually, they were the same ones that Bondy had given us for our victory over the British in the elimination trials in August, and that had been stored in his safe—he still knows how to make the occasional economy, Bondy, even in his moment of glory. But with each of the coins he had now included a little personal message. Mine read, "To John. I always knew you were the best. And now the world does. Thanks. Alan Bond, *Australia II*. 1983." That little piece of paper is very dear to me. I value it more than I do the krugerrand.

Everyone made a little speech at the lunch, and some of them were quite emotional. The Major stood up and said that it had been the most wonderful experience of his life. He talked about the camaraderie and the commitment to each other that had been so strong in all of us. And his eyes filled with tears when he said, "I have been very close to units of men in the army during my career, but I have never known anything like this was. And I know that I never shall."

I remember being very touched at what Colin Beashel said. "I would like to thank John for training me and teaching me. I learned more in 18 months with him than other people learn in a lifetime. And I consider myself to have been very privileged. I've just sailed with the greatest skipper in the world."

The sadness that hung over each of us as we prepared to go home to Australia was almost crushing. I hate the end of a regatta at the best of times. I am famous for the speed with which I depart—win, lose, or draw. I hate the atmosphere. It reminds me of a morgue. Where once the contestants had gathered, full of hope and ferocity and ambition, now, when the battle has been won, there is just emptiness—boxes being packed, boats being crated up, the maintenance men taking over, the nuts-and-bolts end of our sport to the forefront, the gladiators gone in search of new fields to conquer, new windmills at which to joust. And now this deadly pall was creeping across Newport.

Founders' Hall was a scene of desolation. Bags and trunks littered the room where the crew had sat just a few days before in tense, formal silence, as I had said to them, "We are not here by luck or because of some failing on the part of others. We are here because we deserve it." Here in this room we had suffered together and we had fortified ourselves for the times when we were required to dig in and fight back. "The important thing is for us to do it for each other, to make the others proud to be on the same team . . . so that we can at the end of it hold our heads high."

And here we had sat on that appalling evening when we were 3–1 down. When I had steeled myself and stood before them, saying coldly, "Nothing has changed. We still have to win three boat races." That awful evening when Beasho had shut himself in his little room at the top of the stairs, unable to listen to any more discussion, when Grant had walked out into the night to find Alex because he could not bear to be alone with his own demons before we faced the red boat for the fifth, and perhaps the last, time.

Here on the big dining-room table, where now there were only packages and coats, is where Hughey and Schnacks and I sat and plotted the recutting and restitching of the great sails that eventually drove us to victory. This high-paneled Colonial room in the heart of this historic seafaring town would never rid itself of the ghosts of the men of *Australia II*. Never.

On the morning Rasa and I were leaving, I walked down to the dock to say good-bye to the packers and the maintenance men, and, in my own way, to the boat. She was nearly ready now for the long tow back to New York. Her mast was down, and some of the boys were still working away at details for her departure. Beasho was there, and so was Ya—the spotters of the wind—and I thanked them once more, from the bottom of my heart. Splash and Damian were there, too—the big, hard, international oarsman, master of the starboard main winch, and the tough-as-nails carpenter from Williamstown who had flogged along beside him during that final tacking duel with *Liberty*. Words almost failed me as I said my good-byes to them. I walked around the boat, upon which everything was now marked, positions logged, in readiness to begin the defense of the Cup. Essentially, she was ready for her next voyage, in a distant land. I glanced down below deck and I saw a package marked "flags." In there was the beloved kangaroo with the boxing gloves, symbol of our battle mode, symbol of our victory. I stood there by myself for a few minutes, right by the mast, in the spot where Ya had wrestled with those monstrously crucial decisions about the windshifts. And then I stepped off *Australia II*, for the last time.

I drove a borrowed car up to Founders' Hall once more to say good-bye to the others—to Hughey, the Major, Scoop, Skippy, Grant, Chink, Will, Robbie, and Scotty. Even then I knew that we would sail together no more, that we would not again close ranks against a common enemy. Oh, of course, we would meet again at home, but never quite like this, in the intimate camaraderie of men who have gone to the wall for each other. I looked around Founders' Hall for the last time. No, the ghosts of the men who sailed the white boat from Perth would never leave this place. Perhaps in 200 years' time a ghostly chime would be heard in the cool of certain autumn mornings. DING DING DING DING—at precisely 7½ minutes to eight. ORDER! ORDER!

Hughey and I walked out of Founders' Hall together, and before I went, he showed me his old car in which we had driven so often. In enormous white letters he had painted across the hood: "WE 1." A big piece of lettering from a very big man. He and I would never sail together again. Finally, after standing there for a while, both of us hating the final parting, I just said, "Good-bye, Hughey," and I left him standing there alone. But I knew that, as with all of the others, we would be lifelong friends and companions. We were bound together. All of us. Uniquely. For all the days of our lives.

I gathered up Rasa and the children and we set off for the little airport at Newport, where we boarded a plane for New York. We took off, and as the plane banked to the south, I could see Newport Bridge to the left and I could see the berth where we used to keep *Australia II*. I could see the lonely acres of the former America's Cup racecourse out beyond the harbor entrance. I turned quickly to see if I could see Dennison Street, but I was not in time. It was over now.

By the time we landed in New York, I, like just about every member of the crew, felt quite ill. After being strung out so tightly all summer, with scarcely a cold among us, we suddenly collapsed physically, as our systems went from somewhere near breaking point to a normal, everyday life without that killing pressure. We were all having great difficulty adjusting to the real world, and we seemed completely susceptible to every virus in the air. I suppose it was just flu, but it was an amazing physical letdown.

We spent the weekend at the Mayfair-Regent on Park Avenue. On Sunday, the five of us went for a stroll in Central Park in search of what I had read was the North American Yacht Championships, being held on the boating lake. I stood for a while, watching these lovely, five-foot-high, remote-controlled yachts racing across the smooth water, when suddenly a man came up to me and said, "Are you who I think you are?" I smiled and said, "Maybe." He said, "You are John Bertrand. We are honored to have you here. Would you like to have a try?" He handed me a black control box, about nine inches long, and showed me the knobs and handles. Before I knew what was happening, I was in another yacht race—and doing badly at that. I was pushing and pulling and twisting, and I felt as if I were wearing boxing gloves. Nothing could urge my boat forward, and Rasa reported that just before I finished next-to-last, I swung around in anger at my failure to make it go and snapped, "Where the hell's Hughey?" I suppose the old competitive fires are doused only very slowly.

Our New York visit was a lovely time for us. As my special "thank you" to Mad Dog, I had arranged for him and Alex to stay at the Mayfair-Regent, and on Monday morning we all went out together. Now there were seven of us, and we strolled down Fifth Avenue, my navigator and Alex looking for an engagement ring. I went to have a haircut, and when I walked into the salon, everyone stood up and applauded, and they would not take my money. A professor of philosophy sat next to me and told me that New York had very nearly come to a grinding halt as I had headed *Australia II* up to the winning line. "It was like the day Neil Armstrong landed on the moon," he said. Cab drivers shook my hand, people did double-takes on the streets, and others rushed up to me and said, "Congratulations." It was wonderful, and it made me feel fantastic.

Then we all walked down to the New York Yacht Club. I introduced myself to the doorman and told him I wanted to take my children and my navigator to experience the enormous tradition that dwelled behind our victory. He said, "Of course, Mr. Bertrand." He called the manager, who made a rare exception for our children, gave the shirtsleeved Mad Dog a jacket, and introduced us to the Club's curator. Then they took us all through the model room to see the great racing yachts that had sailed where we had sailed. And at the end of the tour, Grant and I each had reached the same conclusion—that every American defender was about three years in front of the challenger in its refinements. Year after year, they had had a technical advantage. The defenders were always a little bit more sophisticated in their rigs, with finer spars, smaller shrouds, and smaller crosstrees. The visitors were always duplicating the previous time, therefore always just a shade inferior.

The curator was very proud, and rightly so, of this fabulous collection of models, but he was worried that the two boats that had fought out the 1983 America's Cup would not be presented to the Club. I gave him my personal assurance that we Australians would definitely not break with that grand tradition. At last they asked us if we would like to walk down to that hallowed room where the America's Cup had stood for so many years. And there we saw the empty space. The carpet was worn where so many people had walked to examine the "Auld Mug" over the years. And now it was gone. I had taken it away. In the place where it had once rested in splendor, there was just a gap. It would soon have to be re-covered. Unaccountably, I felt embarrassed at the mess I had made of the carpet.

The old curator, who had worn white gloves to polish the Cup for 30 years, told us of the day the battle was finally lost. The club had no television or radio, so the only contact with the outside world was through a workman's radio in the basement, and a bricklayer had to keep rushing up the stairs to keep members informed of the progress of the race. They tend to be a touch hidebound at the NYYC—"We want no part of new-fangled inventions like televisions and radios." The curator was also interesting as he told us about the attitudes of the members when all was lost. "The elder gentlemen just kept drinking, saying little," he told us, "but the younger ones were up banging their fists in their palms, saying 'Right. Now we are going to get it back.'" That's the Americans, as I think of them.

It was a wonderful visit, and young Lucas walked out of there with his eyes gleaming, having seen those models of the *Shamrocks*, the big boats his great-great-grandfather had prepared for battle, and about which I had told him so much.

On Tuesday, October 4, we flew from Kennedy Airport to San Francisco to await our Qantas flight to Honolulu. We were taken to the VIP lounge, and when we walked through the door, I thought I recognized a few familiar faces—Benny, Warren, Scoop, Ya, Robbie, Beasho and his dad, Will, and Splash. By extraordinary coincidence, we were all on that same plane leaving America. Again we were aware of all of the old ties. For us it was like stumbling on an oasis in the desert. Once more, we felt this comfortable, easy feeling when we were together, and realized how much we missed it when we were apart. Very strange that, but even Rasa noticed it, and so did the others.

When finally the plane they had sent to take us home did arrive, we were all led out to see it. There, right on the tail, carefully painted, was a huge flag—the kangaroo with the boxing gloves. It absolutely blew us away. And when we finally got on board, the scene was beyond belief. The pilot and crew, the stewards and stewardesses were all in tears, trying to explain to us how our exploits had united the nation as nothing had done since the soldiers returned from World War II. These were the first Australians we had met who had been in Australia during the races, and their tales of the excitement and the ecstasy as we sailed tight-hauled over that finish line were nothing short of astounding. Australia truly had gone berserk. The captain told us that Sydney Airport had indeed been paralyzed during the final stages of Race 7. There were, he said, no pilots available to take the planes out—and, in any event, the passengers would not embark. He told us of one group of about a hundred people clustered around a good-sized transistor radio in the airport lounge. They were all aghast when the radio's owner announced that he, as an American, had to leave to board his Pan Am flight. "There are 15 minutes to go in the race, and *Australia II* leads by almost two boatlengths," the commentator was reporting from Rhode Island. And with that, the crowd passed the hat and *bought* the transistor from the departing *Liberty* supporter. After all that, however, he could just as easily have stayed where he was. The crowded Pan Am flight was at this time stranded—at the gate. The incoming passengers had refused to disembark and sat enraptured by the commentary on the desperate battle in progress 12,000 miles away. "With 12 minutes of this race left, *Australia II* has increased her lead to a little more than two boatlengths as they race on down toward the spectator fleet to the right, closehauled, each boat with a spinnaker on the foredeck."

The crew of the 747 with the kangaroo on the tail struggled to explain exactly what it had been like back home. With moist eyes, they told us of the huge flag, perhaps the biggest in the world, that had been strung out on top of Sydney Harbor Bridge. How the headline in the *Sydney Morning Herald* read, "The Biggest Thing Since Peace in 1945—Triumph Unites Nation." A huge spinnaker flew from Sydney Town Hall, and at a party at the Royal Perth Yacht Club, there were 2,000 people cheering. In the course of the revelry, they doused the Prime Minister with champagne, but no one cared—certainly not Bob Hawke. When the race was over, and millions of exhausted Australians blinked in the light of dawn, the television stations played "Advance Australian Fair," our national anthem. And the entire nation felt an overwhelming need to weep, just as we did on board the boat, as our fanatical determination finally gave way to that mysterious pathos that accompanies achievement beyond one's wildest dreams.

Finally we took off from San Francisco, and left the shores of the United States, in which I had spent 126 days. Peace descended over the crew of *Australia II,* and, after 10 hours of flying, Rasa and I and the children landed in Hawaii for a few days' holiday, during which I would prepare myself for our homecoming, which I suspected might be less than tranquil. I did as I had said I would. I sat on the beach and smiled. My flu went away and, restored to health, we set off for home.

Our arrival in Melbourne was nothing short of extraordinary. In a big private room were gathered all of our friends and family, which was just wonderful. Mum was there, and Rasa's dad, Leon, who I believe was not quite certain whether I had managed to keep my regular job as a milkman. There were all of our relations. Rasa's sister was there, and so was my brother, Lex, a very successful dentist and still one hell of a yachtsman—one of the coaches to the Australian Olympic team going to Los Angeles. He and I just slapped each other on the shoulders. There was no need for speeches between two people as close as we have always been. On reflection, I thought that Mum looked pretty pleased with both of us.

Beyond the room were hundreds of press and television people, and beyond them was a crowd of about three or four hundred people, who had turned up to watch the return of a native son. The excitement went on for the entire day. Arkaringa Crescent, where we live, had been re-named Bertrand Crescent, and the police had cordoned it off. It was completely decorated with green and gold ribbons. Our house was decorated in green and gold, and a huge sign read, "WELCOME HOME, JOHN AND RASA, LUCAS, ANDRE, AND SUNSHINE." There were balloons everywhere, and all the kids on the street had done pictures of *Australia II* that were hung all over the garden wall. All the friends and neighbors were there, and we turned it into a party for the rest of the day. We had champagne and we played Men at Work, and it turned out to be a lovely day. The phone never stopped ringing from the radio stations and newspapers, and we did not care. We danced and sang and laughed long into the evening. It was nice to be home. And it was especially nice to sleep in our own big bed once more—the first time I had been in our bedroom for more than four months. But I still awoke, sweating, at 3:10 A.M., as the red boat glided by us.

In the following days, I began to understand just what an impact our victory had had on ordinary Australian people. On the day of the Melbourne Marathon, we went as usual to the end of the street to watch them all pounding along the road that skirts Port Phillip Bay. Suddenly Andy Morrison, a friend of ours who was competing, spotted me, rushed up and kissed me on the cheek, and then rejoined the race! He was too out of breath to speak, but his action alerted the other competitiors that I was there, and they all began to stop and shake my hand. I was holding a kind of inspection parade in the middle of the Melbourne Marathon, and the runners were all congratulating me. Everywhere I went, there were stories of that fateful night. I gave a couple of little talks at our local primary schools, and the teachers told me how the students fell asleep at their desks all through that morning—how youngsters under the age of 11 had been dragged from their beds by ecstatic parents at five in the morning to see this once-in-a-lifetime piece of history in the making. Among dozens of people who said they simply could not bear to watch it, I met a cab driver who made me laugh because he said his television was in the bedroom, so he shut himself in the bathroom and was so nervous he shaved himself three times.

Ross Lloyd, my manager at North Sails, told me of the morning he arrived at the loft after "the boss had done his stuff against the Yanks." The place was packed with television people, with cameras everywhere, and many of our regular customers just stopped by in order to feel involved.

All along the bayside, down toward our house, the yacht clubs stayed open all night, some with large television screens and more than 300 people in attendance. Come the dawn, they were all outside on the edge of the road, opening bottles of champagne and stopping motorists to give them a drink. No one could remember anything like it. Especially old Ross, who was driving the North Sails van. It took him three hours to get to work.

A friend of ours related that he was piloting his plane across the Nullarbor Desert, hundreds of miles from nowhere, and the progress of *Australia II* was being relayed through air-traffic control in this remote and desolate area, deep in the vastness of the Outback. "*Australia II* is now in the lead as they approach the fifth and last buoy." Almost unable to contain his excitement, he kept going, feverishly tuning in his radio, waiting for the next call. "*Australia II* still leads, and she is now 15 minutes from the line." On he flew, waiting, waiting, waiting . . . and then the words came, the words that small-plane pilots all over the airways Down Under had hoped to hear, "Australia has now won the America's Cup." He put his little plane into a long, lonely victory roll, high above the desert, as his small tribute to our victory, in the style of the old Battle of Britain aviators.

We heard from the wheat planters up beyond the Victorian borders toward the Murray River. Men who had scarcely ever seen the sea and whose lands were immortalized by Banjo Paterson:

It's west by south of the Great Divide
The grim grey plains run out
Where the old flock masters lived and died
In a ceaseless fight with drought
Weary with waiting and hope deferred
They were ready to own defeat
Till at last they heard the master word
And the master word was Wheat.

Well, the crop would be a little late that year. Dozens and dozens of these hardy farmers were up all night watching us, and they said our victory completely screwed up the planting schedules. But when their tractors finally got under way, they displayed the kangaroo with the boxing gloves. On one occasion, soon after we arrived home, Rasa and I went up to those lands for a visit, and they held a ball for us. People traveled 200 miles to attend. When we left in the small hours, there was an old man waiting at the gate of the farm. He had driven miles and miles to see us, and all he wanted to do was to shake my hand and have me sign a book for him. He told me that years before, he had owned the farm where the ball was held, and he knew I would eventually come through this gate. He cried when I told him I was honored that he had come so far to meet me.

A couple of months later, I met a girl in New Guinea who worked for the Education Department. She told me that two months after the Cup was over, a tribesman came out of the hills and wanted to know, in his pidgin English, "what happened to the big white boat from Australia?"

We were world news, no doubt about that. We even made the front page of the newspaper in Peking. Derryn Hinch, one of Australia's top radio documentary reporters, had just finished broadcasting from the Great Wall, where he was working with a group of senior Australian lawyers. They were on their way to an airport when we won, and they were driving in a bus through Peking. Well, they succeeded in persuading the Chinese driver to make a detour via the American Embassy, where they all got out. With tears of joy rolling down their cheeks, they walked up to the gates and sang "Waltzing Matilda" at the top of their lungs, right in the middle of Peking, before the astonished eyes of the guards of the United States Marines.

The managing director of Gillette in Australia had placed dozens of bets with his colleagues in Gillette's offices all over the world, collecting some heavy odds when we were 3–1 down, and now he was poised to collect a fairly substantial sum of money. He reported that he called his foreign offices, and when he was put through to executive offices, he just said, "HA! HA! HA!" and put the phone down. Everyone knew who it was, and everyone paid up.

Another friend was in Paris, calling home to Australia every five minutes for an update on the final two legs of Race 7. He did not know until afterward that the race was being beamed live into his hotel room on a television cable hookup. The French newspaper *Le Matin* headlined their front page the next day with "Bertrand's Crew Smashes 132 Years of American Supremacy."

And now we were all home again, and there was enormous civic pride in our accomplishment. Melbourne held a parade for us local boys—Damian, Will Ballieu, Splash Richardson, and myself. However, in Perth, there was the most gigantic parade, with estimates that almost half a million people witnessed the homecoming of the Western Australian syndicate. Each member of the crew and every member of the backup staff had his own parade car with a big nameplate on the front. The crowd at Fremantle Town Hall went wild as we set off, and they lined the route by the thousands all the way to the Esplanade in Perth. They roared and applauded as we entered the area selected for the grand finale, but when Alan and Eileen Bond drove slowly in, standing in an open Rolls-Royce and waving, the crowd went beserk. They chanted endlessly, "B-O-N-D-Y! B-O-N-D-Y! B-O-N-D-Y!" It might have been the most exuberant welcome-home since Julius Caesar reentered Rome 47 years before Christ.

Within days of his arrival, Bondy was presented with a new number plate for his car, "AB 001." And every new license plate issued in Western Australia now bears the words, "Home of the America's Cup." Not even Caesar could top that. I am told he had to use the same dreary old number plate on his chariot right up until that unforeseen setback involving Brutus and Cassius.

For most of the *Australia II* crew, life underwent a few changes, but in broader terms, it went on very much as before. Damian Fewster had a card printed up that read, "DAMIAN FEWSTER, Bow Man, *Australia II*." Asked, on coast-to-coast television, what it was like to be a national hero, he replied, "Oh, it's all right. Should make it easier for me and Blackie to pick up a few sheilahs." His mum was formally appointed as secretary to arrange his dinner appointments, to which I believe he is often accompanied by the aforementioned Blackie (presumably just in case there should happen to be a few sheilahs around while Damian is addressing the gathering).

Actually, I did hear of an unscheduled stop my bow man made. He went to the vast offices of the Melbourne business tycoon Dick Pratt, former master of the *Challenge* syndicate, and at that moment involved in a board meeting. Damian, slightly less than elegant in his dusty carpenter's overalls, announced to the receptionist that he had just called in to "see my old mate Dick." Well, against some people's better judgment, Dick Pratt was summoned, and, after having a cheerful cup of tea with young

Fewster, he took him into the boardroom to meet the assembled lords of big business. I am told there was a sharp round of applause and much laughter when Damian responded to an introduction to a Knight of the Realm with, "Hiya, Mike," which is, I suppose, as near as you get to immortality around here.

Scotty McAllister went back to Perth to run his father's wheat farm, and the Major retired from the army and set out on a new career in the real estate business. Also, he told me he entered the round-Hawaii canoe race!

Skippy, Scoop, and Chink are all working full time for the Bond Corporation, and Splash left Melbourne Grammar School for a new career as marketing manager for a new computer farming data bank. Will Ballieu is still making boats, and Ya is still painting them at the yacht club. Beasho went to the Los Angeles Olympic Games as Australia's Star Class representative, and will ultimately take over from his dad at the marina on Elvina Bay—no doubt still without any shoes.

Hughey has returned to Sydney as managing director of Sobstad Sails and is continuing to have his elegant wooden cruiser built by his mates. He is a real Soul of the Sea, Hughey. His house is full of lovely polished marine wood, and, as the son of a boat contractor on Sydney Harbor and the brother of a racer, as well as the husband of a racer (Dixie herself was championship class), his future is forever bound up in racing boats. He may very well end up as skipper of *Australia III*.

Grant Simmer has become a director and one of three partners in the North Sails Australian operations. I recommended him to the position because I decided to give up sailmaking, as I also decided to give up racing boats.

Since my return, I have been asked to speak and lecture at many, many national corporations—particularly in the field of computers and in those companies where there are large sales forces. The theme of my talks has been motivation, preparation, psychological warfare, and the art of not giving up. It was during these enlightening and fascinating contacts with men at the very heart of Australian business that I finally decided I would like to enter this most exciting and demanding world.

As the America's Cup ended, I knew more or less that I would not be able to do it again. Four months in a 12-Meter in that kind of a campaign is as long as most sailors spend in racing boats in a lifetime. And I had done it four times.

But all through my career, I have always progressed to a different boat, or taken up a different challenge, and now I feel there is not another yachting challenge that I wish to undertake. I have to feed off my ambitions, I have to feel that fanatical determination to win that has characterized all of my racing over the years. To ask me to try to defend the America's Cup is to ask the wrong man. It would be like calling Sir Edmund Hillary and asking him whether he might not like to go up Mount Everest again, just for fun.

I gave my life, and almost my soul, to the winning of the America's Cup, but I am afraid that someone else will have to helm the next Australian 12-Meter. I gave it my all, and I do not think anyone should ask more of me. I could not give it my all again.

I have a wife and three young children, and I am embarking on a new career in international business. I owe my start in this new venture in no small way to Bob Hawke, the Prime Minister. He has been extremely kind to me since I returned, and he understands that I must broaden my horizons now and set new goals for myself.

Rasa and I are settling down in a new house in Melbourne, and I am devoting as much time as I can to our young family. The memory of Newport 1983 will be with me always, but now I have other fields, other peaks to try to scale. I regard my pursuit of yacht racing's Holy Grail as complete. A long, long chapter in my life is, essentially, over. I practiced for it for 30 years, and finally I was lucky enough to be able to steer a very great crew over the line to claim the elusive prize.

Recently, Rasa and I went for a walk along the cliff near our house. The sea was calm and the sun was going down, casting its fiery red-and-orange glow over the waters where I had learned to sail half a dozen miles and 30 years away. As we walked, Rasa looked up and saw one lone seagull making a long, easy line along the sky, black against the setting sun. We both watched him move lazily into a fast, swooping shallow dive toward the water, and Rasa turned to me and said, "John, do you think that might be Jonathan coming to visit you?"

"Yeah, that'd be him," I said brightly, "still practicing, poor bastard."